CISTERCIAN STUDIES SERIES: NUMBER TWO-HUNDRED-FIVE

UNDERSTANDING RANCÉ:

The Spirituality of the Abbot of La Trappe in Context

David N. Bell

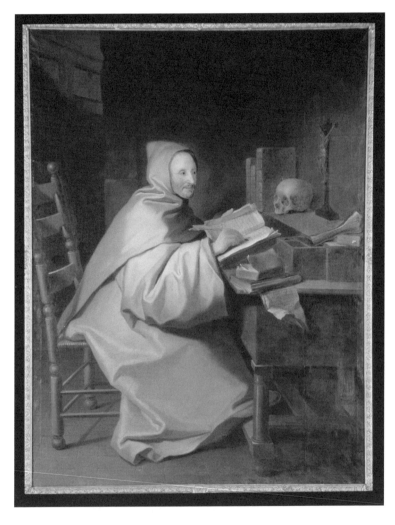

Cistercian Studies Series: Number Two-Hundred-Five

Understanding Rancé

*The Spirituality of the
Abbot of La Trappe
in Context*

by
David N. Bell

✝

Cistercian Publications
Kalamazoo, Michigan

© Copyright, Cistercian Publications 2005

The work of
cistercian publications
*is made possible in part
by support from*
WESTERN MICHIGAN UNIVERSITY
to The Institute of Cistercian Studies

*Available in the UK and Europe from
Alban Books
14 Belford Road   West End
Edinburgh EH4 3BL*

Cistercian Publications books are available
through the following addresses:

The United States: Liturgical Press
Saint John's Abbey   Collegeville, MN 56321-7500
sales@litpress.org

The United Kingdom and Europe: Alban Books Ltd
14 Belford Road   West End
Edinburgh   EH4 3BL
sales@albanbooks.com

Canada: Bayard Books
49 Front Street East, Second Floor
Toronto Ontario M5E 1B3
cservice@novalis-inc.com

Library of Congress Cataloguing-in-Publication Data

Bell, David N., 1943-
Understanding Rancé : the spirituality of the Abbot of La Trappe in
context / by David N. Bell.
     p. cm. — (Cistercian studies series ; no. 205)
Includes bibliographical references and index.
ISBN 0-87907-105-2 (pbk. : alk. paper)
1. Rancé, Armand Jean Le Bouthillier de, 1626-1700. 2. Trappists—
France—Biography. 3. France—Church history—17th century. I. Title.
II. Series.
BX4705.R3B45 2005
271'.12502—dc22
2004021261

Cover design by Elizabeth King

*Text set in Monotype Van Dijck, drop initials in Monotype Castellar
Typography by Gale Akins at
Humble Hills Press, Kalamazoo, Michigan*

PRINTED IN THE UNITED STATES OF AMERICA

TO THE MEMORY OF

Alban John Krailsheimer

1921-2001

✝

Table of Contents

Abbreviations xi

Introduction xv

PART I

Chapter 1   RANCÉ'S BIOGRAPHERS 3

Chapter 2   RANCÉ'S FRANCE 27

Chapter 3   RANCÉ'S ORDER 52

Chapter 4   RANCÉ'S SINS 74

Chapter 5   RANCÉ'S JOY 97

Chapter 6   RANCÉ'S READING 121

Chapter 7   RANCÉ'S ENEMIES 145

Chapter 8   RANCÉ'S CONVERSION 169

Chapter 9   RANCÉ'S MONASTICISM 197

Chapter 10   UNDERSTANDING RANCÉ 234

PART II BIBLIOGRAPHY

I: Works of Rancé.

I.A.i   Printed works
        (excluding letters, *dubia* and *spuria*)   253
II.A.ii Unprinted and untraced works 284

I.B   Letters   286
I.B.i   Collections of letters   287
I.B.ii Single letters   296

I.C   *Dubia* and *spuria*   302

I.D   Selections from the works of Rancé   308

II: Biographies, biographical material, and
        controversial literature

II.A   The seventeenth and eighteenth centuries 311
II.B   The nineteenth and twentieth centuries 334
II.C   Biographies in encyclopedias, dictionaries,
        and other similar compendia 350
Index   355

Acknowledgements

I T IS A PLEASURE to express my gratitude to the abbots of Cîteaux, Gethsemani, Mount Melleray, Roscrea, Septfons, Tamié, Vina, and especially la Trappe for giving me the freedom of their monastic libraries, and to the librarians of these communities for their liberal assistance. I am also, as always, indebted to the miracle-workers in Inter-Library Loans at my own university whose skill in obtaining the most obscure material in an amazingly short time is second to none. There are others, too, whose help has been indispensable, but who prefer to remain anonymous. Without all this assistance, this book would not have been possible.

The bibliography which forms the second part of this study is a revised, corrected, and much expanded version of the first two parts of my 'Armand-Jean Le Bouthillier de Rancé: A Bibliography of Printed Sources' published in *Cîteaux: Commentarii cistercienses* 51 (2000) 219-284. A great deal of it is new, but I am grateful to the *rédactrice-en-chef* and the Editorial Board of *Cîteaux: Commentarii cistercienses* for permission to reproduce those parts which are not.

Finally, I am more indebted than I can say to Father Chrysogonus Waddell OCSO, who first introduced me to the real Rancé (whom, at the time, I disliked because I misunderstood), and whose help, advice, and counsel over the years has been as generous as it has been invaluable.

DNB

✝

Abbreviations

Barbier	Antoine-Alexandre Barbier, *Diction-naire des ouvrages anonymes*, third edition revised and enlarged by Olivier Barbier, René and Paul Billard (Paris, 1872-9, repr. 1964).
Bell, 'Bibliography'	David N. Bell, 'Armand-Jean Le Bouthillier de Rancé: A Bibliography of Printed Sources', *Cîteaux: Commentarii cistercienses* 51 (2000) 219-284.
Bell, 'Library'	David N. Bell, ' The Library of the Abbey of La Trappe in the Eighteenth Century. A Preliminary Survey', *Cîteaux: Commentarii cistercienses* 49 (1998) 129-158.
BMS	Bulletin of Monastic Spirituality (included in *Cistercian Studies [Quarterly]*).
BN	*Catalogue général des livres imprimés de la Bibliothèque Nationale (Auteurs)*. Paris 1897-1981.
Bourgeois/André	Émile Bourgeois & Louis André, *Les sources de l'histoire de France: XVIIᵉ siècle (1610-1715)*. Paris, 1913-32; rpt. Nendeln/Liechtenstein, 1976.
Broekaert	Jean D. Broekaert, *Bibliographie de la Règle de saint Benoît. Éditions latines et traductions imprimées de 1489 à 1929*. Studia Anselmiana 77-78. Rome 1980. The descriptions of the editions in Broekaert supersede those in Anselm M. Albareda, *Bibliografía de la Regla*

	Benedictina. Montserrat: Monestir de Montserrat 1933, but Albareda's long introduction (in Catalan) remains invaluable, above all for its magnificent illustrations.
BSM	Bulletin de spiritualité monastique (included in *Collectanea Cisterciensia*).
Canivez	Joseph-Marie Canivez, *Statuta Capitulorum Generalium Ordinis Cisterciensis ab Anno 1116 ad Annum 1786*. Louvain, 1933-1941.
CCCM	*Corpus Christianorum Continuatio Mediaevalis.* Turnhout.
Cioranescu	Alexandre Cioranescu, *Bibliographie de la littérature française du dix-septième siècle*. Paris, 1966. Three volumes.
DAC	*Dictionnaire des auteurs cisterciens*, ed. Émile Brouette, Anselme Dimier & Eugène Manning. Rochefort, 1975-1979.
DBF	*Dictionnaire de biographie française.* Paris, 1933—.
De la sainteté	Armand-Jean de Rancé, *De la sainteté et des devoirs de la vie monastique*, cited by volume and page number of the first edition. Paris, 1683; rpt. Farnborough, 1972.
DHGE	*Dictionnaire d'histoire et de géographie ecclésiastiques* Paris, 1912—.
DLF XVII	*Dictionnaire des lettres françaises. Le XVIIe siècle*, ed. Patrick Dandrey. Paris, 1951; rpt. with revisions 1996.
DLF XVIII	*Dictionnaire des lettres françaises. Le XVIIIe siècle*, ed. François Moureau. Paris, 1960; rpt. with revisions 1995.
DNB	*Dictionary of National Biography.* Oxford, 1885-1901 [and reprints].

DTC	*Dictionnaire de théologie catholique.* Paris, 1903-1972.
DS	*Dictionnaire de spiritualité.* Paris, 1937-1995.
Dubois	Louis Dubois, *Histoire de l'abbé de Rancé et de sa réforme, composée avec ses écrits, ses lettres, ses règlements et un grand nombre de documents contemporains inédits ou peu connus.* Paris, 1866 [1st ed.], 1869 [2nd ed.].
François	Jean François, *Bibliothèque générale des écrivains de l'Ordre de Saint Benoît.* Bouillon, 1777-1778; rpt. Louvain-Héverlé, 1961.
Jedin-Dolan VI	*History of the Church*, ed. Hubert Jedin & John Dolan, vol. VI, Wolfgang Müller *et al.*, *The Church in the Age of Absolutism and Enlightenment.* New York, 1981.
Krailsheimer, *Legacy*	Alban J. Krailsheimer, *Rancé and the Trappist Legacy.* Cistercian Studies Series, 86. Kalamazoo, 1985.
Krailsheimer, *Rancé*	Alban J. Krailsheimer, *Armand-Jean de Rancé, Abbot of la Trappe. His Influence in the Cloister and the World.* Oxford, 1974.
Lekai, *Cistercians*	*The Cistercians. Ideals and Reality.* Kent OH, 1977.
Lekai, *Strict Observance*	*The Rise of the Cistercian Strict Observance in Seventeenth Century France.* Washington, 1968.
Lekai, 'Bibliography'	Louis J. Lekai, 'A Bibliography of Seventeenth Century Pamphlets and Other Printed Material Related to the Cistercian Strict Observance', *Analecta Sacri Ordinis Cisterciensis* 19 (1963)105-144.

Letter/s

The Letters of Armand-Jean de Rancé, Abbot and Reformer of La Trappe, presented by Alban J. Krailsheimer. Cistercian Studies Series 80-81. Kalamazoo, 1984), and/or *Correspondance*. Édition originale par Alban John Krailsheimer (Paris, 1993). The letters are cited in the same way—by year, month, and day—in both volumes: e.g. Letter 910104 = 1691 January 4. In cases where distinction is necessary, the two versions are cited as Letter/s (English) and Letter/s (French).

Mensáros

Aurèle B. Mensáros, 'L'Abbé de Rancé et la règle bénédictine', *Analecta Cisterciensia* 22 (1966)161-217.

PG

Patrologia Cursus Completus, Series Græca.

PL

Patrologia Cursus Completus, Series Latina.

Tournoüer

Henri Tournoüer, *Bibliographie et iconographie de la Maison-Dieu Notre-Dame de la Trappe au diocèse de Sées, de Dom A.-I. Le Bouthillier de Rancé, Abbé et Réformateur de cette abbaye, et en général de tous les religieux du même monastère*. Documents sur la province du Perche; iv: 2. Mortagne, 1894-1896.

Introduction

THIS BOOK IS NOT a biography of Rancé. There are already too many biographies of Rancé, and since the publication in 1974 of Professor A. J. Krailsheimer's *Armand-Jean de Rancé, Abbot of la Trappe. His Influence in the Cloister and the World* (with a revised edition in French in 2000), there is really little need for further studies of his life. There is, however, need for further studies of his thought and his monastic spirituality, and neither of these can be understood without taking into account his times, his country, his Order, his background, his learning, his conversion, and his character. This present volume is an attempt to deal with some of these issues and is not so much a book about Rancé as around Rancé. I do not expect that it will persuade people who do not like Rancé to like him; it may, however, serve to explain why he said and did what he said and did in the way that he said and did it. I should also add that the *Further Readings* appended to each chapter are, wherever possible, restricted to material in English. If English sources do not exist, one obviously has no choice but to cite those in French. In principle, however, this little book does not require the reader to be bilingual.

Since we shall begin in the middle of things, it may be useful to present here a bald and simple narrative of Rancé's life with some places and dates, both to remind those who know and to inform those who do not of what happened in the seventy-four years between his birth on 9 January 1626 and his death on 27 October 1700. I would emphasize that it is no more than a bald and simple narrative, deliberately devoid of explanation and interpretation, since those are matters for subsequent chapters. Nothing here is new, therefore, nor is it intended to be, and my essential sources have been the accounts presented by Professor Alban Krailsheimer.

Those who wish for more detail cannot do better than to read the relevant chapters in his *Rancé and the Trappist Legacy*.[1]

Rancé's life may be conveniently divided into two parts. The first takes us from his birth in 1626 to his entry into la Trappe as regular abbot in 1664; the second extends from 1664 to his death in the same monastery in 1700. The first part may be subdivided into three smaller sections, each shorter than the last. First of all we have the years of his boyhood and adolescence to 1643 when, at the age of seventeen, he took his MA degree at the University of Paris. Secondly, we have the period from about 1643 to 1657, when he was enjoying the life of a young man about town. And thirdly there are the years of indecision, the period from 1657 to 1663, when he had decided to forsake the world, but was by no means sure what to put in its place.

Armand-Jean Bouthillier de Rancé[2] was born in Paris to Denis Bouthillier and Charlotte Joly—who had married in Dijon in 1619—and was one of a number of children. One brother and four sisters preceded him; one sister and one brother came afterwards. There seems also to have been at least one child who died at birth or in infancy. The family was well-to-do and enjoyed a close relationship with Cardinal Richelieu, who was Rancé's godfather. Rancé's natural father, Denis, held important positions at court, and Rancé's uncles and aunts included secretaries of state, bishops and archbishops, nuns and abbesses.

Rancé's elder brother, Denis-François, was born in 1620, but had never enjoyed good health and died, not expectedly, in 1637 at the age of seventeen. Had he survived, he would have followed two of his uncles into the Church and Armand-Jean would have become a Knight of Malta. As it happened, the death of the Bouthillier firstborn changed the family's

---

1. See page 26 under Further Reading.
2. After Rancé entered la Trappe he ceased to use the family name Bouthillier and signed his letters 'fr. Armand-Jean, abbé de la Trappe'. For further details, see Letters (English) 1:xxvi.

plans, and Armand-Jean, now eleven years old, found himself transferred from a military to an ecclesiastical career. That this was not unforeseen is confirmed by the fact that Armand-Jean had already been tonsured in 1635.

Continuity was here essential. Before he died, Denis-François possessed a number of valuable benefices and it was economically essential to keep them in the family. Thus, after his brother's death, Armand-Jean found himself commendatory abbot or prior—absentee landlord, in effect—of five religious houses, including the cistercian abbey of la Trappe.

The young Rancé had been educated at home by tutors, a common practice at the time, and one of these, the admirable Jean Favier, remained a life-long friend and correspondent.[3] The young boy was obviously an intelligent, perhaps even precocious, student, and his education had clearly been effective, for in 1639, at the age of thirteen, Armand-Jean published a commentary on the greek poet Anacreon,[4] and dedicated it (with a letter in Greek) to his godfather Richelieu. How much of the work is due to Rancé and how much to his tutors remains undetermined.[5]

The five years from 1637 to 1642 were nothing if not eventful. In 1637, as we have seen, Denis-François died, and that same year Rancé's father bought a country estate at Véretz, near Tours. Rancé would come to know it well. Then, in October of the following year, his mother died. 1639 saw the publication of his first book, and in about 1642 he was admitted to the Collège d'Harcourt of the University of Paris. But 1642 was also a year of tragedy: the husband of one of his sisters was brutally murdered by the husband's brother-in-law, and just a few days later Cardinal Richelieu died, leaving

---

3. On Jean Favier (1609-1703), see Élie Jaloustre, *Un précepteur auvergnat de l'abbé de Rancé* (Clermont-Ferrand, 1887) which, despite its age, remains indispensable.
4. Part II, I.A.i [1639 Ἀνακρέοντος Τηΐου τὰ μέλη].
5. For a brief discussion, see the notes to Part II, I.A.i [1639]. The greek letter is Letter 410110 (French), which gives a french translation but not the greek original.

the Bouthilliers bereft of a powerful protector. Worse was to come, for the ascendancy of Cardinal Mazarin foreshadowed nothing but gloom for the Bouthillier family. We shall discuss the matter further in Chapter Two.

After taking his MA in 1646, Rancé began to make his way in society. A number of his close friends went on to high office in the Church, and we shall meet some of them later (especially the bishops of Luçon and Grenoble, Henri Barillon and Étienne Le Camus). Others were to be found frequenting the fashionable *salons*. Some had influential connections at court. But of all the noble families with which he was acquainted, none was more important than the house of Montbazon, and Rancé's relationship with the beautiful and voluptuous Madame de Montbazon will be the subject of a later chapter.

In 1648 Rancé was ordained to the diaconate by Paul de Gondi (the future Cardinal de Retz) and in 1651 to the priesthood by his uncle, the archbishop of Tours. By this time he was head of the family—his father having died in 1650—and the owner of the estate at Véretz. By 1654 he had received his doctorate in theology from the Sorbonne and in the same year his uncle appointed him one of the two archdeacons in the diocese of Tours. But his uncle's hope that his nephew would succeed him as archbishop was to be frustrated by Mazarin, and Rancé's friendship with Mazarin's enemy, Cardinal de Retz—a friendship courageously maintained in a formidably adverse political climate—could only have a deleterious effect upon his ecclesiastical career.

In 1655 the young *abbé* was sent by his uncle to Paris as a delegate to the General Assembly of the Clergy of France. This was the decennial *Grande Assemblée* to which each ecclesiastical province sent four deputies, and which was frequently used as a channel for the ecclesiastical advancement of young and ambitious aristocrats. Rancé, it appears, conducted himself efficiently and effectively, but he also found the proceedings intolerably tedious, and before the long-drawn-out Assembly had come to an end, he had discreetly withdrawn to his estate at Véretz. He clearly enjoyed his life as a country

squire, and contemporary records show him to have been a
good conversationalist, a superb horseman (riding was his
passion), something of a fop in his manners and attire, and a
man who knew how to tread a delicate path through the quag-
mire of french politics in the middle of the seventeenth century. That in itself was no small achievement.

His life as a popular and fashionable *abbé*-about-town came
to an end in 1657 with the unexpected death of the woman he
loved: Marie d'Avaugour de Bretagne, duchesse de Montbazon.
As we shall see later, this was merely the last and most terrible event in a succession of circumstances, but it was unquestionably a turning-point in his life. Following the death
of the duchess he withdrew to Véretz and took the first
definitive steps which would lead, in due course, to the dark
forests and miasmic lakes of that soon to be notorious place

> Where, 'midst her gloomy waste of wood,
> And girt by many a rushing flood,
> Whose deep and melancholy moan
> Seems but the never-ceasing groan
> Of those who, felled by secret blow,
> Sink in the hungry gulph below—
> La Trappe her mitred forehead reyars,
> Grey with the storms of thousand years.[6]

It took Rancé some six years to come to a final decision as
to exactly what to do and where to do it. During that time he
consulted a number of people, both men and women, all of
whom had a deep influence upon him and some of whom we
shall meet in later chapters. Rancé was a man who always
needed encouragement and moral support. Then, in the spring
of 1658, he set off on a tour of the houses of which he was
commendatory superior, and in July of that year he arrived at
la Trappe. Three of these houses at least (including la Trappe)
were in poor condition, both physically and morally—of the

6. John W. Cunningham, *De Rancé. A Poem* (London, 1815) 109.

other two nothing is known—but at that time Rancé did little to correct the problems. Given his own uncertainty as to the direction he should take, this is understandable. A second tour followed in 1659, but Rancé was still unsure of the path he should follow. Further consultations took place, more advice was sought, and it seems to have been Gilbert de Choiseul, then bishop of Comminges and later bishop of Tournai, who first suggested to Rancé that he become a monk and take over one of his benefices as regular superior. Rancé— said Choiseul almost thirty years later—was appalled at the idea, but it is hard to say how appalled. Thirty years is a long time, and memory, which can sometimes be more creative than retentive, is a fickle thing.

Be that as it may, by 1660 Rancé had begun to see clearly. God *was* calling him to the monastic life, whether he liked it or not, and over the next two years he gradually freed himself of his estates and possessions. Véretz was sold, other benefices were transferred—one of them went to Jean Favier, his old friend and former tutor—and in August 1662 he contacted the authorities of the cistercian Strict Observance[7] and asked them to send a few religious from the abbey of Perseigne to the dilapidated Common Observance house of la Trappe to take over 'the unedifying assortment of half a dozen monks living in undisciplined squalor'.[8] This was done on 17 August (not without resistance from the half-dozen monks) and Rancé himself went to the abbey to oversee the work of rebuilding and restoration. He stayed there from September 1662 to January 1663, and those few months seem to have provided him with the final confirmation he needed that the cistercian life was indeed the life for which he was destined. He took the habit at Perseigne on 13 June 1663.

His year's novitiate—a year was standard at the time— can only have been a shattering experience, physically,

7. I am here using the terms Strict and Common Observance for the sake of simplicity, even though anachronistically. The story of the rise of the two Observances will be the subject of Chapter Three.
8. Krailsheimer, *Legacy*, 24.

psychologically, and spiritually. By October his health had broken down and he was obliged to return to la Trappe to recuperate. Then, after his recovery and return to Perseigne, he was sent off to another nearby abbey to restore order there. This was hardly a normal responsibility for a cistercian novice, but neither Rancé nor his novitiate can be termed normal. By June 1664, however, the year of trial was over, and on 14 July he entered la Trappe as its regular abbot. There can be no doubt that he came with reform in mind, and the blueprint for that reform had probably been drawn up at Perseigne when Rancé read a book—which we shall discuss in detail later—by Julien Paris, abbot of Foucarmont. It was *Du premier esprit de l'ordre de Cîteaux*, first published in 1653.

Rancé had been at la Trappe only a few weeks when he was summoned to Paris to meet with the superiors of the Strict Observance. This was in September 1664, and at the meeting Rancé found himself instructed to accompany Dom Dominique Georges, the saintly abbot of Val-Richer, to Rome to plead the cause of the Strict Observance in what has been called the War of the Observances.[9] He was there for more than eighteen months, and what he did and what was done during that time we shall discuss in Chapter Three. As it happens, the roman mission was a failure (though Rancé was not to blame) and he did not enjoy his time in the city. Nor did he enjoy the endless politicking. He returned gladly to la Trappe in May 1666 and, apart from short absences on official business, never left again.

His time as abbot was not easy. This was (and is) true of many abbots, but Rancé, as Professor Krailsheimer has observed, had 'an unhappy genius for incurring hostility unnecessarily':[10] sometimes, *pace* Krailsheimer, even necessarily. The period from his entry into the abbey to about 1675 was dominated by problems with the abbots of the Common Observance who, by definition, were firmly opposed to his

9. See Chapter Three.
10. Krailsheimer, *Rancé*, 42.

reforms; and also by strained relations with his superiors in the Strict Observance who, as far as Rancé was concerned, were not strict enough. At the same time, he was involved in a bitter controversy with Guillaume Le Roy, commendatory abbot of Hautefontaine and a former friend, on the question of 'fictions'—the question, that is, of what methods an abbot may legitimately use to instill humility into his monks. The conflict began in about 1671 and lasted for almost a decade. Then, from 1683 to (officially) 1692, came a battle with Dom Innocent Le Masson, General of the Carthusians, as to whether the Carthusians could or could not justly be accused of laxity. And finally, from 1684 to 1693, there was a controversy with the learned Maurist Jean Mabillon on the question of monastic studies. Further consideration of all these controversies will be found in the following pages.

There were also a number of other disputes of lesser moment. One of these concerned the question of whether professed monks might leave the cloister to take care of indigent parents. Another concerned the problem of the mortality at la Trappe—it was undeniably high, especially between 1674 and 1676—and the question of whether Rancé's strict regulations were too strict for anyone but supermen. And every one of these disputes and controversies occurred in the omnipresent atmosphere of the Jesuit/Jansenist conflict which tormented the french church throughout much of the seventeenth and eighteenth centuries. It was, in essence, a conflict between a more lenient (Jesuit) and a more rigorous (Jansenist) attitude to human sinfulness (we will say more about it in Chapter Two), but Rancé had continual difficulties with both parties. There were Jansenists who thought he was not Jansenist enough, or at least not sufficiently Jansenist in a public way; and there were Jesuits who thought he was too Jansenist. The situation was not helped by the fact that Rancé himself was no irenic peacemaker, but a proud, sometimes haughty, man who was more than ready to defend his views at formidable length and in no uncertain terms.

His continual labours took their toll, as also did the

austerity of his life, and by 1694 he could no longer walk unaided and was forced to enter the infirmary at la Trappe. He was certainly suffering from some form of rheumatism, perhaps rheumatoid arthritis, and was also having trouble with breathing and digestion. In May 1695 he resigned as abbot and was succeeded by Dom Zozime Foisil whom we shall meet again in Chapter One. Zozime, however, had little opportunity to exercise his talents, for he was abbot for only three months before dying unexpectedly in March 1696. He was succeeded by Armand-François Gervaise, who is a story in himself, and under Gervaise's well-meaning but erratic and tactless government, the regular life at the abbey came close to collapse. Gervaise was forced to resign in 1698 and was succeeded by Dom Jacques de La Cour who entered on his abbacy in April 1699.

By that time Rancé's life was drawing to its close. The english poet and essayist Joseph Addison visited him in September 1700, when he had only a month to live, and reported to Dr John Hough, bishop of Lichfield, that he 'has still his senses entire, tho they are forc'd to carry him on his Strawbed to the Masse which he still frequents at the most unseasonable Hours'.[11] He still had his 'senses entire', in fact, until his very last moments, and he was perfectly lucid when he died on 27 October 1700 between one and two o'clock in the afternoon. He was seventy-four. He was given the last rites by Monseigneur Louis d'Aquin, bishop of Séez, who has left us a somewhat too edifying but nevertheless moving account of his last hours.[12]

Both during his lifetime and afterwards Rancé was a controversial figure. He tended to evoke extreme reactions—he was either loved or loathed—and this is reflected in the two dozen biographies which have been produced in the course of the last three centuries. The earliest of these tend to be

11. *The Letters of Joseph Addison*, ed. Walter Graham (Oxford, 1941; rpt. St Clair Shores, MI, 1976) 24 (Letter 20).
12. See Part II, II.A [1701 Aquin].

hagiographical panegyrics, but that is understandable. After Rancé's death there was a concerted movement to have him canonized, and certain of the early biographies clearly reflect this goal. Why else would Dom Pierre Le Nain spend so much time relating his supposed miracles? As it happens, the attempt came to nothing, not as a result of any victory by the Devil's Advocate, but primarily because of death and politics. His staunchest supporters did not long survive him, and the eighteenth century was a very different world from that which formed the character of Rancé.

He remains a controversial figure. I have talked with many Cistercians of the modern Strict Observance and count many of them among my closest friends, but it is rare to find among them any true admirers of Rancé or, indeed, any who have actually read much of what he wrote. And most of them do not care for the designation 'Trappist'. There are, of course, exceptions, most notably Father Chysogonus Waddell of the abbey of Gethsemani, whose perceptive studies of Rancé's thought and ideas are essential reading.[13] Part of the problem lies in the stubborn legend of Rancé as an inhuman, hyper-ascetic autocrat who regarded his monks as no more than a crowd of criminals justly confined to the prison of the cloister. Part of it comes from a failure to understand the culture, religion, and spirituality of seventeenth-century France. Yet another part of the problem is a result of the fact that, among English readers, Rancé is so rarely read. Apart from his letters, the only one of his works available in complete English translation is his *magnum opus, De la sainteté et des devoirs de la vie monastique*.[14] But that volume was published in 1830 and is itself a fairly rare book. Furthermore, the translation is defective, sometimes seriously so. This present study is merely an attempt to place Rancé in context, and if we do that, we can see not only why he said what he said, but also that he

13. His articles will be found listed in my 'Armand-Jean Le Bouthillier de Rancé: A Bibliography of Printed Sources' (see Further Reading, xxvi) 276-277.
14. See Part II, I.A.i [1683 *De la sainteté*].

could hardly have said anything else. His spirituality undoubtedly reflects his temperament—it could not be otherwise—but it also reflects the political, social, cultural, ecclesiastical, and spiritual world in which he lived.

We said above that reaction to Rancé is rarely indifferent. He was, and is, either loved or loathed, and this is revealed in the pendulum-swing of his biographies. Early adulation gives way to spiteful criticism; spiteful criticism is followed by further (if somewhat tempered) adulation; and it was not until Professor Krailsheimer's biography of 1974 that we were offered a fair and balanced assessment of the life and works of the abbot of la Trappe. But even Professor Krailsheimer occasionally teeters on the brink of hero-worship, and I cannot say that I myself am wholly guiltless of it. Rancé can do that to a person.

Let us begin, therefore, by relating the history of these diverse biographies and seeing how the portrait of Rancé changed and developed over the three hundred years from his death in 1700 to the new millenium.

FURTHER READING

For any study of la Trappe or its most famous abbot, the bibliography compiled at the end of the nineteenth century by Henri Tournoüer remains indispensable: *Bibliographie et iconographie de la Maison-Dieu Notre-Dame de la Trappe au diocèse de Sées, de Dom A.-I. Le Bouthillier de Rancé, Abbé et Réformateur de cette abbaye, et en général de tous les religieux du même monastère,* Documents sur la province du Perche, iv:2 (Mortagne, 1894-1896). The final part of the work—*Iconographie de l'abbaye de la Trappe et de l'abbé de Rancé*—was published in 1973 by Lucien Aubry, Eric de Jessé, Jean Lebrun, and Philippe Siguret (Cahiers percherons, 39).

For Rancé himself, see David N. Bell, 'Armand-Jean Le Bouthillier de Rancé: A Bibliography of Printed Sources', *Cîteaux: Commentarii cistercienses* 51 (2000) 219-284, which contains an index of subjects. The second part of this present volume contains a considerably revised and much expanded version of the first two parts of that bibliography: Rancé's own writings, and biographical and controversial literature. It does not contain the third part of the bibliography which lists studies of Rancé's thought and ideas. I am indebted to the *rédactrice-en-chef* and the Editorial Board of *Cîteaux: Commentarii cistercienses* for permission to reproduce the relevant sections of that article.

On the famous portrait of Rancé by Hyacinthe Rigaud, reproduced as the frontispiece to this book (the original is at la Trappe), see Lucien Aubry, 'A la recherche du vrai portrait de Rancé. Essai sur l'iconographie du Réformateur de la Trappe', *Cîteaux: Commentarii cistercienses* 23 (1972) 171-208, Roger Judrin, 'Le portrait de Rancé', *Cahiers Saint-Simon* 1 (1973) 3-4, and Michèle Ménard, 'Le portrait de l'abbé de Rancé par Hyacinthe Rigaud', in *Réformes et continuité dans l'ordre de Cîteaux: De l'Étroite Observance à la Stricte Observance. Actes du Colloque. Journées d'Histoire Monastique, Saint-Mihiel, 2-3 octobre 1992,* Textes et Documents, VI (Brecht, 1995) 53-57 (with an english summary on page 206).

A full account of the various biographies of Rancé will be found in Chapter 1 and/or in the bibliography which forms Part II of this study. My account of the facts of Rancé's life presented in this introduction is dependent primarily on Alban J. Krailsheimer, *Armand-Jean de Rancé, Abbot of la Trappe. His Influence in the Cloister and the World* (Oxford, 1974) Chapters 1-3, and the same author's *Rancé and the Trappist Legacy* (Kalamazoo, 1985) chapters 2-4. Both are excellent, but the former requires a reading knowledge of French, as the abundant french quotations are untranslated. Some of the dates in the first of these two studies are incorrect and have been corrected in the revised french translation, *Armand-Jean de Rancé, abbé de la Trappe 1626-1700* (Paris, 2000), but in both versions the date of his death is given incorrectly. He died on 27 October 1700, not 26 October: see Louis Dubois, *Histoire de l'abbé de Rancé et de sa réforme, composée avec ses écrits, ses lettres, ses règlements et un grand nombre de documents contemporains inédits ou peu connus* (Paris, 1866) 685, n. 3.

.

✝

PART I

✝

Chapter 1

RANCÉ'S BIOGRAPHERS

RANCÉ HAS NOT, in general, been well served by his biographers. As we said in the Introduction, it is not that there are too few biographies; there are, on the contrary, rather too many and they vary widely—wildly even—in quality and reliability. Some of the best written are the most untrustworthy; some of the more turgid contain valuable information and insights. But in too many cases, the authors are busy grinding away at their own particular axes.

The history of rancéan biography begins about 1674 with the arrival at la Trappe of a lawyer's clerk from Châtillon-sur-Seine. Charles Maisne had come to the abbey to try his vocation, but weak health prevented him from embracing the monastic regimen in all its austerity. But since he did not wish to give up the monastic life entirely, he stayed on at the monastery as a secular—he was not alone in this—and over the next five or six years gradually became indispensable to Rancé as his secretary. Unfortunately, he gravely abused his position, betrayed Rancé's confidence, and, in the long run, did more harm than good. He himself certainly thought he was doing the right thing in 'protecting' Rancé, but there can be no doubt that he took his protection too far. By about 1680 the only way to Rancé was through his secretarial *éminence grise*.

By the early 1680s, it is clear that Maisne had conceived the idea of compiling a dossier on Rancé with a view to his eventual canonization. He therefore wrote to a number of the abbot's friends, asking them to send him whatever letters and documents they might have in their possession. Some did, some did not; though precisely who sent what is unknown. It seems, too, that in his efforts to prepare the way for Rancé's canonization, Maisne had the cooperation of Pierre de Maupeou, a young man who had also tried his vocation at la Trappe, but, like Maisne, had also been forced to abandon his design for reasons of health. Maupeou's brother Grégoire, a former Dominican, also entered the abbey, but was stronger than Pierre and stayed—though not without causing problems.[1] Pierre himself went on to become curé of Nonancourt near Dreux, about forty kilometres from la Trappe, and was installed there by 1691. The sixteenth-century church is still standing.

It is clear that Maisne supplied Maupeou with a considerable number of documents, but it also appears that over the years cooperation turned into rivalry. Maisne, like many others, clearly saw Rancé's canonization as a foregone conclusion and intended to profit from it in any way he could. At some stage, therefore, he began to retain any documents which came into his possession—he was not prepared to share his saint—and Maupeou lost an important source. Maupeou himself was devoted to Rancé and, in 1685, had already published a rather ineffectual reply to Daniel de Larroque's popular *Véritables motifs de la conversion de l'abbé de la Trappe*, a work we shall examine in detail in Chapter Seven.[2] Soon after Rancé died on 27 October 1700, he appeared in print yet again in 1701 with his *Éloge funèbre du Très-Révérend Père Dom Armand Jean Bouthillier de Rancé, abbé et réformateur du monastère de la Trappe*,[3] which, he tells us, was composed at the request of Françoise-Angélique d'Étampes de Valençay, abbess of les Clairets, who was equally devoted to Rancé and whom we shall meet again in a moment. Maupeou began the work on 11 November 1700 and finished it in about three weeks.

Then, a year later, Maupeou published the two volumes of his *La vie du Très-Révérend Père Dom Armand-Jean Le Bouthillier*

1. See Krailsheimer, *Rancé*, 105.
2. Part II, II.A [1685 Maupeou].
3. Part II, II.A [1701 Maupeou].

de Rancé, Abbé et Réformateur du monastère de la Trappe[4] on which, obviously, he had been working for some time. Rancé himself had, in a sense, authorized the work, for in 1697 he had written to Maupeou expressing his confidence in him as his biographer.[5] The resulting life, however, is a superficial, hagiographical work—a contemporary report describes it as *une apologie et non une histoire*[6]—and it is by no means always reliable. When Maupeou lacked documentary sources, he did not hesitate to supply the necessary material from his own imagination, and a considerable number of his statements are simply wrong. But, like the other early biographies, Maupeou's apology contains a certain amount of material (especially letters) unavailable elsewhere.

Despite its obvious deficiencies, Maupeou's *Vie* may truly be called the first life of Rancé, even though it had been preceded by a much briefer sketch published a year earlier by Monseigneur Louis d'Aquin, bishop of Séez, who had attended Rancé on his deathbed. The bishop first published an account of Rancé's last hours[7] and then incorporated part of this into his *Imago R.P. Domni Armandi-Joannis Le Bouthillier de Rancé, abbatis de Trappâ. Portrait de Dom Armand-Jean Le Bouthillier de Rancé, Abbé Régulier et Réformateur du Monastère de la Trappe, de l'Étroite Observance de Cisteaux*, published in 1701.[8] This is a Latin/French bilingual work with the latin text on the left and an amplified french translation on the right, but apart from providing Rancé with a splendid epitaph and telling us of his salutary death, Aquin's *Imago*, together with the revised editions of 1704 and 1708,[9] is of limited value.

Meanwhile, while Maupeou was preparing his biography and Maisne his dossier, another monk of la Trappe had been accumulating material for a life of its illustrious abbot. This

---

4. Part II, II.A [1702 Maupeou].   5. Letter 971003.
6. Quoted in Philippe-Irénée Boistel d'Exauvillez, *Histoire de l'abbé de Rancé, réformateur de la Trappe* (Paris, 1868 [rev. ed.]) iv.
7. Part II, II.A [1701 Aquin *Relation*].
8. Part II, II.A [Aquin *Imago*].   9. See *ibid*.

was the prior, Jean-Baptiste de La Tour, a former Dominican who had entered the abbey in 1695. He was a learned man, though plagued with ill health, and he took his task seriously. He interviewed the older members of the community, talked with Rancé as often as he could (or as often as Charles Maisne would let him), and made a collection of copies of letters to and from Rancé and of any other relevant documents he could find in the abbey archives. His declining health prevented him from completing the work, but his accumulated documentation did not go to waste.

Sometime at the beginning of the 1700s someone or some group at the abbey contacted Jacques Marsollier, archdeacon of Uzès, and commissioned him for the sum of three thousand francs[10] to prepare a new life of Rancé. It is possible, though not certain, that Maisne was behind the choice; what is certain is that Marsollier was given access to what he calls certain 'Mémoires de la Trappe' compiled by a 'learned religious',[11] who can only have been Jean-Baptiste de La Tour. Marsollier had not known Rancé personally, but had already published a history of ecclesiastical tithing, a history of the Inquisition, a somewhat inaccurate life of Cardinal Ximenez, a rather better life of Henry VII of England, and a life of St François de Sales for which he had not done quite enough research. In due course, he would publish a flawed apology for Erasmus and lives of Henri de La Tour d'Auvergne, duc de Bouillon, and Jeanne de Chantal.[12] He was, therefore, a professional historian, but although he wrote well, he also wrote too hastily. His books were indeed popular, but they are not always reliable. Marsollier used part, though clearly not all, of La Tour's documentation to prepare his own *La Vie de Dom Armand-Jean Le Bouthillier de Rancé, Abbé régulier et Réformateur du monastère de la Trappe, de l'Étroite Observance de Cisteaux* which appeared in 1703.[13] It is a well-written work,

10. See Exauvillez, *Histoire de l'abbé de Rancé*, iv.
11. See the 'Avertissement' to his *Vie de Dom Armand-Jean Le Bouthillier de Rancé* (Part II, II.A [1703 Marsollier]).
12. His works are listed in *DLF XVIII*, 848.   13. Part II, II.A [1703 Marsollier].

but—as Professor Krailsheimer has said—it is also incomplete and uncritical.[14] It is also decidedly partisan, but it, too, includes a certain amount of material unavailable elsewhere. We might add, however, that it was not well received at la Trappe.

By 1703, then, there were already in circulation two biographies of Rancé, neither satisfactory. Yet while Maisne, La Tour, Maupeou, and Marsollier had been collecting their own data, a number of Rancé's friends, including the influential Bossuet (at this time bishop of Meaux), had been in contact with Dom Pierre Le Nain, a monk of la Trappe and a close friend and staunch admirer of Rancé, with the intention of producing yet another life of the reformer, a life which would be comprehensive, authentic, and not controlled by Maisne. Pierre Le Nain was the younger brother of the learned historian Sébastien Le Nain de Tillemont, a Jansenist, who had composed an admirable *Mémoires pour servir à l'histoire des six premiers siècles de l'Église*—a work much esteemed by Edward Gibbon—and an equally sound *Histoire des empereurs et des autres princes qui ont régné pendant les six premiers siècles de l'Église*.[15] The younger brother, alas, did not possess the elder's critical sensibilities, but he had the inestimable advantage of having once (before the advent of Maisne) been Rancé's secretary and of being wholly familiar with the enormous mass of his abbot's correspondence. He had known Rancé for many years and was intimately acquainted with his ideas, ideals, and moods.

Pierre Le Nain was born in Paris on 25 March 1640 and had studied first at the *Petites Écoles de Port-Royal* and then at the parisian abbey of Saint-Victor. He entered la Trappe in 1668 where, in due course, he was appointed sub-prior. He died on 12 December 1713 and a full account of his life was published two years later by the *abbé* d'Arnaudin.[16] A number of his writings remain in manuscript, but he left works of spirituality as well as history and biography. He was responsible for

14. Krailsheimer, *Rancé*, 59.
15. See *DLF XVII*, 743-746.
16. See Further Reading, 25.

compiling the *Méditations sur la règle de s. Benoist, tirées du Commentaire de Monsieur l'Abbé de la Trappe sur la mesme Règle,* first printed in 1696,[17] which is a good piece of work. Le Nain's own spirituality, as we might expect, echoes his beloved abbot's, and some of his *Homélies sur quelques chapitres du prophète Jérémie*[18] still make for rewarding reading.[19] His *magnum opus* was a nine-volume *Essai de l'histoire de l'Ordre de Cîteaux, tirée des Annales de l'Ordre et de divers autres historiens,* published between 1696 and 1699. But the *opus* is *magnum* in size rather than reliability, and it is not so much a scholarly history as an uncritical collection of pious biographies.

At some time in the early 1700s, then, Le Nain had been contacted by Bossuet or his friends with a view to publishing a sound and accurate life of Rancé, and there is every evidence that he was eager to espouse the task. How much access Le Nain had to material collected by Maisne and La Tour is uncertain, but by 1706 he had completed a first draft of the biography. Considerable delays then followed, partly because Le Nain was asked to make certain modifications to his text regarding Rancé's position *vis-à-vis* the Jansenists and Jesuits, and partly because of official opposition to yet another life of the Great Reformer. Le Nain, in fact, died at the end of 1713, before his book was published, but two years later, in 1715, there appeared the three duodecimo volumes of *La vie du Révérend Père Dom Armand-Jean Le Bouttillier de Rancé, Abbé et Réformateur de la Maison-Dieu Notre-Dame de la Trappe, de l'Étroite Observance de l'Ordre de Cîteaux.*[20] It was published without place, date, or official approbation, undoubtedly as a result of its Jansenist leanings, and a second edition with major changes by an unknown editor was published in 1719. It is an adulatory and hagiographic work, but, as with the other early biographies, it cannot be ignored.

17. Part II, I.D [1696 *Méditations*].
18. Paris, 1706 (two volumes).
19. Two other spiritual tractates are included in the *abbé* d'Arnaudin's biograhy of Le Nain (see Further Reading, 25) on pages 197-360.
20. Part II, II.A [1715 Le Nain].

By 1713, then, there were three biographies of Rancé, but the story is far from finished. The next to appear came neither from la Trappe nor from France, but from la Trappe's colony in Italy, the abbey of Buonsolazzo near Florence. The author was Joseph Dominique d'Inguimbert, known in religion as Father Malachie/Malachia, who was born in Carpentras in 1683. He studied at Aix and Paris before taking the cistercian habit at the abbey of Casamari near Rome. In 1719 he was sent to Buonsolazzo where his talents were recognized by the grand duke of Tuscany and by Cardinal Annibal d'Albani, nephew of Pope Clement XI, who brought him to Rome. By 1723 he was librarian to Cardinal Corsini, and when the cardinal was elected Pope Clement XII, he named Inguimbert titular archbishop of Theodosia and then, in 1735, bishop of Carpentras. When Inguimbert returned to his native city he took with him his large personal library, added to it another large collection, made the whole available to the public, and left it to Carpentras where it is now the *Bibliothèque Inguimbertine*. After more than twenty years devoted to his city and his see, he died on 6 September 1757.

Inguimbert's *Genuinus Character Reverendi admodùm in Christo Patris D. Armandi Johannis Buttilierii Rancæi, abbatis monasterii B. Mariæ Domus Dei de Trappa*[21] appeared in 1718, and his *Vita di D. Armando Giovanni Le Bouthillier di Ransé, Abate Regolare, e Riformatore del Monastero della Trappa*[22] was published seven years later in 1725. Both are essentially derivative, being based primarily on the previous lives by Marsollier and Le Nain and the *Imago R.P. Domni Armandi-Joannis Le Bouthillier de Rancé* of Louis d'Aquin, and one of their main purposes was to defend Rancé against accusations of Jansenism and disrespect for the Holy See. Neither adds anything significant to the information already provided by the other biographers.

So let us return to la Trappe. We said earlier that Jean-Baptiste de La Tour had been collecting material from about

---

21. Part II, II.A [1718 Inguimbert].
22. Part II, II.A [1725 Inguimbert].

the time of his arrival at la Trappe, but that ill health had prevented him from making full use of what he had collected. By the time of his death in 1708 he had certainly prepared some sort of draft life of Rancé, but it was not something ready for publication. To follow the story further we must now introduce a friend of La Tour who had entered la Trappe with him in 1695: a former Carmelite named Armand-François Gervaise,[23] a turbulent priest who deserves a biography of his own.

Gervaise was born in Paris in about 1660 (his father was a physician), well educated by the Jesuits (he completed his studies with eminent success), and entered the Discalced Carmelites as frère Agathange. He appears to have been well respected in his Order and rose to become prior of Grégy in the diocese of Meaux. But in 1695, as we have seen, he abandoned the Carmelites to enter la Trappe. He was the last choir-monk to be professed by Rancé himself. In the same year, ill-health forced Rancé to retire as abbot, and his successor, Dom Zozime Foisil, appointed Gervaise prior. Then, when Zozime unexpectedly died in March 1696, Rancé—encouraged by Bossuet—appointed Gervaise as abbot in his place. It was a disastrous choice, but as we shall see in later chapters, deep spirituality does not always go hand in hand with good sense.

Problems and friction immediately arose within the community. Gervaise had an inflated opinion of his talents as an organizer and spiritual director—and as if this were not enough, he entered on an unfortunate attempt to make a trappist foundation at the abbey of l'Estrées near Dreux. The monastery had been abandoned since 1672 and, at the time, was held *in commendam* by François de Montmorency-Laval, bishop of Québec. But since the buildings were vacant, and since the cistercian nuns of Colombe, near Longwy, had been obliged to leave their own priory because of one of Louis XIV's numerous wars, the General Chapter housed them in the deserted monastery. This, however, was not at all agree-

---

23. He also appears as François-Armand.

able to the bishop of Québec, who offered the abbey to Dom Gervaise. The latter then sent a group of Trappists to l'Estrées, forced the nuns out, and took over the buildings. The prioress immediately appealed to the king who, in turn, ordered the newly established Trappists to leave (they had, in any case, technically infringed the royal ban on new foundations) and the nuns to return.

Shortly after this fiasco Dom Gervaise antagonized the formidable abbess of Les Clairets, Reverend Mother Françoise-Angélique d'Étampes de Valençay, a daughter of a very powerful family. She was a devout but haughty woman, very conscious of her position, and she had not found Gervaise sufficiently respectful. It is infinitely unlikely that Gervaise had been deliberately rude or discourteous—imprudent would be a better term—but the abbess perceived his conduct as a slight and she had no hesitation in exercising her considerable family influence to bring about his downfall.

Gervaise had also antagonized Charles Maisne. Again, he had not done so deliberately, but, again, he seems to have acted undiplomatically. We must remember, however, that the situation was extremely delicate. Gervaise was abbot, that is true, but Rancé was still alive and Maisne, his amanuensis and second self, was a formidable power in the abbey. To govern the house in such circumstances demanded the utmost prudence and discretion, and discretion was something conspicuously lacking in Dom Gervaise. Maisne therefore put it about that Gervaise was not showing sufficient respect for his ailing former abbot and was even imperilling the reform. As it happens, neither accusation was true, but both were damaging; and although Gervaise tried to recoup the situation by resigning his spiritual directorship of les Clairets and abandoning the resettlement of l'Estrées, he had lost the battle.

In July 1698 he submitted his resignation to the king, but it was not immediately accepted. The situation at the abbey immediately began to degenerate, and there were five months of vituperative in-fighting which culminated in the depar-

ture of Gervaise in December of the same year. With him
went his friend Jean-Baptiste de La Tour. Gervaise was succeeded by Jacques de La Cour who is not here our concern.

Gervaise then became a sort of gyrovague, wandering from
monastery to monastery, never staying too long, and producing a considerable number of historical works of mixed quality.[24] They are well written and easy to read, but not always
reliable either in facts, balance, or opinions. He then antagonized the unreformed Cistercians by publishing a grossly
biased *Histoire générale de la Réforme de l'Ordre de Cîteaux en
France*, and his irate adversaries succeeded in obtaining a *lettre
de cachet* from the king to have Gervaise confined to the abbey
of le Reclus in the diocese of Troyes, which was a sort of
borstal for rebellious religious. There he died on 21 September 1751, still faithful to the memory of Rancé and still ob-
serving, so far as was possible, the monastic rule of la Trappe.

When Jean-Baptiste de la Tour had left La Trappe in 1699
with Gervaise, it had not been for friendship alone. His
infirmities were too grave for the austere regime of the monastery and he had only a few more years to live. He therefore
entrusted his unfinished, or at least unpolished, life of Rancé
to Gervaise in the hope that the latter would complete what
he, La Tour, had been unable to do. Gervaise assented willingly, and the conspicuous defects of the three biographies
already available by 1713 merely encouraged him in his work.
By 1720 he had produced a more complete, more reliable, and
more detailed account than anything that had appeared earlier, but permission for publication was refused by the state
censors. Part of the problem was that there were already
three biographies of Rancé; part of the problem may well
have been the machinations of Gervaise's enemies. He had,
after all, left la Trappe under a cloud, and there were doubt-
less those who would have seen the reputation of Rancé sullied by a life coming from his pen. Maisne and the duc de
Saint-Simon in particular had no time at all for him. Gervaise

24. For a complete list, see *DTC* 6:1339-1340. See also *DLF XVIII* 536-537.

himself certainly thought that his enemies were behind the censors' refusal, and he may have been right.

This did not, however, stop him from publishing other related works. In 1724 the learned Maurist Dom Vincent Thuillier published an attack on Rancé's attitude to monastic studies in his *Ouvrages posthumes de D. Jean Mabillon et de D. Thierri Ruinart, Bénédictins de la Congrégation de Saint Maur*, a work which included an entirely Benedictine view of the 'Histoire de la Contestation sur les Études Monastiques'.[25] Gervaise immediately replied with an *Apologie pour feu M. l'abbé de la Trappe, Dom Armand-Jean Bouthillier de Rancé, contre les calomnies et les invectives de D. Vincent Thuillier,*[26] a piece which, as Jean François put it, was 'très-vive'.[27] Furthermore, since Gervaise could not publish his own life of Rancé, which corrected many of the errors that had appeared in the earlier biographies, he published, in 1742, an important *Jugement critique, mais équitable des vies de feu M. l'abbé de Rancé, réformateur de l'abbaye de la Trappe. Écrites par les Sieurs Marsollier et Maupeou. Divisé en deux parties où l'on voit toutes les fautes qu'ils ont commises contre la vérité de l'Histoire, contre le bon sens, contre la vray-semblance, contre l'honneur même de M. de Rancé, et de la Maison de la Trappe.*[28] That the book (published under a false imprint) is *critique* is not in doubt; few would call it *équitable*. It is, in fact, a biting, acid, and sometimes malicious criticism of Maupeou and Marsollier, though less so of Le Nain, but it certainly reveals Gervaise's mastery of his sources. Other material from his unpublished biography appeared in his biased *Histoire générale de la Réforme de l'Ordre de Cîteaux en France* which, as we have seen, would in due course lead to his imprisonment at le Reclus.

When he died on 21 September 1751 Gervaise's life of Rancé remained still in manuscript. A further attempt was made to publish it in the 1780s,[29] but to no avail. Then, in 1791-92, when the monks of la Trappe were expelled from their abbey

25. Part II, II.A [1692 *Ouvrages posthumes*].   26. Part II, II.A [1724 Gervaise].
27. François, 3:137.   28. Part II, II.A [1742 Gervaise].
29. See Lekai, 'Problem of the Authorship' (cited under Further Reading, 25) 159-160.

in the tumult of the French Revolution, they took with them a copy of Gervaise's manuscript. During the years of exile a start was made on revising and editing the text, but it had not been completed by the time the Trappists returned to France in 1815. At that time the manuscript came into the possession of the abbey of Sept-Fons where, for the moment, we must leave it.

By 1815, however, the public was fascinated by Rancé and la Trappe. In 1813 Mary Schimmelpenninck had published her *Narrative of a Tour Taken in the year 1667, to La Grande Chartreuse and Alet by Dom Claude Lancelot, Author of the Port Royal Grammars; including Some Account of Dom Armand Jean Le Bouthillier de Rancé, Reverend Father Abbé, and Reformer of the Monastery of Notre Dame de La Trappe*.[30] The author was a deeply pious Englishwoman of Quaker stock (her maiden name was Galton: the Schimmelpenninck came from her marriage in 1806 to a Dutch tobacco trader) who was much involved in the anti-slavery movement and who was also clearly captivated by Port-Royal. Her *Narrative* contained some thirty pages devoted to Rancé and the reform, but it was no more than a brief sketch of his life. Far more significant was the first full-scale english life which appeared a year later, Charles Butler's *The Lives of Dom Armand-Jean Le Bouthillier de Rancé, Abbot Regular and Reformer of the Monastery of La Trappe; and of Thomas à Kempis, the Reputed Author of 'The Imitation of Christ'*.[31] The title of the work is somewhat misleading since the life of Thomas à Kempis appears only as an appendix. Butler compiled his life of 'the venerable Martyr of penitential austerity'[32] from Maupeou, Marsollier, and Le Nain, but added material from Rancé's own works, the *Relations de la mort de quelques religieux de l'abbaye de la Trappe*, and the 1708 *Description du plan en relief de l'Abbaye de la Trappe présenté au Roy par le frère Pacôme*.[33] Butler's life of Rancé is an interesting

30. Part II, II.B [1813 Schimmelpenninck].
31. Part II, II.B [1814 Butler].
32. Butler, 1.
33. See *ibid.*, 2.

and well-written little volume, though none of the many quotations is footnoted, and its accuracy inevitably reflects the accuracy, or otherwise, of its sources.

The first german biography to appear was the *Leben des Dom Armand Johanns Le Bouthillier de Rancé, Abt's und Reformators des Klosters La Trappe. Ein Beitrag zur Erfahrungs-Seelenkunde*, published in 1820 by Leopold Friedrich Gunther von Göckingk.[34] This, however, is little more than a germanized version of Marsollier and does not tell us very much that we do not already know either about Rancé or about psychology. Yet another french life appeared in 1842. This was the *Histoire de l'abbé de Rancé* by Philippe-Irénée Boistel d'Exauvillez,[35] but since the revised version of 1868 was more important, we shall leave Exauvillez for later discussion.

Infinitely more significant was the appearance in 1844 of Chateaubriand's *Vie de Rancé*,[36] and things were never quite the same again. The book is actually less a life of Rancé than a life of Chateaubriand, and it certainly tells us more about the latter than the former. It was a product of his old age (he died four years after its publication) and was written at the command of his confessor, the *abbé* Séguin.[37] The author evinces a Romantic fascination with Rancé's conversion, and especially his relationship with Madame de Montbazon— Chateaubriand had been reading Daniel de Larroque— but the fame of its author guaranteed the book a wide dissemination. Furthermore, its translation into most european languages ensured that the Rancé most people knew was the Chateaubrianized Rancé of legend, not the man himself.

34. Part II, II.B [1820 Göckingk].
35. Part II, II.B [1842 Exauvillez].
36. Part II, II.B [1844 Chateaubriand].
37. 'C'est pour obéir aux ordres du directeur de ma vie que j'ai écrit l'histoire de l'abbé de Rancé. L'abbé Séguin me parlait souvent de ce travail, et j'y avais une répugnance naturelle. J'étudiais néanmoins; je lus, et c'est le résultat de ces lectures qui compose aujourd'hui la Vie de Rancé' (*Vie de Rancé. Édition critique avec une introduction, des notices, des variantes et des notes*, ed. Fernand Letessier [Paris, 1955] 1:10).

There was, of course, a reaction. In 1864, Stanislas Lapierre, abbot of Sept-Fons, published a *Circulaire*[38] in which he referred to the book as a 'roman dans le genre de ceux de Walter Scott', and asserted that it was not a book to be in the hands of any monk, much less a young monk.[39] And in the same *Circulaire* he was happy to announce the imminent publication of a new, authoritative, long-awaited biography of Rancé by a certain *abbé* Louis Dubois. Two years later this new and authoritative biography duly appeared—the two solid volumes of the *Histoire de l'abbé de Rancé et de sa réforme, composée avec ses écrits, ses lettres, ses règlements et un grand nombre de documents contemporains inédits ou peu connus*[40]—and for almost a century it remained the 'standard' biography of the Great Reformer.

To understand the history of this 'standard' biography—a history brilliantly presented by Father Louis Lekai in 1959[41]—we must return to Sept-Fons where, it will be remembered, the Trappists who returned to France in 1815 had deposited a manuscript copy of Armand-François Gervaise's unpublished life of Rancé. When Dom Stanislas, the author of the *Circulaire*, became abbot of Sept-Fons he realized the need for a new and comprehensive biography which would go further than those of Maupeou, Marsollier, Le Nain, Aquin and those who followed them. He therefore took the two substantial manuscript volumes of Gervaise (which had already been the subject of some editorial revision) and gave them to Dom François Couturier, abbot of Port-du-Salut, for final revision and early publication. The revisions, as Lekai has said, 'added little or nothing to the amount of factual information originally presented by Gervaise',[42] and were mainly concerned with toning down his

38. Part II, II.B [1864 La Pierre].
39. *Ibid.* The *Circulaire* is unpaginated. The *abbé* Bonhomme calls it 'a bad novel rather than a biography' (Exauvillez, *Histoire de l'abbé de Rancé*, xi).
40. Part II, II.B [1866 Dubois].
41. Lekai, 'Problem of the Authorship', cited under Further Reading, 25.
42. *Ibid.*, 160.

more vituperative outbursts.

Couturier, however, died in 1854, before the work of revision was quite complete, and the task of bringing the work to final publication was then entrusted to the *abbé* Louis Dubois, a priest in the diocese of Dijon. Dubois was offered all the assistance he needed by and from the Order, but took little advantage of it, and the two substantial volumes which finally saw public light in 1866 were little more than Couturier's revision of Gervaise's already partly revised manuscript. The personal contribution of Dubois, says Father Lekai,

> remained strictly in the field of editorial activity. He divided the text into small chapters, now and then re-arranged and rephrased a few paragraphs, polished the style and eliminated the last vestiges of a still latent Gallicanism.[43]

In other words, Dubois was essentially a plagiarist, and the 1866 biography (with a revised edition appearing in 1869) was, in actuality, more than two hundred years old. This is not to say that it does not contain a huge amount of invaluable information, but that information must always be carefully authenticated, and the portrait of Rancé that emerges from its more than fifteen hundred pages is a portrait painted by Gervaise.

The revised version of Exauvillez's life, which appeared in 1868,[44] took advantage of the newly-published work of Gervaise/Dubois and the title-page informs us that it was 'revue, corrigée et augmentée par l'abbé R. Bonhomme, Prêtre du diocèse d'Évreux'. The book was indeed much enlarged, and the *abbé* added a useful introduction on the history of rancéan biography, but it added nothing to what was already known. It was, however, much shorter than the huge *Vie* of Gervais/Dubois and (as the learned *abbé* tells us) very much

43. *Ibid.*, 161.
44. See Part II, II.B [1842 Exauvillez].

cheaper. The same may be said of two new german lives, both of which appeared in 1897: one by Franz Büttgenbach, the other by Bernhard Schmid.[45] The former, which has neither footnotes nor bibliography, is based on Gervaise/Dubois; the latter is primarily indebted to Gervaise/Dubois and Marsollier, but also utilizes Chateaubriand (an unfortunate choice), Louis Du Bois's *Histoire civile, religieuse et littéraire de l'abbaye de la Trappe* (1824),[46] and (for the dispute over monastic studies) Henri Didio's excellent *La querelle de Mabillon et de l'Abbé de Rancé* (1892). Neither biography is of major consequence.

There now followed a period of more than thirty years when no further Life appeared. Then, in 1929, Henri Bremond published a volume which, in its way, was destined to have almost the same impact as the pseudo-autobiography of Chateaubriand. This was '*L'Abbé Tempête*': *Armand de Rancé, Réformateur de la Trappe*, translated into English the following year as *The Thundering Abbot. Armand de Rancé, Reformer of La Trappe*.[47] It is a brilliant book, written by a brilliant scholar who also published an *Histoire littéraire du sentiment religieux en France* which is a tour-de-force of recondite information. But, as Professor Krailsheimer has said, '*L'Abbé Tempête*' is also 'brilliantly perverse. ... With cavalier disregard for evidence, [Bremond] presents a masterly and entertaining caricature of a Rancé as remote from historical reality as that of Chateaubriand'.[48] Unfortunately, the book is a splendid read, and people generally prefer amusing inaccuracy to turgid precision.

Reaction was immediate. In 1930 Georges-Abel Simon published a *Réponse à 'L'Abbé Tempête'*, a pamphlet of a dozen pages,[49] and 1930 and 1931 saw the publication of three new

45. Part II, II.B [1897 Büttgenbach] and [1897 Schmid].
46. This is not the Louis Dubois of the 'standard' biography. The name was—and is—common.
47. Part II, II.B [1929 Bremond].
48. Krailsheimer, *Rancé*, xi.
49. Part II, II.B [1930 Simon].

biographies of Rancé, all intended to correct the misrepresentations of the past, whether by Chateaubriand or by Bremond. Two were in French—by Albert Cherel (1930) and the vicomte Du Jeu (1931)[50]—and one was in English, by Ailbe J. Luddy (1931),[51] a cistercian monk well known for his studies and translations of Bernard of Clairvaux.

None of these works was particularly successful. Simon corrected some of Bremond's more glaring inaccuracies, but made others of his own;[52] and Albert Cherel's volume is, as Aurel Mensáros has said, 'rich in reflections, but lacking in all desirable references'.[53] Cherel's study was written at the request of his brother-in-law, Pierre du Roure, a monk of Cîteaux (where he took the name of Frère Robert), and the result is, if not panegyrical, at least adulatory. Du Jeu's work is likewise pro-Rancé, but more balanced (save when he is speaking of trappist observances) and more inclined to use evidence from Rancé's letters. He also provides a brief and judicious assessment of the abbot at the end of the volume.[54]

More important is *The Real De Rancé* of Ailbe Luddy, who calls Bremond's work a 'nasty book':

> Not that it contained anything opposed to Christian faith or morality, but because it presented to the reader as an authentic portrait of a saintly monk what was really a caricature. How anyone could seriously offer this ugly amalgam of half-truths, suspicions, insinuations, and 'likely guesses' as a study of De Rancé passes comprehension.[55]

Luddy had a point. One does get rather tired of Bremond's

50. Part II, II.B [1930 Cherel] and [1931 Du Jeu].
51. Part II, II.B [1931 Luddy].
52. See Mensáros, 175, n. 73.
53. *Ibid.*, 177.
54. Du Jeu, *Monsieur de la Trappe*, 207-210.
55. Luddy, *The Real de Rancé*, xi (slightly abbreviated).

innuendos and rhetorical questions. Luddy's own account was intended to redress the balance, but although it is a thorough and painstaking piece of work, it lacks the pungency—and therefore the popularity—of Bremond.

One of the main problems besetting almost all these biographies was a deficiency of sources. The authors had at their disposal the early lives, the two tomes of Gervaise/Dubois, and Rancé's own writings. But Rancé wrote a great deal, and of that great deal, some is repetitive, some is tedious, some demands an appreciation of a literary genre rare after the nineteenth century, and some remained in manuscript. Of manuscript material, by far the most important was the substantial mass of the abbot's correspondence, scattered throughout the monastic and secular libraries of France. Some of this had been gathered together in an odd sort of way in 1701-02 in the *Lettres de piété écrites à différentes personnes*,[56] though precisely who did the gathering remains unclear. Other letters had been well edited in 1846 by Benoît Gonod, librarian of Clermont-Ferrand.[57] But it was not until the 1970s and the ground-breaking work of Professor Alban Krailsheimer that scholars were provided with the necessary material for a fundamental reassessment of the ideas and influence of the abbot of la Trappe.

In 1984 Professor Krailsheimer published his *Letters of Armand-Jean de Rancé, Abbot and Reformer of La Trappe*, and followed this nine years later with his magisterial edition of Rancé's *Correspondance*.[58] Prior to this, however, in 1974, he had made use of his preliminary researches into Rancé's letters to publish his *Armand-Jean de Rancé, Abbot of la Trappe. His Influence in the Cloister and the World*, which (in the revised french translation published in 2000) remains the best biography to date.[59] The book is a masterpiece. It does not confuse a biography with an encyclopedia, and it presents Rancé

56. Part II, I.B.i [1701 *Lettres*].
57. Part II, I.B.i [1846 Gonod].
58. Part II, I.B.i [1984 Krailsheimer] and [1993 Krailsheimer].
59. Part II, II.B [1974 Krailsheimer], with reference to reviews.

in his world and his times. Krailsheimer presents an astonishing amount of information; he writes beautifully; and no student of Rancé can afford to ignore his work.

Four years later, in 1978, there appeared a curious little volume written and published by members of The Order of the Magnificat of the Mother of God, an Order which

> was requested by the Blessed Virgin at La Salette (France) in 1846, and was founded in Canada in 1962. This religious Order, destined to form the Apostles of the Latter Times, received a mission for the preservation of the deposit of the Catholic Christian Faith and the safeguard of the Universal Church.[60]

This little book is entitled *The Holy War or The Story of Abbot de Rancé*[61] and is based on the Gervaise/Dubois biography supplemented by the other early biographies (Maupeou, Marsollier, and Le Nain) together with limited reference to Chateaubriand, Marie-Léon Serrant,[62] Bremond, Cherel, Du Jeu, and the 'Manuscrit de Septfons'.[63] It is not, in fact, the story of abbot de Rancé, but rather the story of abbot de Rancé's involvement in the War of the Observances and the eventual triumph of the Trappist Reform. It presents nothing new and is written from the standpoint of piety, but it contains good english translations of a considerable amount of material unavailable elsewhere.

Much more important was a second volume from the pen of Alban Krailsheimer which appeared in 1985 as *Rancé and the Trappist Legacy*.[64] This is a deceptively simple volume which

60. I quote from their website on the Internet, URL http://www.magnificat.ca/english/.
61. Part II, II.B [1978 Apostles of the Infinite Love].
62. Marie-Léon Serrant, *L'Abbé de Rancé et Bossuet: ou, Le grand moine et le grand évêque du grand siècle* (Paris, 1903).
63. *The Holy War*, 172.
64. Part II, II.B [Krailsheimer].

was intended for a wider audience than the 1974 biography (in which passages in French were not translated), but it contains much of value both in information and balanced judgement. It remains the best popular introduction in English to the man and his influence. A biography by Ivan Gobry, which appeared six years later in 1991, however, is a grave disappointment.[65] It is certainly well written, but it does little more than reproduce Gervaise/Dubois, and the author appears to ignore entirely the seminal work of Krailsheimer. There are also far too many inaccuracies and misrepresentations, and it is difficult to understand why the book was ever published. It can safely be ignored.[66]

Anna Maria Caneva's *Il riformatore della Trappa. Vita di Armand-Jean de Rancé*, published in Italian in 1996 and in french translation a year later,[67] is much better, though it adds nothing to the work of Krailsheimer. It is, however, accurate, well written, easy to read, and cheap to buy.

In summary, then, the period from 1701 to 1996 witnessed the publication of no less than two dozen biographies of the abbot of la Trappe. This constitutes a substantial quantity of material. Most of it, however, is derivative, and a number of the biographies reveal more of the biographer than the biographee. The early lives by Maupeou, Marsollier, Le Nain, and Gervaise/Dubois retain their (mixed) value, as also does Gervaise's *Jugement critique* and, to a limited extent, Aquin's *Imago* and its later revisions; but from Butler in 1814 to Caneva in 1996, only the work of Krailsheimer is of major significance. I should add, perhaps, that I am speaking here of *biographies* of Rancé. Krailsheimer did not deal specifically with Rancé's spirituality—that was intentional, not an oversight[68]—and

---

65. Part II, II.B [1991 Gobry].
66. See Lucien Aubry's justly critical review in *Collectanea Cisterciensia* 54 1992) BSM [263]-[264].
67. Part II, II.B [1996 Caneva].
68. As the author himself says, Rancé's spirituality 'deserves full-scale treatment by a specialist, and I have neither the space nor the competence to attempt it' (Krailsheimer, *Rancé*, xvi).

the last forty years have seen a large number of studies devoted to this important subject.[69] In 1975 Yves Chaussy said
that 'Rancé is almost unknown to the general public and his
works are no longer read'.[70] As it happens, the comment was
untrue in 1975. It is infinitely more untrue now.

Yet Rancé remains elusive, partly because few take the
trouble to understand the soil from which his ideas sprang,
and partly because the misrepresentations which we see from
Chateaubriand through Henri Bremond to (it must be admitted) Louis Lekai—who did not like Rancé—have had a
singular tenacity. The idea of the thundering abbot, the over-
zealous penitent, the hyperascetical ascetic, the inflexible and
inhuman lord of la Trappe who would not even let his monks
visit their dying parents is still all too common, and there are
still few who would agree with Professor Krailsheimer's comment that

> first-hand acquaintance with Rancé and with
> the present community of la Trappe has, I
> hope, not impaired my judgement or impar-
> tiality, but has certainly filled me with
> respect, enthusiasm, and ultimately real
> affection for a man of uncommon gifts who
> still has much to offer.[71]

I do not know many Trappists today who could be said to
have respect, enthusiasm, or affection for their great founder,
and fewer still who would agree that his works still have much
to offer. I think they are wrong in this, and my own immer-
sion in the life and works of the Great Reformer has, I happily admit, led me to the same end as it led Professor
Krailsheimer.

69. They will be found listed in my 'Bibliography' (see page 282 of the index
to that article).
70. Yves Chaussy, 'Un livre sur Rancé', *Cîteaux: Commentarii cistercienses* 26
(1975) 221.
71. Krailsheimer, *Rancé*, xvi.

Let us, then, try to put Rancé in perspective. He was unquestionably a man of his times and, as we said in our Introduction, he cannot be understood without taking into account his country, his Order, his background, his learning, his conversion, and his character. Let us therefore begin with his country, with France during *le grand siècle*, and try to appreciate how the grand gestures and black-and-white contrasts of the 1600s differ so radically from the politically correct overall greyness of our twenty-first century.

FURTHER READING

On Charles Maisne, see Krailsheimer, *Rancé*, 39, n. 1 and the references in the index, 371. There is a good account in Dubois (1866) 5-6.

Of Rancé's biographers, my account of Pierre de Maupeou is drawn from comments in his own life of Rancé, comments by the other early biographers, especially Gervaise in his acerbic *Jugement critique* (see n. 28 above), Rancé's letters to Maupeou, and a few references in other letters. See also the index to Krailsheimer, *Rancé*, 371 s.v. Maupeou, Pierre. For Jacques Marsollier, see the brief bibliography in *DLF XVIII*, 848. Pierre Le Nain (*DAC* 451-452) is the subject of the valuable biography by the *abbé* d'Arnaudin, *La Vie de Dom Pierre Le Nain, religieux et ancien soûprieur de l'abbaïe de la Trappe* (Paris, 1715 [two editions]). See also G. Müller, 'Pierre Le Nain', *Cistercienser-Chronik* 25 (1913) 33-38. Armand-François Gervaise has not, oddly, been the subject of a full-length biography, though he certainly deserves it. An essential bibliography is provided by Jean Besse in *DTC* 6:1339-1340 and Anselme Dimier in *DHGE* 20:1091-1093. To these must be added Louis J. Lekai's brilliant article, 'The Problem of the Authorship of Rancé's "Standard" Biography', *Collectanea OCR* 21 (1959) 157-163 and *idem*, 'The Unpublished Second Volume of Gervaise's "Histoire générale de la réforme de l'ordre de Cîteaux en France" ', *Analecta SOC* 17 (1961) 278-283. On Louis d'Aquin, see Louis Duval, *Un ami de l'abbé de Rancé. Mgr Louis d'Aquin, évêque de Sées* (Alençon, 1902), which is no more than a pamphlet of fourteen pages, and the full-length study by Lucien-Victor Dumain, *Mgr Louis d'Aquin, évêque de Séez (1667-1710)* (Paris, 1902). For Joseph Dominique d'Inguimbert, bishop of Carpentras, we have the brief biography by Robert Caillet, *Monseigneur d'Inguimbert, archevêque, évêque de Carpentras (1683-1757), un prélat bibliophile et philanthrope* (Lyon, 1952). For further information, the reader must be referred to the bibliographies in *DTC* 7:1934-1936, *DS* 7:1733-1735, *DAC* 382-383, and *DHGE* 25:1175-1176. The bibliography on Chateaubriand is immense and we obviously cannot deal with it here. The best edition of his life of Rancé (there is no english translation) is by Fernand Letessier, *Vie de Rancé. Édition critique avec une introduction, des notices, des variantes et des notes* (Paris, [1955], two volumes). Letessier's admirable introduction is essential reading. Henri Bremond is the subject of one full-length study in English and about half a dozen in French. In English we have Henry Hogarth's *Henri Bremond: The Life and Work of a Devout Humanist* (London, 1950); in French, the most important studies are by Albert Autin (1946), Francis Hermans (1965), André Blanchet (1975), and Émile Guichot (1982). There is also an italian study by Armando Savignano published in 1980.

For Gervaise's enemy and Rancé's friend, Reverend Mother Françoise-Angélique d'Étampes de Valençay, abbess of Les Clairets, see the delightful article by Chrysogonus Waddell, 'Armand-Jean de Rancé and Françoise-Angélique d'Étampes Valençay: Reformers of Les Clairets', in *Hidden Springs: Cistercian Monastic Women, Book Two. Medieval Religious Women, Volume Three*, ed. John A. Nichols and Lillian T. Shank (Kalamazoo, 1995) 599-673.

For the true origin of the *abbé* Louis Dubois's *Histoire de l'abbé de Rancé et de sa réforme, composée avec ses écrits, ses lettres, ses règlements et un grand nombre de documents contemporains inédits ou peu connus* (Paris, 1866[1], 1869[2]), see Lekai's 'Problem of the Authorship', cited above.

Mary Anne Schimmelpenninck (1778-1856), a most interesting woman, has left us her own autobiography, posthumously published: *Life of Mary Anne Schimmelpenninck, edited by her relation Christina C. Hankin* (London, 1858 [two volumes]). There were three later editions.

Chapter 2

RANCÉ'S FRANCE

WHEN CHARLOTTE JOLY, wife of Denis Bouthillier, gave birth to a boy-child on 9 January 1626, France had been ruled either through or by Louis XIII for twenty-five years. Louis had succeeded his father, Henry IV, in 1610, but since he was only nine at the time, his mother, Marie de Médicis, ruled the country as regent and continued to do so until 1617. She was not a great success, being dominated by italian advisors, too pro-spanish, and unable to control the unruly french nobles. On the other hand, she did promote the advancement of Armand-Jean du Plessis, Duc de Richelieu, that extraordinary man, and it was as a result of her influence that he was made cardinal in 1622 and prime minister of France in 1624.

Richelieu dominated the young Louis, which was, in general, no bad thing, and it was primarily a result of his vigorous efforts that the political power of the great french families was drastically curtailed, that France was transformed into the dominant military power in Europe, and that the foundations were established for the age of absolutism.

On a more parochial level, the cardinal was also well-disposed to the family Bouthillier and, as we saw in the Introduction, he was godfather to the young Armand-Jean whose name echoes that of his illustrious sponsor. Towards the end of the sixteenth century, it seems, the Bouthilliers, then a family of lawyers in Angoulême, had been of service to the Du Plessis, and the greater family had not forgotten its debt to the lesser. Rancé's first published work, his commentary

on Anacreon which appeared in 1639,[1] was dedicated to the
cardinal, but at that time Richelieu had only three more years
to live. He died on 4 December 1642—Rancé would be seventeen a month later—and his successor, Cardinal Mazarin, was
no friend to the Bouthilliers and, as we shall see, no friend to
Rancé either.

Mazarin was a mixed blessing to France. On the one hand,
he continued Richelieu's absolutist policies and brought the
Thirty Years' War to a successful, if not entirely happy, conclusion. But at home his insensitivity to the problems of the
people—those usually provoked by war: too little food and
too high taxes—caused widespread unrest, and certain fool-
hardy actions on the part of Mazarin resulted in a protest by
the *Parlement* of Paris, a protest which soon evolved into the
widespread armed insurrection known as the Fronde.

The Fronde was actually a series of revolts which lasted
for five years, from 1648 to 1653, and, in its second and final
phase, was less concerned with high taxation than with a fear
on the part of the french nobility of the growing power of
the monarchy. As it happens, the Fronde was unsuccessful,
the revolt of the nobles was suppressed, the crown emerged
from the conflict stronger than ever, Mazarin (who had been
directing events from Germany) returned to France in triumph, and Armand-Jean Bouthillier de Rancé found himself
in difficulties. Why?

In December 1648 he had received minor orders, the sub-
diaconate and the diaconate, from the hands of Jean-François-
Paul de Gondi, who at the time was coadjutor archbishop of
Paris. But Paul de Gondi was one of the leaders of the Fronde
and a staunch opponent of Mazarin, a man he generally de-
spised—save when it was opportune not to. And to make
matters worse, Rancé's relationship with Gondi was not
merely that of a deacon to his bishop. The two became fast
friends, and remained so until 1679 when Gondi—or Cardinal de Retz, as he had become in 1652—died in disgrace (or at

1. Part II, I.A.i [1639 Ἀνακρέοντος Τηΐου τὰ μέλη].

least partial disgrace). On the collapse of the Fronde in 1653 and Mazarin's triumphant return, Retz had been imprisoned, had escaped, and had fled into exile; and friends of the one cardinal were no friends of the other. Mazarin himself now began to instruct his young protégé, Louis XIV (whom we shall meet in a moment), in the arts of war and diplomacy; he amassed a colossal fortune (despite his addiction to gambling); he founded what, in time, would become the *Institut de France*; and—his crowning achievement—concluded the Treaty of the Pyrenees in 1659 to the great advantage of his country and his king. He died in 1661.

Mazarin's enmity, as we saw in the Introduction, doomed any hopes that Rancé might succeed his uncle as archbishop of Tours, and, in any case, by the time of his ordination to the priesthood in 1651, France was no longer what it was. Louis XIII had been dead for eight years, and the throne was now occupied by his thirteen-year-old son who was to reign for more than seven astonishing decades. Louis XIV, the Sun King, was born in 1638. He was not particularly well educated academically, but his mother indoctrinated him in basic Catholicism together with an unhealthy amount of superstition. Mazarin taught him the craft of kingship. The Fronde showed him the need for a strong, centralized government as well as making him darkly suspicious of the activities of the french nobility. He was a magnificent specimen of manhood, dramatically active below the waist ('he kept his Mistrisses very avowedly', said Gilbert Burnet[2]), but diligent, interested, unflagging, and hard working in the exercise of his kingship. He was also an effective, though overconfident, military leader; but if we say that his quest for military glory was more for France than for himself, we must not forget that in Louis's eyes, France and Louis were much the same thing. 'L'État, c'est moi', he would say in 1655. It was under the Sun King that *la gloire*, that rarefied yet real concept which has remained so important a part of the french mentality, took on reality.

2. Gilbert Burnet, *History of his Own Time* (London, 1724-1734), 1:207.

Louis was also a munificent patron of the arts, and in the course of his long reign there was a marvellous flowering of painting, sculpture, music, architecture, landscape gardening, building technology, the decorative arts, and, of course, literature and language. This is the age of Malherbe, Guez de Balzac, Descartes, Corneille, Pascal, Molière (a caricature of Rancé may possibly be seen in some lines of *Tartuffe* [1664][3]), Racine, Boileau-Despréaux, La Fontaine, La Rochefoucauld, Madame de Sévigné, Madame de La Fayette, La Bruyère, a host of *mémorialistes* (including the greatest of them, Saint-Simon), and, not least, the great preachers.

'Sermons', says Gerald Cragg, 'were one of the few means of moulding public opinion; they were almost the only vehicle of criticism in matters of high public concern.'[4] This is true. They sometimes functioned as the newspapers of the day. The two greatest orators of the time were undoubtedly Rancé's friend, Jacques-Bénigne Bossuet, and the Jesuit Louis Bourdaloue. Their styles were very different. Bossuet often spoke with little preparation, but he was known for the clarity of his thought, his subtle merging of theology and practical ethics, his magisterial grasp of his subject, and the splendour of his language. Bourdaloue prepared and wrote out his discourses with the greatest care, but his immense popularity was due to a large extent to the power and beauty of his voice, and that, alas, we cannot hear. He spoke very quickly but very clearly, and the common description of him as 'the king of preachers and the preacher of kings', though too much of a cliché, is not unjust.

On the other hand, there is no doubt that much of this preaching was over-elaborate, mannered, precious, and pedantic. Even such a notable orator as Esprit Fléchier was known for his love of sonorous words and pretentious

3. See Krailsheimer, *Rancé*, 77, who suggests that 'such a view cannot survive acquaintance with Rancé's letters'. But that is to confuse Rancé himself with Rancé as he was perceived by others.
4. Cragg, *The Church and the Age of Reason* (cited under Further Reading, 49) 35.

periods, and many sermons were no more than dramatic displays of linguistic pyrotechnics. The medium was more important than the message. What, then, of Rancé?

That he was eager to preach is clear from a letter to Jean Favier, his old tutor, written late in 1643 when he was sixteen,[5] and it seems that his public preaching (which began four years later) was well received. How well received is difficult to say. His early and panegyrical biographers naturally laud his eloquence and his popularity, and they may be right. He certainly took great pains with his style and oratory—he was satirized for doing so[6]—but when André Félibien des Avaux writes to the duchesse de Liancourt and says that she will, of course, remember with what eloquence the young *abbé* used to express himself when he was still at court,[7] there is no reason to disbelieve him. Rancé preached his first sermon in 1647, when one of his sisters was received into the convent of the Annonciades in Paris, and other sermons followed.[8] His delivery, we are told by Gervaise/Dubois, was 'moving, majestic, and fervent'.[9] He showed something of the torrent of words so admired in Bourdaloue, but did not speak so quickly, and (according to Marsollier) possessed 'most of the qualities which make a great orator'.[10] He may also have had a high opinion of his own capabilities, for on one occasion, when he met a friend in Paris, François de Harlay de Champvallon (later archbishop of the city), and was asked what he was doing that day, the young Rancé replied, 'Ce matin, prêcher comme un ange; ce soir, chasser comme un diable': 'This morning I'll preach like an angel; this afternoon I'll hunt like a devil.'[11] Angels and devils notwithstanding, if

5. Letter 431100.
6. See Chrysogonus Waddell, 'The Cistercian Dimension of the Reform of La Trappe (1662-1700): Preliminary Notes and Reflections', in *Cistercians in the Late Middle Ages: Studies in Medieval Cistercian History VI*, ed. E. Rozanne Elder (Kalamazoo, 1981), 148-149 (for note number 77, read 78).
7. [André Félibien des Avaux], *Description de l'abbaye de la Trappe* (Part II, II.A [1671]), 93-94 of the 1689 edition.
8. Dubois (1869) 1:49-51.   9. *Ibid.*, 50.
10. *Ibid.*, 50-51 (following Marsollier).   11. *Ibid.*, 51.

he was as good a preacher as he was a horseman, his displays in the pulpit must have been spectacular. But even if they were merely impressive, they would have stood him in good stead in his advancement in society; and it may well be that the success, in later years, of la Trappe was due in part to the eloquence of its abbot in an age when eloquence was esteemed and effective. This was the *grand siècle*, the 'Great Century', and it was an emotional age. Tears flowed more easily and more copiously than with us, and sentiment was often mistaken for conviction.[12] But when Félibien des Avaux again tells us that, at la Trappe, Rancé's words were like a devouring fire which set ablaze those who heard them,[13] who are we to disagree?

The *grand siècle* was a century of extremes. On the one hand we have the artificial elegance of Versailles; on the other the filthy and dangerous rookeries of parts of Paris. On the one hand we have opulence, wealth, and splendour; on the other the chronic poverty of too many wretchedly-dressed peasants living 'in a pore one roome & and one story open to the tiles, without window', whose diet might consist of little more than 'rie bread & water'.[14] On the one hand we have the Jardin du Luxembourg, frequented by crowds of persons of quality, citizens, strangers, gallants, ladies, friars, scholars, and 'jolly Citizens; some sitting & lying on the Grasse, others, running, & jumping, some playing at bowles, & ball, others dancing and singing';[15] on the other we have a crowd of ten thousand assembled at the Old Market in Poitiers to watch a man being broken on the wheel. The executioner began with his arms, and then proceeded to the knees, thighs, and stomach.

12. See Anne Vincent-Buffault, tr. Teresa Bridgeman, *The History of Tears: Sensibility and Sentimentality in France* (New York, 1991). The author is concerned primarily with the eighteenth and nineteenth centuries, but what is said of the eighteenth century is equally true of the seventeenth.
13. [Félibien des Avaux], *Description*, 93.
14. John Locke, quoted in Lough, *France Observed* (cited under Further Reading, 49) 40-41.
15. John Evelyn, quoted in Lough, 114.

The wretched criminal was still alive after the twentieth stroke, and when the executioner went to strangle him, as was the custom, the rope broke twice. The crowd loved it.[16] Putting it another way, in *le grand siècle* everything was *grand*, including disparities and distinctions. It was not a century of shades of grey, it was a century of blacks and whites. It was, furthermore, a century of absolutism. Indeed, as we have said above, it was The Age of Absolutism, and we are not speaking here only of absolutism in politics. 'The Absolute', as Lucien Aubry has rightly said, 'is a feature of all the reforms of the age',[17] and Rancé's reform was no more than a part of this. We must note, however, that absolutism and innovation have never been happy bedfellows—unless, of course, the innovations have been introduced by the absolute power. Nor, for that matter, has innovation ever been welcomed by the Church. 'Keep what has been committed to you', says the writer of the first letter to Timothy, 'and avoid profane novelties (*novitates*) of words' (1 Tim 6:20). What this means is that the numerous reforms of the seventeenth century had to show themselves to be re-forms and not new forms; and if they were re-forms, they had to show themselves to be solidly based on the established authorities of the past. As Professor Krailsheimer has said, 'authority, in the sense of precedent, was the only effective defence against charges of innovation or singularity, but it was an argument that all respected'.[18] It was indeed, but the continual citation of authority on authority can be wearisome to modern minds and there are parts of Rancé's *De la sainteté et des devoirs de la vie monastique* which make for tedious reading. Rancé himself made it perfectly clear that, in his view, his reform was precisely that: a re-forming of the Cistercian Order in accor-

16. See John Lauder's account quoted in Lough, 108-109
17. Lucien Aubry, 'Rancé's Spirituality: Total Service to God', *Cistercian Studies Quarterly* 35 (2000) 49.
18. Alban J. Krailsheimer, 'Bernard and Rancé', *Cîteaux: Commentarii cistercienses* 42 (1991) = *Bernardus Magister. Papers presented at the Nonacentenary Celebration of the Birth of Saint Bernard of Clairvaux*, ed. John R. Sommerfeldt (Kalamazoo, 1992) 548.

dance with the undisputed authority of the Rule of Saint Benedict. And if, in looking to the future, he looked to the past, so did everybody else.

French literary society in the seventeenth century was wholly convinced that the perfection of literary beauty had already been achieved by the great writers of classical antiquity. Their writings were the only admissible models, and they were models which exemplified the universal quest for universal truth. This is the era of *le classicisme* or *l'esprit classique*—the terms are not quite translatable—with its emphasis on the Glories of Antiquity, the importance of reason and objectivity, a distaste for personal comment and personal reference, a complete command of one's subject, and, above all, good taste. It also demanded that one wrote in accordance with *les règles des bienséances et des genres*, 'the rules of propriety and style', which meant that grand subjects were elucidated in grand language, trifling subjects were avoided, and the end result was a formal, balanced, and harmonious whole in which each separate part was as carefully crafted as each piece of a jigsaw puzzle. If the pieces of the puzzle are not carefully crafted, they obviously will not fit, and the final picture will be at best distorted and at worse unrecognizable. *Classicisme* began to give way to Romanticism, *le romantisme*, in the latter part of the seventeenth century, but by that time Rancé's literary style had been formed and fixed. In the *Querelle des Anciens et des Modernes*—the literary dispute between those who stayed firmly committed to the models of classical antiquity and those who preferred the call of the senses and the emotions and the spirit of progress—there is no doubt where Rancé stood. He had been solidly trained in the classics from his earliest years (remember Anacreon) and, as we shall see in Chapter Six, he never lost his love for the literary glories of Greece and Rome.

Unless we bear in mind the grandness of the *grand siècle*, unless we bear in mind the grandness of its gestures and public displays, unless we bear in mind its classical ideals and its recourse to authority, we will never understand *la grande vie* and *la grande réforme* of *le grand réformateur*.

But for the moment all that takes us a little too far. We must therefore retrace our steps to 1655 and seek Rancé in Paris where he is immersing himself, not without success, in ecclesiastical politics. The Assembly of the Clergy was the guiding body of the French Church and, in later years, would operate safely under the tutelage of the Sun King.[19] Its major preoccupations were normally clerical taxation and clerical privileges, but in 1655 there were more pressing matters to consider: the consequences of the Fronde and the question of Jansenism. Rancé's uncle, the archbishop of Tours, had already appointed the young *abbé* to an archdeaconry in 1654, and the next year exerted his considerable influence to have him serve in the Assembly where he acquitted himself well and competently. It was all part of the uncle's scheme to have his nephew succeed him as archbishop, but, as we have seen, his scheme was doomed to disappointment.

In 1655, as we have said, the Assembly of the Clergy was deeply concerned with Jansenism, and the reason we are speaking of Jansenism here, and not in a chapter on seventeenth-century french spirituality, was that Jansenism was as much a cultural and political phenomenon as a theological and spiritual one. Like many earlier movements—Arianism, Apollinarianism, Adoptionism, Catharism, and so many others—it began with theology, but soon became inextricably commingled with politics. The origins of the movement lay in the dense pages of the posthumously published *Augustinus* (1640) of Cornelius Jansen, the flemish bishop of Ypres, who, as a literal follower of Saint Augustine, had reiterated the latter's strict predestinationism. Without God's unsolicited grace not one of us can do a good action, and 'of our own power we can only fall'.[20] Who will be saved? Those whom God chooses to be saved, and there's an end to the matter.

19. See John McManners, *Church and Society in Eighteenth-Century France* (Oxford, 1998) 1:148.
20. Augustine, *Enarratio in Ps.* 129.1; *PL* 37:1696.

Jansen's followers, understandably, were accused of being crypto-Calvinists, for it was Calvin, above all, who established the doctrine technically known as Double Predestination. This is the teaching that God actively predestines some for eternal life in heaven and actively predestines the rest to eternal damnation in hell. In a few rare passages Augustine himself maintains this doctrine,[21] though his preference was for Single Predestination, *i.e.*, the theory that God actively predestines some for eternal life, but leaves the rest to their own devices. While it is true that their own devices must ineluctably lead them to Hell, it cannot be denied that there is a difference between watching a man walk to the edge of a cliff and fall over and actively pushing him to his death. Neither case does much for our conception of God—in the one case he may be called an accessory before the fact; in the other he is a murderer—and Calvin's doctrine met with stubborn resistance.

The Jansenists, in fact, were not Calvinists, and they wholly (and at considerable length) rejected the accusation that they were. Yet when the movement began to flourish in France after about 1640, its theological principles were of less consequence than their corollaries: strict morality and austere piety. This, inevitably, led the Jansenists into conflict with the Jesuits, whose views on the human condition and its inevitable sinfulness were less rigorous and more humane. This is a matter we shall consider in Chapter Four. But 'Jansenism' in France (like Puritanism in England) was a term which encompassed a wide spectrum of ideas. At one end we have someone like the staunchly augustinian Jean Du Vergier de Hauranne, *abbé* de Saint-Cyran, a close friend of Jansen himself and the main force behind the success of Jansenism in France; at the other we have Madame X or Monsieur Y who were simply happy to attend *salons* where the *Lettres provinciales* of Blaise Pascal, written in 1656, were read and admired as much for their style and wit as for their content. In between

21. See Bell, *Many Mansions* (cited under Further Reading, 49) 325-326.

the two was a host of different people, including Rancé, with a host of different ideas.

Much of the 'Jansenism' of the period was no more than a desire for a reform, or at least a cleansing, of the French Church. We have seen already that the age was an age of extremes, and the french bishops (of whom, at the time, Rancé did not think particularly highly[22]) were a varied collection of prelates who ranged from saintly men who truly sought to conquer the world, the flesh, and the devil to those who embraced all three with relish. To corruption and moral equivocation Jansenism opposed honesty and ethical idealism, and in a society which had refined and elevated the game of follow-my-leader to an art-form and way of life, it opposed independence and self-respect. It was certainly theologically pessimistic and it certainly held a bleak and gloomy view of depraved humanity, but many of its foremost advocates were men and women of the highest integrity, though their writings are often tinged with a displeasing air of insufferable self-righteousness.

Where did Rancé stand in this jansenist atmosphere? His biographers have struggled both to condemn him[23] and to exonerate him,[24] but the truth is far simpler: Rancé was loyal to his friends and his faith. If his friends were Jansenist, so be it: he did not forget them. If the principles of his faith coincided with Jansenism, so be it. But if they conflicted with Jansenism, again, so be it. But given the fact that his faith had been moulded by Jansenism, it is hardly surprising that, in many matters, Rancé and the Jansenists were in wholehearted agreement. But what do we mean by *moulded*?

As early as 1644 Rancé had been reading Antoine Arnauld's

---

22. See Letter 580824.

23. The Jesuit François Le Lasseur is the classic example: see his 'L'Abbé de Rancé et le jansénisme', in *Études religieuses, philosophiques, historiques et littéraires, par des Pères de la Compagnie de Jésus*, 20ème année, tom. 10, Lyon, 1876, 321-351 and 481-517.

24. As does Dubois. Krailsheimer provides a judicious assessment (Krailsheimer, *Rancé*, ch. 15 [319-328]).

uncompromising *De la fréquente communion*,[25] published just
the preceding year. In this important work, Arnauld maintained, with great eloquence, that sinners could in no way
atone for continual sin by frequent communion without full
and proper preparation, heart-felt repentance, and the living
of an austere and evangelical life. The book aroused a whirlwind of controversy and the fury of the Jesuits, who maintained, not without reason, that their doctrines had been
seriously misrepresented; and there is no doubt that in his
exposition Arnauld saw communion more as a reward for righteousness than as a remedy for sin. Rancé, however, clearly
appreciated the book, as he also appreciated Pascal's *Lettres
provinciales*, which he had heard read in the *salons* in the mid-1650s.

In the weeks and months after the death of Madame de
Montbazon in 1657, both the people and the books from whom
and from which he sought advice and illumination tended
strongly in a jansenist direction, sometimes theologically, sometimes morally. The Oratorian Claude Séguenot, for example,
the Port-Royal solitary Arnauld d'Andilly, the saintly and
ascetic Nicolas Pavillon, bishop of Alet, the young Guillaume
Le Roy, commendatory abbot of Hautefontaine (with whom
he would later come into bitter conflict), and a number of
others all had strong jansenist leanings. And as for his reading matter in those difficult days, he tells Robert Arnauld
d'Andilly at Port-Royal that he is reading *Petrus Aurelius* with
enjoyment,[26] and *Petrus Aurelius* was a mammoth study of
episcopal authority by none other than the Jansenist Saint-Cyran himself. In the same letter he also asks for anti-Jesuit
pamphlets. A few weeks later he has finished *Petrus Aurelius*,
but over the next few months he will annotate it.[27] As Professor Krailsheimer has said, Rancé's reading programme 'could
hardly have been more Jansenist'.[28] True, but we should not

25. See Letter 440317.
26. Letter 580626.
27. Letter 581214.
28. Krailsheimer's comment to Letter 580626.

be too surprised. As we shall see in a moment, the religious tastes of the reading public readily embraced jansenist and anti-Jesuit writings, and some of the most popular spiritual literature of the day came from the ready pens of the Jansenists and their sympathizers.

It appears, then, that Rancé had had 'jansenist' (in the widest sense) leanings for some time, and that the spiritual counsel of men like Claude Séguenot and Nicolas Pavillon was pleasing to his ears. But if this were the case, what does it tell us about his supposed worldliness before his conversion, and what does it say about his undoubted love for Madame de Montbazon, whose bed was said to be the most welcoming in France? Is it conceivable that a man of 'jansenist' morality could be so flagrantly immoral?

The answer, of course, is yes, he could, especially in seventeenth-century France where sin, as we shall see, was perceived and handled very differently from anything to which we are accustomed today. In any case, the various sexual scandals which have rocked the Roman Catholic Church in recent years have revealed, all too graphically, how religiosity can easily coexist with libertinism. I cannot help but recall a wonderful scene in the movie 'Needful Things' where the devil, wickedly played by Max von Sydow, is sitting in a comfortable chair before a blazing fire and listening, with every sign of enjoyment, to the Bach-Gounod setting of 'Ave Maria'. In the age of absolutism, which was also the age of absolute contrasts, asceticism and debauchery were frequent bedfellows (Ivan the Terrible, tsar of Russia, is perhaps the extreme example); and, in any case, chastity, as Professor Krailsheimer delicately puts it, was not 'a necessary part of an *honnête homme*'s qualifications'.[29] An *honnête homme*, we might add, was not an 'honest man', but a cultivated person, and honesty had no necessary place in his accomplishments. The archbishop of Narbonne was only one of many high prelates

29. Alban J. Krailsheimer, *Studies in Self-Interest from Descartes to La Bruyère* (Oxford, 1962) 212.

to keep 'a very fine mistress in the town',[30] and if one could not afford a mistress, the brothels of the larger cities catered to every taste. Members of the religious orders were 'talkt of as the lecherousest people that lives',[31] and the accusation was not always simply a common *topos*. Seventeenth-century french society was a Janus-faced society which,

> in spite of its worldliness, frivolity, and vice, prided itself, and with reason, on its power of appreciating what was intellectual and scholarly, and though scandalously irreverential in the very temple of God, had an insatiable craving for religious discourses.[32]

It was also a society that had an insatiable craving for religious literature. Henri-Jean Martin[33] tells us that between 1598 and 1643 a third of all books printed in Paris were connected with religion,[34] and between 1666 and 1700 the proportion rose to more than forty percent.[35] Religious literature in the seventeenth century, he writes, was of 'oceanic proportions'[36] and a huge amount of it was devotional. It also tended to be in French rather than Latin, though Latin, if not Greek, was an accomplishment of every educated man. But French or Latin, much of it was by no means easy reading. Many popular works were both subtle and profound, and the spirituality they advocated could be demanding. Rancé's voluminous writings must be seen against this background, and the numerous printings and editions of many of his works should not surprise us—even without taking into account

30. John Locke, quoted in Lough, *France Observed*, 185.
31. John Lauder, quoted in *ibid.*, 191.
32. *The Catholic Encyclopedia* (New York, 1907) 2:718.
33. Most of what follows is based on Martin's masterly survey, *Print, Power, and People in 17th-Century France*, cited under Further Reading, 49.
34. *Ibid.*, 73.
35. *Ibid.*, 529.
36. *Ibid.*

the later fame of la Trappe and the renown of its charismatic abbot. But what sort of religious literature are we talking about here? What and who were being read in Rancé's France? The Bible certainly, in a variety of formats, and, since the Council of Trent had emphasised Tradition as well as Scripture, the Fathers of the Church. In the first fifty years of the seventeenth century, the Paris printers issued hundreds of volumes of patristic texts and studies, and the variety—from Abelard to Zozimus—is astonishing. Rancé was intimately familiar with a very large number of them,[37] and in his appreciation of authors like Ambrose, Athanasius, Augustine, Basil (a particular favourite), Cassian, Chrysostom, Eusebius, Gregory the Great, Jerome, John Climacus (about whom we shall say more later), and many others, he was far from being alone. Nor would he have had difficulty in finding editions. Medieval writers, including Bernard of Clairvaux, were likewise readily available, and at this period Aquinas, Bonaventure, and a number of other well-known scholastics experienced an important revival.

In the first half of the century, medieval spirituality was still immensely popular, particularly the *Imitation of Christ*—it appeared in innumerable editions—and certain works attributed (incorrectly) to Johannes Tauler. Translations of the writings of Luis de Granada were widely read and constantly in demand, and Teresa of Ávila enjoyed a huge following, though by Rancé's time she had fallen into a certain desuetude. A voluminous literature was produced by Capuchin and (especially) Jesuit authors, and their writings reached a large and interested public. Of Saint François de Sales, Pierre de Bérulle, and their colleagues, we shall speak later, but it is interesting to note that when Reverend Mother Louise-Henriette d'Albon, recently appointed superior of the Visi-

---

37. See Bernard Duymentz, *Les citations des Pères de la période patristique et médiévale chez Rancé*. Mémoire de Diplôme d'Études Approfondies en théologie catholique, soutenance du 12 juin 1991 en la Faculté de théologie catholique de Strasbourg. 1991. Typescript. Frère Bernard is a monk of la Trappe. We shall say more of Rancé's sources in Chapter Six.

tation convent at Riom in 1687, complained that her nuns did
not much care for the saints of old, Rancé recommended that
she turn to François de Sales and the Jesuit Alfonso de
Rodriguez, whose *Pratique de la perfection chrétienne* Rancé knew
in the translation by the *abbé* François-Séraphin Régnier-
Desmarais.[38] He also clearly appreciated the writings of Jeanne-
Françoise de Chantal.[39] But not only were the writings of the
saints esteemed, there was also an intense interest in their
lives, and hagiography (which included not only lives of saints,
but also lives of *beati*, miracle-workers, pillars of the Church,
and those considered by the society of their time to have
been just plain good) was a vast field which expanded at an
amazing rate.

In the second half of the century, however, we detect certain changes. Apart from the fact that Jansen's *Augustinus* first
appeared in 1640 and Arnauld's *De la fréquente communion* in
1643, Latin gives way to French, large folio volumes give way
to handy duodecimos, and theologians address themselves to
the educated laity and not simply to fellow theologians. But
the intense interest in 'religion' in the broadest sense remains—indeed, it even increases—and much of what is being read takes on a decidedly jansenist flavour. Take, for
example, Isaac-Louis Le Maistre de Sacy's translation of the
Bible. The author was the fourth son of Catherine Arnauld,
one of the daughters of Antoine Arnauld, and was held in
high esteem by the Jansenists as a spiritual director. He was
also confessor to the nuns and solitaries of Port-Royal, the
convent located some sixteen miles from Paris which had been
reformed in 1608 by Mother Angélique Arnauld. Sacy's translation met with astonishing success and papal condemnation,
and precipitated a pamphlet war with the Jesuits which helped
its sales enormously. But Jansenism also came to be associated with Gallicanism—that is to say, the desire of the French
Church to preserve its autonomy *vis-à-vis* the papacy—and
the end result was that in the minds of many, Jansenism/

38. See Letters 870918 and 881213.
39. See Letter 890400.

Gallicanism was much the same as Nationalism. It was something truly french, and pro-jansenist booksellers like Guillaume Desprez (the publisher of Sacy's translation of the Bible) could rely on a large, eager, and appreciative audience.[40]

There is nothing unusual, therefore, in Rancé's jansenist reading. In this, as in most other things, he was a man of his times, and if he had gallican sympathies (which he did) and found jansenist ideas sympathetic, he was far from being alone. The austere spirit of Port-Royal, if not of Jansen himself, was omnipresent, and both jansenist and jesuit writings were as eagerly discussed in the fashionable *salons* as were the latest scandals, the sonnets of Voiture or Benserade, or the precise meaning of certain words in the french language.

It is difficult to overestimate the importance of the *salons*. They were held regularly in private houses, commonly once a week, and invariably presided over by the mistress of the house. The company was select, literate, cultivated, and regular in its attendance, and the topics of conversation included politics, literature, philosophy, art, religion, and, naturally, gossip and the talk of the town. The prototype of the *salon* was that held in the parisian town-house—the *Hôtel de Rambouillet*—of Catherine de Vivonne, marquise de Rambouillet. She was a charming and intelligent woman, born in Rome in 1588, who had been married to the marquis de Rambouillet at the age of twelve. She presided over her *salon* for more than thirty years—from about 1618 to 1650—and over that period entertained most of the eminent writers, wits, and conversationalists of the day. Malherbe attended, as did La Rochefoucauld and Saint-Évremond. Corneille was for a time an *habitué*, as also was Rancé's great friend Bossuet. Indeed, Bossuet would occasionally use the *salons* to try out his sermons. Whether the young Rancé joined the assembly at the *Hôtel de Rambouillet* is unknown, but it would not be at all surprising.

Madame de Rambouillet's *salon* was not the first of its kind,

---

40. For Desprez, see Martin, *Print, Power, and People*, 535-536.

but it certainly laid the foundations for what a proper *salon* should be; and when Madame de Sablé and her friend Madame de Longueville opened their own *salons* a little later, they based them on that of Madame de Rambouillet. So did Madame de La Sablière and Madame de La Fayette. All four women were friends and correspondents of Rancé. The influence of the *salons* on french literature was immense, and they were also of first importance in offering to women a means of exercising sometimes very considerable influence and power. It is true that they could degenerate into mutual admiration societies in which the preciosity of the conversation was more important than its content, but they could also offer a cultivated and enjoyable refuge from the turbulent politics of the times. In the very midst of the Fronde, the question (which divided the literary world) as to whether Isaac de Benserade's sonnet on Job was superior to Vincent Voiture's sonnet on Uranie, or vice-versa, was being hotly debated at the *Hôtel de Rambouillet*. This was a society with which Rancé was intimately familiar, and although he left it far behind when he entered the walls of la Trappe, the concern of the *salons* with linguistic elegance, precise terminology, and polished style may clearly be seen in his writings.

One other matter demands discussion before we conclude this chapter. I am speaking here of the devil, whom we mentioned briefly above. But the movie in which he appears—'Needful Things'—is a modern movie, and the portrayal of Satan by Max von Sydow is a modern portrayal. Satan here is certainly malevolent, there is no doubt of that, but he is also urbane and sophisticated. Things were very different in Rancé's France. There the devil roamed loose in all his medieval crudity, seeking whom he might devour, and there the reality of evil was dramatically apparent. The period from about 1570 to 1670 saw the peak of the witchcraft delusion in France. A magician executed in Paris in 1571 stated that there were a hundred thousand witches in the country, and Church and State clearly believed him.[41] It was a

---

41. Rossell H. Robbins, *The Encyclopedia of Witchcraft and Demonology* (London-New York, 1959) 210.

period in which we witness mass persecution by civil judges and the publication of the classic works of the french demonologists: Jean Bodin's *Démonomanie des sorciers* in 1580; Nicolas Remy's *Demonolatreiæ* in 1595; Martin Antoine Del Rio's *Disquisitionum magicarum* in 1599; Henri Boguet's *Discours des sorciers* (dedicated to the commendatory abbot of the cistercian abbey of Acey) in 1602; Pierre de Lancre's *Tableau de l'inconstance des mauvais anges* in 1612; Jacques d'Autun's *L'incrédulité savante et la crédulité ignorante au sujet des magiciens et des sorciers* in 1671; and a number of other lesser works.[42] Neither the reality of witchcraft nor the possibility of demoniacal possession was in question.

The french nuns appear to have been particularly susceptible.[43] Father Urbain Grandier, accused and convicted of bewitching the Ursulines of Loudun, had been burned at Loudun in August 1634,[44] and in 1647, when Rancé made his debut as a preacher at the convent of the Annonciades, the nuns of Louviers in Normandy were sorely beset. Both they and three of their spiritual directors were accused—or, in the case of Sister Madeleine Bavent, accused themselves[45]— of orgiastic rites, cannibalism, and desecration; and the sordid affair resulted in the execution of Father Thomas Boullé who, after the usual tortures, was burned alive in the Old Market Square in Rouen on 21 August 1647. Just over a decade later, between 1658 and 1662 (while Rancé was seeking his true path after the death of Madame de Montbazon), the possessed Ursulines of Auxonne accused their Mother Superior (Barbara Buvée) of witchcraft and a wanton variety of

42. Details of all these works will be found in Yve-Plessis's *Essai* (cited in Further Reading, 49) *passim*.
43. See Robbins, *Encyclopedia*, 207-212 and the individual entries listed on page 212. The primary sources are listed in Yve-Plessis's *Essai*.
44. The classic account is Aldous Huxley's *The Devils of Loudun*, first published in 1952. It appeared as a movie ('The Devils'), directed by Ken Russell, in 1971.
45. The prurient will find Madeleine Bavent's confession set out in pornographic detail in Le R.P. Desmarets, *Histoire de Magdelaine Bavent* (Paris, 1652) = Yve-Plessis, no. 1340.

sexual assaults, though the end result was happier than had occurred at Louviers. The *Parlement* of Dijon heard the case against Buvée in January 1661 and, after rigorous examination, dismissed the charges in August 1662. When Buvée moved to another convent, the hysteria gradually disappeared.

But unquestionably the most dramatic example of Satan's presence in Rancé's France is the extraordinary *Chambre Ardente* affair which lasted from the early 1670s to July 1682. It involved divination, witchcraft, poisoning, sorcery, Satanism, and Black Masses. It also involved Madame de Montespan, the king's mistress, and a great many ladies and gentlemen of Louis's entourage. While it is true that police commissioner Nicholas de La Reynie used torture to elicit confessions, there cannot be the least doubt that strange things had been happening at court and that the *abbé* Guibourg had indeed performed blasphemous masses which, at least on one occasion, involved the sacrifice of a child. The details of the matter are not here our concern and may be read elsewhere,[46] but they provide an extraordinarily vivid glimpse into the mentality of seventeenth-century France.

In this hot-house atmosphere, Rancé himself may not have been wholly innocent of magical matters (he was fascinated by astrology and alchemy and certainly had an interest in occultism[47]), and rumours of a horrific vision at Véretz after the death of Madame de Montbazon (normally dismissed by modern biographers)[48] may not be wholly imaginary. The possibility of such visions was discussed in overwhelming detail in the 976 quarto pages of Pierre Le Loyer's *Discours et histoires des spectres, visions et apparitions des esprits, anges, démons et âmes, se monstrans visibles aux hommes*, published at Paris in 1605. But even if the young Rancé did experience such a vision, it is really of little consequence. What is much more important is the all-pervading belief in the reality of evil and the pres-

46. See Frances Mossiker, *The Affair of the Poisons* (London, 1969).
47. Dubois (1869) 1:33-35.
48. See David N. Bell, 'A Vision and an Invasion: Two Episodes in the Life of Armand-Jean de Rancé', in *Cistercian Studies Quarterly* 38 (2003) 459-463.

ence of Satan in the France of his time, and there is not the least doubt that Rancé shared these beliefs. His friend Bossuet also shared them and preached two sermons on demons: one at Metz in 1653 and the other at Paris in 1660.[49] To Rancé and his brothers at la Trappe, therefore, 'the Devil and all his works' was in no way an abstract concept, and the battle against Satan was a battle against a real and omnipresent adversary. Indeed, they knew it at first hand, for although la Trappe was a fortress against the powers of evil, it was not impregnable.

In 1683 the abbey experienced a violent outbreak of demonic manifestations. Cries and shrieks resounded through the house, the doors shook to thunderous poundings, a frightful cacophony erupted in the dormitory, and lustful thoughts abounded in a wholly extraordinary manner. Rancé thought he might have to have the whole abbey exorcized, but on the feast of All Saints the monks invoked the angels, saints, and all the company of heaven to come to their aid, and their prayers were speedily and happily answered. Satan was vanquished, the demons retreated into darkness and silence, and peace was restored to la Trappe.[50] Saint Bernard had had similar problems at Clairvaux more than five centuries earlier,[51] and neither he nor Rancé had the least doubt about the actuality of evil.

By 1683, however, Rancé had been abbot of la Trappe for almost two decades. Twenty years earlier he was just experiencing the last stages of his long conversion and setting out on the path which would lead him inexorably to the ruined buildings of la Trappe and its handful of unreformed and recalcitrant monks. He still had his year's novitiate to com-

49. Jacques-Bénigne Bossuet, ed. Joseph Lebarq, *Œuvres oratoires de Bossuet* (Lille, 1890-97) 1:340-359 and 3:213-235. The sermons are discussed in more detail in my 'A Vision and an Invasion' cited immediately above.

50. Dubois (1866) 2:35-36. See further Bell, 'A Vision and an Invasion', 464-469.

51. See Bernard, *Super Psalmum Qui habitat, sermo* 7.8, cited by Dubois in *ibid.*, 2:34-35.

plete at Perseigne, but after that was over (not without problems), he entered la Trappe as its new and regular abbot on 14 July 1664.

In that year the Sun King was in his mid-twenties and, since the death of Mazarin in 1661, had ruled France alone. Three years later, in 1667, he would rapidly and successfully invade the Spanish Netherlands, and in 1672 he would launch his armies against Holland. Neither of these events had a direct influence on the new abbot, but Louis's foreign policy certainly affected him indirectly, and Rancé's negotiations with the Common Observance in Rome cannot be divorced from the wider background of seventeenth-century European history. To these matters we must now turn our attention.

FURTHER READING

It is obviously impossible to provide here a comprehensive bibliography for seventeenth-century France, but for a useful general survey of the period, see John Lough's *An Introduction to Seventeenth-Century France* (London-New York, 1954). The same author's *France Observed in the Seventeenth Century by British Travellers* (Stocksfield, 1985) offers a fascinating collection of observations. For further information, readers may be referred to the invaluable *Bibliography of French Seventeenth-Century Studies* published since 1952 by the Modern Language Association of America. Those interested in the lives of Louis XIV, Richelieu, Mazarin, and Retz will have no difficulty in finding an abundance of material both in English and French. A sound account of the Fronde may be found in Orest A. Ranum, *The Fronde: A French Revolution, 1648-1652* (New York, 1993). As to the Church, the old study by Gerald R. Cragg, *The Church and the Age of Reason 1648-1789* (Penguin Books, 1960), remains a sound introduction to the whole period, and for France in particular we have Jedin-Dolan VI (with excellent, though now inevitably outdated, bibliographies) and Henry Phillips, *Church and Culture in Seventeenth-Century France* (Cambridge-New York, 1997).

There is likewise a mountain of material on seventeenth-century french literature, but Antoine Adam's *Grandeur and Illusion: French Literature and Society 1600-1715* (London, 1972) remains indispensable. A convenient summary of the period is provided by P. J. Yarrow in his *A Literary History of France, Volume II: The Seventeenth Century 1600-1715* (London-New York, 1967), and further information may be found in William D. Howarth, *Life and Letters in France: The Seventeenth Century* (London, 1965), and volumes 3 and 3A, edited by Nathan Edelman and H. Gaston Hall respectively, of *A Critical Bibliography of French Literature* (Syracuse, 1947-). For an excellent succinct summary of *classicisme*, see *The Oxford Companion to French Literature*, ed. Sir Paul Harvey and Janet E. Heseltine (Oxford, 1969), 139-140.

For printing and publication in the seventeenth century, we need look no further than the superb study by Henri-Jean Martin, tr. David Gerard, *Print, Power, and People in 17th-Century France* (Metuchen-London, 1993), supplemented by Martin's *The French Book: Religion, Absolutism, and Readership, 1585-1715*, tr. Paul and Nadine Saenger (Baltimore-London, 1996). Useful material may also be found in the older study by David T. Pottinger, *The French Book Trade in the Ancien Régime, 1500-1791* (Cambridge, MA, 1958).

For french Jansenism we are fortunate in having an excellent study by William Doyle, *Jansenism: Catholic Resistance to Authority: From the Reformation to the French Revolution* (Basingstoke-New York, 2000), but the earlier study by Alexander Sedgwick, *Jansenism in Seventeenth-Century France: Voices from the Wilderness* (Charlottesville, 1977), is equally good and more specifically directed to the period with which we are here concerned. Sedgwick's final chapter on 'The Nature of Jansenism' is essential reading. Those more interested in the personalities involved will find much to their taste in James D. Crichton's *Saints or Sinners? Jansenists and Jansenisers in Seventeenth-Century France* (Dublin, 1996). An excellent concise summary of the rise of Jansenism and the jansenist conflict will be found in Jedin-Dolan VI:24-57 (with bibliography on pages 592-595).

The question of Single and Double Predestination is briefly considered in David N. Bell, *Many Mansions: An Introduction to the Development and Diversity of Medieval Theology West and East* (Kalamazoo, 1996), ch. XVII (323-328).

The nature and importance of french preaching in the first half of the seventeenth century is well served by Peter J. Bagley, *French Pulpit Oratory, 1598-1650: A Study in Themes and Styles* (Cambridge, 1980) and Thomas Worcester, *Seventeenth-Century Cultural Discourse: France and the Preaching of Bishop Camus* (Berlin-New York, 1997). But both, alas, stop short of Bossuet who has an extensive bibliography of his own. In English there are two old but still sound works: William J. Sparrow-Simpson, *A Study of Bossuet* (London, 1937) and

Ernest F. Reynolds, *Bossuet* (New York, 1963). There is also a brilliant chapter on Bossuet in Alban J. Krailsheimer's *Studies in Self-Interest from Descartes to La Bruyère* (Oxford, 1962) 173-195 (Chapter Ten). So far as I know, the most recent biography in French is Jean Meyer's *Bossuet* published in 1993.

The place of witchcraft, demonianism, magic, and the occult is too often overlooked in studies of the period, and that is a major omission. The best accounts—the works of Robert Mandrou—are to be found only in French, but important information may be found in the old but reliable compendium by Rossell H. Robbins, *The Encyclopedia of Witchcraft and Demonology* (London-New York, 1959). A number of papers in *European Witchcraft* (New York, 1969), edited by E. William Monter, also have immediate relevance. The grim story of Urbain Grandier and the Ursulines of Loudun may be read in Aldous Huxley's *The Devils of Loudun*, first published in 1952. But for primary sources, R. Yve-Plessis's *Essai d'une bibliographie française méthodique & raisonnée de la sorcellerie et de la possession démoniaque* (Paris, 1900; rpt. Nieuwkoop, 1971), supplemented by the microfiche collection (99 volumes) edited by Robert Mandrou, *Sorciers, démonologues, magistrats, théologiens et médecins aux XVIᵉ et XVIIᵉ siècles* (Paris, 1975), remains essential. For Rancé himself, the Véretz vision of 1657, and the poltergeist activity at la Trappe in 1683, see David N. Bell, 'A Vision and an Invasion: Two Episodes in the Life of Armand-Jean de Rancé', in *Cistercian Studies Quarterly* 38 (2003) 459-469.

Chapter 3

RANCÉ'S ORDER

THE STORY BEGINS in 1098 with the foundation of the New Monastery, the *Novum monasterium*, of Cîteaux as a consequence of Robert of Molesme's intention to live a life based more strictly on the Rule of Saint Benedict. The way of life of the earliest cistercian monks was formidably austere, and it was inevitable that over the ensuing centuries, changing times and circumstances would demand accommodations and adaptations in the interpretation of the Rule. Nowadays it is common to hear of a cistercian 'Golden Age' which came to an abrupt end on the last day of the twelfth century (or perhaps on 20 August 1153, the date of the death of Bernard of Clairvaux) to be followed by long years of inexorable decline, but the idea is false. There certainly were examples of laxity and decadence, and the pages of Joseph-Maria Canivez's *Statuta Capitulorum Generalium Ordinis Cisterciensis ab Anno 1116 ad Annum 1786* make for interesting reading, but adaptation and decadence are not necessarily the same thing and it is all too easy to attribute to the Highest Common Denominator the faults and vices of the Lowest Common Factor.

We must also remember that cistercian history in France did not take place in a vacuum. From about 1315 onwards the country was ravaged by famine, plague, pestilence, and war. From the outbreak of the Hundred Years' War in 1337, the mother-house of Cîteaux was virtually isolated; and the records of the General Chapter reveal a dismal litany of pillage, arson, looting, murder, starvation, destruction, and the abandonment of both monasteries and monastic lands. Regular visitation inevitably petered out, and the poorly attended General Chapter of 1390 pointed to this as the main reason for the desolation and decay in communities of both men and women. 'Alas!', said the Chapter, there scarcely remains in any one of them 'any religious observance, or any form of real devotion, or any vestige of what our Order requires'.[1] Added to this was the scandal of the Great Schism of the western Church which had a disastrous impact on papal authority. And no sooner had the Great Schism come to an end with the election of Pope Martin V in 1417 than large parts of France were again plunged into bloodshed with a protracted struggle between the Burgundians and the Armagnacs for the control of France.

Plague and pestilence, with their inevitable consequences of social and psychological unrest, had just as devastating an impact on the monasteries as on the general population; and the period of restoration, which began in the second half of the fifteenth century and continued until the outbreak of the Wars of Religion in 1559, unhappily (for the monasteries) coincided with the insidious spread of the commendatory system.

The system of commendatory superiors had its origins in the desire of the Avignon popes to establish greater control over ecclesiastical offices. Previously, monastic communities had normally elected their own abbot (which is not to say that there was no outside interference), but this privilege was now suspended. Henceforth abbots would be appointed by the pope or secular ruler, and the abbots so appointed were usually secular prelates who received their abbacies as a reward for services rendered. Rarely did they live in their monasteries and, for the most part, they were simply absentee landlords whose main concern was the collection of a substantial portion of the monastic revenues. Not all commendatory abbots were bad—in the eighteenth century we

---

1. Canivez, 3:579 (1390.8)

find a surprising number who were deeply concerned about
their communities—but there is no doubt that from its in-
ception to the time of Rancé, himself a commendatory abbot, the system was a catastrophe for the cistercian Order. In
1467 the *Parlement* of Paris informed Louis XI that

> in the monasteries all forms of regular disci-
> pline have disappeared; the divine services are
> performed improperly and without devotion.
> ... As the material establishments are being
> ruined, so are the spiritual ones. Such condi-
> tions are common among the monks who, for
> lack of discipline, lapse into lax life and often
> apostatize. ... Until the benefices return to
> regular abbots it remains impossible to re-
> verse the ruinous trend.[2]

In 1514 the Fifth Lateran Council called for the abolition of
the system, as, later, did the Council of Trent, but it was too
well entrenched, the lobby groups too powerful, and the royal
government too refractory. In 1579 the Ordonnance of Blois
reconfirmed an earlier decision that there should be free elec-
tions at Cîteaux, La Ferté, Pontigny, Clairvaux, and Morimond, but they were the only exceptions to the general rule.
By the end of the century most cistercian abbeys in France
were held *in commendam* and the General Chapter (attended
now by fewer and fewer abbots) could do nothing to remedy
the situation. Monastic morale was as low as it ever had been.

We can hardly be surprised, in such circumstances, to witness decline and decadence. The dramatic drop in monastic
populations was a direct result of the commendatory
system,[3] and with few religious, little money, little food,
dilapidated buildings, no spiritual direction, no growth, no

2. Quoted in Lekai, *Cistercians*, 103.
3. This is of first importance. The undoubted decline in numbers does *not*
necessarily indicate a corresponding decline in interest. For an essential discussion, see Louis J. Lekai, 'Moral and Material Status of French Cistercian

guidance, and no *esprit de corps*, what else was to be expected?

And then, when the Wars of Religion ran their terrible course from 1559 to 1598, the monasteries suffered even more than in the Hundred Years' War. Cîteaux itself was sacked in 1574, again in 1589, and again in 1595, and what happened to Cîteaux happened to more than half of the french abbeys. In fact, the history of most french monasteries followed very much the same course: an initial period of expansion and prosperity; pillage and plunder during the Hundred Years' War; further decay as a consequence of the commendatory system; yet more pillage and plunder in the Wars of Religion; a momentary rekindling of monastic fervour in the late seventeenth and eighteenth centuries (an important point too often ignored); and final eclipse in the tumult of the French Revolution.

On the other hand, we must not think that the Order was ignorant of the need for reform. Indeed, the entire late medieval Church and the monastic Orders in general were well aware of the problems, and a glance at the religious history of the fifteenth, sixteenth, and seventeenth centuries reveals an astonishing variety of valiant attempts at changing, cleansing, and purging. Certain Benedictines, with a stroke of genius, circumvented the dangers of the commendatory system by doing away with permanent abbacies altogether. They grouped themselves into congregations of varying numbers of abbeys, placed the abbeys under the firm centralized control of a General Chapter—a principle borrowed from the Cistercians—and the Chapter appointed superiors for individual monasteries who governed their communities for a specific, limited term. The best known of these congregations are the Cassinese Congregation in Italy, the Valladolid Congregation in Spain, and the Bursfeld Congregation in Germany. The Cistercians, as we shall see, did exactly the same

---

Abbeys in the Seventeenth Century', *Analecta Cisterciensia* 19 (1963) 199-266, and the same author's 'Cistercian Monasteries and the French Episcopate on the Eve of the Revolution', *Analecta Cisterciensia* 23 (1967) 66-114.

thing, though not always for exactly the same reasons.

The Order of Cîteaux had always been more centralized than other Orders and its institution of a General Chapter had proved so successful that it was imposed on all Orders by the Fourth Lateran Council in 1215. But by the fifteenth century, as we have seen, attendance at General Chapter was poor (understandably so, given the dangers or impossibility of getting there[4]) and its decrees, for the most part, were ineffectual. For a number of reasons, therefore, some good, some less so, the abbot of Cîteaux attempted to step into the breach and in his own person centralize the authority hitherto exercised by the General Chapter. In the circumstances it was a reasonable move, but it was not well received by the four 'proto-abbots'—the abbots of La Ferté, Pontigny, Morimond and, above all, Clairvaux—who saw it as no more than a selfish quest for self-aggrandizement on the part of the mother-house.

Tensions between Cîteaux and Clairvaux escalated throughout the last thirty years of the fifteenth century, culminating in the resignation of Pierre de Virey, abbot of Clairvaux, in 1496. His successor, a more amenable man, was able to establish a better relationship with the mother-house which, at that time, was being governed by an intelligent and energetic abbot, Jean de Cirey.

Jean de Cirey was also a reformer, and in 1487 he had been entrusted by Pope Innocent VIII with the reform of the entire cistercian Order. Special attention was to be paid to attendance at General Chapter, regular visitation, the responsibilities of commendatory abbots, and certain important matters related to taxes and dues within the Order. But pope and abbot were not alone in their desire for reform. His

---

4. There is a hair-raising letter written by Lazarus Padway to the abbot of Buckfast describing his journey to Cîteaux in 1471. Lazarus was the sole representative of the english abbots and tells of a journey beset by robbers, armed enemies, difficulties, and dangers. See *Letters from the English Abbots to the Chapter at Cîteaux 1442-1521*, ed. Charles H. Talbot (London, 1967) 46-50 (letter 7 [in Latin]).

Majesty Charles VIII was just as interested and, in December 1493, he had called together at Tours a council of ecclesiastics and superiors (including Jean de Cirey, who played an active role) to consider the matter. As it happened, the king did not follow through on his ideals, being distracted by his invasion of Italy in 1494, but this did not deter Jean de Cirey. He called a meeting of more than forty french abbots at the Collège Saint-Bernard in Paris in February 1494, and drew up as a basis for reform the sixteen 'Articles of Paris', the *Articuli Parisienses*, which were approved by the General Chapter of the same year and again in 1502. Nicholas Cotheret, the grouchy librarian of Cîteaux whose *Annals* are a vital, if unashamedly biased, source of information on the later history of the Order, draws particular attention to Article XI, which is 'an eloquent appeal to abbots to work for the benefit of their communities both in word and example in a spirit of selfless dedication'.[5] Rancé, later, would do exactly that.

The Articles make it clear that the abbots were seeking reform, not revolution. They wished to return to the old ways, not to introduce novelties. Reformation, they said, was re-formation, it was not the creation of a new Order. The abbots also recognized that many of their troubles stemmed from the historical, political, and economic circumstances of the times, but despite that, they still stated their intention to reform the Order 'in the whole and in the parts, in the members and in the head, in matters spiritual and in matters temporal',[6] for both monks and nuns.

They were not successful. That they were honestly committed cannot be doubted, but with the commendatory system still firmly entrenched, the authority of General Chapter still feeble, and the impact of the Reformation looming on the horizon, little could be achieved. And when the Wars of Religion swept through France a few decades later, the prime

5. Louis J. Lekai, *Nicolas Cotheret's Annals of Cîteaux, Outlined from the French Original* (Kalamazoo, 1982) 55. The text of the *Articuli Parisiensis* can be found in Canivez, 6:87-97.
6. Canivez, 6:90 (1494.39).

concern for almost all monasteries was not reform but survival.

The fifteenth century also saw major administrative changes within the Order. The essential organizational and administrative principles set forth in the twelfth-century *Charter of Charity* were two: affiliation—every abbey was affiliated to one of the five proto-abbeys—and visitation. Visitation, however, meant regular visitation by responsible abbots, and in the fifteenth century this was no longer possible. Abbots, as we have seen, were too often commendatory, and the political situation in France often made regular visitation difficult or impossible. Furthermore, the prevailing tendencies of nationalism, self-government, and cultural distinction were inevitably felt within the Order, and the end result was fragmentation into provinces and congregations.

On the other hand, we must not see this fragmentation merely as a political inevitability or as a sign of decline and decadence. On the contrary. The rise of the autonomous congregations was closely associated with regional attempts at serious reform, and one of the most important—the Congregation of Castile—had begun as early as 1427. Its founder, Martin Vargas, was a bold and charismatic reformer who recognized the commendatory system as the major problem in cistercian life and adopted, almost wholesale, the benedictine congregational idea which had proved so successful in Italy. He did it, we might add, in the teeth of determined opposition from the General Chapter, which was terrified of losing its control over the spanish houses; but there can be little doubt that Vargas was right. At that time and in those circumstances, regional reform was the only way to go. Vargas's reform was dramatically successful, and when Pope Eugene IV, who was normally politically short-sighted, disregarded protests from Cîteaux and approved the Congregation of Castile in 1437, he, like Vargas, saw more clearly than the General Chapter.

Other congregations or semi-congregations (their legal status is not always clear) appeared in Italy, Spain, Portugal,

Germany, Austria, Switzerland, Poland, Bohemia, and Ireland. They varied in their loyalty to Cîteaux, but, on the whole, they were remarkably successful, and an examination of their histories reveals a healthy amount of intellectual and spiritual renewal.

In France, however, the situation was different. The only french congregation to arise was that of the Feuillants, begun in the late 1570s by Jean de La Barrière, the fiercely ascetic former commendatory abbot of Feuillant (a cistercian house near Toulouse). The new congregation flourished—-Sixtus V's unstinting praise was well deserved—though its success was watched with growing nervousness by the abbot of Cîteaux and the General Chapter. Quite whether it was 'cistercian' or not was a moot point—despite its independence it persisted in calling itself the 'Congregation of Our Lady of Feuillant of the Cistercian Order'—but what we see in its discipline and austerity would not be seen again until Dom Augustin de Lestrange established La Val-Sainte in Switzerland in 1791. Feuillantine discipline, in fact, proved too arduous and austere, and by the end of the sixteenth century Jean de La Barrière had been deposed and the harshness of the original rule considerably mitigated. But the Congregation remained spiritually sound and intellectually active, and the french Feuillants of the seventeenth century produced an impressive amount of solid and scholarly literature.

Meanwhile, faced with the triumphant progress of the Reformation, the Catholic Church had taken itself in hand and, over eighteen years from 1545 to 1563, held that long and intermittent exercise in self-analysis known as the Council of Trent. The effects of the council were profound. It imparted to the Church a sense of direction and cohesion, it provided a great stimulus to the Counter Reformation, and it called for general reform. In France, however, the Wars of Religion prevented the implementation of its ideals until the sixteenth century; but once those wars had drawn to a close and stability had been restored under Henry IV—a gallant soldier and an admirable king—the spirit of the Counter Reformation seemed eager to make up for lost time and swept through France like a fire.

In these circumstances, combined with the triumph of Catholicism and the development of absolutism under Henry, regional reformation was out of place and out of date. What was wanted was something on a national level, and at Cîteaux, under a number of capable and energetic abbots, the call went out for general reform. It is no coincidence that two of these abbots had played an active role in the Council of Trent. But reform, and reform there was, did not stem from any official resolution or decree. It trickled into the Order from the pillaged and plundered abbey of La Charmoye in Champagne where, in 1598, a devout nineteen-year-old of italian ancestry, Octave Arnolfini, had just been appointed commendatory abbot.[7]

Arnolfini (like Rancé in later years) took his responsibilities seriously and realized that he could not restore the monastic buildings or monastic discipline unless he truly embraced the monastic life. He therefore entered Clairvaux, completed his novitiate, was professed in 1603, and returned to La Charmoye as its regular abbot. Over the next few years, Arnolfini met and befriended Étienne Maugier and Abraham Largentier, the nephew of Denis Largentier, abbot of Clairvaux, and the three young men composed a document in which they stated unequivocally their desire for reform and their intention to observe the Rule of Saint Benedict 'without making use of any dispensations'.[8] The major dispensation to which they were referring was the dispensation to eat meat. The Rule of Saint Benedict permits meat only to the sick, but by the late fifteenth century meat was being eaten in the abbeys of the Order on Tuesdays, Thursdays, and Sundays, except in Advent, part of Lent, and on certain specified days of abstinence.[9] A return to the Rule therefore de-

7. Much information on Arnolfini may be found in Louis Lekai's *Strict Observance* (see page 255 of the index). There is hardly anything else in English.
8. Quoted in Lekai, *Strict Observance*, 30.
9. See Lekai, *Cistercians*, 112. Those seeking more details on the matter must refer to Canivez, 8 (index) 98-99 s.v. *Carnium, esus*.

manded a return to perpetual abstinence, and this had been a feature of many of the reform movements (including the Feuillants) long before Arnolfini and his friends signed their statement in 1606. But whereas the Feuillants had been a limited, local movement, Arnolfini and his devout followers—the Abstinents as they came to be called—envisaged a universal reformation of the whole Cistercian Order. It was the beginning of the Strict Observance.

The details of its rise and development have been chronicled elsewhere in a work of great (if biased) brilliance—Father Louis J. Lekai's *The Rise of the Cistercian Strict Observance in Seventeenth Century France*—and we need not reiterate the whole story here. Suffice it to say that it occurred in four major phases.

In its first phase, the abstinent ideals of Arnolfini received encouragement from Denis Largentier of Clairvaux, and with his support a number of houses affiliated with Clairvaux joined the new movement. The General Chapter of 1618 had no hesitation in approving the reform in principle, but realizing that there was also strong opposition to perpetual abstinence, the Chapter was not prepared to impose it on the whole Order. Instead it proposed a compromise solution: meat would not be eaten from 14 September (the feast of the Exaltation of the Holy Cross) to Easter. But the compromise antagonized many and satisfied none. Both the royal and papal courts realized that help and advice were needed in the matter (for the urge to reform was not restricted to the Cistercians) and in 1622 Pope Gregory XV appointed Cardinal François de La Rochefoucauld as apostolic visitor to oversee the movement. Since the cardinal was a devout man with a passion for reform, it is hardly surprising that he immediately came under the influence of the Abstinents, and in 1623 he issued a revolutionary document proposing the establishment of an autonomous, abstinent, reformed congregation, centred on Clairvaux.

To this hair-raising proposal the General Chapter of 1623 reacted with horrified alarm, but since the desire for reform

was still strong, and since abbot Nicolas Boucherat II of
Cîteaux supported it, the Abstinents were nevertheless
granted a certain autonomy. With Boucherat's permission and
encouragement they formed themselves into, not a congregation, but a vicariate—a congregation in all but name—to be
administered by Étienne Maugier who, in turn, would act
under the authority of the abbot of Cîteaux. It could have
been a very satisfactory resolution of the situation and, as
Louis Lekai has said, 'had Maugier been satisfied with these
generous concessions, the reform could have expanded peace-
fully on a voluntary basis and an embarrassing chapter of the
history of the Order could have remained unwritten'.[10]

The second phase of what was rapidly becoming the War
of the Observances[11] opened in 1624-1625 with the deaths of
Largentier of Clairvaux and Boucherat of Cîteaux, two staunch
supporters of the Abstinent movement. Their successors at
both abbeys were far less sympathetic, and, for the Abstinents,
the situation was worsened when the reforming cardinal La
Rochefoucauld's appointment as apostolic visitor expired in
1628. But then, four years later, the cardinal made an unexpected return when he was appointed as visitor for a further
three years, and by that time the leadership of the reform
movement had passed to Jean Jouaud, abbot of Prières, a brilliant and dynamic young man in his early thirties with
influential friends at court.

The powerful alliance of La Rochefoucauld and Jouaud resulted, in 1634, in a proposal for a radical and overall reorgani-
zation of the Cistercian Order under the absolute and total
control of the Abstinents, or, as we may now call them, the
Strict Observance. Reaction to the proposal was as prompt
as it was predictable: the new abbot of Cîteaux, Pierre Nivelle,
and the four proto-abbots—the abbots of La Ferté, Pontigny,
Clairvaux, and Morimond—immediately appealed to the pope,
the king, and Cardinal Richelieu, and a large number of

---

10. Lekai, *Cistercians*, 142.
11. Such is the title of chapter XI in Lekai's *Cistercians*.

abbeys outside France threatened to leave the Order unless the proposal was withdrawn.

The appeal to Richelieu seemed at first to be promising, but with the wily cardinal there was always a price: to ensure even the possibility of his assistance the Order would have to elect him as abbot of Cîteaux and abbot general. Nivelle accordingly bowed, resigned, received the bishopric of Luçon as compensation, and in November 1635, after a legally dubious election, Richelieu gained the coveted abbacy. He immediately did an about-face, allied himself with Jouaud (an old acquaintance), and gave his full support to the Strict Observance.

As a consequence, the number of houses controlled by the Strict Observance doubled from fifteen to thirty, though not all the abbeys joined the movement willingly. But from this time on the conflict between the two Observances became more and more embroiled in national and international politics. The Strict Observance tended to turn for support to the king in Gallican France; the Common Observance tended to turn to the pope in curial Rome. And when Richelieu died in 1643, the Common Observance took immediate advantage of his death and, in a chaotic, contested, and—once again—legally dubious election, elected Claude Vaussin to the abbacy of Cîteaux. Vaussin was a worthy opponent for Jean Jouaud, but his election was successfully contested by the Abstinents and, after a great deal of legal wrangling and political lobbying, a new election was called for May 1645. The two candidates were Jouaud and Vaussin, but since there were more than twice as many anti-Abstinent electors as there were others, the result was a foregone conclusion. Vaussin was again elected as abbot general and his election was quickly confirmed by pope and king, both of whom were eager to impose some sort of stability on what had become a violent, confused, and explosive situation.

With the re-election of Vaussin we begin the third phase of the War of the Observances. Again the Strict Observance contested the election—the lawsuits dragged on for years—

and again the whole issue became entangled in politics. Once again the Strict Observance looked for, and found, support in France; once again the Common Observance found it in Rome. And France being France, it is understandable that the Strict Observance made large gains—until, that is, the accession of the Sun King.

Louis XIV, as we have already seen, was the epitome of an absolute monarch and looked with a jaundiced eye on any threat to centralized authority. As far as he was concerned, the reform movement of the Strict Observance was a threat to the authority of the abbot of Cîteaux—the abbot general—and, in any case, Louis preferred to keep on good terms with those foreign abbots (especially in Germany) who had never supported the Abstinent cause. Vaussin took advantage of the situation to seek royal permission to refer the whole business to Rome for papal arbitration, and once approval had been granted, he himself went to Rome to plead the case for the Common Observance in person. Once in Rome, Vaussin never denied the need for reform—indeed, he emphasized it—but pointed out that a need for reform was not the same thing as domination by the Strict Observance. To this argument the pope lent a sympathetic ear and, in consequence, appointed a special Congregation for Cistercian Affairs and invited representatives of both Observances to Rome in the hope of establishing some common ground for the reform of the entire Order.

At these meetings, which took place in 1664, the chief negotiator for the Common Observance was, once again, Vaussin. The Strict Observance was represented by Dominique Georges, abbot of Val-Richer, and Armand-Jean de Rancé, abbot of la Trappe. But why Rancé? He had, after all, spent only six weeks at la Trappe after his abbatial blessing and already he was being plucked from his norman retreat and plunged into serious negotiations of the first importance for his Observance and his Order. Why? There are perhaps five reasons. He was well connected in an age when connections were of first importance and he was eloquent in an age when eloquence was effective. He was also wholly committed to the cause of the Strict Observance; he was obviously competent, for his short time at la Trappe had produced a striking improvement in the material and spiritual condition of the abbey; and, perhaps most important, he clearly possessed that indefinable something, that charisma, which makes one person heard while another is not.

Professor Krailsheimer has suggested that Rancé was an odd choice.[12] It is, perhaps, less odd when one remembers that Jouaud was seeking, if not total victory (for the circumstances were against him), at least as much of a victory as possible, and in such a case you do not send in those too eager to compromise. Dom Georges, like Rancé, had joined the Order after a long and distinguished career in the world, and, again like Rancé, he had good contacts and important friends. We are talking politics here, not theology; though when it came to theology Rancé knew his material, and Father Lekai's comment that he had a 'lack of understanding of authentic Cistercian spirituality'[13] is, as we shall see, untrue.

But however eloquent the Abstinents, their cause was doomed. Victory was never a real possibility and the best they could hope for was a reasonable compromise. A compromise there was, though few on either side found it reasonable, and the apostolic constitution *In suprema* was promulgated on 19 April 1666. Rancé himself had left Rome two months earlier, having been away from la Trappe for about two years. Among other things, *In suprema* required the same basic discipline for both Observances, save that the Strict Observance would practise perpetual abstinence and the Common Observance (in accordance with the old dispensation) could eat meat three times a week except during Advent and Lent. And although the pope granted the Strict Observance formal legal standing, he certainly did not grant it autonomy. The whole Order would still be governed by the abbot of

12. Krailsheimer, *Rancé*, 21.
13. Lekai, *Cistercians*, 149.

Cîteaux and the General Chapter.

We now enter the fourth and final phase of the controversy. The Apostolic Constitution was formally read at the General Chapter of 1667, which was surprisingly well attended, and was immediately and vigorously challenged by Rancé on the grounds that it had been composed under undue influence from the Common Observance and that certain matters had been inserted into the text without the pope's knowledge or consent. In obedience to pope and king he would give provisional assent to the document, but only until the king would permit another appeal to Rome which, he hoped, would result in a more auspicious and honest solution to the controversy.

Pope Alexander VII, however, was mortally ill at the time of the Chapter and died a few days after it was adjourned. His successor, Clement IX, had no interest at all in Rancé's protest, and the situation for both sides was then thrown into further confusion by the death of Claude Vaussin in 1670, a chaotic and inconclusive General Chapter in 1672, and the death of Jean Jouaud in 1673. The abbacy of Cîteaux, meanwhile, had passed into the hands of Jean Petit, who shared with Louis XIV an absolutistic approach to administration and was determined to establish his own authority on what was no longer an Order but a Disorder. His opponents were Claude Le Maître, abbot of Châtillon, and Rancé, on whom the mantle of Abstinent leadership had fallen after the death of Jouaud.

Rancé now decided to lobby his influential friends at court and address the king directly. This he did in 1673 in his *Requeste présentée au Roy par le Révérend Père Abbé de La Trappe*,[14] a pamphlet of eight eloquent pages which was hailed by certain of his contemporaries as a masterpiece of prose. At the same time Le Maître had drawn up a collective (and less flowery) document, the *Requeste présentée au Roy par les Abbez, Prieurs, et Religieux de l'Estroite Observance de l'Ordre de Cisteaux*.[15] Both

14. Part II, I.A.i [1673 *Requeste*].
15. *Ibid.*

were presented to Louis on 22 August 1673. As a consequence, Louis (who was sick of the whole business) established a special committee to investigate the charges brought by the Strict Observance and appointed as chairman of the committee the archbishop of Paris, François de Harlay de Champvallon, an old friend of Rancé.

All looked well for the Strict Observance and the committee was inundated with a flood of documents in support of the Abstinent cause. Rancé himself contributed a further *Éclaircissement sur l'état présent de l'Ordre de Cisteaux*,[16] published in 1674, which told the story of the immensely successful carmelite reform of Saint Teresa in Spain, pointed out how that reform could not have succeeded without royal support— Louis could hardly have missed the inference—and demanded, as a basis for successful reform, full autonomy for the Strict Observance.

There was, however, a problem. At just this time Louis had been at war with Holland for about a year, and the Dutch, aided by Austria and Spain, were holding him at bay. What Louis did not want, therefore, was the possibility of a host of anti-Abstinent German abbots ganging up against him. As a consequence, and despite Rancé's friends on the committee and at court, in April 1675 the Council of State rejected the claims of the Strict Observance, though it opened the way for a further appeal to Rome if the contesting parties so wished. In 1675, however, the pope was Clement X, a good friend to the Common Observance, and there was little point in the Strict Observance pursuing the matter. But then, in 1676, happily for one party and unhappily for the other, Clement died to be succeeded by Innocent XI, an austere pontiff with jansenist leanings, an admirer of Rancé's revitalization of la Trappe, and perhaps the greatest pope of the seventeenth century.

The Strict Observance naturally took advantage of the situation and their appeals fell on receptive ears. A bull was

16. Part II, I.A.i [1674 *Éclaircissement*].

prepared which gave the Strict Observance full autonomy, but since Innocent was in continual conflict with Louis—the king's absolutism inevitably clashed with the pope's stubborn resistance to any infringement on the rights of the Church—he was not prepared to promulgate the document without consulting the french court. Louis, understandably, would have none of it, and despite his sympathy for the reform, he categorically refused to see the authority of Cîteaux threatened by the establishment of a second cistercian Order. Both Observances were back where they started, and both continued to publish pamphlet after pamphlet supporting their cause.

It took a further four years for the controversy to be resolved, but the General Chapter of 1683 took careful heed of a set of recommendations drawn up by a committee chaired by the Abstinent abbot of Cadouin, Pierre Mary. Rancé himself was ill and was not present at the assembly. In essence, the Chapter granted the Strict Observance almost complete autonomy, though the abbot of Cîteaux still preserved his place at the apex of the cistercian pyramid. There were to be annual meetings of all Strict Observance superiors, but they were to be held under the presidency of the abbot general— the abbot of Cîteaux—at a time and place decided by him. On the other hand, if, in any monastery, a majority of monks were in favour of reform, then the Strict Observance (which then comprised sixty houses) could take over the abbey with the consent of the abbot general or, at least, of its father immediate, *i.e.* the abbot of the mother-house of the daughter-house in question. As Louis Lekai has pointed out, the compromise was much the same as that negotiated between Étienne Maugier and Nicholas Boucherat sixty years earlier in 1624,[17] and whether anything had really been gained by the sixty weary years of fighting is a moot point.

Rancé, as we have said, did not attend the Chapter of 1683. In fact, the only Chapter he ever did attend was that of 1667.

---

17. Lekai, *Cistercians*, 150.

Nor did he attend any of the annual assemblies of the Strict Observance. The reform at la Trappe proceeded independently, in much the same way as reform had proceeded earlier in the various Congregations; and from 1672, Rancé simply ignored Cîteaux and the abbot general, though at no time did he question his authority. In any case, by 1672 Rancé was involved in a bitter conflict with his former friend Guillaume Le Roy, abbot of Hautefontaine, something we shall discuss in more detail in Chapter Six. But since neither that conflict nor a number of others can be understood without an understanding (not necessarily an appreciation) of Rancé's ascetic spirituality, it is to an examination of the bases of that spirituality that we must now turn. Before doing so, however, let me draw attention to six important points which arise out of our present discussion.

□ First, questions of decline and decadence can only be considered after taking into account the political, economic, and social conditions of the time and place.

□ Second, there was what we can only call an omnipresent atmosphere of reform pervading the whole of the french Church from the fifteenth century onwards. After the Council of Trent the desire for reform became more acute, and the effects of that Council were profound and wide ranging.

□ Third, the practical responses to this quest for reform took different forms in different places. Many of them were limited and local, but many of them were dramatically successful.

□ Fourth, although the commendatory system was in general a disaster for monastic Orders, we must note that Rancé was neither the first nor the last commendatory abbot to become regularized and seek the renewal of his community. We certainly cannot say that this was a tradition, but we should remember that there was a considerable number of other examples.

☐ Fifth, the desire for perpetual abstinence was not something unique to the Strict Observance, but was part of the way of life of a number of contemporary regional reforming movements.

☐ And finally, the reform of la Trappe itself must be seen against this wider background. To no small extent, Rancé's monks were Feuillants *redivivi* and there is no reason to be surprised at the success of Rancé's reform. Many of the regional reform movements, from the Benedictine Congregations onwards, were regularly successful, and it would be more surprising had the attempt at la Trappe met with failure. We must also remember that from about 1662, 'Trappist' (if we may be permitted the anachronism: 'rancéan' would be a better term) and 'Strict Observance' were not necessarily the same thing; and whereas the latter may be seen as a national movement counting some seventy houses in France at the Revolution, including five nunneries,[18] the former manifested itself most clearly on localized, limited levels such as la Trappe itself, Sept-Fons, Tamié, Orval, and their dependent houses.

18. See Lekai, *Cistercians*, 152 and the list in *ibid.*, 473-479.

FURTHER READING

There is now a considerable literature in English on the history of the cistercian Order during its first two centuries, though the material is not always reliable. In this regard we might note that the re-dating of the early documents and the hypothesis of wholesale forgery suggested by Constance H. Berman in *The Cistercian Evolution. The Invention of a Religious Order in Twelfth-Century Europe* (Philadelphia, 2000) cannot be sustained, and the book must be read in conjunction with three essential rejoinders: Brian P. McGuire, 'Charity and Unanimity: The Invention of the Cistercian Order. A Review Article', and Chrysogonus Waddell, 'The Myth of Cistercian Origins: C. H. Berman and the Manuscript Sources', both to be found in *Cîteaux: Commentarii cistercienses* 51 (2000) 285-297 (McGuire) and 299-386 (Waddell), and Michael Casey, 'Bernard and the Crisis at Morimond: Did the Order Exist in 1124?', *Cistercian Studies Quarterly* 38 (2003) 119-175.

Once we go beyond 1300, however, sources in English become far fewer, and for a competent overall survey of cistercian history from the fourteenth century to the French Revolution we are still dependent on Louis J. Lekai's *The Cistercians. Ideals and Reality* (Kent OH, 1977). This admirable volume now requires revision and its bibliographies are inevitably out of date, but it remains a generally reliable handbook. The same author's *The Rise of the Cistercian Strict Observance in Seventeenth Century France* (Washington, 1968) is a work of genius and remains a sure, if biased, guide to this most complicated controversy. Father Lekai was a member of the Common Observance—now called the Order of Cîteaux—and had little time for the Strict Observance and no time at all for Rancé. This shows in his work, but his study remains indispensable.

Father Lekai also led the way in the study of seventeenth- and eighteenth-century cistercian history and his published papers are essential reading. They may be found listed in his bibliography in *Studiosorum Speculum: Studies in Honor of Louis*

J. Lekai, O.Cist., ed. Francis R. Swietek and John R. Sommerfeldt (Kalamazoo, 1993) 423-428. The same volume also contains an article on 'The Papacy and the Reform of the Cistercian Order in the Late Middle Ages' by Bernhard Schimmelpfennig (337-354).

For the wider background of monastic reform we now have the useful survey by Peter King, *Western Monasticism. A History of the Monastic Movement in the Latin Church* (Kalamazoo-Spencer, 1999). Chapters 9-11 are particularly important, as is the Select Bibliography on pages 437-461. The Maurists are well served by Maarten Ultee's *The Abbey of St. Germain des Prés in the Seventeenth Century* (New Haven-London, 1981), with a bibliography on pages 193-204.

There is (alas) no study of the Feuillants in English, but excellent accounts in French (with comprehensive bibliographies) will be found in *DTC* 5:2265-2268 and (especially) *DS* 5:274-287 (by Maur Standaert). To these may now be added *Les Feuillants et l'abbé Jean de La Barrière: 2ᵉᵐᵉˢ Rencontres cisterciennes en Comminges: Actes des rencontres, avril 1994, Labastide-Clermont et Toulouse* (s.l., [1994?]). For lists and summaries of Feuillantine writings we are still heavily dependent on the four volumes of Jean François, *Bibliothèque générale des écrivains de l'Ordre de Saint Benoît* (Bouillon, 1777-1778; rpt. Louvain-Héverlé, 1961).

Information in English on the *dramatis personæ* of the various reform movements (other than Rancé) is minimal. Apart from the information provided by Lekai and Krailsheimer, one is often dependent on the articles in the standard French *repertoria*: the *DTC*, *DS*, *DAC*, and the incomplete *DHGE* and *DBF*. The earlier articles in these otherwise invaluable collections are now seriously in need of revision.

Those interested in the various Congregations have no recourse but to turn to studies in other european languages, especially French (for the Feuillants), German, Italian, and Spanish. Lekai's account in *The Cistercians*, 126-137, is sound, but unfortunately brief. Similarly, the only comprehensive account of the commendatory system is the old article by

R. Laprat in the *Dictionnaire de droit canonique* (Paris, 1942) 3:1029-1085.

For the account of the seventeenth-century cistercian reform presented here I am dependent on Lekai and Krailsheimer, together with the important studies by Polycarpe Zakar, *Histoire de la Stricte Observance de l'Ordre cistercien depuis ses débuts jusqu'au généralat du cardinal de Richelieu (1606-1635)* (Rome, 1966), Julius D. Leloczky, *Constitutiones et Acta Capitulorum Strictioris Observantiae Ordinis Cisterciensis (1624-1687)* (Rome, 1967), and Thomas Nguyên-Dình-Tuyên, 'Histoire des controverses à Rome entre la Commune et l'Étroite Observance de 1662 à 1666', *Analecta Cisterciensia* 26 (1970) 3-247 (an excellent study and edition), supplemented by the relevant *statuta* in Joseph-Maria Canivez, *Statuta Capitulorum Generalium Ordinis Cisterciensis ab Anno 1116 ad Annum 1786* (Louvain, 1933-1941). I have not, however, always followed my sources in their interpretation of the facts.

Chapter 4

RANCÉ'S SINS

ONE OF THE GREATEST difficulties faced by modern men and women in coming to an appreciation of the spirituality of Rancé—or indeed of the spirituality of seventeenth-century France in general—is that we approach the whole concept of spirituality from different premises. We tend, nowadays, to be spiritual optimists, and that is a fairly recent phenomenon. It was not, in general, the approach of seventeenth-century Catholic writers, and it was not the approach of the vast majority of medieval writers either. The true nature of medieval spirituality, in fact, is often misrepresented by modern scholars precisely because they approach it with a modern mentality.

We must begin with Augustine of Hippo, the most important single formative influence on the development of western theology. In the course of his bitter controversy with Pelagius, Augustine found himself asserting ever more strongly the absolute need for grace and the utter depravity of human beings. In his view, the first sin committed by Adam and Eve was, in a sense, an infinite sin. Before that first sin, humanity was wholly sinless; that first sin therefore brought about a change in kind or state, not just a change in degree. What had previously been unsullied was now sullied. Subsequent sins might sully it more, but the difference is now no more than quantitative. The difference between no sin and sin is infinite; the difference between one sin and a billion sins is large but finite.

It is this first, infinite sin which has been inherited by

humankind, and Augustine can therefore refer to the whole human race as *una massa peccati, una massa damnati, una massa perditionis*, 'one lump of sin, one lump damned to Hell, one mass of perdition'.[1] But there is more to it than that. Not only have we all inherited Adam's sin, we have also inherited his guilt. How? Because when Adam and Eve were in Eden, we too were in Eden, for *in potentiality* (though not yet in actuality) we existed in their loins. Since, therefore, we were, in that sense, *in* Adam, what Adam did we did; and when Adam fell, we fell in Adam. But since we did (in potentiality) what Adam did, it means we are every bit as guilty as Adam for the deed he committed. And since the deed he committed was an infinite sin, Adam was an infinite sinner, and so are we. When we come into this world, we come into it totally corrupt, totally guilty, and fit only for damnation. Our free will has lost its freedom to do good. It is now free only to sin. As Augustine himself says, 'Of our own power we can only fall'.[2]

The corollary of this depressing doctrine is, of course, predestination. Since we cannot, of our own power, do even one good act—absolute darkness cannot put forth any light—we cannot therefore earn, warrant, deserve, or merit divine grace. And since we cannot merit grace, we can receive it only as a free gift from God. And to whom will God give his grace? To those to whom he wills. In other words, to those he predestines to receive it. The augustinian view of human beings—wholly sinful and wholly guilty—cannot be separated from the doctrine of predestination.

Most modern theologians accept, in some form, the doctrine of original sin. They may prefer to say that something happened in the course of evolution which makes us more egocentric—perhaps it is no more than the instinct for self-

---

1. All these expressions occur more than once. For a classic example of *una massa peccati*, see Augustine, *De diversis quaestionibus ad Simplicianum* I, *quaest.* 2 *argumentum* and §16; *PL* 40:111, 121; for *una massa damnati, De civitate Dei* XXI.xii; *PL* 41:727; for *una massa perditionis, Enchiridion* 107; *PL* 40:282.
2. Augustine of Hippo, *Enarratio in Ps* 129.1; *PL* 37:1696.

preservation—but most of them would admit that human beings, for some reason, find it easier to sin than to do good. Our own experience confirms the view. Sin is far too enjoyable. But very few modern theologians are prepared to accept the doctrine of original *guilt*. That is a quite different matter. Something may have happened in the course of evolution which has made us selfish, but we are not guilty of that something. A baby boy born with AIDS may suffer the consequences of his parent's actions, but he cannot be said to be guilty of them.

This may be an obvious point, but it is a very important one. Modern theologians might reject the idea of Original Guilt, but the great majority of post-Tridentine *spirituels* accepted it without question. So did the great majority of medieval writers. One of the most popular and widely-read treatises of the Middle Ages was the twelfth-century *Meditationes piissimæ* attributed (incorrectly) to Bernard of Clairvaux. It was to be found in virtually every monastic library, often in multiple copies, and its second chapter begins thus:

> In my outer form I come from parents who condemned me before they gave me birth. Sinners themselves, they have begotten in their sin a sinner and have nourished him with sin. Wretches themselves, they have brought forth a wretch into the wretched light [of this world]. Nothing have I from them save wretchedness, sin, and this corruptible body I carry about. Truly, I am hastening towards those who have departed this place in bodily death. When I look on their tombs, I find in them nought but ashes and worms, stench and horror. What I am, they have been; what they are, I shall be. And what am I? A human being [come] from liquid moisture, for at the very moment of conception I was conceived from human semen, and then that froth co-

agulated, increased a little, and was made flesh.
After that, weeping and wailing, I was deliv-
ered into the exile of this world, and behold!
I am now dying, full of iniquities and abomi-
nations.[3]

And so it continues: we are nothing but slime from slime, a
fetid sperm, a bag of excrement, food for worms, ensnared by
our senses, entangled in vice, itching for pleasure, possessed
by passion, polluted by fantasies, and ever inclined to wickedness. We are conceived in sin, born in misery, live in pain,
and die in agony.[4] 'Why then do we so desire this life in which
the longer we live, the more we sin?'[5]

Pope Innocent III said the same thing in the thirteenth
century. In the very first chapter of his immensely popular
De miseria conditionis humanæ, he tells us that we are fuel for the
fire, food for worms, a mass of putridness. We are formed
from dust, clay, and ashes, and—what is worse—'from the
foulest sperm' (*de spurcissimo spermate*). We are conceived in
the itch of the flesh, the heat of desire, the stench of lust,
and the disgrace of sin, and in the end we will be what we are
now: a mass of rottenness, stinking and filthy.[6]

Generally speaking, this is not our modern viewpoint. It
was, however, the viewpoint of Rancé and of much (though
not all) seventeenth-century french spirituality. 'The state
to which we have been reduced by the sin of our first father',
said Pierre de Bérulle (to whom we shall return later),

is so deplorable that it has more need of tears
than of words, more need of a continual abase-

---

3. *Ps.*-Bernard of Clairvaux, *Meditationes piissimæ de cognitione humanæ conditionis*
ii.4; *PL* 184:487CD.
4. *Ibid.* iii.10 (491B), iii.8 (490AB), xii.33 (503B-4A), iii.7 (489D), iii.8 (490B),
in that order.
5. *Ibid.* ii.5; 488B.
6. *Lotario dei Segni* (*Pope Innocent III*), *De Miseria Condicionis Humane*, I.1, ed., tr.
Robert E. Lewis (Athens, GA, 1978), 92-95.

ment of our soul before God than of any
worldly speeches or thoughts which are too
inconsequential to portray its reality. For in
this condition, we possess the right only to
nothingness and hell. We can do nothing but
sin, and we are no more than a nothingness
opposed to God, deserving of his anger and
his everlasting wrath.[7]

Jean-Jaques Olier, who founded the Society of Saint-Sulpice in
Paris in 1642 (it was intended to train directors for the seminar-
ies established by Olier), was of exactly the same opinion. He,
too, speaks of us as 'nothingness', and tells us that if there is
anything at all in us which is not corrupted by sin, that is due to
God's grace alone. We sinned with and in Adam, and that first
fault, which is our doing as well as his, 'is the root cause of the
seed of evil which pollutes every hour of every day'.[8] Furthermore, not being satisfied with the depravity which comes from
original sin, 'we have also committed and blackened ourselves
with a thousand crimes, which is why, in truth, we are sin in
ourselves and nothing but sin'.[9] Sin, says Saint John Eudes, another contemporary of Rancé, is cruel homicide and dreadful
deicide. It is homicide because sin alone kills both body and soul
together; it is deicide because sin and the sinner crucified Christ
on the cross and continue to crucify him daily. Sin transforms
the children of God into children of Satan; it is the worst of evils
and the greatest of misfortunes.[10] And 'so long as you are not
willing to die, and suffer all sorts of scorn and torments rather
than commit a single sin, then know that you are not truly Christian.'[11]

7. *Œuvres complètes du cardinal de Bérulle: Œuvres de piété*, ed. Jacques-Paul
Migne (Paris, 1856) 958.
8. Jean-Jacques Olier, *Introduction à la vie et aux vertus chrétiennes. Pietas seminarii*,
ed. François Amiot (Paris, 1954) 33. 9. *Ibid.*, 34.
10. *Œuvres complètes du Vénérable Jean Eudes, Tome I: Le royaume de Jésus* (Paris,
1905) 174-175.
11. *Ibid.*, 177.

Given that we are born not only sinful but guilty, given that sin is homicide, and given that each of us has committed 'a thousand crimes', Rancé is being no more than logical when, in a famous—or infamous—passage, he likens monks to criminals and prodigals:

> Religious congregations are gangs of criminals and public penitents who are lacking in the fidelity they owe to God. They have angered him by their disobedience and can expect nothing from his goodness until they have satisfied his justice by chastisements worthy of their sins. They are prodigal children who have forsaken their Father's house and squandered the goods they have received from him. . . . With their hearts deeply penetrated by the awareness of their crimes, they must repair the ravages caused by their pride and disobedience by whole-hearted abasement and profound humiliations.[12]

Much has been made of this passage, but the opprobrium into which it has been cast by many modern writers is unjust and unnecessary. Apart from the fact that Rancé is simply following Saint John Climacus (as we shall see in Chapter Six), 'crimes' (*crimes*) is a word commonly used by seventeenth-century spiritual writers for sins, and Rancé's sentiments were far from being unique. He himself was a 'criminal' (*criminel*), a man 'condemned to hell by the number and seriousness (*grandeur*) of his sins', and he believed 'that the only way to appease God's wrath was to engage himself in penitence which would end only with [the end of] his life'.[13] Rancé may be less philosophical than Bérulle or Olier—he does not dwell on this Neo-Platonic 'nothingness'—but he certainly

12. *De la sainteté*, 1:392-393.
13. Letter 640630.

shares with them their overwhelming sense of sin, guilt, and utter unworthiness.

For us today, however, sin, while always serious, is—in a casuistic sense—less serious than it was for Rancé. For us today it is not especially easy to commit mortal sin. It takes a certain dedication. But in seventeenth-century France, 'most sins were mortal; a venial sin would be something like speaking an idle, frivolous word, or stealing something of no consequence like an apple or a pin'.[14] In seventeenth-century France, average men and women believed they were far closer to everlasting torment than we in the twenty-first century think we are. The conflict between the Jansenists and Jesuits, therefore, must not be seen as a mere theological quibble. The questions of Probabilism, Laxism, and Rigorism, which we shall discuss in a moment, were considered to be of profound importance for the salvation of one's soul. The questions being posed, in fact, were as simple as they were fundamental. First, when is an act a sin? And second, if it is a sin, how sinful is it? We need to say more about this since it impinges directly on Rancé's own penitential spirituality—a spirituality which cannot be understood outside its contemporary context.

The term casuistry has a bad name, but, in principle, it was no more than the application of general moral principles to specific situations. The Bible and the Church both provided certain general guidelines for ethical conduct, but it was the business of one's confessor to apply those guidelines specifically and determine the state of his penitent's soul. Some actions—murder, theft, drunkenness—were obviously sinful; others—usury was much in question—were more doubtful. If, then, we have done or are thinking of doing an action whose permissibility or sinfulness is in doubt, we may need more than one opinion on the matter. Such opinions

---

14. John McManners, *Church and Society in Eighteenth-Century France, II: The Religion of the People and the Politics of Religion* (Oxford, 1998) 2:246. The statement is equally true of France in the seventeenth century.

may come from two sources. They may come from recognized authorities, in which case they are referred to as extrinsic opinions; or they may come from the application of sound, logical argument, in which case they are referred to as intrinsic.

Let us suppose, then, that we are contemplating an action and we are not sure whether it is sinful or not. We consult our confessor who, in turn, consults his written authorities and/or examines the question logically. He may then arrive at two conflicting probable opinions: one which says that the action is probably sinful, and one which says it probably is not. Then, according to Probabilism, the confessor may rely on the probable opinion—either extrinsic or intrinsic—which suggests that the action is permissible, even though a *more* probable opinion suggests that it is, in fact, sinful. In other words, we are given the benefit of the doubt.

Probabilism was first formulated by Bartolomé de Medina (1527-80), a Spanish Dominican, but in the seventeenth century it came to be associated particularly with the Jesuits. It was clearly a more benign way of looking at human sin, but, equally obviously, it could be abused; and if we end up by saying that even the very slightest degree of probability is sufficient to excuse us from sin, then we have what was known as Laxism. Taken to its logical conclusion, Laxism made it far more difficult to be sinful than to be good.

Probabilism and Laxism had been attacked and satirized by Blaise Pascal, Rancé's contemporary, in his *Provincial Letters* and defended, not wholly successfully, by the Jesuit Georges Pirot in his *L'Apologie pour les casuistes contre les calomnies des jansénistes* in 1657.[15] But Pirot himself slid into Laxism and his book was censured in 1659, the year of its author's death. Laxism itself was condemned by Pope Alexander VII in 1665 and 1666, and again by Innocent XI in 1679.

The opposite of Probabilism was Tutiorism or Rigorism.

---

15. The *Apologie*, in turn, engendered further attacks and further rebuttals: see Cioranescu, 3:1635, nos. 55102-55105.

This system maintained that after we have formulated our opinion, either extrinsically or intrinsically, we should follow the safer (*tutior* in Latin) or more prudent view, *viz.* the view which is more in accord with the moral principle. To follow the 'less safe' opinion—that normally followed by the Jesuits—required that that opinion be not just probable, but virtually certain. In other words: if in doubt, don't!

It will not come as a surprise to learn that most of the augustinian Jansenists favoured Tutiorism, and in their view, the Jesuits were overlooking human sin, making a mockery of the confessional, and rendering the road to salvation far too easy. This was especially the view of the Jansenist Pierre Nicole (1625-95) with whom Rancé enjoyed a long correspondence and whose *Essais de morale* he greatly admired.[16] What, then, of Rancé himself?

That Rancé was deeply interested in the Jansenist/Jesuit dispute is certain. As early as 1644, when he was eighteen, he wrote to his old tutor Jean Favier on the question;[17] and fourteen years later he sent a letter to Robert Arnauld d'Andilly asking for pamphlets against the Jesuits.[18] Nor is there any doubt where his sympathies lay. Rancé might not have been— was not, in fact—a Jansenist, but he was certainly augustinian, and he had no time at all for what he saw as jesuit Laxism. He had too strong a sense of his own sinfulness, and in his view, the path which led to eternal life was not broad and easy, but narrow and demanding. The way of life which he instituted at la Trappe was the *tutior* way to salvation. Six years after Rancé's death, Dom Pierre Le Nain wrote that Rancé had never had a '*grande liaison*' with the Jesuits. Indeed, he and they really had nothing in common, and 'in a word, la Trappe is the reverse of Jesuit morality'.[19] On the other hand, as we saw in Chapter Two, Rancé esteemed the Jesuit Alfonso Rodriguez and recommended the reading of his *Pratique de la*

16. See Letters 751202, 780315a, and 890826.
17. Letter 440317.
18. Letter 580626.
19. See Krailsheimer, *Rancé*, 327 for the text of the letter.

perfection chrétienne.

Yet in the same letter Dom Le Nain also tells us that Rancé had continual problems with the Molinists, who were 'always at his heels during the last years of his life',[20] and Rancé himself speaks of them disparagingly in a letter written in 1675. 'The good thing about the Jansenists', he says, 'is that when you do not speak ill of them, they speak well of you', but as for the Molinists, 'unless you share their passions, and unless you accept all their ideas and arguments, they regard you as their enemy.'[21] Who were these Molinists and why was Rancé so opposed to them? Once again, this is not a question of theological obscurantism: it is a question which pertains directly to the salvation of one's soul.

Molinism began with Luis de Molina (1535-1600), a Spanish Jesuit, and was a valiant attempt at resolving the problem of predestination. We saw above that the augustinian tradition of total human depravity requires that grace be a free gift—it cannot be earned or merited—and that the only ones who receive this grace are those whom God has chosen to receive it. All others are inevitably doomed. But how are we to make sense of this doctrine? How can we explain to those suffering in hell that God is actually good and just and not merely a random executioner, choosing some for eternal life and some for eternal torment at his own whim? In short, how can we reconcile predestination with free will?

One attempt had been made back in the eighth century by Hincmar, archbishop of Reims, and we need to say a few words about Hincmar's ideas if we are to understand the views of Molina and, more importantly, the views of Rancé and his Jansenist and jansenizing friends.

Hincmar's solution was to make a distinction between predestination and foreknowledge. The two are not the same. To know something in advance is not necessarily to make it happen. If you see someone drop a glass, you know in advance

20. *Ibid.*
21. Letter 751100a.

that the glass will hit the floor and break, but you are not responsible for the damage. But if *you* take the glass and deliberately drop it, you both foreknow and predestine its destruction.

God, says Hincmar, is omniscient and therefore knows everything in advance. When the universe came into being, he knew exactly what was going to happen to all things at all times in all places. He therefore knew in advance what each of us would do and whether we would be good or wicked, but God does not force us to be good or wicked. That is up to us. Then, for those of us who God knows will be good, he predestines heaven, and for those of us who he knows will be wicked, he predestines hell.

This scheme certainly has advantages. First, it recognizes the universal saving will of God. God does indeed want everyone to be saved, but not everyone will cooperate with him in achieving salvation. Christ has truly died for us all, but not all will take advantage of his sacrifice. Secondly, in Hincmar's scheme, God is neither the author of evil nor a random executioner. He does not compel us to act wickedly. But if, through our own free choice, we *do* act wickedly, then we must accept the consequences. Thirdly, Hincmar does not deny human free will. God, as we have said, does not force us to be either good or wicked. That is up to us. And although God knows in advance what choices we will make, he predestines only the *consequences* of those choices, he does not predestine the choices themselves.

There were, however, two major problems with this neat solution. One was that it was contrary to Scripture, for Romans 9:18 states specifically that God has mercy on whom he wills, and he hardens the heart of whom he wills. It is *God* who does this, not us. He makes some of us vessels of mercy and he makes others vessels of wrath. This, said Hincmar's opponents, is an unambiguous statement that God directly affects human beings: he does not leave them to their own devices and predestine only their eventual end. And who was Hincmar to contradict Saint Paul?

Secondly, Hincmar's idea that we use our own free will to choose either good or evil, and that God knows in advance what we will choose, is contrary to the teaching of Augustine. The whole point of Augustine's teaching is that, because we are born sinful and guilty—'one lump of sin'—we can *never* choose good unless we are first given the grace to do so. Thus, for Hincmar to say that 'God foreknows those who will do good' is absurd. *No one* can do good without grace, and those who receive grace are those whom God has predestined to receive it. We are back where we started.

For biblical Augustinians, therefore, Hincmar's solution cannot work, and Luis de Molina was aware of this. His own solution was to expand the idea of God's omniscience to include not only things which have happened and will happen, but things which *might* have happened had circumstances been different. In other words, God not only knew in advance that George W. Bush would become president of the United States in the year 2000; he also knew what would have happened had George W. Bush died at birth or been born Georgina.

This idea is essential to Molina's argument. God not only knows what we have done and will do, but what we *would have done* in other circumstances. What circumstances are we talking about? The circumstances of our sinfulness. We cannot, in fact, do a single good action, just as Augustine said. Our will is not, in fact, free to do good, but free only to sin. But God, being wholly omniscient, knows in advance what we *would* have done *if* we had had perfect free will, unaffected by original guilt and original sin. So to those whom God foreknew *would* have cooperated with his grace and done good actions had they been able to so, he makes his grace available; to those whom he knows would not, he does not. He hardens their hearts and makes them vessels of wrath because they deserve it. Even if they could have done good, they would not have done so, and they alone, not God, make themselves fit for hell.

Molinism was widely accepted by the Jesuits. It was emphatically rejected by the Jansenists and those—like Rancé—

with jansenist leanings. Why? There were two main reasons. First, it makes the gift of grace dependent on (hypothetical) human actions. This, in turn, transforms grace into wages and detracts from the absolute sovereignty of God. Secondly, the idea that God's grace was there to be used or not, just as one (hypothetically) saw fit, contradicted the jansenist idea that grace was irresistible. Grace was a free gift from God, just as Augustine had said it was, but if God infused it into a human soul, its effect on that soul was irresistible. It transformed the soul and the will, whose seat was in the soul; and the will, freed by grace, was then free to try to fulfil God's commands. Grace was not like an apple on a tree, which some would choose to pick and some would not. Grace was like an aspirin: once inside you, it produced certain effects whether you liked it or not.

In Rancé's case, his own conversion had brought home to him the reality of God's intervention. For reasons known only to himself, God had elected to show a sinner and reprobate the way to salvation. Rancé had not earned this grace and, emphatically, did not deserve it. The all-powerful and sovereign Deity had freely bestowed it upon him, and Rancé could only be infinitely grateful for such an infinite gift. As far as he was concerned, Jesuits, Probabilists, Laxists, and Molinists were all cut from the same cloth, and not one of them had a correct notion of the awesome nature of God and the awful consequences of sin.

The reception of so great a free gift, however, inevitably has its darker side. It is not always pleasant to be given something one knows one does not deserve, and a gift of this nature must inevitably arouse feelings of humility and remorse and a desire to make amends. That this was true of Rancé cannot be doubted. But in his feelings of remorse and in his desire to make amends—'I know (he wrote) that many centuries of the life I want to embrace cannot for a moment make satisfaction for that which I led in the world'[22]—he was once

22. Letter 630430.

again a man of his times. It was not just Rancé, but the whole
post-Tridentine world which was in travail. If we do not appreciate this, Rancé's spirituality can appear masochistically
unbalanced; if we do appreciate it, we will see that his spirituality was no more than we would expect.

The Council of Trent did not accomplish all that it tried
to do, but it did accomplish a very great deal. It gave the
Church a clearly defined system of doctrine, it established a
solid foundation for the renewal of ecclesiastical discipline,
and it engendered a remarkable revitalization of spiritual life.
But in the wake of the Council there came about what Pierre
Janelle has called the 'cycle of remorse' which, as he says, 're-
appeared in full force after the Council of Trent, when the
Church had made its children rueful for their past lascivious-
ness'.[23] The concept was not new. Janelle draws attention to
the twelfth-century 'Archweeper' of Jean de Hauteville, but
the same principle lies at the back of such works as the pseudo-
Bernardine *Meditationes piissimæ* and Innocent III's *De miseria
conditionis humanæ* which we discussed above. As a matter of
fact, the tradition lasted well into the nineteenth century
and may be clearly seen, for example, in the writings of John
Henry, Cardinal Newman. Religion, he said,

> is founded in one way or other on the sense
> of sin; and without that vivid sense it would
> hardly have any precepts or any observances.
> Its many varieties all proclaim or imply that
> man is in a degraded, servile condition, and
> requires expiation, reconciliation, and some
> great change of nature.[24]

And Newman's own prayer could easily be that of Rancé:

> I am in myself nothing but a sinner, a man of
> unclean lips and earthly heart. I am not wor-

23. Janelle, *Catholic Reformation* (cited in Further Reading, 96), 142.
24. Erich Przywara, *A Newman Synthesis* (New York, 1945) 27.

thy to enter into His presence. I am not worthy of the least of all His mercies.[25]

Expressions such as these are not so common in the twenty-
first century. We are spiritual optimists, and a besotted preoccupation with our sins is not generally considered psychologically advisable or spiritually beneficial.

The two main themes of the 'cycle of remorse' were the
remorse of Saint Peter after he had denied Christ and the
remorse of the Magdalene after her conversion. The story of
the former is told in the long, rambling, unfinished epic poem
Lagrime di San Pietro by Luigi Tansillo (1510-1565); the story
of the latter appears in the six hundred and eight lines of the
Lagrime di S. Maria Maddalena by Erasmo di Valvason (1523-
1593).[26] Both poems were immensely popular in their day;
both were translated into French as well as other european
languages; both spawned innumerable imitations. But the
essential feature of all of them are torrents of tears. In the
Lagrime della Maddalena, Mary never stops weeping from the
moment of her conversion to the end of her life, and while
Anne Vincent-Buffault's *History of Tears*[27] is concerned primarily with the eighteenth and nineteenth centuries, the seventeenth century was even wetter.

To this general atmosphere of contrition and tears we must
add that Rancé was a convert, and great conversions are always accompanied by an equally great desire to make amends.
'What is the business of a monk?', asks Rancé, and answers
the question in the words of Saint Bernard: 'It is to weep for
our own sins and for those of all others.'[28] 'Bathe your face
continually in the bitter waters of penitence', says Rancé;
'Let your only care be to pour out your tears, and leave it to
God to dry them.'[29] It is inevitable, therefore, than penitence

25. *Ibid.*, 200.
26. See Janelle, *Catholic Reformation*, 142-148.
27. See Chapter 2, n. 12.
28. *De la sainteté*, 1:394.
29. *Ibid.*, 1:458.

and penance must play a fundamental role in his spirituality. The situation could not be other. The whole tenor of seventeenth-century french spirituality was penitential, and in being penitential, the french *spirituels* were doing no more than imitating Christ, the Great Penitent. Rancé is in no way unusual in referring to Christ in this way. It was a standard theme. 'Let us respectfully consider Jesus Christ', says Jean-Jacques Olier, 'doing penance for our sins.'

> Let us honor in him the holy Spirit of penitence, which animated the whole of his life and afterwards filled the hearts of all the penitents of the Church.[30]

Jesus Christ was 'the penitent one'[31] who 'lived a life of penitence'[32], and therefore, says Olier,

> In honour of and in union with Jesus Christ Our Lord, penitent before God for my sins and for the sins of the whole world, I declare my intention to do penance all the days of my life, and to regard myself in all things as a poor and miserable sinner, an utterly unworthy penitent.[33]

Penances, he continues,

> have been established in the Church to continue the holy penitence of Jesus Christ; and those holy souls who are especially called to this should [offer themselves as] victims for

---

30. Olier, *Introduction à la vie et aux vertus chrétiennes*, 23.
31. *Ibid.*, 24 and many other places. Olier's expression (also used by a number of other writers) is 'Jésus-Christ pénitent'.
32. *Ibid.*, 125.
33. *Ibid.*, 73. The whole of Olier's seventh chapter on the virtue of penitence 62-83) repays careful reading.

> the sins of the world, and render satisfaction
> to God in the very Spirit of Jesus Christ.[34]

It stands to reason, therefore, that we should eschew all luxury, groan on wood and straw, be content with the poorest rooms and furniture, and wear the most lacklustre clothes.[35]

These are quotations from Olier, not Rancé, but if one did not know it, it would be difficult to tell them apart. And similar passages can easily be found in the multitudinous writings of the other seventeenth-century *spirituels*. When, therefore, we read, as we may often read, that Rancé 'over-emphasizes' penitence and penance, this is nonsense. He might emphasize them too much for our modern taste, but the majority of his contemporaries would simply have nodded their heads and said 'Of course!' They might not always have agreed with the ways in which penance was manifested at la Trappe, but they would have had no doubt about the principle.

All this is not to say that Rancé was simply another member of the 'French School'. He was not, and to see why he was not we must say something about this school and its teachings. Its greatest representatives were Cardinal Pierre de Bérulle (1575-1629), the founder and first Superior-General of the Oratory, his successor as Superior-General, Charles de Condren (1588-1641), Jean-Jacques Olier (1608-1657), the founder of Saint-Sulpice, Madeleine de Saint-Joseph (1578-1637), the first french prioress of the Great Carmel in Paris, and John Eudes (1601-1680), who was so important in the development of devotion to the heart of Jesus and of Mary. Rancé had certainly read Bérulle's *Office de Jésus* and Condren's *L'Idée du sacerdoce et du sacrifice de Jésus-Christ*: both had been sent to him by the Jansenist Pasquier Quesnel.[36]

The principles of the School were five. First, the adoration and worship of the sovereign majesty of God who became incarnate in Jesus Christ. Secondly, a profound Christo-

34. *Ibid.*, 126.
35. *Ibid.*
36. See Letters 730301 and 770321.

centrism in which Christ is central to all our devotion, thoughts, and spirituality. Thirdly, an eastern—actually Neo-Platonic—conception of our human participation in what Bérulle and his followers call the 'states' (*états*) of Christ from his infancy to his glory. Fourthly, the vital importance of holy communion through which we share in Christ's infinite life. And fifthly, the idea that only when we have wholly annihilated our own self-will, only when Christ has become all in all, only when we have realized our own—once again, essentially Neo-Platonic—nothingness, can we be wholly united—identified, even—with Christ himself.[37]

The precise degree to which Rancé was directly influenced by Bérulle remains a matter of debate, but he certainly cannot be called 'bérullian'. He shares with the French School its adoration of a sovereign God (and its corollary: the all-important nature of grace as a free gift). He shares with it a profound devotion to Christ and the Eucharist. And he shares with it the idea that (as he himself says), 'the surest way to purify oneself before God is to despoil and annihilate oneself in one's own eyes'.[38] But he does not share its philosophical basis and he is, as always, his own man. Rancé is not a Neo-Platonist and his idea of what the seventeenth-century french *spirituels* liked to call *abandon* or 'abandonment' of one's self is far more down to earth.

For Rancé, abandonment is certainly not Quietism, a system which he denounced as the chimaeras of fanatics and absolute impiety,[39] but rather 'the trusting acceptance of God's providence and the cooperation with him in obedience which together were seen as essential Christianity'.[40] The concept is clear in most of the spiritual writers of the time, including Rancé's great friend, Bossuet, and it finds its culmination in the posthumously published *L'abandon à la providence divine* of

37. For the French School, see the literature cited in Further Reading, 95.
38. Letter 830211c.
39. Letter 970414.
40. *A Dictionary of Christian Spirituality*, ed. Gordon S. Wakefield (London, 1983) 1.

the Jesuit Jean-Pierre de Caussade.[41]

For Jeanne-Françoise Frémyot de Chantal (whom Rancé admired[42]), the trust we place in providence and in the love of the Bridegroom relieves us from all anxieties, and imbues us with the confidence that he will furnish us with all we need—provided we strive to please him by doing his will and trusting in his goodness.[43] The gift of grace may be 'purely a result of God's mercy', as Rancé says, but God will call us to account for it. If we have indeed received grace, we are obliged 'to follow its promptings and profit from them'.[44] God may be liberal, but he gives his gifts only to those souls 'who preserve and make good use of that which they receive from his mercy'.[45]

God is the source and end of all our feelings, wrote Rancé to Henri Barillon, bishop of Luçon, 'and we must receive the orders of his providence with a resignation worthy of the blessing which comes from belonging to him'.[46] And to his sister:

> You could not do better than submit yourself to God's guidance in everything, and accept with total resignation any conflicts that may come your way, wherever they may come from. It is enough to know that Providence rules everything, and that there is nothing that God does not do or permit for the sanctification of those who are his.[47]

Abandonment, therefore, is

---

41. See *ibid.*, 81-82. Caussade's *L'abandon* is easily available in more than one english translation.

42. See Letters 840420 and 890400.

43. *Francis de Sales, Jane de Chantal: Letters of Spiritual Direction* (cited in Further Reading, 90) 245.

44. Letter 831112.   45. Letter 820916.

46. Letter 910730.   47. Letter 891013.

> that giving of oneself to God in which one
> wishes to do his will whatever the situation
> and at the same time not only accepts the
> situation as the current context for this but
> actively wills it, as it were endorses it, since
> faith interprets it not as mere happening but
> as divine providence.[48]

The Spirit of God blows freely, says Rancé, so abandon your-self (*abandonnez-vous*) to his inspiration, and follow, in perfect simplicity, the promptings of his Spirit.[49] It is in this willing surrender to God and his will—this 'trustful surrender to the Holy Spirit', as Martinus Cawley puts it[50]—that we find our joy in God.

Joy. This is the other side of the coin. With Rancé, all is not, in fact, gloom and doom, compunction and contrition, weeping and wailing. It is true that we are utterly sinful. It is true that all we do here on earth is 'to offend God and dis-please him'.[51] It is true that because of what we are, we should live out our entire life 'wholly consecrated to the works of penitence and the exercises of mortification, especially fast-ing, solitude, and silence'.[52] But to what end? Not only to the attainment of heaven—though death must necessarily be the crowning summit of the life of any religious—but to a joyful contentment in the knowledge that one is trying—if unsuc-cessfully—to fulfil and to accept God's will. And if God wills that we suffer, so be it. There can be joy in suffering, and Rancé refers to his favourite saint, John Climacus, John of the Ladder, 'unquestionably the greatest and most enlightened solitary ever to appear in the Church of God',[53] to support his case.[54]

---

48. *Dictionary of Christian Spirituality*, 2.   49. *De la sainteté*, 1:293-294.
50. Martinus Cawley, 'The Psalms on the Deathbed at la Trappe', *Cistercian Studies Quarterly* 35 (2000) 311.
51. Letter 910627.   52. Letter 670910.   53. Letter 800618.
54. See Chapter 5, n. 63, for a translation of the relevant passage.

But this is to take us into a new realm. It is to take us into a discussion of Rancé's understanding of monasticism and monastic joy, and of the harsh and stark contrast—essential for understanding any of the french spiritual writers of the seventeenth century—of the things which pertain to heaven and the things which pertain to earth.

FURTHER READING

The most complete account of seventeenth-century french spirituality is to be found in the informative but idiosyncratic pages of Henri Bremond's *Histoire littéraire du sentiment religieux en France depuis les guerres de religion jusqu'à nos jours* (Paris, 1916-1933; rpt. 1967-1968 [eleven volumes in twelve]). This is an astonishing repository of recondite information which provides a vital background for an appreciation of Rancé's spirituality. Much of the material provided by Bremond cannot be found elsewhere. The first three volumes were translated into English as *A Literary History of Religious Thought in France from the Wars of Religion down to Our Own Times*, tr. K. L. Montgomery (London, 1928-1936 [three volumes]). The translation ends with volume three of the French original: *La conquête mystique - L'école française* (1921). On Bremond himself, see the references in Further Reading to Chapter One.

Useful shorter summaries may be found in Jedin-Dolan VI:75-93 (with bibliography [now in need of revision] on pages 596-598), Louis Cognet, tr. P. J. Hepburne-Scott, *Post-Reformation Spirituality* (London, 1959), *The Study of Spirituality*, ed. Cheslyn Jones, Geoffrey Wainwright, and Edward Yarnold (Oxford-New York, 1986), 379-419, and Michael J. Buckley, 'Seventeenth-Century French Spirituality: Three Figures', in *Christian Spirituality: Post-Reformation and Modern*, ed. Louis Dupré and Don E. Saliers (New York, 1991) 28-68.

For the French School of spirituality, see Raymond Deville, tr. Agnes Cunningham, *The French School of Spirituality: An Introduction and Reader* (Pittsburgh, 1994), and the solid introductions and excellent bibliographies in the Classics of Western Spirituality translations of *Bérulle and the French School: Selected Writings*, ed., intro. William M. Thompson, tr. Lowell M. Glendon (New York-Mahwah, 1989), and *Francis de Sales, Jane de Chantal: Letters of Spiritual Direction*, tr. Péronne M. Thibert, selected and introduced by Wendy M. Wright and Joseph F. Power (New York-Mahwah, 1988). There is also a great deal of valuable information in Pierre Janelle's *The Catholic Reformation* (Milwaukee, 1963), but the book is seriously flawed by its lack of source-references.

For the positive and negative sides of casuistry, the old study by Kenneth E. Kirk, *Conscience and its Problems: An Introduction to Casuistry* (London, 1927) remains sound and useful, but may now be supplemented by Albert R. Jonsen, *The Abuse of Casuistry: A History of Moral Reasoning* (Berkeley, 1988), and the collected papers in *Conscience and Casuistry in Early Modern Europe*, ed. Edmund Leites (Cambridge, 1988).

On the controversy between the Jansenists and the Jesuits, the reader may be referred to Jedin-Dolan VI:41-57 (with a bibliography on pages 593-595) and the studies by Sedgwick and Crichton cited in Further Reading to Chapter Two. The final part of the story is the subject of Dale K. Van Kley's *The Jansenists and the Expulsion of the Jesuits from France, 1757-1765* (New Haven, 1975). Pierre Nicole is well served by Edward D. James, *Pierre Nicole, Jansenist and Humanist. A Study of His Thought* (The Hague, 1972).

On Probabilism, Probabiliorism, Laxism, Tutiorism or Rigorism, Equiprobabilism, and so on, the reader may be referred to the concise entries (with bibliographies) in *The Oxford Dictionary of the Christian Church*, edd. Frank L. Cross and Elizabeth A. Livingstone, 3rd ed. (Oxford, 1997) or, for longer accounts, the still reliable articles in the old *Catholic Encyclopedia* (New York, 1911) (now available on the Internet). Molinism has a study to itself: Thomas P. Flint, *Divine Providence: the Molinist Account* (Ithaca, NY, 1998), and a summary of Hincmar's ideas will be found in David N. Bell, *Many Mansions: An Introduction to the Development and Diversity of Medieval Theology West and East* (Kalamazoo-Spencer, 1996) 326-330.

Chapter 5

RANCÉ'S JOY

JOY, LIKE LOVE, is a word with many shades of meaning. It may refer to worldly happiness; it may refer to other-worldly serenity. There is the overwhelming joy of meeting up again with a long-lost love; there is the quiet joy of a lazy hour under the cherry-tree with a cup of coffee and the cat. There is also a monastic, more precisely a trappist, joy, and Rancé gave his monks a conference on this very subject.[1] He begins by distinguishing sharply between dedicated monks within the monastic enclosure and worldly people outside it, and he dwells on the infinite difficulties experienced by those *extra claustrum* in fulfilling God's will:

> Not a moment ago, my brothers, I was think-
> ing how hard it is for people living in the world
> to conform their lives to God's commands and
> regulate their conduct by his desires. God
> continually provides them with precepts and
> instructions: he warns them and presses
> them. But the difficulties they encounter—
> or which they themselves create—in carry-
> ing out what Jesus Christ ordains are infinite.[2]

And since, for Rancé, it is in willing service to God's will—that service which is perfect freedom—that we find our true

---

1. 'Armand-Jean de Rancé: A Conference on Spiritual Joy', introduced and translated by David N. Bell, *Cistercian Studies Quarterly* 37 (2002) 33-46 (cited below as 'Conference' with paragraph number of the translation).
2. 'Conference' §1.

joy, it follows that worldly people outside the monastery are in deep trouble. This is not to say that they cannot be joyful. They can. But the joy they feel is a worldly joy. It is founded on the desires of the flesh and its basis is a dissipated and dissolute heart. Theirs is a false and wicked joy, the consequence of cupidity, and the Holy Spirit has rightly forbidden it.[3] To find joy in worldly things is merely to attach oneself to worldly things, and those who attach themselves to worldly things are necessarily doomed. The bedrock of Rancé's spirituality, and the bedrock of seventeenth-century french spirituality in general, is a sharp, almost violent, contrast between that which is of the world and that which is not. Present-day cistercian monasticism is much exercised with the problems of breaking down barriers between those within and those without the cloister (witness the on-going discussions on cistercian Lay Associates); Rancé and the other reformers were concerned with erecting them. As we saw in Chapter Two, la Trappe stood as a fortress against the powers of darkness. In the world outside the cloister the devil was going about as a roaring lion, seeking whom he might devour; and his notable successes within the enclosing walls of the nunneries of Loudun, Louviers, and Auxonne (to say nothing of the royal court) were clear evidence that stone and mortar alone could not keep him out.

Hence Rancé's uncompromising definition of a monk: 'He is a man who, by a solemn vow, has renounced the world and all that comes through the senses and passes away. He lives only for God, and concerns himself only with eternal things.'[4] Again and again Rancé returns to this stark contrast of *transitoria* and *eternalia*, and the equally stark demand that one renounce the former in favour of the latter. In 1698, when he was sick and confined to the infirmary, he published the

3. 'Conference' §3.
4. *De la sainteté*, 1:1: 'Un homme qui ayant renoncé par un vœu solemnel, au monde & à tout ce qu'il y a de sensible & de perissable, ne vit plus que pour Dieu, & n'est plus occupé que des choses éternelles.'

two volumes of his *Maximes chrétiennes et morales*, and the first
of the *Maximes* sets the tone for all the others:

> Happy are those who live perfectly detached
> from earthly things and truly conscious of
> heavenly things. The spirit of penitence is
> found only where the former are utterly de-
> stroyed and the latter are alive and wholly
> present.[5]

The terminology is the technical terminology of seventeenth-
century french spirituality— *dégagement parfait des choses de la
terre'*, *'sentiment véritable de celles du ciel'*—but the principle
comes straight from the New Testament and the Fathers.
And by a 'true consciousness'—*sentiment véritable*—of heavenly things, Rancé means what Saint Paul means when he
says 'It is no longer I who live, but Christ who lives within
me' (Gal 2:20). As we saw in the last chapter, Christ was
himself the Great Penitent, and true penitence is no more
and no less than the imitation of Christ. It has nothing to do
with hair-shirts, scourges, chains, and whips.[6] Rancé's *sentiment véritable'* is an experiential knowledge of Christ in the
soul and, for Rancé, the Kingdom of God was not only imminent, it was already present in the heart of the believer. But
when Christ comes in glory, his coming will be dramatically
different for those who are of the world and those who are
not:

> Those who can rejoice are those who will pos-
> sess the Kingdom which Jesus Christ has pro-
> mised to those who have fought for the faith

5. Rancé, *Maximes chrétiennes et morales* (Paris, 1698 [Part II, I.A.i (1698)
Maximes]) 1.
6. In very exceptional circumstances Rancé permitted the use of the scourge—
the 'discipline'—and a penitential belt. The evidence comes from the *Relation
de la mort* of Frère Zénon de Montbel. But Rancé was virtually unique in
making no standard provision for their use.

and preserved it. But for [worldly] madmen,
the only thing they have known is how to
ignore the fact that they have no part in this
Kingdom and have closed its gates forever.[7]

The 'spirit of the world (1 Cor 2:12) gleefully leads all too
many people into those 'works of the flesh' which are listed
in detail in Galatians 5:9-20: 'enmity, contention, emulation,
anger, quarrels, dissension, sectarianism, envy, murder, drunkenness, drinking parties, and the like'; and those who take
part in these worldly things will have no share in the Kingdom of God. 'But if they have no share in the Kingdom of
God, how can they find any joy in the coming of Jesus Christ?
How can they rejoice at the approach of a Judge whose justice
is unyielding, since they can expect nothing but eternal damnation?'[8]

But there is more to it than this. Rancé's morality (like
Saint Paul's) is indeed an eschatological morality, but the
eschaton is not just a matter for the future. Christ, as we have
read, has *already* begun to be present in the heart of the true
religious, for the less self-will (*volonté propre*) we have, the
more we are indwelt by the spirit of Christ. Rancé, says Father Chrysogonus Waddell,

remains firmly within the tradition in which
heaven is not simply the kingdom to come,
but the kingdom already inchoatively but
really present. At early Clairvaux as at later
la Trappe, the kingdom was perceived as still
to come—and this meant a spirituality of
desire and gradual growth; but the kingdom
was also already present to the monk formed
in the wisdom of discipline and prayer—and
this meant a spirituality of joy.[9]

7. 'Conference' §11.
8. 'Conference' §15.
9. Chrysogonus Waddell, 'The Abbot de Rancé and Monastic Revival', in *The*

In 1963 Dom Jean Leclercq wrote a brief article, based on passages selected from the second edition of *De la sainteté et des devoirs de la vie monastique*, entitled 'La Joie de Rancé'.[10] In it he discussed the preconditions for joy: joy in God, joy in one's brethren, and joy in death. As to the preconditions for joy, Dom Leclercq rightly maintained that they were to be found in monastic renunciation, a *désoccupation*[11] with the things of this world and a corresponding 'occupation' with the things of God. But the essential precondition for this joy in God is charity,

> that consummate charity which banishes all fear and has us serve God here on earth as the angels serve him in heaven, i.e., not from any fear of punishment, but solely for truth and righteousness, solely for the love they have for Jesus Christ and for the consolation they find in pleasing him.[12]

It is this 'consolation'—the same word in both French and English—which brings with it peace, tranquillity, and joy, though contentment or serenity might be a better word.

But we cannot love God unless we also love our neighbour. This principle is a commonplace of the monastic tradition, and few expressed it more clearly than Baldwin, the twelfth-century abbot of Forde and later archbishop of Canterbury:

> We should not deceive ourselves in thinking we love God if we do not love our neighbour.

Spirituality of Western Christendom, II. The Roots of the Modern Christian Tradition, ed. E. Rozanne Elder (Kalamazoo, 1984) 161.

10. Jean Leclercq, 'La Joie de Rancé', *Collectanea Cisterciensia* 25 (1963) 206-215, reprinted in *idem, Témoins de la spiritualité occidentale* (Paris, 1965) 376-389.

11. This, too, is a technical term of seventeenth-century french spirituality: see *ibid.*, 208, n. 3.

12. *Ibid.*, 209, quoting Rancé, *De la sainteté*, 1:56.

> For if we do not love our neighbour whom we
> see and who, as it were, stands beside us in
> the place of God, to whom shall we pay the
> debt of charity? How else can we offer benefits
> to God, who in himself needs nothing, save
> by offering them to someone in whom God
> does have a need? It is God who, in his mem-
> bers, asks and receives. It is he who is loved
> or despised. The love of our neighbour, there-
> fore, is the tie of love and the bond of peace
> by which we maintain and preserve in our-
> selves the love of God and unity of spirit.[13]

This is precisely the view of Rancé, save that in his opinion our neighbours are primarily the members of the reformed community of la Trappe, and it is this charitable interaction with our confrères, the *caritas fraternitatis* of the Rule of Saint Benedict,[14] that leads to what Dom Leclercq calls '*la joie dans les frères*'.[15]

But let us now turn to the other side of the coin. It is all very well to speak of a voluntary surrender to God and his will, but how can we know his will? Sometimes, true, it is clearly set out in Scripture, but Scripture is all too often am-biguous and, in any case, we will not always find specific in-structions for life in a seventeenth-century french monastery in the words of a first-century galilean rabbi. For Rancé, what is essential here is obedience; and by obedience, he means unlimited and unquestioning obedience to God, Saint Benedict, and the abbot who stands in the place of Christ.[16]

13. Baldwin of Forde, *Sermon* 15, 64-66; *CCCM* 99:245. Cf. also *ibid.*, 14, 22; 222.
14. *Regula S. Benedicti* 72, 8, quoted by Rancé in *De la sainteté*, 1:258 and by Leclercq on page 212.
15. Leclercq, 211-213.
16. In this, Rancé is (once again) at one with the whole cistercian tradition. For two admirable discussions of the nature and need for obedience, see Baldwin of Forde, *Sermons* 2 and 7; *CCCM* 99, 23-43 and 103-123.

'For Rancé', says Bernardo Bonowitz, 'it is absolutely clear that no distinction should be made between the direct will of God and the will of God as communicated by the Rule or the abbot's instructions'.[17] Rancé was not alone in maintaining this. 'God's will', wrote François de Sales, 'is known not only by [the demands of] necessity and charity, but also by obedience; so much so that anyone receiving a command [from their superior] should believe that it is the will of God.'[18] The same principle appears in a host of other spiritual writers. *Vir obediens loquetur victoriam*, says Rancé, quoting Proverbs 21:28, 'an obedient man shall speak of victory'.[19]

In Rancé's opinion, then, obedience is no more than a mechanism for the reduction of self-will, but it clearly puts enormous responsibility on the abbot. On the other hand, Rancé's view of abbatial responsibilities is equally formidable. La Trappe was emphatically not a democracy and Rancé is insistent that the abbot is the only true superior in the house.[20] In stating this, he echoes not only the Rule of St Benedict, but the whole absolutist atmosphere of *le grand siècle*. For Rancé's great friend, Bossuet, 'independence and liberty are the temptations of the Devil, obedience and discipline the way to God. . . . The *autorité légitime* so constantly invoked is a precise and concrete reference to the rule set up on earth by God.'[21] The same rule is set up by God in the monastery and resides in the person of the abbot, and a monk who cannot obey his abbot as king and God has no place at la Trappe.

But if the monks must have absolute confidence in their abbot, so the abbot must know his monks with a deep and

17. Bernardo Bonowitz, 'Monastic Sanctification in Rancé's Conferences and Instructions on the Epistles and Gospels', *Cistercian Studies Quarterly* 35 (2000) 319.
18. François de Sales, ed. André Ravier, *Correspondance: Les Lettres d'amitié spirituelle* (Paris, 1980) 175 (Letter 80). For a useful summary of François de Sales' teaching on obedience, see *ibid.*, 835-837.
19. 'Conference' §19.
20. See *De la sainteté*, 1:151-152.
21. Alban J. Krailsheimer, *Studies in Self-Interest: From Descartes to La Bruyère* (Oxford, 1962) 188.

penetrating intimacy. Ideally, therefore, the abbot ought to be their only confessor, though circumstances (numbers not least) may sometimes require the relaxation of this ideal.[22] The confessional is an essential and illuminating window on the state of the soul, and we know that at la Trappe, Rancé was assiduous in fulfilling his confessional duty. We also know that he was by far the most popular of the abbey's confessors. The monks go to him, André Félibien des Avaux tells us,

> as to a source of living and beneficial water by which they are refreshed, and they never leave without being strengthened and filled with new graces. For I will tell you here in passing that when they enter the novitiate, they begin with a general confession to him to reveal their inner conscience, and thereafter they make their confession to no other but him. It is in this way that he knows their spirit perfectly, that he sees whether they have a true vocation to embrace the austere life of the house, and that he judges their capacity for the tasks he intends for them. The wholly individual care he takes for the conduct of their souls does not offend or constrain them. On the contrary, they find it so agreeable that they have difficulty in making their confession to others, even when he gives them freedom to do so. And even though he is so assiduous in correcting them that, in public, he may appear severe, he nevertheless speaks to each one of them with so great a love and tenderness that they never have greater joy than when they can talk to him.[23]

22. See *De la sainteté*, 1:159-160.
23. André Félibien des Avaux, *Description de l'abbaye de la Trape. Nouvelle édition, avec figures* (Paris, 1689) 60-61.

Rancé's emphasis on the importance of the confessional was neither new nor remarkable. What is remarkable was his obvious effectiveness as a spiritual director. Indeed, he was widely sought as such outside the cloister, but he hardly ever acceded to any of the multitudinous requests. Félibien, naturally, writes in the florid idiom of his times, yet there is no reason to disbelieve his account. But let us return to obedience.

Rancé, like other reformers of his time, makes it clear that obedience must never be unwilling. It must spring from love, not constraint. So, too, must all the other monastic observances:

> Do not imagine that the integrity with which you keep all your rules, your fidelity in your fasts, your vigils, your work, your mortifications, your silence, and your other austerities are enough to acquit you of this obligation. The love of God is a wholly interior disposition, and, although it expresses itself in works and shows itself in outward actions, it nevertheless resides in the heart. It is the heart that truly loves. Love is an affection of the heart, and when the heart is not involved, there is no true love.[24]

François de Sales puts the matter neatly: 'We must do everything from love and nothing from constraint. We must love obedience more than we fear disobedience.'[25] Such, he says, is the general rule of the Order of the Visitation and it is written in capital letters. And what is more, just as loving obedience is required of a monk, so the abbot's commands must likewise arise out of love—or, more accurately, out of loving discernment. The love we are speaking of here is not the amor-

24. *De la sainteté*, 1:133.
25. François de Sales, *Correspondance*, 169 (Letter 80).

phous sentimentality of modern pop songs. Nor is it a diffuse
and discursive sense of generalized benevolence. It is partly
the 'intense will' of augustinian love,[26] and partly that laser
beam of concentrated fire which can come only from a heart
which has truly experienced that essential component of the
religious life: *conversio morum*, 'conversion of one's way of life'.
In Rancé's own case, the conversion had been nothing if not
dramatic. The conversions of his monks might have been less
sensational, but none the less real for all that.

Not one of Rancé's confrères and not one of his friends
would have disagreed with his concept of authority or the
need for discipline and obedience. 'God's will is known by
obedience',[27] said François de Sales, and Jeanne de Chantal,
his devoted friend, makes it eminently clear that obedience
to God and one's ecclesiastical superiors are fundamentally
the same thing.[28] It was the tenor of the times. Not everyone,
however, would have agreed with what Rancé commanded. In
his opinion, obedience promoted humility,[29] of that there was
no doubt, and if humility had to be achieved by humiliations, then humiliations there must be. On this matter, however, there was rancorous disagreement between Rancé and a
former friend, Guillaume Le Roy, commendatory abbot of
Hautefontaine, and we shall say more on the matter in our
next chapter.[30]

It remains true, however, that the essential purpose of obedience was to diminish *amour propre* or *volonté propre*—self love
or self will—for they are simply two different names for the

26. See, for example, Augustine, *De Trinitate* 11.5; *PL* 42:988, *ibid*. 15.38; 1087,
ibid. 15.41; 1089, *De patientia* 22; *PL* 40:623.
27. See n. 18 above.
28. See *Francis de Sales, Jane de Chantal: Letters of Spiritual Direction*, tr. Péronne
M. Thibert, selected and introduced by Wendy M. Wright and Joseph F.
Power (New York-Mahwah, 1988) 252-253 and 257-258.
29. See, for example, Letter 711203a.
30. For a sound and balanced account, see François Vandenbroucke, 'Humiliations volontaires? La pensée de l'abbé de Rancé', *Collectanea Cisterciensia* 27
(1965) 194-201, translated into English as 'De Rancé on Deliberate Humiliations', *Cistercian Studies* 8 (1973) 45-52.

same thing. Obedience, said Bossuet in a sermon on Saint Benedict, is 'the guide to life, the rampart of humility, the mainstay of perseverance, the life of the spirit, and the certain death of self-love'.[31] The more we have of self-will and self-love, the less we have of God's will and God's love—both his for us and ours for him. Self-love, says Rancé, is that 'love of independence, that self-will which we cherish'.[32] Sin and self-will prevent us from perceiving the promptings of the Spirit of God, and they certainly hinder us from following them. What Rancé did at la Trappe was to provide an environment in which the quest for the diminution of self-love and self-will might be most effectively accomplished. Or, putting it another way and returning to the main theme of this chapter, it was an environment designed to turn the heart from *temporalia* to *eternalia*, from joy in the world to joy in fulfilling the will of God.

Rancé accomplished this task not only spiritually, but physically, physiologically, and mentally. Physically, la Trappe was a fortress, a prison, and a tomb. It was a bulwark against the powers of evil which, as we have seen, were real, present, and evident in Rancé's France; and it was a gaol and reformatory for sinful 'criminals'. As a gaol, it was a place for penance and penitence; as a reformatory, it was a *schola caritatis*[33] where one was diligently trained in the love of God and one's neighbour. It was also a sepulchre for those who had died to the world. 'I regard our monastery as my tomb',[34] wrote Rancé, and he advised nuns to look on their cells as their graves.[35] This idea may be abhorrent to life-affirming men and women in the twenty-first century; to Rancé it was no more than obvious, and not one of his friends would have disagreed.

---

31. Jacques-Bénigne Bossuet, ed. Bernard Vélat, *Oraisons funèbres; Panégyriques* (Argenteuil, 1936) 612.
32. 'Conference' §19.
33. The term was actually a creation of William of Saint-Thierry (it does not appear in Bernard). *Schola Christi*, however, is not uncommon in Augustine.
34. Letter 820212 and many other places.
35. Letter 790526.

Once you had permanently entered the monastery, once you had taken your final vows, once you were interred in your monastic tomb, you did not ever leave again. Not only was the world outside the cloister full of perils, but Rancé took the benedictine concept of *stabilitas* literally and unreservedly. This was not the view of everyone. Some ten years before the publication of *De la sainteté et des devoirs de la vie monastique* Rancé had been asked by the Jansenist Pierre Floriot to give his opinions on the latter's *Morale du Pater*.[36] One of the points involved precisely this question of 'stability': if a monk's parents are sick or indigent, should the monk be released from the monastery to help them? Rancé had no doubts on the matter. Final vows are, by definition, final, and the answer is No. Such vows are not taken lightly and they are taken only after long preparation. Once taken, however, they stand. Rancé is no more than logical. This is not to say that sick or indigent parents should not be helped in all possible ways, but leaving the monastery is not one of them.[37] When Rancé returned to the theme in his *De la sainteté* he dealt with it at greater length and suggests how such parents might be assisted;[38] but despite his logic and his formidable citations of authority after authority, the question remained a matter of dispute and many, perhaps most, people remained unconvinced.

Yet Rancé, as we have said, is no more than logical. If you have taken final vows, you have died to the world. And since your parents are part of the world, you have also died to them. A monk, as we have seen, is 'a man who, by a solemn vow, has renounced the world and all that comes through the senses and passes away'.[39] For Rancé and the other *spirituels* of his time, this was the key to the religious life: a monk lives only

36. This is the usual brief title for Floriot's *Morale chrétienne rapportée aux instructions que Jésus-Christ nous a données dans l'oraison dominicale* (Tours, 1672). It is a huge tome of more than a thousand pages.
37. See the good discussion in Krailsheimer, *Rancé*, 71-72.
38. See *De la sainteté*, 2:74-79.
39. See n. 4 above.

for God. If you have truly renounced the world, then renounce it! But belonging, as they did, to *le grand siècle*, their ideas and intentions were also *grand*. 'Today', says Lucien Aubry, comparing our times with theirs, 'the Absolute no longer exists, but in the seventeenth century every slope ran that way. Religion easily became heroic.'[40] Life at la Trappe, therefore, was a heroic rejection of the world and all that it stood for: a heroic renunciation of 'concupiscence of the flesh, concupiscence of the eyes, and pride of life' (Jn 2:16).

It is this renunciation of concupiscence that introduces us to the physiological component of life at la Trappe. Life at the abbey was hard, there is no doubt about that, and the grim and sudden onset of monastic mortality in 1674 can be attributed to two factors: the unhealthiness of the site (something emphasized by Rancé and regarded by him as laudable) and a diet which was, in fact, inadequate for monks spending long hours in hard, manual labour with very little sleep (and that uncomfortable).[41]

Much of the problem lay in the interpretation of the pauline phrase 'concupiscence of the flesh'. Augustine, in his earlier days, had been a Manichean, and Manicheanism was a dualistic system which saw created matter, and flesh in particular, as inherently evil. And although, after his conversion to Christianity, Augustine overcame his earlier Manicheanism rationally, emotionally it tended to linger; and one of the characteristics of the whole augustinian tradition is a distrust—fear might be a better term—of 'the flesh'. There is no doubt that this attitude can be dangerous. If interpreted too literally, it can lead one to try to diet one's way into Paradise, and to suggest that a man or woman's sinfulness can be directly estimated from their bodily weight. But mortification of the flesh was a standard theme of the monastic movement, and in hoping to reduce concupiscence by reducing nourishment,

---

40. Lucien Aubry, 'Rancé's Spirituality: Total Service to God', *Cistercian Studies Quarterly* 35 (2000) 49.
41. See the balanced discussions in Krailsheimer, *Rancé*, ch. 5 (83-101) and *Legacy*, 43-44 and 84-86.

Rancé was merely echoing his beloved Desert Fathers, Benedict, Bernard (let us remember the appalling mortality at Cîteaux in 1111-1112), and his reforming contemporaries. In fact, the diet at la Trappe was less austere than that of the first Feuillants and less rigorous than that proposed by Dom Augustin de L'Estrange for la Val-Sainte.

On the other hand, it is easy to misread the mortality at la Trappe. That an inadequate diet contributed to early deaths cannot be doubted. But when we roll our eyes and utter horrified exclamations at the ulcers, abscesses, fevers, coughs, tuberculosis, gangrene, pain, agony, and suffering that fill the pages of the *Relations de la mort de quelques religieux de l'abbaye de la Trappe*, we do so from a modern standpoint. An inadequate diet frequently contributed to early deaths among the peasantry of seventeenth-century France. We, in general, strive to live as long as we can. The business of a trappist monk was quite the contrary: it was not to live but to die. La Trappe was *supposed* to be a tomb, and if one suffered in making the transition from this life to the life to come, what were those sufferings compared with the sufferings of Christ who had borne upon his shoulders the sins of the world?

> If, in the order of God, all Christians live only to die; if the whole of their lives should be simply a preparation for death; and if (as Saint Augustine says) some one who does not have a sincere will to die is not worthy of a happy death, what, then, should be the disposition of a monk? . . . His life should be no more than a continual desire for and meditation on death, and his principal occupation is to await its arrival and have it unceasingly in his thoughts.[42]

In short, a monk flees the world to die well, and if he does not

42. *De la sainteté*, 2:30-31.

think he should suffer, he need only read Saint Paul. We should imitate the Desert Fathers who preferred the sanctity of their souls to the length of their lives', and God obviously approved of their decision since he gave them the power to work miracles.[43] We said above that life at la Trappe was a heroic rejection of the world and all it stood for. It was also a heroic preparation for death, which is eternal life.

It cannot come as a surprise, therefore, to find that Dom Leclercq ended his article on 'La Joie de Rancé' with a discussion of '*la joie dans la mort*', joy in death.[44] The desire to die, he says, 'is not inspired by any morbid gloom, but by an impatient longing "to be with Christ", as Saint Paul says';[45] and the *Relations* bear witness not to a grim and brooding preoccupation with death, but to an absorbing interest in the culminating triumph of a monk's life. In dying, he was going home. The *Relations* may not be much to our modern taste, for we have sanitized death and do not much care to be reminded of it. But seventeenth-century France was a society 'in which it was impossible to avoid being conscious of [death's] shadow and its arbitrary empire over humankind'.[46] For any Christian, therefore, whether lay or religious, 'it was important to prepare for dying, to rehearse for it, to ensure that the wiles of the Devil were anticipated and guarded against'.[47]

Part of this preparation lay in the study of the Fathers. Rancé's views on monastic studies—the mental component of life at la Trappe—have often been misunderstood, though Rancé is actually perfectly clear about what he means. When he says that 'the study of theology is the extinction of piety',[48] he is not talking about the intellectual demands of

---

43. *De la sainteté*, 2:472 and the entire discussion from page 472 to 496.
44. Leclercq, 'Joie de Rancé', 213-214.   45. *Ibid.*, 214.
46. John McManners, *Church and Society in Eighteenth-Century France, II: The Religion of the People and the Politics of Religion* (Oxford, 1998) 2:28.
47. *Ibid.*
48. Letter 880629 (save in the case of Franciscans and Dominicans, whose business it is).

lectio divina. By 'theology' he means the erudite philosophiz-
ing of later scholasticism, something he refers to as '*les grands
sciences*' and which Professor Krailsheimer translates as 'deep
learning'.[49] It is this which is incompatible with prayer. Studying theology or philosophy in this sense will dry up a monk's
heart, take away the spirit of prayer, and put him off manual
labour,[50] for 'erudition is the reef on which humility is ship-
wrecked, and vanity, the commonest consequence of study,
has often produced a thousand fatal wounds in the hearts of
those who are learned'.[51] In his opinion, the only reason monks
take up study is 'to try to regain by their learning a distinction which they once had, but which, through strict discipline and the regularity and holiness of [monastic] life, they
have no longer'.[52] We must remember that Aquinas read
Cassian's *Collations* to cure him of 'any aridity that might be
produced by the study of theology'.[53] Reading 'doctrinal
books', therefore, can be decidedly harmful: one should excite
one's piety, not accumulate unnecessary knowledge.[54] Indeed,
there is nothing more dangerous than theological reading,[55]
and in writing to a nun in 1684, Rancé commends her on
putting aside her *livres curieux*, her 'curious books'. She should
read in their place the ascetic works of Basil the Great and
John Climacus.[56] Too much reading of the wrong kind merely
distracts our spirits and weakens our hearts.[57]

It follows, then, that in the protracted controversy over
the place of monastic studies, there could really be no agreement between Jean Mabillon and Rancé. They were arguing
from different premises. On the one hand, Mabillon was perfectly correct in asserting that the labour of the mind could
be used to the greater glory of God, and that there can certainly be a true spirituality of scholasticism. We may see it in
both Aquinas and Bonaventure.[58] On the other hand, Rancé

49. Letter 920619.
50. Letter 780206.
51. Letter 801005.
52. Letter 910307.
53. Letter 711212.
54. Letter 850212a.
55. Letter 840206.
56. Letter 84/2.
57. Letter 850823.
58. As Rancé himself
admits: see Letter
880629 cited at n. 48
above.

was perfectly correct in maintaining that, for monks, the labour of the mind should be devoted to a better understanding of God's revelation in Scripture and not, let us say, to a better understanding of the complexities of Molinism and the precise nature of God's omniscience. As Patrick Ryan has said, 'the disputants were to a large extent arguing past each other, for the Benedictines had brought in reflections on clerical studies without realizing that de Rancé considered the monastic life to be basically non-clerical, as was ancient monasticism'.[59] Both Rancé and Mabillon were concerned with the quest for God, but it cannot be denied that the emphasis was different. For Rancé, there is no need for 'deep learning': the moral admonitions of the Fathers were sufficient not only for monks, but also for those who must direct a diocese.[60]

Rancé, therefore, did not despise study. Far from it. We should study the lives and writings of the Desert Fathers, John Cassian, John Climacus, Basil the Great, and Ephrem Syrus. We should study Augustine's Enarrations on the Psalms, his Tractates on the Gospel of John, and the *Moralia* on the Book of Job of Gregory the Great. We should study Saint Bernard. And if the Visitandine nuns of Reverend Mother Louise-Henriette d'Albon do not care for the saints of the distant past, they should study François de Sales and Alfonso Rodriguez! Indeed, we can even include such up-to-date works as the pastoral writings of Étienne Le Camus, bishop of Grenoble, or Henri Barillon, bishop of Luçon.[61] But Rancé has no time for what we might call academic erudition. A monk will have all that he needs

> if he can say with the holy Apostle, 'I judged
> myself to know nothing among you save Jesus,
> and him crucified' (1 Cor 2:2). It is there, my

59. Patrick Ryan, 'De Rancé's Anti-Intellectualism', *Cistercian Studies* 8 (1973) 39.
60. See Letter 870710.
61. For all these authors, see Letters 681030, 711212, 831207, 84/2, 870918, 880629, and elsewhere.

brothers, that he will learn the nature of unlimited obedience, an insatiable desire for reproaches and humiliations, unconquerable
patience in suffering, total resignation to the
whole will of God, poverty without reserve,
constant charity in the midst of injustice,
unswerving attachment to the things which
are eternal, and perfect renunciation of
everything that does not last forever.[62]

And so we come back to the fundamental premise of Rancé's
spirituality: live in perfect detachment from earthly things;
have an unswerving attachment to those which are eternal.
And for Rancé, this absolute contrast between *transitoria* and
eternalia is reflected in the absolute contrast between worldly
pleasure and monastic joy. For just as God's will is eternal and
unchanging, so the joy that comes of submitting to God's
will is likewise eternal and unchanging. And if God wills that
we suffer, so be it.

Anybody who weeps because God wants him
to weep is happy, and when he is what God
wants him to be, his realization and experience of this comfort him. It is exactly the same
with those who suffer. If they accept their
sufferings, however real and biting, it is
enough, for the preservation of their tranquillity and peace, that they see themselves
in the order of God and in the situation in
which he has been pleased to put them. It is
in just this spirit that Saint John Climacus
says that the sorrow which a truly converted
soul has for its sins contains a spiritual cheer-
fulness and joy, just as wax encloses honey,
and that the real and profound sorrow of peni-

62. *De la sainteté*, 1:197-198.

tence receives the consolation of God as purity of heart receives the light of heaven.[63]

That these ideas were no airy-fairy hypotheses ungrounded
in reality is confirmed by the many visitors to la Trappe,
both during and shortly after Rancé's lifetime. One of the
earliest accounts is to be found in André Félibien des Avaux's
Description de l'abbaye de la Trappe first published in 1671 (we
have translated some excerpts from it already). Of all that
happens at the abbey, he tells the duchesse de Liancourt, what
Christians might find most comforting is to see what contentment may be found in bearing the easy yoke of Jesus
Christ. Christians would see, in fact,

> one of the great miracles of the love of God,
> namely, that for the monks, the joy which
> comes from [living] in penitence is equal to
> the suffering which comes from penitence it-
> self. Indeed, this joy takes the place of all other
> joys, for the vows taken by these anchorites
> are followed by a perseverance in virtue which
> endures to the very last moment of their
> lives.[64]

Again and again the various visitors to la Trappe testify to
the joy shown on the monks' faces, and to the love shown by
them for their abbot and by their abbot for them. Despite
the austerity, the humiliations, the hard and wearing labour,
the privations, fasts, silence, and solitude, these devoted men
clearly knew what they were about and rejoiced in the lot
they had chosen. When you belong to God utterly, says Rancé,

---

63. 'Conference' §26 quoting John Climacus, *Scala paradisi, grad.* 7.[49]; *PG*
88:811D; *John Climacus: The Ladder of Divine Ascent*, tr. Colm Luibheid and
Norman Russell (New York-Toronto, 1982) 141.
64. Félibien des Avaux, *Description de l'abbaye de la Trape*, 114.

when you have truly given yourself to him and the things of
heaven, when your heart is entirely in his service, then,

> when you are with him as much as you desire,
> all your troubles will blow away like so much
> smoke. And just as he will then be the abso-
> lute master of your heart, so he will inspire
> in it all the impulses that please him, and he
> will strengthen you in that holy peace which
> is the consolation of those who belong to him
> and who, by a special grace, know only him
> and who have taken him alone as their por-
> tion.[65]

That this is a formidable task and a formidable achievement
is not in question, but it must be remembered that Rancé's
monks were not without help. I am speaking here not of human help, but of divine assistance. Rancé himself was, above
all, a man of prayer and was convinced that any true prayer
for help would not go unanswered. 'Faith, humility, and obedience are three primary weapons in the Christian armoury,
and prayer the indispensable means of forging them.'[66] As to
how one should pray, that was up to the individual. The Rule,
he wrote, 'allows great freedom in this matter and wishes us
to act as we feel moved by the Spirit of God. In short: each
unto his own'.[67] His own advice on the matter is well presented in the eleventh chapter of *De la sainteté*[68] and (to my
mind) even more clearly in the *Conduite chrétienne, adressée à
Son Altesse Royalle Madame de Guise*, first published in 1697. It
is not for nothing that each of the monastic day offices begins
with the plea 'O God, come to my assistance. O Lord, make
haste to help me'; for without that assistance and without
prayer (which, according to Rancé, involves listening as much

65. Letter 941117.
66. Krailsheimer, *Rancé*, 332.
67. Letter 830508.
68. There is a good summary in Krailsheimer, *Legacy*, 94-95.

as asking), there can be no progress whatever. As Augustine said, 'Of our own power, we can only fall'.[69]

Nothing in all that we have said here is original. I do not think, in fact, that there is anything original in anything Rancé says. His interpretations of the material might be his own—witness the controversies over humiliations, over *stabilitas*, over monastic studies—but he always takes the greatest pains to support whatever he says by lengthy and, it must be admitted, sometimes wearisome citations of the relevant authorities. Such, again, was the tenor of the times.[70] But what authorities? What and who were the sources of Rancé's vision of the monastic life? Whom did he read and how did he interpret what he read? The question is as interesting as it is important, and we shall examine the matter in our next chapter.

69. See Chapter Four, n. 2.
70. We discussed the matter in Chapter Two.

FURTHER READING

In the past, the positive aspects of Rancé's spirituality tended
to be overlooked. All was seen in the light of gloom, pessimism, and penance. More recently the balance has been re-
dressed in a number of studies of which the following are the
most important to have appeared in English: Lucien Aubry,
tr. Alban J. Krailsheimer, 'Rancé's Spirituality: Total Service
to God', *Cistercian Studies Quarterly* 35 (2000) 47-54; Bernardo
Bonowitz, 'Monastic Sanctification in Rancé's Conferences and
Instructions on the Epistles and Gospels', *Cistercian Studies
Quarterly* 35 (2000) 317-326; Chrysogonus Waddell, 'The
Cistercian Dimension of the Reform of La Trappe (1662-1700):
Preliminary Notes and Reflections', in *Cistercians in the Late
Middle Ages*, ed. E. Rozanne Elder (Kalamazoo, 1981) 102-161;
idem, 'The Abbot de Rancé and Monastic Revival' in *The Spirituality of Western Christendom, II. The Roots of the Modern Christian Tradition*, ed. E. Rozanne Elder (Kalamazoo, 1984) 145-
181; Krailsheimer, *Rancé*, ch. 16 (329-337) 'Spiritual Lessons';
and Krailsheimer, *Legacy*, ch. 7 (87-102) 'Teaching on the Monastic Life'.

Until the late 1950s little had been written in any language
on any aspect of Rancé's spirituality. The earlier works had
been primarily concerned with his supposed Jansenism (see
Chapter Two, nn. 23-24) and his controversy with Mabillon,
though in 1929 Albert Cherel had published a charming if
lightweight paper on 'Rancé directeur d'âmes' (*La Nouvelle
Revue des Jeunes* 1 [1929] 1022-1030; repr. in *Collectanea OCR* 11
[1949] 257-263) and Robert Trilhe had written some
'Remarques sur l'abstinence établie par l'Abbé de Rancé' in
Revue Mabillon 27 (1937) 108-118. But there was little else.
Then, in 1954, Vincent Hermans published (for private circulation) his mimeographed *Spiritualité monastique* which contains summaries of Rancé's major works, an assessment of
his spirituality, and concludes that '1. His great virtue and
authentic holiness are beyond question; 2. He was himself
sincerely convinced of the correctness of his monastic ideal;

3. He recovered in fact almost all the observances of the ancient Cîteaux, *but not its true spirit*' (Hermans, *Monastic Spirituality*, tr. by monks of Mepkin Abbey [Mepkin, 1958] 2:404). Whether this last statement, emphasized in the original, is correct is a matter of dispute. I do not think it is. Hermans' study, however, was not intended for general distribution.

Then, in the 1960s, there was a spate of activity. Denise Pezzoli led the way with her *Thèse és Lettres* on 'La spiritualité de l'abbé de Rancé' presented to the University of Lille in 1957. This is a fine study, though now inevitably dated, but it was never published as a book. Three articles deriving from it appeared in the pages of *Collectanea Cisterciensia* in 1960 and 1961 and will be found listed in my 'Bibliography', 272. At about the same time, Marie-Gabriel Petitcolin, a monk of Cîteaux, published a useful account of Rancé's monastic theology entitled 'Armand Le Bouthillier de Rancé: Abbé de la Trappe (1626-1700)' in *Revue Mabillon* 51 (1961) 157-163 (repr. in *Théologie de la vie monastique d'aprés quelques grands moines des époques moderne et contemporaine* [Ligugé, 1961] 67-73).

1963 was the three-hundredth anniversary of Rancé's entry into la Trappe, and the Strict Observance celebrated the event with an issue of *Collectanea Cisterciensia* dedicated to Rancé. The articles included—some of which pertain directly to his spirituality—will be found listed in my 'Bibliography'. The trend continued with some fifteen solid studies by Lucien Aubry, François Vandenbroucke, and Marie-Pierre De Grox— the latter's 'Un monachisme volontaire. L'idéal monastique de l'abbé de Rancé, réformateur de la Trappe', *Cîteaux: Commentarii cistercienses* 20 (1969) 276-354, is particularly important—and then, from 1976 onwards, there appeared a series of important papers on a variety of aspects of Rancé's life and thought by Father Chrysogonus Waddell. Some of these we have noted above; the others will be found listed in my 'Bibliography', 276-277. It is true that Father Waddell's *apologiæ* for the Great Reformer may sometimes be overstated, but these studies are essential reading for any understanding of Rancé's spirituality. For other articles on the subject, the

reader may be referred to my 'Bibliography', 282 s.v. 'Spirituality'.

Chapter 6

RANCÉ'S READING

THAT RANCÉ WAS LEARNED is not in doubt, and despite his views on monastic studies, he was an avid reader to the end of his life. The breadth of his reading was astonishing, but of all the mass of material he read, three books in particular—or, more precisely, two books and one series of books—were seminal to his conception of the monastic life and monastic spirituality. The first book was the *Ladder of Divine Ascent* by Saint John Climacus. The second was *Du premier esprit de l'ordre de Cisteaux* by Julien Paris, abbot of Foucarmont, first printed in 1653 with two later augmented editions in 1664 and 1670. The third was a series of Jansenist or jansenizing works which he was reading as early as the 1640s and which he was certainly studying with great attention after the death of Madame de Montbazon in 1657.[1]

Professor Krailsheimer has said that in the late 1670s, when Rancé was embroiled in bitter polemic,

> his critics were not slow to advertise his inexperience of religious life on a humble level and his fundamental ignorance of the monastic tradition represented by Benedictine and Cistercian usage. These charges are fair, and relevant: in 1664 when he took up his abbatial staff he knew far more about the Eastern solitaries, especially his favourite St. John Climachus, than Western monasticism. This

1. We discussed the matter in Chapter Two.

knowledge he had moreover acquired under
the guidance of Andilly, and largely through
his editions, at a time when he was not himself contemplating community life.[2]

Pace Professor Krailsheimer, the charges were not entirely fair.
Thanks to Julien Paris not least, Rancé (as we shall see) knew
a great deal about cistercian usage, but there is no doubt that
he had long been fascinated with the desert tradition and that
it formed the bedrock of his thought. For him, Climacus was
'unquestionably the greatest and most enlightened solitary
ever to appear in the Church of God'[3] and he never hesitated
to recommend that he be read nor to use him as an authority
for some of his more controversial practices.

John Climacus, or John of the Ladder, was born about 570
and entered the monastery of Mount Sinai as a novice when
he was sixteen. After his monastic profession he spent some
years as a solitary, and then returned to the monastery where,
in due course, he was elected abbot. He died *c.* 649, when he
was just about eighty. His *Ladder of Divine Ascent* (or *Ladder
of Paradise* or *Heavenly Ladder*—*Klimax* in Greek or *Scala Paradisi*
in latin translation) is a remarkable and penetrating study of
monastic virtues and vices (especially vices) and we shall discuss its contents in more detail in a moment.

Rancé's earliest quotation from Climacus appears in a letter to the Reverend Mother Louise Rogier of the convent of
the Visitation at Tours dated 30 June 1664. It was written
just four days after his profession at Perseigne, and he tells
Mother Louise that he has resigned himself wholly to God's
providence and surrendered himself utterly to his eternal
designs. 'I remember having read in Saint John Climacus that
a creature who has been so unfortunate as to lose the good
graces of his God should not stop the flow of his tears until
he is told either by God himself or one of his angels that his

2. Krailsheimer, *Rancé*, 19.
3. Letter 800618 quoted earlier in Chapter Four, n. 53.

sins have been forgiven.'[4] It is understandable that, in a lachrymose age, such a sentiment would appeal to a converted and remorseful Rancé.

Robert Arnauld d'Andilly's translation of the *Scala Paradisi—Traité de S. Jean Climaque des degrez pour montrer au ciel, traduit de grec en françois*—was first published in 1652 and there is no doubt that Rancé had read it. It was a popular work.[5] There were two copies in the library of la Trappe in the eighteenth century,[6] though whether either or both belonged to Rancé is impossible to say. But he need not have waited for Andilly's translation. A latin version of the work had first appeared in 1492 (other latin translations followed) and Matthew Rader's *editio princeps* of the greek text was published in 1633. Latin or Greek made no difference to Rancé. There was a duodecimo copy of '*S^ti. Joannis Climaci opera quædam*' in the library of la Trappe in 1752, but—again—we do not know when or how it came there.

That Rancé did not penetrate to the true heart of Climacus's spirituality is—to us—evident, but he cannot be blamed for that. No seventeenth-century Frenchman with no experience of the Orthodox tradition could have done so. Yet it is easy to see why the book appealed to him. The ladder of divine ascent has thirty rungs: twenty-three of them deal with monastic vices; seven with monastic virtues. That is as it should be. Both seventh-century greek monks and seventeenth-century french *spirituels* were in perfect agreement that we are very much more bad than we are good and that the road from vice to virtue is long, difficult, painful, and violent. Climacus therefore begins his *Ladder* with a consideration of renunciation. So, we might add, does Dorotheus of Gaza, whom Rancé translated.[7] Renunciation of what? Of the world and

4. Letter 640630. The reference to Climacus is a very loose paraphrase of his *Scala paradisi*, grad. 1.[6]; *PG* 88:633D.
5. See Henri-Jean Martin, tr. David Gerard, *Print, Power, and People in 17th-Century France* (Metuchen/London, 1993) 425.
6. They are listed in the 1752 catalogue of the la Trappe library: see Bell, 'Library' (cited in Further Reading, 144) 130-133.
7. Part II, I.A.i [1686 *Les Instructions*].

all that it stands for. We must depart from Egypt, escape from Pharaoh. Death can come at any time; the devil is out to destroy us; evil and wickedness are abroad. What then can we do? We can flee the world, utterly reject *temporalia* in favour of eternal goods, and leave our houses, families, and friends to enter the silence, solitude, austerity, and asceticism of the monastery. Whether Sinai or la Trappe makes no difference.

In the monastery we learn detachment: the second step of the *Ladder*. Rancé would call it *dégagement*. And it leads to 'a resolute abandonment of everything in our own country [Climacus means our familiar surroundings] that hinders us from attaining the goal of the religious life'.[8] In the dispute over monastic stability—the question of whether monks can leave their monastery to look after indigent parents—Rancé can therefore turn to Climacus in the absolute conviction that he will support him. And he does. 'It is better to cause grief to your parents than to the Lord',[9] says Climacus, and 'Love of God extinguishes love of parents'.[10] 'Do not let the tears of your parents or friends fill you with pity', he says, 'for if you do, you will weep forever in the life to come.'[11] We cannot, perhaps, call this humane, but we can certainly call it logical. As Climacus says, 'it is impossible to look at the sky with one eye and the earth with the other'.[12] Rancé's definition of a monk does no more than echo this theme.

In the monastery we are in exile from the world, and when we combine this exile with obedience we have the two golden wings on which the devout soul steadily ascends to heaven.[13] A long discussion on obedience in step four of the *Ladder* exactly represents Rancé's thinking, for obedience is the total renunciation of our own life, the sepulchre of self-will, and death freely and willingly accepted. A corpse, says

8. John Climacus, *Scala paradisi*, grad. 3.[1]; *PG* 88:664B.
9. *Ibid.*, 3.[12]; 665C.
10. *Ibid.*, 3.[16]; 668A.
11. *Ibid.*, 3.[17]; 668B.
12. *Ibid.*, 3.[23]; 668D.
13. *Ibid.*, 4.[1]; 677C.

Climacus, does not argue, and a monk is a living corpse. But
we must be watchful in this matter. It is all very well to be
obedient, but if a monk finds himself taking pride in his obedience, all that he has gained falls away. Pride is a manifesta-
tion of self-will and self-love, and both Climacus and Rancé
look upon it with dread. Hence the disputed practice of 'humiliations' which we mentioned in the last chapter. What are
we talking about here?

Humility itself is no more than the recognition of one's
true position, and a false Uriah Heepish humility is just as
sinful and dangerous as pride. But in Rancé's France, one's
true position—morally speaking—was viewed (as we have
seen) far more pessimistically than it is today. For both
Climacus and Rancé, the contrast between good and evil was
seen, not in shades of grey, but in stark black and white. On
the one hand we have the absolute perfection of God; on the
other we have the absolute imperfection of sinful humanity.
All our actions are by definition imperfect, and to praise a
monk for doing something well is to open the door to pride.
A 'vigilant and loving superior', therefore,

> will take care to train a monk by reproaches,
> sharp reproofs, stinging words, public embar-
> rassment, hard work, and degrading occupa-
> tions.[14]

But there is more to it than this. Even if a monk has, in all
conscience, tried to do something well, a discerning superior
can still find fault. If, for example, a monk has been reading to
his brethren in the refectory more carefully, clearly, and distinctly than usual, his superior can justly say to him that he
reads like someone proud and presumptuous, that his voice
reveals more of his own vanity than the simplicity and humility of a monk, and he may then add 'more or less strong
words as he judges it to be more advantageous and more use-

---

14. *De la sainteté*, 1:314.

ful not only for the monk in question, but also for those of
his brethren who are witnesses to the reproof'.[15] In other
words, a monk cannot, by definition, do anything right, and
minor lapses may warrant major rebukes.

It is not difficult, however, to misunderstand this idea and
see it as the deliberate invention of non-existent faults—in
which case a superior would be lying. It is true that superiors
may sometimes be mistaken and incorrectly accuse monks of
doing things they have not done, but that is very different
from systematic humiliation for spurious reasons. Guillaume
Le Roy, a former friend of Rancé and commendatory-abbot
of Hautefontaine, certainly misunderstood Rancé's idea and
accused him of using 'lies or inventions' (*mensonges ou fictions*)
to gain his ends. Rancé replied to Le Roy's criticisms in a long
*Lettre d'un abbé régulier sur le sujet des humiliations et autres pra-
tiques de religion*, but the letter—more accurately the book—
was actually published by André Félibien against Rancé's
wishes.[16] Rancé then wrote to Le Roy to apologize for its appearance, which caused him, he said, 'extreme displeasure',[17]
but his apology fell on deaf ears. In *le grand siècle*, people's
convictions were likewise *grand*, and the bitter quarrel, which
expanded to include a collection of other unrelated controversies, dragged on for years.[18]

But where did Rancé get the idea? From Climacus of course.
The principle pervades John's discussions of penitence, mourning, vainglory, pride, and humility.[19] There is a proverbial
saying, he says, that 'reproof is the washtub of the soul's
passions'. Even worldly people, when they have accused someone to their face of being utterly worthless and then boasted
about it to others, will say 'I gave him a real scrubbing'. And
so they did![20]

---

15. *Ibid.*, 1:316.
16. See Part II, I.B.ii [1677 *Lettre*].
17. Letter 770414.
18. See Krailsheimer, *Rancé*, 370 s.v. Le Roy, Guillaume.
19. *I.e.*, steps 5, 7, 22, 23 and 25 of the *Ladder of Divine Ascent*.
20. John Climacus, *Scala paradisi*, grad. 8.[25]; *PG* 88:833B.

From Climacus, too, comes (in part) Rancé's notorious metaphor of the monastery as a prison and its inhabitants as criminals;[21] and both Climacus and Rancé are at one in believing that theology and mourning have nothing in common. A theologian sits in a professorial chair; a mourner—and a monk is nothing but a mourner—spends his days, like Job, in rags on a dung-heap.[22] Climacus, like Rancé, has no time for academic erudition, for 'deep learning', for *les grandes sciences*.[23]

And so it goes on. Repentance, the imitation of Christ, the gift of tears, the remembrance of death, silence, abstinence, poverty, mortification, sleep (or lack of it), personal prayer, the importance of the Psalms, simplicity, discernment, and above all, humility through which (as Dorotheus of Gaza says) every device of the Enemy is destroyed:[24] all were ideas dear to Rancé's heart. But with Climacus as with Rancé, all is not gloom and despondency. 'Tears', says Climacus, 'over our departure [from the world] produce fear; but when fear begets fearlessness, joy appears. And when joy is unceasing, holy love bursts into flower.'[25] For Climacus, too, joy lies in the knowledge that one is striving to fulfil the will of one's Creator. We must hold fast to the blessed and bitter joy of holy compunction,[26] he says, and this bitter joy which wells up in the soul of the monk is a testimony to his progress on the long path to perfection. Climacus is not the first to speak of this joy-in-sorrow, but it is more clearly formulated in his writings than in those of any of his predecessors.

There are times, as one reads Andilly's eloquent translation of Climacus, that one could be reading Rancé himself. It

21. Step 5 of the *Ladder*. See Chapter Four, n. 12 where the relevant passage is translated.

22. *Ibid.*, 7.[24]; 805CD.

23. See Chapter Five, n. 49.

24. *Dorothée de Gaza*, *Œuvres spirituelles*, ed./tr. Lucien Regnault and J. de Préville (Paris, 1963) 186. Dorotheus is quoting abba Isaiah (see *ibid.*, 186-187, n. 2).

25. John Climacus, *Scala paradisi*, *grad.* 7.[56]; *PG* 88:813BC.

26. *Ibid.*, 7.[9]; 804C. 'Bitter joy' is χαρμολύπη in Greek, a rare word and (I think) a coinage of Climacus.

is true, as we have said, that Rancé did not and could not appreciate Climacus's holistic teaching on deification and the true nature of *apatheia*,[27] but neither could Andilly nor anyone else of his era. Yet there cannot be any doubt that the ideas of Climacus formed Rancé in a fundamental way (and, we may add, caused a number of his problems). And his approach to many later writers tends to be illuminated by the harsh and unforgiving light of the desert.

Thus, the Bernard of Rancé is not really Bernard of Clairvaux. Rancé, in fact, seems to have seen little difference between Bernard's teachings and those of the Desert Fathers, Climacus, John Cassian, and Ephræm Syrus.[28] He can easily cite selected passages from Bernard in his defence of the practice of humiliations,[29] in support of his principle of strict *stabilitas*,[30] and as evidence for his teaching on the need for prudent severity on the part of a monastic superior.[31]

But Rancé's introduction to the cistercian life did not come from Bernard. It came from that remarkable book written by Julien Paris which we mentioned at the beginning of this chapter: *Du premier esprit de l'ordre de Cisteaux*. Julien Paris, in fact, deserves a study to himself and his account of what he saw as early Cîteaux is a notable achievement. The author was first a monk of Prières and then abbot of Foucarmont from 1645 to his abdication in 1671 (he died the following year). He was, as Louis Lekai has said, 'a stern ascetic, an uncompromising reformer, but also a dedicated antiquarian, keenly interested in history',[32] and the position he takes in his *Premier esprit* may justly be accepted as the 'official stand of the Reform'.[33] On the other hand, to say that the work is 'not a systematic treatise', as Lekai has done,[34] is not true. Certainly it con-

---

27. See David N. Bell, '*Apatheia*: The Convergence of Cistercian and Byzantine Spirituality', *Cîteaux: Commentarii cistercienses* 38 (1987) 141-164.
28. See Letter 711212.
29. As, for example, in Letter 720718.
30. Letters 730927 and 821222a.   31. Letter 781112a.
32. Lekai, *Strict Observance*, 184.   33. *Ibid.*
34. *Ibid.*

tains a copious amount of illustrative material, but the thread
that runs through it is clear enough and there is no doubt
that it exercised a profound influence on Rancé. He probably
came across it during his novitiate at Perseigne in 1663-1664
and he was certainly quoting from it extensively by the end
of 1664.

But Julien Paris's understanding of early cistercian life has
about it a decided flavour of the Desert.

> Those souls called by God to the religious
> life must know that this way of life is no
> more than a revival and imitation of that
> of the first Christians. Jesus Christ him-
> self revealed its principles to us from the
> cross and wrote them in our souls with his
> own blood. It was not established or in-
> tended for pleasure, to gratify flesh and
> blood, but, on the contrary, to mortify the
> senses or, more accurately, to kill off all our
> faculties, both of body and soul.
>
> Whoever, then, is called to this vocation
> must, from the moment he enters [the mon-
> astery], renounce his own self and swear
> enmity against his imperfections, his pas-
> sions, his desires, his comforts, and the
> most innocent of bodily pleasures in order
> to embrace the cross of Jesus Christ and all
> that it teaches: especially penitence, pov-
> erty, humility, chastity, and obedience—and
> all until death.
>
> From the moment he enters, he must not
> only renounce the world and all the goods,
> honours, and pleasures it offers; [he must
> also renounce] himself and sacrifice himself
> to a life of penitence and labour like that of
> Jesus Christ. Let none enter, then, who do
> not wish to do so, but those who *do* enter

must, so to speak, swallow down death at
the first gulp. If they do not, they will gain
nothing.[35]

For Paris, Climacus, and Rancé, a monk is a living corpse,
a dead man walking, and the monastery is the grave in
which he has been buried alive.

But what does Julien Paris actually say, and just what
was the *premier esprit* of the Cistercian Order? The book is
divided into four parts, and the author begins, logically, with
the foundation of Cîteaux by Robert of Molesme in 1098. He
then goes on to explain how the abbey grew and developed,
and how it became the mother-house of an Order. He is well
aware of the importance of Stephen Harding in this matter,
and his consideration of Stephen leads him to detailed analysis of the Charter of Charity, the *Carta caritatis*. He discusses
cistercian uniformity, the practice of visitations, the importance of the General Chapter, the election and deposition of
abbots, and then presents a series of 'reflections necessary
for understanding this first Statute [i.e. the *Carta caritatis*] of
the Order of Cîteaux'. Then, in Chapter Four of Part One, he
turns his attention to the fundamental theme that runs
through his whole lengthy treatise: the nature and importance of the Rule of Saint Benedict. It was unswerving fidelity
to this Rule which encapsulated the *premier esprit* of the Order, and the decline of the Order after the Golden Age of the
past (which Paris sees through the rose-coloured spectacles
of the seventeenth century) is entirely due to a lack of zeal in
keeping the Rule. Paris's logic is then inexorable: if the decline of the Order was due to a failure to keep the Rule in its
entirety, the Order may accordingly be restored and re-formed
by re-establishing '*l'entière Observance de la Règle de S. Benoist*'.

In the rest of Part One the author examines characteristic
cistercian usages: the habit, monastic profession, the *opus Dei*,

35. Julien Paris, *Du premier esprit de l'ordre de Cisteaux* (Paris, 1664), 'Directoire
pour la conduite et l'instruction des novices' (added at end with separate
pagination) 7-8.

the sacraments, fasts and abstinence, solitude and silence, manual labour and *lectio divina*, 'mental prayer' (*oraison mentale*), and hospitality and alms-giving. His discussion is intended to demonstrate how all these usages are in accord with the principles set forth in the holy Rule, and how—in the matter of abstinence—the meat-eaters of what would later be called the Common Observance were wrong, wrong, wrong. We must not forget that *Du premier esprit de l'ordre de Cisteaux* is not a cool academic study of early cistercian history, but a political—sometimes polemical—treatise in support of the Abstinent cause.

Part Two of the work is devoted to the administration of the Order and begins with a discussion as to why it was exempted from episcopal control. The author then examines the type of government envisaged in the Charter of Charity, the authority of General Chapters, the powers of abbots (a section heavily indebted to Climacus), and the responsibilities of other monastic superiors (claustral priors, conventual priors, sub-priors, cellarers, infirmarians, and all the others). We then find a discussion of the nature and importance of penance and penitence and a concluding chapter which summarizes the admirable qualities exhibited by the Order in the course of its first three centuries. And all of this is rooted in the admonitions of the Rule of Saint Benedict and elaborated by quotations from Saint Bernard.

The third part of the work makes for depressing reading, for it is here that we see the decline of the Order. Its abbots and religious have alienated themselves from the *premier esprit* of their Fathers, and the reasons for this—as Saint Bernard had long ago made eminently clear—are three in number. First, they have become vain and ambitious. Second, they have lost their taste for austerity and the penitential life and spend too much time worrying about their health and bodily comforts. And third, they have become unfaithful to their religious vocation. Paris then discusses these problems at considerable length, quoting both cistercian and non-cistercian sources, though he willingly acknowledges the efforts of certain popes (especially Benedict XII), kings, and 'Christian Princes' to restore the ancient discipline. Ultimately, he says, the religious superiors are to blame, and not just superiors within their own abbeys. The General Chapter itself has failed to maintain the observance of the Rule of Saint Benedict and the abbots of Cîteaux have done no better.

The fourth part of the work then addresses the fundamental question: how can the *premier esprit* of the Order be restored? The answer, as we saw above, is simply by the restoration of the wholehearted observance of the Rule of Saint Benedict. In the first chapter of this final part, Paris paints an idealised picture of the halcyon days of the first Cistercians, though he supports his case—once again—by copious quotation from cistercian and non-cistercian sources. In the second chapter he makes it clear that the renewal of this spirit is not just an aspiration, but an obligation, and he again cites Saint Bernard to support his case. And how is this restoration to be achieved? How is one to implement *l'entière observance* of the Rule? Simply by re-instituting the principles established in 'the first Statutes and the ancient Constitutions', by which the author means primarily the Charter of Charity, the decrees of the General Chapters, and the early cistercian usages. Novices, therefore, must be educated in these things, which means that those responsible for the formation of novices must live them, and monks must do away with all those dispensations and mitigations which have insidiously contaminated the *premier esprit* of the Order over the centuries. Good examples may be seen in the rise of the various cistercian Congregations—something we considered in Chapter Three— and the author's fervent hope is that the french abbeys will see fit to follow in their footsteps.

Such, in summary, is the teaching contained in Julien Paris's lengthy treatise. That Rancé studied it assiduously is not in question, and there is no doubt that it provided him with a detailed, if slanted, account of the foundation and nature of the Order to which he belonged. Rancé's own *La Règle de saint Benoist, nouvellement traduite et expliquée selon son véritable esprit* which first appeared in 1688[36] is clearly indebted to the work of Paris, and in his insistence on *l'entière observance* of the Rule he follows directly in his footsteps.

On the other hand, Rancé's own commentary on the Rule is *selon son véritable esprit*, 'according to its true *spirit*', and not 'according to its true *letter*'. The distinction is significant. Despite his own rigorism, Rancé realized that, although much in the Rule must remain immutable, there are certain areas where changes could and should be made. An obvious example is the fact that the Order no longer accepted young oblates and did not provide education for schoolboys. What should and should not be mitigated, of course, called for the most delicate discernment, but then, as Rancé himself said, 'discernment (*discrétion*), when free from all laxity and fleshly indulgences, is a greater virtue than penitence'.[37] In Rancé's view, both the saints of the Desert and the saints of early Cîteaux were animated by a greater zeal and a stronger spirit than was to be found among the religious of his own time.

Of all the saints of early Cîteaux, Bernard was by far the most important. It is true that the Bernard depicted by Rancé is not a wholly accurate picture of Bernard of Clairvaux, but the Bernard he portrays is, in reality, little different from the Bernard portrayed by seventeenth-century french *spirituels* in general. Of all the authorities cited by Rancé in his *De la sainteté*, Bernard is the most common; and towards the end of the work he speaks of the saint as having more authority for his abstinent monks than did a thousand others.[38] His intimate acquaintance with Bernard's writings was made all the easier by the publication in 1667 of the superlative edition of the *Opera S. Bernardi* by the great Maurist scholar, Jean Mabillon;[39] and to be able to quote an authoritative text of an authoritative source was of inestimable value to Rancé in defending his programme of reform and in answering the call

36. Part II, I.A.i [1688 *La Règle*].
37. Letter 75/2.
38. *De la sainteté*, 2:541.
39. The classic edition is the second edition of 1690.

of Julien Paris for the restoration of *le premier esprit* of the Order.

Only one sermon on Saint Bernard has survived among the writings of Rancé. It was preached on 20 August, the feast day of the saint, and is based on Psalm 4.4 *Mirificavit Dominus sanctum tuum*, which Rancé translates as 'God has made his saint admirable'.[40] He begins his discourse by explaining why this 'great saint' is justly called 'great', and this leads him into an account of selected episodes from Bernard's life, beginning with his influential involvement in the conflict between Pope Innocent II and the antipope Anacletus II. But Bernard was dedicated not only to the political unity of the Church, he was equally dedicated to its doctrinal unity, and Rancé moves on to speak of Bernard's opposition to Abelard, Gilbert de la Porrée, and other dangerous heretics. In this, we are told, Bernard maintained the faith by his doctrine, his arguments, his holiness, and his courage. Blessings attended him wherever he went, and his influence was felt from the courts of kings to the dwellings of the common people. Miracles, too, followed in his train: the sick were healed, the blind saw, paralytics walked again. In fact, says Rancé, there is just too much to tell. Even if he had days to speak of the saint, it would not be enough, and he will therefore confine himself to speaking of three ways in particular in which Bernard may be seen as a model for monks: in the mortification of his spirit; the mortification of his senses; and his love of humility.[41]

Even when he was in the world, the world meant nothing to Bernard. His intimate acquaintance with popes, kings, and

40. The sermon is *Conférence LXXXII* in the *Conférences ou instructions sur les épîtres et évangiles des dimanches et principales fêtes de l'année, et sur les vêtures et professions religieuses* (Paris, 1698 *&c.* [Part II, I.A.i [1698 *Conférences*]) and is conveniently reproduced in the *Collection intégrale et universelle des orateurs chrétiens. Deuxième série* (Paris, 1866), ed. Jacques-Paul Migne, cols. 578-593. The latter is the edition cited here.

41. *Conférence LXXXII*, col. 583: 'La mortification du cœur, celle des sens, et l'amour des humiliations', but 'humiliations' is not being used here in the technical sense which caused such problems for Guillaume Le Roy.

princes had not the least effect on his profound humility, and in the bustle of the world he remained wrapped in his own holy solitude. Furthermore, his mortification of the spirit was matched by his mortification of the flesh. Witness the joy he found in afflicting his body. Witness his vigils and fasts and abstinence. The ruin of his own health was of no consequence, and he treated his ailments not with medicinal care but with a rustic brutality. And if he was ill and recovered? He simply returned to his austerities and mortifications. Indeed, if God had preserved his life, it was only that he might offer it back to God as a living sacrifice. Rancé calls him a martyr, a victim of penitence who ate his bread in the water of his tears. He lived only to crucify his body, to walk in hard ways, and 'the penitence of this incomparable man condemns our own laxity and laziness, and covers us with confusion'.[42]

The third great virtue of this great saint was humility. Indeed, it is the foundation of all other virtues, and equalled his love of renunciation and penitence. But the quality and greatness of humility is judged by the quality, greatness, and dignity of the one who is humiliated; and in Bernard's case, the one who was humiliated was one of the glories of the Church, whose wisdom, teaching, mortifications, miracles and holiness were known and recognized everywhere. But not only did he humble himself, he dishonoured and degraded himself. How could he, a slave to sin, seek praise from others? If such a saint saw himself as no more than an unfaithful servant, deserving only to be beaten, how can we esteem ourselves? Let us beware, then, lest we be condemned by his consummate humility. Let us emulate his mortifications. Indeed, the purpose of this feast, says Rancé, is not only to sing the praises of so great a saint, but to enable us to profit from his example and his teaching on monastic observance and submission to the Rule. To be sure, there are those who will criticize our endeavours, who will regard what we try to do as excessive. So be it! They are merely dominated by their cupidity and

42. *Ibid.*, col. 587.

know hardly anything of the teachings of the saints. And, in the face of their laxity, the Church still sings to Bernard's glory these blessed words: '*Mirificavit Dominus sanctum suum*'.

Such, concludes Rancé, are the ideals at which we should aim, and we must strive to make ourselves worthy of God's help and the saint's intercession by the ardour of our prayers and the sincerity of our intentions. Sustained by Bernard's example, by his teachings and by his prayers, we might then run a joyful course and win that immortal crown destined for those who have kept and defended the faith.

There is no doubt that the Bernard of this important sermon is Bernard the ascetic, Bernard the humble, whose glory lies in his mortifications and his humility. He is certainly not Bernard the mystic—a matter we shall discuss in due course; neither is he the sentimentalized Bernard of legendary lactations. He is, in fact, the Bernard of Julien Paris, but that is not surprising. The portrait painted by Rancé may have been conveniently appropriate to his intentions—the establishment of the Strict Observance—and his own desert spirituality, but it was also, as we have said, the Bernard of the seventeenth century. In his own sermon on the saint, Bossuet says much the same thing and portrays him in much the same way.[43] And if it be objected by modern scholars that this reveals only one side of the abbot of Clairvaux and that the picture so presented is gravely distorted, the same may be said for the fuzzy, warm Bernard often presented in contemporary works of pseudo-spirituality and inner development. Too many modern writers mistake the real nature of medieval spirituality, and one can make a sound case that the seventeenth-century understanding of Bernard of Clairvaux contains more of the truth than much that has appeared in more recent times.

The third thing to have a profound effect on Rancé were the jansenist works he had been reading in the years before

43. Jacques-Bénigne Bossuet, ed. Bernard Vélat, *Oraisons funèbres; Panégyriques* (Argenteuil, 1936) 287-314, preached at Metz on 20 August 1653.

and after his decision to enter the cloister. This is a matter we discussed in Chapter Two, and, as we saw there, his reading programme 'could hardly have been more Jansenist'.[44] Arnauld's *De la fréquente communion*, Pascal's *Lettres provinciales*, Saint-Cyran's *Petrus Aurelius*, and other such works were welcome food to his ascetic soul, and when combined with his love of Climacus and his absorption of the principles set forth by Julien Paris, how could his outlook be other than austere and abstinent?

His approach to these writers was not (if we may express it thus) holistic. He drew from them their spirit rather than their specific doctrines. Consider the case of Pasquier Quesnel. Early in his relationship with Rancé, Quesnel was (as Professor Krailsheimer has said), 'a prime recruiting and publicity agent for la Trappe'.[45] Later in his life he was one of Rancé's severest critics; nor could he ever forgive Rancé for failing to give public support to the jansenist cause. But in 1671, long before the unhappy ending of their friendship, Rancé wrote to Quesnel warmly praising his *Abrégé de la morale de l'Évangile*.[46] Two years later Quesnel sent Rancé a copy of Bérulle's *Office de Jésus*,[47] and two years after that a copy of his own edition of Leo the Great,[48] a book which was placed on the Index for its patently gallican sympathies. Then, in 1680, Quesnel sent Rancé his *Jésus-Christ pénitent*,[49] a book which could hardly fail to appeal. Indeed, in his letter thanking the author, Rancé speaks of the book as being 'full of holy and Christian ideas and principles'. 'There is nothing more effective', he continues, 'for teaching people a truth they have no desire to know, namely, that it is penitence that must open for them the gates of the Kingdom of Jesus Christ.'[50] In July of the following year, however, Rancé writes for the last time to Quesnel expressing his condolences on the death of his mother,[51] and that is the end of what, for more than a

---

44. See Chapter Two, n. 28.
45. Krailsheimer, *Rancé*, 253.
46. Letter 711125.
47. Letter 730301.
48. Letter 750704.
49. Letter 800411.
50. Letter 800411.
51. Letter 810722.

decade, had been a very cordial relationship.

Quesnel's *Abrégé de la morale de l'Évangile* would, in due course, be expanded and developed to become his *Le Nouveau Testament en françois, avec des reflexions morales sur chaque verset*, published at Paris between 1687 and 1692, but the principles of what used to be called 'Quesnellism'—simply his own variety of Jansenism—may clearly be found in the earlier work. The 1671 edition already contained five of the 101 propositions which would later be condemned in the bull *Unigenitus* (1713), and if the other essential tenets of jansenist thought are not presented systematically, it is not difficult to extract them. We see strict predestinationism, the irresistibility of grace, the stark contrast between the love of God and the love of the world, our total inability to do any good without the gift of the grace of Jesus Christ, the principle that Christ died only for the elect, the true and invisible Church of the saints, and a number of other opinions echoing jansenist thought. But Rancé, as we have said, was not a Jansenist. Nor was he formally 'quesnellian', though he was clearly sympathetic to much of what Quesnel wrote. He would not have disagreed with the idea that faith is the first grace and the source of all the others. He certainly would have agreed that the love of the world and the love of God are wholly incompatible. He would have agreed that when God wishes to save a soul, that soul is saved—had he not had personal experience? He would also have agreed that fear restrains only our hands, for so long as the heart is not (by grace) led by a true love of righteousness, it remains attached to sin. All these ideas would, in due course, be specifically condemned in the bull *Unigenitus*, and if Rancé was not a jansenist *ad litteram*, he had certainly absorbed the jansenist spirit.

But it must not be thought that Rancé's reading was confined to Climacus, Bernard, Julien Paris, and the Jansenists. His letters reveal familiarity with a wide range of authors and writings, and an inventory of the sources he used for his *De la sainteté*[52] is

---

52. See Bernard Duymentz, *Les citations des Pères de la période patristique et médiévale chez Rancé*, cited under Further Reading, 143.

nothing if not impressive. A long list would make for tedious reading, but the writers range from classical and patristic authorities in Greek and Latin, through a variety of medieval writers, through fifteenth- and sixteenth-century saints and *spirituels*, to such writers of his own times as Arnauld d'Andilly, Godefroi Hermant, Pierre Bérulle, Lazare Bocquillot, his old friend Bossuet, Charles de Condren, Pierre Floriot, Pierre Nicole, Étienne Le Camus, Henri Barillon, Louis-Isaac Le Maître de Sacy, Saint-Cyran, and Jean-Baptiste Santeul.

Even before he entered la Trappe Rancé had possessed a fine library, and much of it—exactly how much we do not know— he brought to la Trappe with him and had a new library built to accommodate it. According to André Félibien des Avaux, when he went from Perseigne to la Trappe in March 1664, he arranged for his will to be read in the Chapter House of la Trappe—the date was 12 March—and confirmed his intentions by word of mouth. He made especial mention of his books,

> which he placed in the hands of the monks [of la Trappe], on condition that they could neither be moved from the abbey nor deposited anywhere else for any reason at all. His intention was that they should serve for the use and instruction of the reformed religious of his own monastery.[53]

If, however, through unforeseen circumstances, the abbey was to return into the hands of the 'anciens religieux'—those who had been in possession of the house before Rancé took over—and the reform cease to be, the library was to be given to the Hôtel-Dieu in Paris, sold, and the proceeds used to provide for the poor and the sick.[54] In order to facilitate this,

---

53. André Félibien des Avaux, *Description de l'abbaye de La Trape. Nouvelle édition, avec figures* (Paris, 1689) 13-14.
54. *Description de l'abbaye de la Trappe avec les Constitutions, les Reflexions sur icelles; la mort de quelques Religieux de ce Monastère, plusieurs lettres du R.P. Abbé, et une brière relation de l'Abbaye de Septfons* (Lyon, 1683) 100.

Rancé himself made an inventory of his collection[55] which, to my sorrow, appears not to have survived.

As it happened, the reform did not fail and the books remained at la Trappe. A decade later, however, Rancé changed his mind on the matter and on 3 March 1675 wrote to Nicolas Pinette, former treasurer to Gaston of Orléans who had since retired to the Oratory, saying that after giving the matter much serious thought, he had now come to the conclusion that there was, in fact, nothing less useful to his monks than the library:

> Our occupations and our manual labour do not allow us the leisure to make any great use of the library, and my brothers and I therefore beg you to find someone who can purchase the collection. We shall use the money for the relief of the poor, for their prayers before God will be of greater help to us than any reading of these books.[56]

But since Rancé had already made a legal bequest of his collection to la Trappe in 1664, Pinette was unable to comply with his wishes. Rancé, however, still went ahead with his plan and sold

> a large number of finely bound and printed volumes, but for much less than they were worth. With the money he then bought other books more useful for his monks, such as the 'Library of the Fathers' in twenty-four volumes,[57] and other similar works.[58]

---

55. *Ibid.*   56. Letter 750303a.

57. A copy of Marguérin de La Bigne's *Maxima Bibliotheca Veterum Patrum et antiquorum scriptorum ecclesiasticorum* (Lyon, 1677) in twenty-seven folio volumes is listed in the 1752 catalogue of the library of la Trappe as 'Bibliothèque des Pères'.

58. Pierre Le Nain, *La vie de Dom Armand-Jean Le Boutillier de Rancé, Abbé & Reformateur de l'Abbaye de la Maison-Dieu-Notre-Dame de la Trappe* (Paris, 1719²) 165.

The earliest catalogue we have of the library of la Trappe dates from 1752,[59] but although it certainly contains much of Rancé's original library, it is impossible to specify just which books had belonged to him. We may suggest with some confidence that the latin and græco-latin editions of pagan authors—Herodotus, Thucydides, Xenophon, Polybius, Pausanias, Isocrates, Homer, Terence, and so on—came from his collection; and the same may be said for most of the bilingual editions of early Christian Fathers—writers such as Philo, Clement of Alexandria, Cyril of Jerusalem, Cyril of Alexandria, Eusebius of Caesarea, Gregory of Nazianzus, Gregory of Nyssa, John Chrysostom, and Isidore of Pelusium. Similarly, it is possible that the numerous writings of the 'M[rs]. de Port-Royal'[60] had originally belonged to Rancé. There are also the editions that he himself prepared and the works that he wrote,[61] and a study of his multitudinous sources point to many other volumes in the 1752 catalogue that we may suspect came from his own collection, but which we cannot conclusively prove to have done so.

One thing is certain, the abbot of la Trappe was immensely learned, and (to a bibliophile) few things could more dramatically reveal his true conversion than his intention to sell his library. In fact, he never lost his taste for the classics, though he would not permit himself the pleasure of reading them. In 1691 Claude Nicaise, a canon of Sainte-Chapelle in Dijon and an old friend of Rancé (they had first met in Rome in 1666), sent him a copy of his discourse on the form and figure of the Sirens.[62] On 4 October of that year Rancé wrote to Nicaise acknowledging the gift, but went on to say:

59. Now Rouen, *Bibliothèque municipale*, MS 2240 (Coquebert de Montbret Y.4). For details, see Bell, 'Library', 130-133.
60. Rouen, *Bibliothèque municipale*, MS 2240 (Coquebert de Montbret Y.4) 149-150.
61. See *ibid.*, 153, edited in Bell, 'Library', 152-154.
62. Claude Nicaise, *Les Sirènes, ou Discours sur leur forme et figure*, with illustrations by Franz Ertinger (Paris, 1691). It is a slender volume of about eighty pages.

> I have glanced at your work on the Sirens,
> but I confess to you that I did not dare go
> into it in any detail. All the fabled figures [of
> the past] awoke, and I realized that I was still
> not as dead as I should be. Such a thought
> was followed by a great deal of reflection![63]

It is, I think, a touching and remarkably human admission
for a man who, by many, was regarded as inhumane (especially in his teaching on strict enclosure), obstinate, opinionated, inflexible, vain, and ambitious.   But since we cannot
understand Rancé unless we also understand his failings, or
(what is sometimes more important) what others perceived
as his failings, we must now turn our attention from Rancé's
reading to the writings of his enemies. Who were these
enemies? What were their disagreements with the abbot of la
Trappe? How did they attack him? And how effective was
their propaganda?

FURTHER READING

There are two excellent accounts of the spirituality of Saint John Climacus (or John of the Ladder) in English: John Chryssavgis, *Ascent to Heaven: The Theology of the Human Person according to St John of the Ladder* (Brookline, 1989), and Bishop Kallistos Ware's long introduction to *John Climacus: The Ladder of Divine Ascent*, tr. Colm Luibheid and Norman Russell (New York-Toronto, 1982) 1-70. The Luibheid-Russell translation is fluent and idiomatic, but not always as accurate as the older version by Archimandrite Lazarus Moore, *St. John Climacus, The Ladder of Divine Ascent* (London, 1959), especially in the revised edition published by the Holy Transfiguration Monastery (Boston, 1978). For other works in English, French, German, and Greek, see pages 69-70 (Bibliography III) of the Luibheid-Russell translation.

For Rancé's approach to Saint Bernard, see Alban J. Krailsheimer, 'Bernard and Rancé', *Cîteaux: Commentarii cistercienses* 42 (1991) = *Bernardus Magister. Papers presented at the Nonacentenary Celebration of the Birth of Saint Bernard of Clairvaux*, ed. John R. Sommerfeldt (Kalamazoo, 1992) 547-556, and (in French) Lucien Aubry, 'Rancé et saint Bernard', *Collectanea Cisterciensia* 52 (1990) 140-162. Both articles are useful; neither is wholly satisfactory.

There is hardly anything in either English or French on Julien Paris. In English, see the index to Louis Lekai's *The Rise of the Cistercian Strict Observance in Seventeenth Century France* (Washington, 1968) 259 s.v. Paris, Julien (though Lekai's comments are not always unbiased). In French there is only the brief entry in *DAC* 428. There is nothing at all in *DTC*, *DS*, or *DLF XVII*, and neither the *DBF* nor the *DHGE* has yet reached the letter P.

Rancé's patristic and medieval sources are listed in a useful compilation by Bernard Duymentz, *Les citations des Pères de la période patristique et médiévale chez Rancé*, Mémoire de Diplôme d'Études Approfondies en théologie catholique, soutenance du 12 juin 1991 en la Faculté de théologie catholique de

Strasbourg (also cited in Chapter Two, n. 37). Unfortunately, the work was never published. There is no comprehensive list of Rancé's post-medieval sources.

On the library of la Trappe, see David N. Bell, 'The Library of the Abbey of la Trappe in the Eighteenth Century: A Preliminary Survey', *Cîteaux: Commentarii cistercienses* 49 (1998) 129-158, and for a briefer account in French, but more specifically directed to Rancé's personal collection, the same author's 'La bibliothèque de La Trappe au XVIIe siècle' in *Un Homme et son temps: l'abbé de Rancé. Actes au colloque de La Trappe, 23-29 octobre 2000, pur la troisième centenaire de la mort de Rancé,*ed. Hugues de Seréville (Bégrolles-en-Mauges, 2004) 393-404. I have an edition of the 1752 library catalogue in hand and almost completed.

On the Jansenists in general, see Further Reading to Chapter Two. On Pasquier Quesnel in particular there is hardly anything in English and less than one might expect in French. The old article in *The Catholic Encyclopedia* (New York, 1911) 12:601-603 remains useful, but for a comprehensive account of his theology and spirituality one must refer to *DTC* 13:1460-1535 (by J. Carreyre), *DS* 12:2732-2746 (by Joseph A. G. Tans, with an excellent bibliography), and Joseph A. G. Tans, 'Quesnel et Jansénius', in *L'Image de C. Jansénius jusqu'à la fin du XVIIIe siècle: Actes du Colloque, Louvain, 7-9 novembre 1985*, ed. Edmond J. M. van Eijl (Leuven, 1987) 137-149. There is also a useful article in *DLF XVIII*, 1078-1080. On the Bull *Unigenitus*, the definitive work is now Lucien Ceyssens and Joseph A. G. Tans, *Autour de l'Unigenitus: recherches sur la genèse de la Constitution* (Leuven, 1987). There is also a very sound analysis in *DTC* 15:2061-2162. In English, we are fortunate in having a splendidly readable account by John McManners in his *Church and Society in Eighteenth-Century France* (Oxford, 1998), vol. 2, chaps. 35-38, who also provides a further bibliography.

Chapter 7

RANCÉ'S ENEMIES

RANCÉ MADE ENEMIES EASILY, that must be admitted. To some extent this is understandable. The Common Observance obviously would not and could not care for him, but it is never easy to deal with a person who is utterly and unarguably convinced that he (or she) is right. With regard to his interpretation of the Rule of Saint Benedict, Rancé was inflexible. It is true that within the limits of the Rule he could be accommodating, considerate, and charitable—his monks were well aware of this—but if, for example, the Rule demanded strict enclosure, there was nothing else to be said. If he thought others were wrong, he was prepared to say so, and say so in no uncertain terms. On the other hand, this was the tenor of the times. Seventeenth-century France was a verbose age, and the innumerable controversies provoked a huge number of well-written, lengthy, hard-hitting diatribes. One need only think of the thousands of sometimes tedious pages which chart the course of the War of the Observances. It was not a time for mincing words.

This is not to say that the exchanges could not be courteous. In the long dispute over monastic studies, Mabillon was ever the gentleman—he cannot be called an enemy of Rancé—but courtesy can often be more cutting than vituperation. It is also true that one's former friends can become one's worst enemies, and this we can see with Rancé. It happened to some extent in the case of Quesnel, though we are here dealing with criticism rather than enmity. It happened much more in the controversy over 'fictions' which we discussed in the last chapter. Guillaume Le Roy had been a close friend of Rancé. He had spent time with him at Véretz shortly after his conversion and had been welcomed at la Trappe in June 1671. But his disagreement with Rancé over what he understood—misunderstood, to be precise—of the latter's teaching on the question of 'humiliations' led to a war of words which, as Professor Krailsheimer has said, 'aroused all the worst feelings of anger, resentment, pride, and self-righteousness in the participants'.[1] It is true that Rancé's reply to Le Roy, the *Lettre d'un abbé régulier sur le sujet des humiliations*,[2] was published without Rancé's permission, but it is a cutting and intemperate piece of work, and the bitter quarrel dragged on for years.

Even more bitter was the quarrel with the General of the Carthusians, Dom Innocent Le Masson. Le Masson himself was a man much like Rancé—devout, austere, learned, an excellent organizer, a voluminous correspondent, and an effective and respected spiritual guide—but he did not take kindly to criticism of his Order. He also hated Jansenists and anything that smelled of Jansenism, and Rancé's jansenist leanings could hardly have endeared the one to the other. The problem arose from certain passages in *De la sainteté* which contrasted the Carthusians' primitive austerity with a more lax approach in Le Masson's own times, and in 1683 Le Masson published a detailed refutation of Rancé's comments in a highly critical *Explication de quelques endroits des anciens statuts de l'Ordre des Chartreux. Avec les éclaircissements donnez sur le sujet d'un libelle qui a été composé contre l'Ordre et qui s'est divulgué secrètement*.[3] It is a long and tendentious work[4] which contains a number of harsh comments on Rancé himself (accusing him, amongst other things, of being Jansenius *redivivus*), and in July 1689 Rancé replied with a long letter—a mini-treatise in fact—saying exactly why and where Dom Le Masson was

1. Krailsheimer, *Legacy*, 39.
2. Part II, I.B.ii [1677 *Lettre*].
3. Part II, II.A [1683 Le Masson].
4. For a brief summary, see Krailsheimer, *Rancé*, 164-165.

wrong.[5] The quarrel went from bad to worse, and although, in theory, it was ended by royal command in 1689 (the king imposed silence on both parties), it still rankled seven years later.[6] We might add that the royal command prevented publication of Rancé's reply until a decade after his death.

But although Le Roy and Le Masson were enemies of Rancé, they were, we might say, professional enemies. They disagreed with Rancé on specifically monastic matters. The same is true of the Benedictine Dom Antoine-Joseph Mège who viciously and vituperatively attacked Rancé on his interpretation of the Rule of Saint Benedict,[7] and the same is also true of the even more vituperative attack by another Benedictine, Dom Denis de Sainte-Marthe, who wrote four somewhat hysterical letters attacking Rancé on the matter of monastic studies.[8] But such professional disagreements were inevitable among literate seventeenth-century french gentlemen, each of whom was inflexibly convinced that he was right.

Far more significant was an attack on Rancé which came from a quite different source. It did not reflect professional disagreement—the author was neither a monk nor (at the time) a Roman Catholic—but it presented to the public gaze a vain and ambitious Rancé whose conversion reflected only his own egotism and whose writings contained ideas manifestly abhorrent to any civilized reader. The work in question was *Les Véritables motifs de la Conversion de l'Abbé de la Trappe, avec quelques reflexions sur sa Vie & sur ses écrits Ou Les Entretiens de Timocrate & de Philandre Sur un livre qui a pour titre, Les S. Devoirs De la Vie Monastique* and it was written by Daniel de Larroque.[9]

The book itself is no more than a small duodecimo—just 7 x 13.5 cms—which was published anonymously by Pierre

5. Letter 890720 = Part II, I.B.ii [1689 *Lettre*].
6. See Letter 961018.
7. Krailsheimer, *Rancé*, 49, and see the notes to Part II, I.A.i [1688 *La Règle*].
8. *Ibid.*, 53, 166 and Part II, II.A [1692 Sainte-Marthe], [1693 Sainte-Marthe], [1693 A.D.P.C.E.], and [1694 Thiers].
9. Part II, II.A [1685 Larroque]. I have here followed the capitalization of the original. There was only one edition.

Marteau at Cologne in 1685, but its impact was in inverse proportion to its size. Larroque's account of the *véritables motifs* which led to Rancé's conversion occupy just twenty pages out of two hundred. The rest of the book is devoted to a discussion and criticism of certain passages from Rancé's *De la sainteté et des devoirs de la vie monastique* published two years earlier in 1683.

Daniel de Larroque was born about 1660 at Vitré in Brittany, the son of Mathieu de Larroque, a protestant pastor known and respected for his erudition. Mathieu de Larroque was much involved in the controversies of his times and the author of numerous works, including one attacking Bossuet's treatise on communion in both kinds.[10] He was also a specialist in the history of the early Church and at his death left a manuscript (never published) of an *Histoire ecclésiastique pendant les trois premiers siècles*. His son inherited both his interests and his erudition (though the father was the more learned) and, like his father, studied for the protestant ministry. When the Edict of Nantes was revoked in 1685—a measure, we might add, with which Rancé agreed[11]—he fled first to London, then to Copenhagen, and finally to Holland, where he was given employment as editor of a literary journal by Pierre Bayle. In 1690 he returned to France, expediently converted to Roman Catholicism, and found employment in the book-trade. But in 1693 he wrote the introduction to a satirical work attacking the government for its failure to take appropriate steps in dealing with a famine which, at the time, was causing grave problems in France. This ill-advised move had serious consequences: the book was seized, the printer was hanged, and Larroque spent five years in prison in the château of Saumur.

On his release he found employment in the office of the Marquis de Torcy, Secretary of State for Foreign Affairs, and

10. *Réponse au livre de M. l'évêque de Meaux, de la Communion sous les deux espèces* ([s.l.], 1683). He was neither the first nor the last to do so: see Cioranescu, 1:435, nos. 14975-14977.
11. See Further Reading, 168.

appears to have carried out his duties well and conscientiously.[12] He retired with a pension of two thousand pounds *per annum* and spent his remaining years studying, writing, and enjoying the company of his many friends. He died in Paris on 5 September 1731.

Larroque was a fairly prolific writer with wide interests and a talent for satire which, as we have seen, could get him into trouble. But there is no doubt that he was well read. In his attack on Rancé he reveals his knowledge of Cyprian, Jerome, Rufinus, Athanasius, John Chrysostom, the *Ecclesiastical Histories* of Theodoret and Socrates, and Rosweyde's edition of the *Vitas Patrum*. He had read (and heartily disapproved of) Jansenists like Antoine Arnauld, Pierre Nicole, Le Maître de Sacy, and Saint-Cyran. He had read (with equal approval) their opponents such as François Annat and the Jesuit Denis Pétau (Antonius Kerkoetius). He had read the *Entretiens d'Ariste et d'Eugène* of another Jesuit, Dominique Bouhours, as well as certain works of yet another, Antonio de Escobar y Mendoza, in french translation. He had read Jean de Launoy on the saints, Jean Crasset's life of Madame Helyot, and Edmond Richer's apology for Jean Gerson. He was familiar with Jean Barbier d'Aucour, he had read Mateo Aleman's *Aventuras y vida de Guzman de Alfarache* in the translation by Jean Chapelain, and he knew the pro-Rancéan *Entretiens de l'abbé Jean et du prêtre Eusèbe* of François Du Suel. His favourite work of devotion appears to have been Thomas à Kempis's *Imitation of Christ*, but 'I speak of the original, not of the translations, and above all not the translation put out by Port-Royal which seems to me too polished and too dressed up for the court' (83[13]).

Whether Larroque was paid to write his book on Rancé's 'true motives' is unknown. It is certainly possible, and it would not be surprising to find that the Jesuits had a hand in

12. Both his release and his employment were due to the intervention of the abbess of Fontevrault.
13. Numbers in parentheses refer to pages in *Les Véritables motifs de la Conversion de l'Abbé de la Trappe*.

it, but that is no more than conjecture. So what, according to Larroque, were the *véritables motifs* for Rancé's conversion, and what were the passages in *De la sainteté* which gave rise to Larroque's critical reflections?

The book takes the form of two dialogues between two friends, Timocrate and Philandre (names reflecting the literary fashion of the times), and takes place over two days. Philandre is the more knowledgeable and critical of the two; Timocrate is the defender of Rancé, but is regularly out-argued by Philandre. Rancé's name does not actually appear until page 13, but his (too) considerable literary productions are clearly in Larroque's mind from the start.

The temptation to be an author, says Timocrate, is a great evil, for one almost always succumbs to it. One then ends up writing for the sake of writing, and the results are inevitable: bad books and poor authors. Philandre agrees and adds that if only these gentlemen would take the trouble to study before they write, we might not see the absurd spectacle of authors who know almost nothing of God (disciples of Descartes, not of Jesus Christ) trying to prove his existence. Too many of them, he says, speak of religion simply in order to speak of themselves or to defend their way of life.

Indeed, says Philandre, there is only one real reason for writing on religion: the glory of God. But how long is it since we have seen that? The only difference nowadays between an author who is morally good and one who is not is that in the former we see a few pious sentiments following in the wake of his egocentricity, and in the latter we see none!

This is too much for Timocrate. There *are*, he says, some authors who have written for the glory of God, and who would not have written at all if they did not truly love God and their neighbour. He is thinking especially of the Solitaries of Port-Royal, men like Saint-Cyran, Antoine Arnauld, Pierre Nicole, and Claude Lancelot. Philandre, however, will have none of this. The Solitaries may *appear* to want nothing more than to uphold the morality of the Gospels in a corrupt world, but if you look at their conduct towards the Jesuits, you will see a very different picture. The Solitaries are no more than Jansenists, and in the war between the Jansenists and the Jesuits, the Jansenists give little indication of loving their neighbours! They examine the life of every Jesuit in detail, and if they find any sins at all, they immediately impute them to the whole Society of Jesus, just as the sin of Adam was imputed to the whole human race. And when King Louis XIV (with his discerning spirit and uncommon wisdom) imposed a holy silence on the contending parties, did the Jansenists obey? They did not! The Jesuits ceased to speak immediately; their adversaries are still writing! Does this sort of conduct really have as its only end the glory of God? Or do you not see (asks Philandre of Timocrate) that the whole jansenist machine is powered only by 'a host of criminal and shameful passions' (12)?

To this argument Timocrate cannot reply. On the one hand, he has no intention of re-kindling a war which seems to have died down and, in any case, he is not sufficiently acquainted with the details of the matter to make a proper response to Philandre. But he remains unconvinced:

> Examples of people who write only for the glory of God are not as rare as you think, Philandre. For every one you reject, I can provide a thousand more! But since a single good example may serve to convince you, I will content myself with giving you one against which you cannot possibly have anything to say: it is that of the abbot of la Trappe. Tell me, I ask you, what other purpose could he have in writing? He who passes his days in penitence and humiliations, he who has renounced the world only because he recognised that it is all vanity, he whose happiness consists in forgetting the world and being forgotten by it? (13)

And so we come to the main subject of the book. Rancé

does indeed seem to be an admirable example, says Philandre, but appearances can be deceptive. Philandre has read Rancé. He has read his work on 'the holy duties of the monastic life'—the *De la sainteté*—and if Timocrate had done the same, he would see why Philandre remains unpersuaded. It is certainly true that Rancé's dramatic conversion seems to have edified many, and it is equally true that in his works we can see something that appears to be genuine piety together with a rigid morality and what seems to be great zeal for the monastic life. But we can also see other things as well: ostentation, for a start, and love of self confused with the love of God, and pride disguised as humility. Indeed, what the abbot of la Trappe has written stems not from christian charity, but from a desire to be thought a saint.

Timocrate is horrified. This cannot be! The abbot is admired by everyone. His writings are of inestimable value for devotion. But then, on the other hand, Philandre seems to know more of these matters than Timocrate, and the latter begs his friend to tell him something of Rancé's past life and the events that led to his conversion. Philandre is only too happy to do so, and over the next dozen or so pages he sets forth what, in his view, were the two *véritables motifs* for Rancé's dramatic conversion.

The first motive was his support for Cardinal de Retz and his clash with Cardinal Mazarin. We saw earlier how Rancé's uncle, the archbishop of Tours, had hoped to have his nephew appointed coadjutor bishop of Tours and, in due course, to have him succeed him as archbishop, but Mazarin's return to power in 1653 dashed any such hopes. According to Philandre, Rancé himself had been eager to obtain the archbishopric, and realized too late that in this world—and especially at court—one had to be both astute and prudent. His disappointment in failing to attain his goal may even be called the 'prevenient grace' (25) that led the young *abbé* to the idea that if he could not achieve fame in the world, he would achieve fame by renouncing it. Larroque's account of these events is undeniably slanted, but, as we shall see in the next chapter, the events he recounts did indeed play a significant role in Rancé's conversion.

The second of the two *véritables motifs* was far more dramatic and involved the sudden and unexpected death of Marie de Bretagne-Avaugour, duchesse de Montbazon. We shall have more to say on this matter in the next chapter, but for the moment we will summarize Philandre's version of the events. As a young man about town, Rancé had had many affairs—*commerces tendres* (25)—and the last of them was with the beautiful and notorious Madame de Montbazon. But after narrowly escaping death once, the young duchess had contracted either measles or scarlet fever (Philandre mistakenly speaks of smallpox) and died after just a few days. The date was 28 April 1657.[14] Rancé, we are told, was out of town at the time the tragedy occurred, and when he returned, he hastened, all unknowing, to visit his mistress. But meanwhile, the undertakers had found that the coffin prepared for her was too short, and to make the corpse fit they had removed her head. Thus, on entering her chamber, the duchess's lover was confronted with the sight of a decapitated corpse and a gory head—*toute sanglante* (27)—which had rolled out from beneath a covering cloth.

The story of the severed head is a matter we shall discuss in due course, but it is certainly true that the death of the duchess did indeed play a significant role in Rancé's conversion. According to Philandre, the young *abbé* might, in time, have overcome his disappointment at failing to gain an archbishopric, but the death of the duchess was too much: 'Without the episcopal throne and without his mistress, the world appeared to him unbearable' (30).

Rancé therefore took counsel with 'M^r. l'Evêque d'Aleth'— Nicolas Pavillon—who wisely advised him to retire to la Trappe. But even now Rancé's ambition (which, says Philandre, had always been his overweening vice) would not

14. The date of 26 April in the french translation of Krailsheimer, *Rancé*, 29 is a typographical error.

permit him to enter the abbey as a simple monk: he had to be
abbot and ensure for himself '*le plaisir de commander*' (31). Yet
even that was not enough. Abbot of la Trappe was one thing;
head of an Order was another. In place of his lost archbishopric, Rancé wished to become a 'chef d'Ordre' (33), and
it was with this in mind that he went to Rome in 1664. The
pope, however, would have none of it (there were already too
many Orders) and the disappointed Rancé therefore returned
to France to try to achieve his goal at the royal court. He
presented 'a printed request' to the king—this was the
Requeste présentée au Roy par le Révérend Père Abbé de la Trappe of
1673[15]—but it met only with ridicule. His friends therefore
advised *le pauvre abbé* to retire back to his monastery and make
the best of a bad thing, and this, 'to his inexpressible cha-
grin' (34), he did.

And if all this is not yet enough (says Philandre to
Timocrate), to persuade you of the ambition and vanity of
your so-called saint, read the pages of his *De la sainteté et des
devoirs de la vie monastique*! What will you see there? Apart from
the frightful depictions of his monks (which can only be regarded as satire), you will see his desire to dominate clearly
reflected in his demand for submission and blind obedience.
You will see his impiety in the disrespectful way he speaks of
saints who displease him. You will see his contempt for certain miracles recognized as authentic by the Church. And
you will see his vanity in his extraordinary ideas, in his display of ill-digested knowledge, in his unnecessary neologisms,
and in his desire to make public writings which are good only
for monks and which should have been confined to the cloister.

To this tirade Timocrate replies—in effect—'Prove it!' He
knows Philandre has a copy of *De la sainteté* and he asks his
friend to have a servant bring them the book so that they can
discuss the passages in question. Philandre agrees, the book
is brought in, and Timocrate opens his argument by quoting
Rancé's statement that he only ever intended his books for

15. Part II, I.A.i [1673 *Requeste*].

his monks, and that it is true that they should never have been made public.[16] How, then, can Philandre say that the abbot wrote only to gain a worldly reputation as an author?

The truth of the matter is evident, replies Philandre: Rancé is lying. Everyone knows the infinite pains he takes to perfect his manuscripts before they are printed and the numerous copies he circulates to his friends before his works are made public. Why would he do this unless he had in mind their eventual publication? No. What Rancé is doing here is hiding one vice under another: he is concealing his vanity beneath a lie.

We have now reached page 41 of Larroque's scurrilous account; the rest of the book is taken up with attacking a number of selected passages and themes from *De la sainteté*. We need not deal with all the arguments in detail, but what Philandre brings to the attention of Timocrate certainly reflects those ideas which, outside the walls of la Trappe, had given rise to contention and disagreement. Some of these criticisms we have already mentioned in previous chapters; others, as we shall see, are new.

Philandre begins by attacking Rancé's statement at the very beginning of *De la sainteté* that monastic rules are not to be thought of as human inventions and that the monastic life was instituted by Christ himself. This (says Philandre) is historically incorrect and Timocrate agrees. 'If I am not mistaken', says the latter, 'it is Paul the Hermit who is called the "Father of monks" and there is general agreement that he lived in the third century' (45). The next problem is Rancé's assertion that 'in a solitary, God has brought to an end all duties of charity and justice with regard to the world'.[17] A monk neither succours the poor, consoles the afflicted, visits the sick, or teaches the ignorant. But it can easily be shown that this was never the conduct of earlier ascetics who had no hesitation in leaving their monasteries if either Church or people were oppressed or in difficulties.

16. Larroque, 40, quoting the *Avertissement* to *De la sainteté*.
17. Larroque, 48, quoting *De la sainteté*, 1:17.

The third point introduced by Philandre is more serious, for it is concerned not with historical accuracy, but with contemporary practice. It is Rancé's demand (based, as we know, on the Rule of Saint Benedict) that a monk give total and absolute obedience to his abbot. Philandre finds this appalling. Timocrate, on the other hand, points out that you cannot have a community without some sort of order and without someone at its head. True enough, says Philandre, but while proper order is one thing, it is quite another to put oneself in the place of God and demand for oneself the total obedience due to him. Rancé, in his vanity and pride, wishes to be a king in his convent. And if—as he says—every abbot is a 'vicar of Jesus Christ' and has Christ's authority and power, then in place of one Sovereign Pontiff, the abbot of la Trappe has put a multitude! Philandre then goes on to contrast with this the true humility of the first monks, and adds that if Rancé had really intended to restore the monastic order '*dans son premier état*' (78), he would have gone to the desert, not to an abbey with an income of eight or nine thousand pounds *per annum* set in a fertile and attractive location 'with watered meadows and magnificent forests' (78-79). It would seem that Larroque had never visited la Trappe.

Philandre's next point concerns Rancé's statement that a monastic superior 'needs to know neither the tradition of the Church, nor its history, nor its canons' (85). Not only is this unwise (for the history of the Church tells us much of the innocence, fervour, and humility of the first Christians and early monks), but the abbot of la Trappe also contradicts himself when he says elsewhere that meditation on the Scriptures should be accompanied by reading the works of the Fathers (who advise us on our conduct and christian way of life) and ecclesiastical writers (who relate to us the lives of holy monks) (92)!

But if all this is true, says Timocrate, how in the world could the book have been given official approval by the bishops of Reims, Meaux, Luçon, and Grenoble (i.e. Le Tellier, Bossuet, Barillon, and Le Camus)? Ah, replies Philandre, that is not surprising when you know how official approval is given. An over-worked prelate with innumerable duties and obligations merely reads the preface to a book and glances at the first few pages. He then hands it over to one of the priests in his entourage (who will be a '*Docteur de Sorbonne par honneur*' [95]) and tells him to check the rest. But the priest, who will often have more titles than intelligence, may well have been influenced by the spirit of Jansenism or Port-Royal, and reports back to his bishop that the book is '*plein d'onction*' (95). The bishop then instructs the Doctor to write a letter of approval, and he does so, seeking fine phrases and brilliant expressions. He writes the letter, in fact, much as Lully[18] might write an opera. Episcopal approval, therefore, is quite unreliable.

But it is now sunset and time for the evening stroll. Timocrate has promised to accompany Philandre to the Tuilleries gardens and the coach is waiting at the door. But Timocrate agrees to go only if Philandre will discuss the second volume of *De la sainteté* the following day, and having received his promise, the two friends drive off to take the evening air. So ends the first *entretien* of Daniel de Larroque's account of the *véritables motifs* of the conversion of Armand-Jean de Rancé.

The second dialogue opens on the following day with a discussion of what was, as we have seen earlier, one of Rancé's most contentious principles: that once a monk had entered the monastery and had taken his final vows, he was dead to the world; and if he was dead to the world he was also dead to his parents. If, then, his parents were sick or indigent, the monastery as a whole might come to their aid in whatever way it could, but the monk himself could not leave to attend to their needs. For Philandre, this is a monstrous idea. It fills him with horror. Nevertheless, 'it is this on which [Rancé] most insists and he devotes a quarter of his book to maintaining this pernicious doctrine' (103).

---

18. Jean-Baptiste Lully (1632-1687), Louis XIV's court composer.

Philandre then spends more than thirty pages showing why this pernicious doctrine is unchristian. His arguments are fairly obvious: the obligation to honour one's parents, the demands of christian charity, and so on. But he is well aware that Rancé can adduce numerous examples from the lives of the Desert Fathers—the *vitas patrum*—to support his case. How do we reply to these? Philandre's answer is simple and, indeed, reasonable. Some of these lives do indeed present us with useful lessons—witness the life of Antony written by no less an authority than the great Athanasius—but in others we are confronted with examples which are not at all useful and which should never be imitated. The historians who have recorded these tales are obliged, by their profession, to tell us everything. Sensible Christians, on the other hand, are not obliged to imitate everything. It is just the same as in Scripture: God has left us examples to avoid as well as examples to follow. But the abbot of la Trappe quotes only those Fathers and those passages which support his own ideas and he praises only those saints whose ideas concur with his own. Anyone who does not agree with him—and the Jesuits (those 'new doctors who have never had any calling to speak of holy things' [134]) certainly do not agree—he simply condemns. Is this humility?

Philandre then goes on to speak of the way in which Rancé fails to follow the Rule of Saint Benedict, which permits monks to eat the meat of two-legged birds but not of four-legged beasts. Here, of course, Philandre is referring to the War of the Observances, which we discussed at some length in Chapter Three. Yet once again the abbot of la Trappe has no hesitation in quoting those authorities who support him and decrying those who do not. Indeed, he even goes so far as to deny the authenticity of certain miracles recognized as authentic by the Church if they do not accord with his principles. There is a tale, for example, of Saint Columba and his disciples feeding for three days on the miraculous provision of 'an innumerable number of all sorts of birds' (146), but despite the teaching of the Church, Rancé treats the miracle as false and speaks of it as 'supposed' or 'so-called' (146). Quite apart from the vanity of setting forth one's own personal opinions as if they were absolute truth, such convenient judgements can only be injurious to the good of the Church. The book in which they appear—*De la sainteté*—can hardly be said to have been written solely for the glory of God.

Furthermore, in trying to prove his point, this abbot, who disapproves of monks reading the Fathers and the canons, actually quotes *The Clouds* of Aristophanes, a poet 'filled with mordant satire' (153) and a writer who, because of his indecency, is translated into French only with appropriate omissions. Timocrate is clearly perplexed by this. 'But what I would like to know', he says (with justice),

> is when he read the work. Was it in his youth
> before he had left the world, or after? I find it
> hard to believe that he could have recalled so
> exactly something he had read thirty years
> earlier. It seems more likely, in fact, that he
> had been amusing himself with this comic poet
> in his retreat and that he had been reading
> him to pass the time which he could not
> wholly give to devotion. (157)

But more than that, says Philandre, the sixteenth canon of the fourth Council of Carthage (which he quotes [159]) expressly forbade bishops or priests from reading books by pagans and heretics, and the Council of Aix-en-Provence reiterated the prohibition in 1585. And if it applies to bishops and priests, how much more should it apply to cloistered monks?

But to return to the question of diet. Timocrate now asks Philandre what he thinks of that passage where Rancé refers to Philo's account of certain early Christians who lived in solitude, ate only bread and herbs, and practised hitherto unknown austerities. Philandre replies with a learned discus-

sion in which he demonstrates that the people referred to by
Philo were neither Christians nor monks, but Jewish secta-
ries. Timocrate, as we might expect, is convinced, and finally
returns to something they had discussed earlier but had not
examined in sufficient detail: Rancé's statement that the Old
Testament prophets normally spoke by divine inspiration,
but sometimes gave only their own personal opinion.

Philandre agrees that what a prophet says to his family
over the breakfast-table is to be distinguished from what he
says to the whole people of Israel, but this is not what Rancé
means. His view (which, according to Philandre, he borrowed
from Spinoza) is that he can pick and choose what he finds
appropriate from the writings of the prophets, and that when
they say—as they do say—that they are speaking with the
voice of God, they are lying. It is yet another example of the
vanity and counterfeit humility of the abbot of la Trappe.

Timocrate is finally convinced, and vows that if he had a
say in the matter, he would not now vote for the canonization
of Rancé. Philandre can therefore afford to become a little
more lenient. Earlier in their conversation he has admitted
that there are some fine passages in Rancé's work and that
some of his more hyperbolic statements can be forgiven when
we remember that this is the style of some of his sources,
especially the Spaniards.[19] Yet in France one strives for clarity
and lucid precision, and language which might be appropriate
for a sonnet is not appropriate for a work of devotion. There
are indeed some telling passages in the two volumes of *De la
sainteté*, passages which go straight to the heart, but it would
have been better if the abbot had written just two hundred
pages of this type rather than two oversized volumes in which
good sense has been buried under preciosities and 'brilliant
balderdash' (187). Timocrate—now convinced—totally agrees.
The book, he says, is like a diamond set in lead, a collection of
genuine pearls mixed with artificial.

19. They can be forgiven the vice, says Philandre, since they are born with it.
It probably came from their commerce with Moors and Arabs who think only
'*par métaphore & par Hieroglyphe*' (Larroque, 54).

Philandre now brings up one last point: the perpetual silence of la Trappe. Both he and Timocrate see this as ill advised. It is better, says Timocrate, to allow monks to refresh their spirit by means of decent and holy conversation. We are not, of course, speaking here of vain and worldly chatter, but it is certainly true that discussion of one's problems and difficulties can do much to restore and nourish the soul.

So the conversation ends. Timocrate declares that he now intends to publish what he can remember of their discourses (though Philandre advises caution), and the result, as we have seen, are the two discussions which comprise *Les Véritables motifs de la Conversion de l'Abbé de la Trappe*.

What can we say to all this? How just were the criticisms of Philandre/Larroque? The book is an easy read and Larroque's arguments are subtle. He rarely overstates his case and the issues he raises undoubtedly echo what was being said at the time. Furthermore, when he makes the case that strict enclosure and perpetual silence are, from his point of view (and, we might add, from many a modern point of view) unreasonable, he is not wrong. They *are* unreasonable. The problem lies in the fact that the monastic life is itself unreasonable. The Rule of Saint Benedict is likewise unreasonable. *As a monastic rule*, it is humane and balanced, but monastic rules are not designed as guides to everyday living. They are for people who have decided to live a life which, if I may quote Geoffrey Moorhouse, is *Against All Reason*.[20]

It is therefore easy for those outside the monastery to attack Rancé's apparent inhumanity in his doctrine of strict enclosure, and it is easy to attack, on psychological grounds, the principle of perpetual silence. But as far as Rancé was concerned, he was simply following the Rule of Saint Benedict. He was following the same Rule in maintaining that an abbot stands in the place of Christ and that he must command absolute obedience (whether he likes it or not). Similarly, as we saw in the last chapter, his idea that 'in a solitary, God has

20. Geoffrey Moorhouse, *Against All Reason* (London, 1969).

brought to an end all duties of charity and justice with regard to the world',[21] simply reflects his conception of absolute renunciation. If you really wish to renounce the world,
renounce it! There is no middle way. As John Climacus had
said, you cannot look up and down at the same time.[22] That
all these principles give rise to difficulties is not in doubt,
and monastic obligations (as Rancé was well aware) sometimes conflict with biblical obligations. But a religious who
has taken final vows cannot be expected to act as a secular,
and if one does not wish to enter a monastery, one need not
do so. Larroque, it will be remembered, was neither a monk
nor (at heart) a Catholic; his conversion was mere expedi-
ency, and his comments reflect his heritage.

Sometimes, from a logical and historical point of view, his
objections are sound. Historically, for example, monasticism
was not instituted by Jesus Christ, and although Philo's
Essenes may have been members of a religious community,
they were certainly not Christians. But if one goes to the
trouble of reading what Rancé actually wrote and thereby
appreciating what he actually meant, his own arguments are
logical. Indeed, it cannot be denied that he often explains himself at inordinate length and his citation of authority after
authority can be tedious. Sometimes, too, Larroque mis-
understands him, as he certainly does in his echoes of the
debate over monastic studies. He was not alone in this, however, and Rancé is still misunderstood on the question.

Sometimes Larroque is wrong. His account of the conflict
between cardinals de Retz and Mazarin and its impact on
Rancé, while grounded in fact, is too slanted and gossipy to
be reliable, and his cynical if amusing account of the *modus
operandi* of episcopal approbation does less than justice to the
bishops he mentions. Bossuet, Barillon, and Le Camus had
certainly read *De la sainteté* and had offered both suggestions
and criticisms. It is also somewhat startling to read of the
wealth of la Trappe and its idyllic location in a bucolic land-

21. See n. 17 above.
22. See Chapter 6, n. 12.

scape of meadows, streams, and forests. No visitor to the site, I think, would have agreed.

What, then, of Larroque's suggestion that Rancé longed to be recognized as an author, and what of his main contention that he was vain and ambitious? The question of the verity of the *véritables motifs* of his conversion we shall leave until our next chapter.

As to Rancé's desire to be recognized as a writer, it cannot be denied that Larroque has a point, though he certainly overstates his case. It is true that some of Rancé's works were leaked to the outside world by others, and it is also true that pressure from Bossuet played a role in the publication of *De la sainteté*. The first we hear of the work, in fact, is in a letter from Rancé to Bossuet written in June 1682,[23] in which Rancé asked him not to show the manuscript to anyone. It contains, he says 'some instructions which I have given to our brothers regarding their duties and the principal obligations of their profession'.[24] Moreover, the version which Bossuet has is defective. It is not as systematic as it should be; Rancé has made additions and changes which do not appear in the manuscript; some of the ideas expressed are appropriate only for la Trappe; and much of the teaching will not be approved by those outside the monastery since it no longer accords with contemporary practice. Initially Bossuet prudently agreed with Rancé, but afterwards it was he, more than anyone, who pressed Rancé—against the latter's inclinations and in spite of his opposition[25]—to publish the work.

A similar story may be told of the *Relations* (initially leaked by Nicolas Pinette[26]) and the commentary on the Rule of Saint Benedict which, according to Rancé, was published only under pressure from friends.[27] This may be true. Rancé's origi-

23. Letter 820627. See further the notes to Part II, I.A.i [1683 *De la sainteté*].
24. He says much the same thing in Letter 870703a, written five years later, and also in Letter 871005.   25. See especially Letter 830530a.
26. See Letter 760100b. We met Nicolas Pinette, former treasurer to Gaston of Orléans, in Chapter Six. See further the notes to Part II, I.A.i [1677 *Relations*].   27. Letter 89/5.

nal intention may well have been to circulate certain of his writings only within his own community, but it must be remembered that disavowal of authorship and the assertion that what one had actually published had been published only reluctantly or under pressure was a standard literary pretence of the times. As Larroque says, Rancé certainly took pains to seek approval for his work from Bossuet, Barillon, and Le Camus, and was eager for their suggestions and criticisms. Nor was Larroque the only one to satirize him for taking too much trouble over his literary style.[28] I do not think Rancé was unhappy to see his works in print, nor do I believe him when he protests his reluctance. And once the works were in print he was not unhappy to revise them. *De la sainteté* itself went through three editions, apart from the publication of its accompanying volume, the *Éclaircissemens de quelques difficultez que l'on a formées sur le livre De la sainteté et des devoirs de la vie monastique*,[29] which went through two. But this is not to say that Rancé wrote simply to gain renown as an author, nor is it to say that his published works were simply a reflection of his yearning for recognition, power, and fame.

On this matter, Larroque is wrong. Rancé certainly did not go to Rome to seek fame, glory, or promotion, and the *Requeste présentée au Roy* is not a request for his own advancement. Nor is there the slightest reason to believe that in demanding from his monks the obedience demanded by the Rule of Saint Benedict, he was acting only from a sense of self-aggrandizement. In citing his sources, he is not making a display of his knowledge, but grounding his arguments (as was expected at the time) in precedent, authority, and tradition. On this score—and it is his main score—Larroque's portrait of Rancé is grossly inaccurate, which is not to say that Rancé was all sweetness and light. In his replies to Le Roy and Le Masson, for example, he could be intemperate and authoritarian, and if opinionated means being wholly convinced of the rightness of one's own opinions—grounded, of

28. See Chapter Two, n. 6.
29. Part II, I.A.i [1685 *Éclaircissemens*].

course, in authority—then opinionated he was. Le Masson had already called him a man who wanted to be seen as '*grand et spirituel*'.[30] As Professor Krailsheimer has said, we can see pride and resentment on both sides,[31] but that is a far cry from saying that Rancé's conversion, writings, and way of life were simply reflections of his ambition and vanity.

However slanted Larroque's arguments, there is no doubt that they were persuasive. His little book had a very considerable impact, especially in promulgating the gruesome tale of the severed head of Madame de Montbazon. And if one did not much like Rancé, and there were many who did not, it merely confirmed their view of him as a proud, stubborn, arrogant, unbalanced, and inhumane ascetic.

Rancé certainly knew of Larroque's book, though not the name of its author.[32] In November 1685 he wrote to Henri Barillon saying that 'I do not know if you are aware that a criticism of the book *On Monastic Life* has been printed in Cologne: the most scathing and violent thing possible. In a word, it is the author who is attacked on the grounds of his [former] life in the world, and not the truths he puts forward.' Some people of the same ilk as its author are delighted with it, he continues, but in general 'it has been scorned and badly received'.[33] It had not, in fact, been scorned and badly received, nor is it quite true that Larroque had attacked Rancé only 'on the grounds of his life in the world'.

Then, in January 1686 Rancé wrote to his sister, Reverend Mother Louise-Marie Bouthillier, telling her that he had seen the book but had 'taken no notice of it'. He himself did not think it worthy of a reply, but he had been told that a rebuttal had already been published.[34] This is true. The work in question was Pierre de Maupeou's *La conduite et les sentimens de Monsieur l'abbé de la Trappe, pour servir de réponse aux calomnies de*

30. Quoted in Krailsheimer, *Rancé*, 166.
31. See n. 1 above.
32. See Letter 861003.
33. Letter 851129a.
34. Letter 860121.

l'autheur des Entretiens de Timocrate et de Philandre sur le livre de la Sainteté et des devoirs de la vie monastique published in 1685.[35] It was not very effective.

Ten days later Rancé wrote again to Barillon saying that the book had fallen flat (which it had not) and that those who had read it felt only scorn (which was also not entirely true). The author, he asserts, is not a little mortified to find that he has not had the prompt approval that scandalmongers usually get, and Rancé himself did not think it worth a stroke of his pen.[36] That, too, must be taken with a grain of salt.

The book was, in fact, an effective libel, widely read and widely quoted, and it undoubtedly reflected a number of commonly held contemporary opinions regarding Rancé and his ideas. Satires work by distorting the truth, not by denying it. I suspect, too, that it disturbed Rancé more than he ever admitted. But of all that Larroque wrote, nothing was to have a greater or longer-lasting impact than his account of the role played by the death of Madame de Montbazon in the conversion of Rancé, and it is to the question of Rancé's conversion that we must now turn.

35. Part II, II.A [1685 Maupeou].
36. Letter 860131a.

FURTHER READING

The most important of Rancé's many enemies are all mentioned in the third chapter of Krailsheimer's *Armand-Jean de Rancé* and discussed in more detail in other sections of his biography. But apart from Krailsheimer's judicious comments, there is hardly anything in English on any of them. Guillaume Le Roy is well served in French by Gérard Namer, *L'abbé Le Roy et ses amis: essai sur le jansénisme extrémiste intramondain* (Paris, 1964), and Innocent Le Masson by Jacques Martin, *Le Louis XIV des Chartreux. Dom Innocent Le Masson. 51ᵉ Général de l'Ordre (1627-1703)* (Paris, 1975), which supersedes the earlier work by the *abbé* Gallois, 'Dom Innocent Le Masson', *Comité archéologique de Noyon. Comptes rendus et mémoires lus aux séances* 22 (1900) 121-312. For a list of their writings and references to other less important studies, see Cioranescu, 1:1258 (Le Masson) and 1277-1278 (Le Roy). For Antoine-Joseph Mège and Denis de Sainte-Marthe, see *ibid.*, 1:1396-1397 (Mège), 2:1810-1811 (Sainte-Marthe), and the notes to I.A.i [1688 *La Règle*] and II.A [1692 Sainte-Marthe] in Part II of this present study.

There is an extensive literature on the controversy with Mabillon over monastic studies, but the old work by Henri Didio, *La querelle de Mabillon et de l'Abbé de Rancé* (Amiens, 1892) remains fundamental. It is a sober and balanced account with a wealth of documentation. The more recent volumes by Blandine Barret-Kriegel, *Jean Mabillon* (Paris, 1988) and *La querelle Mabillon-Rancé* (Paris, 1992), are both unreliable. For a justly scathing review of the first, see the review by Professor Krailsheimer in *Cîteaux: Commentarii cistercienses* 40 (1989) 523-524. For further secondary material, almost all of it in French, see my 'Bibliography', 281 s.v. 'Monastic Studies', but that neither includes nor is intended to include all studies on Mabillon. The primary texts of the controversy are all listed in Part II of this present volume.

There is nothing on Daniel de Larroque in English and no comprehensive study in French. A useful account of his life and works is to be found in the second edition of Michaud's *Biographie universelle ancienne et moderne* (Paris, [s.d.]) 285-286, preceded (284-285) by an equally useful account of his father. Their writings are listed in Cioranescu, 1:1199. Brief notices may be found in *DLF XVII*, 711 (Mathieu) and *DLF XVIII*, 691 (Daniel). At the time of writing, the *Dictionnaire de biographie française* has not yet reached the letter L.

On Rancé's (positive) attitude to the Revocation of the Edict of Nantes, see Alban J. Krailsheimer, 'L'Abbé de Rancé et les Protestants: autour de la Révocation de l'Édit de Nantes (1685)', *Collectanea Cisterciensia* 48 (1986) 297-310, and Yves Krumenacker, 'Le Camus, Barillon, Rancé: trois artisans de la réforme catholique face à la révocation de l'Édit de Nantes', in *Homo Religiosus: autour de Jean Delumeau* (Paris, [1997]) 386-392. Krailsheimer provides the better account.

Chapter 8

RANCÉ'S CONVERSION

CONVERSION is always inexplicable. We might be able to pinpoint certain specific events which appear to have precipitated it, but why such events should have such an impact on one person and no effect on another remains unaccountable. Nor can we explain why, in one case, conversion lasts a lifetime and, in another, no more than a few years. I am not, of course, speaking here of the sort of brief and inconsequential conversion that many of us experience in January after over eating in December.

In 1923 Robert Thouless, then Reader in Educational Psychology in the University of Cambridge, attempted an analysis of conversion in his study of the psychology of religion, and despite outdated terminology and recent advances, his comments remain of value.[1] He was certainly correct in pointing out that what appears to be the moment of conversion—in Rancé's case, the death of Madame de Montbazon in 1657—is not so much the beginning as the end of a long process of unconscious or subconscious incubation.[2] A seed sown in the mind has, for some inexplicable reason, taken root. In Rancé's case it might have been his ordination. We do not know. This seed then begins to grow over a period of time, but is repressed by the conscious mind since the latter has not the least desire to face up to it. And then, says Thouless,

---

1. Robert H. Thouless, *An Introduction to the Psychology of Religion* (Cambridge, 1961 [2nd ed. with a new preface]), chs. XIII-XIV (187-224).
2. Thouless has borrowed the terms from Carl Jung and William James.

> the struggle between a consciously develop-
> ing sentiment and a conscious opposition
> to it would be present to the mind as a pain-
> ful mental conflict. The time may come when
> the development of the complex has so far
> advanced that the resistance is no longer pow-
> erful enough to keep it repressed. There is
> then an outbreak into consciousness of a new
> mental construction which appears to intro-
> spection to have had no period of develop-
> ment in the mind. The system seems to
> have come to the mind from outside, so
> its outbreak has an apparently supernatural
> character.[3]

It is also possible that a combination of external circumstances
may combine to precipitate this dramatic 'outbreak into consciousness', but to date the conversion from this moment is
to confuse its birth with its conception.

Thouless also makes a useful distinction between moral/
intellectual conversion[4] and mystical conversion. For understanding Rancé, this is important. In the former case

> the repressed complex may be a desire to es-
> cape from excessive drinking or from sexual
> indulgence, or from any other kind of
> behaviour which is regarded as sinful. The
> interest behind the complex may be genuinely
> religious in character—a desire to be 'right
> with God'. This interest is often, however,
> supplemented or replaced by others—by a
> wish for the approval of other people or of
> oneself, etc.[5]

3. *Ibid.*, 188-189 (slightly abbreviated).
4. He actually distinguishes moral from intellectual conversion, but not very
successfully. There is a large degree of overlap.
5. *Ibid.*, 191-192 (slightly abbreviated).

We have no knowledge of Rancé's drinking, excessive or otherwise, though we may suspect him of sexual indulgence, but there is no doubt that after his conversion—or, more precisely, the culmination of his conversion—he continually sought approval and felt an urgent need to confirm that what he was doing was right. But his conversion was not 'mystical'. That is to say, it was not precipitated by any ecstatic experience such as certainly happened, for example, to Pascal. The *Mémorial* Pascal wore over his heart, however enigmatic, leaves us in no doubt on the matter:

> The year of grace 1654. Monday 23 November, feast of Saint Clement, pope and martyr, and of others in the Martyrology, vigil of the feast of Saint Chrysogonus, martyr, and others. From about half past ten in the evening to about half past twelve, Fire.[6]

But Rancé, so far as we know, never experienced such an extraordinary revelation. We may certainly call him a *spirituel*; we may not call him a mystic. His conversion was a wholly moral conversion, and this—as we shall see in our next chapter—was to have a marked effect on his conception of the monastic life.

Thouless's somewhat dated account, then, retains its usefulness, and does, I think, throw some light on Rancé's character and conversion. The more recent study by Chana Ullman does not, for our purposes, add a great deal to Thouless's earlier analysis.[7] She defines conversion as

> the process through which a self threatened by intense negative emotions experiences re-

6. See Cole's *Pascal* cited in Further Reading, 195.
7. Ullman, *The Transformed Self* (cited in Further Reading, 194). Ullman freely admits that some of her data 'may be more descriptive of trends in contemporary American society than of universal characteristics of religious beliefs' (192).

lief and happiness as a consequence of its new
attachment to a real or imagined figure.[8]

She draws attention to late adolescence and the twenties as
the most common period for conversion. She emphasizes the
impact of absent or dead parents. She speaks of conversion as
'a search for a perfect authority'[9] and suggests that the 'trans-
formation of the self' may be seen as 'the consequence of
cognitive restructuring and of a more or less deliberate search
for meaning'.[10] All this is indeed relevant to Rancé, but much
of what Ullman says is specific to twentieth-century America
and is more applicable to Thomas Merton than to the abbot
of la Trappe.

Professor Krailsheimer, the *doyen* of rancéan scholars, himself attempted to place Rancé's conversion in perspective in a
little volume published in 1980. Rancé appears there in the
company of a dozen other great converts, ranging from Saint
Paul to Merton,[11] and in his conclusion, Krailsheimer draws
our attention to a number of similarities in the lives of the
converts he discusses. Much of what he says would later be
echoed by Ullman, though she seems to have been unaware of
Krailsheimer's work. He begins with the 'commonplace that
conversion, of whatever kind, follows a period of emotional
confusion and disturbance, often but not always, accompanied by intellectual doubts'.[12] He mentions the 'marked
tension or imbalance in family relationships'[13]—Rancé lost

8. *Ibid.*, 191.

9. *Ibid.*, 193.

10. *Ibid.*, 194. Her conclusions are summarized on pages 191-195.

11. Krailsheimer, *Conversion* (cited in Further Reading, 194). Something similar, but without Krailsheimer's analysis, had been attempted sixty years earlier by Hugh F. Blunt in his *Great Penitents* (New York, 1921; repr. 1967). For
Rancé, see 51-75. The other penitents include John of God, Ignatius Loyola,
Camillus de Lellis, Silvio Pellico, Paul Féval, Hermann Cohen, J. B. Carpeaux,
François Coppée, Huysmans, and Verlaine. Blunt also wrote a companion
volume on women: *The Great Magdalens* (New York, 1928; repr. 1969).

12. Krailsheimer, *Conversion*, 154.

13. *Ibid.*

his elder brother when he was eleven and his mother when he was twelve[14]—and the importance of relationships outside the family (we inevitably think of Madame de Montbazon). He draws attention to their 'sense of isolation, of loneliness even in the midst of friends'[15] and their tendency to autocratic independence. Almost all of them—Rancé certainly—came out of their conversion experience with what the Puritans called the 'conviction of sin', and all were convinced that their conversion had been due to 'Christ's saving love for them'.[16]

> All in their different ways were unusually self-willed individuals who quite suddenly revolted against the insatiable demands of self and submitted to God's love revealed in Christ's suffering. In one way or another self-love, usually in the form of pride, was the sin of which they all became aware.[17]

For all of them, adds Krailsheimer, their conversion was an entirely private affair. That is to say, they were not converted by another person. 'The defeat, and surrender, of their pride and self-will was the outcome of a direct transaction between each of them and God',[18] though after their conversion all were eager to seek from others guidance and support. That Rancé sought such guidance and support is, as we have seen, not in doubt. Whether his conversion was as sudden and as direct as Krailsheimer suggests may be doubted: the hypothesis of 'unconscious incubation' is persuasive. But

---

14. But as Professor Krailsheimer points out, 'The pious paradigm of biographers is so inevitable, that it is hard to be sure how close relations were between Rancé and his mother, or whether he really was the favourite among her eight children' (Krailsheimer, *Rancé*, 5).

15. Krailsheimer, *Conversion*, 155.

16. *Ibid.*, 158.

17. *Ibid.*

18. *Ibid.*, 160.

Krailsheimer is certainly correct in pointing out that the conversion experience initiated a further period of travail. In all his examples, conversion was followed by a lengthy period—more than five years in the case of Rancé—in which the new converts were not at all sure of the course they should follow or even of the direction they should take. Madame de Montbazon died in 1657, but it was not until 1663 that Rancé could write to Reverend Mother Louise Rogier (another convert whom we shall meet again later) and say that

> I am quite sure you will be surprised when you learn of the resolution I have formed to devote the rest of my life to penitence in the habit and reform of Saint Bernard. For a number of years God led me by ways quite unknown to me, but finally, over the last eight or ten months, his mercy has inspired in me the intention I now have and I have begun to see more clearly than I did. I am now convinced that the state he wants me to adopt is the regular [monastic] life.[19]

In 1657 Rancé knew what to give up; he did not know exactly what to put in its place. Conversion, as Krailsheimer rightly says, 'implies total change, but of priorities, not of the components of life and personality'.[20] But once they had found what was, for them, their true path, all these great converts pursued it with superhuman—indeed supernatural—energy. We need only think of Rancé's enormous literary output (Larroque would say too enormous) and his utter devotion to la Trappe and his monks. This is not to say that his devotion was always rightly directed. God might have given Rancé discernment of souls in the realm of spiritual guidance; he had not given him the same discernment as a judge of character. Some of his decisions were unquestion-

19. Letter 630430.
20. Krailsheimer, *Conversion*, 162.

ably imprudent, but conversion bestows upon one neither perfection nor omniscience.

We must also remember two other factors. The first is that dramatic conversions in seventeenth-century France were, if not the rule, at least far from uncommon. The second is the point we made in our second chapter: that in *le grand siècle*, everything was *grand*. As to conversions, we could point to Louise de La Vallière, Madame de Montespan, Madame de La Sablière, Madame de Longueville, the princess Palatine, Madame de Guéméné, and the Reverend Mother Louise-Françoise Rogier who had such a profound effect on Rancé in his years of indecision.[21] Even Madame de Montbazon died, if not in the odour of sanctity, at least repentant in the arms of the Church.[22] Among the men we could mention Cardinal de Retz himself, Retz's father, père de Gondi, Étienne Le Camus, Nicolas Pinette, Henri Barillon, Madame de Montbazon's ill-used admirer Beaufort, the marquis de Laigues, Renaud de Sévigné, and a host of others.[23] In our cynical day and age, when things are seen as a series of greys, the strident black-and-white mentality of seventeenth-century France is difficult, perhaps impossible, to appreciate; but there is no reason to believe that the conversions were not genuine. Sometimes—Retz is a good example[24]—doubts were expressed even by their contemporaries, but those who have not been converted generally have difficulty in understanding those who have:

> When [Retz] made himself cardinal by intrigues, factions and turmoils, he was accused of being an ambitious man who had sacrificed public interest, conscience, and religion to his

21. Some of their tales are told, charmingly if unreliably, in Blunt's *Great Magdalens*.
22. See n. 72 below.
23. See n. 80 below.
24. For an excellent discussion of Retz's conversion, see Salmon, *Cardinal de Retz* (cited in Further Reading, 196), ch. 14 (360-385).

own fortunes. When he abandoned the cares
of earth for those of heaven, when the allure
of another life led him to regard the glories of
this one as no more than chimaeras, they said
his head was turned, and they interpreted
what Christians consider the highest virtue
to be shameful weakness.[25]

The whole phenomenon, in fact, must be seen as part of that
greater phenomenon which brought to seventeenth-century
France an astonishing burgeoning of mysticism and all those
developments so splendidly (though not impartially) described by Ronald Knox in his study of 'enthusiasm'.[26] For-
tunately, it is not our business here to explain it.

All these penitents were public penitents. That was how
things were done in *le grand siècle*. When that most moral of
the king's mistresses, Louise de La Vallière, was about to join
the Carmelites, she threw herself at the queen's feet, maintaining (according to a contemporary report) that since her
offences had been public, it was fitting that her penitence
should likewise be public. Of all these public penitents, Rancé
was one of the best known, and, if we are to believe Daniel de
Larroque, his conversion was precipitated by the sudden death
of his mistress, Madame de Montbazon, and its gruesome
sequel.[27] But who was Madame de Montbazon, how did she
die, and how accurate is Larroque's version of the events?

Marie d'Avaugour de Bretagne was born about 1612[28] as
the eldest of eight sisters. None of the others married. Three
entered religion: two of them became abbesses and the third,

25. Charles de Saint-Denis, sieur de Saint-Évremond, 'Réflexions sur la religion', in *Saint-Évremond, Œuvres en prose*, ed. René Ternois (Paris, 1966) 3:364
(with a good accompanying note).
26. Ronald A. Knox, *Enthusiasm. A Chapter in the History of Religion* (Oxford,
1950).
27. See n. 63 below.
28. It might have been as early as 1610: see Gédéon Tallemant des Réaux,
Historiettes, ed. Antoine Adam (Paris, 1970) 2:1085, nn. 1 and 4.

Catherine-Françoise d'Avaugour de Bretagne, Mademoiselle de Vertus, spent her last twenty years at Port-Royal.[29] The young Marie was educated by nuns—Louis Bossebœuf calls her 'a radiant flower blooming in the shadow of the convent'[30]—and, in these early years, appears to have shown a marked attraction for religion. So much so, in fact, that for a while she actually entered the cloister and her elderly husband, the duc de Rohan, used to call her *sa religieuse*.[31]

On 15 March 1628, when she was sixteen or a little older, she married Hercule de Rohan, duc de Montbazon, who was more than forty years her senior. It was his second marriage. The duke was of a noble family and in 1598 had acquired a country seat at Couzières,[32] not far from what, later, would be Rancé's estate at Véretz. Hercule was the second son of Louis de Rohan VI, prince de Guéméné, comte de Montbazon, baron de La Haye, and his wife Léonore de Rohan, dame du Verger, and came into his inheritance on the death of his elder brother. The duke's first marriage had been to Madeleine de Lenoncourt by whom he had two children, Louis and Marie. Marie, in due course, married the duc de Luynes and then, on the duke's death, Claude de Lorraine, duc de Chevreuse. It is as Madame de Chevreuse that she is best known.[33] She was a charming and veteran intriguer, but quite untrustworthy, for she changed her opinions with the wind. 'I have never seen anyone but her', said Cardinal de Retz, 'in whom vivacity took the place of judgement.'[34] According to the cardinal (who was not unopinionated), Madame de Chevreuse's view was that her only duty was to please her lover of the moment.[35]

When Hercule de Rohan was in his sixties his first wife,

29. On these sisters, see *ibid.*, 1083, n. 12 and Krailsheimer, *Rancé*, 280-288.

30. Bossebœuf, *Le Chateau de Véretz* (cited in Further Reading, 195) 180.

31. Tallemant des Réaux, *Historiettes*, 2:217.

32. Described with illustrations in Bossebœuf, *Chateau de Véretz*, 167-169.

33. See (in French) Victor Cousin, *Madame de Chevreuse* (Paris, 1869 [5th ed.]) and (in English) Michael Prawdin, *Marie de Rohan, Duchesse de Chevreuse* (London, 1971).

34. Cardinal de Retz, *Mémoires*, ed. Maurice Allem (Paris, 1956) 156.

35. *Ibid.*

Madeleine de Lenoncourt, died, but he lost no time in marrying again, this time the young Marie de Bretagne. Marie thus became the step-mother of a considerably older step-daughter. There was little love lost between them.

The second Madame de Montbazon bore her husband three children: a son, François de Rohan-Montbazon, prince de Soubise (who would become a distinguished soldier); and two daughters, Marie-Éléonore and Anne. Marie-Éléonore became a nun and abbess; Anne married Louis-Charles d'Albert, duc de Luynes.[36] Throughout his life Rancé remained in contact with all of them, especially with the prince (who was not especially devout), to whom he wrote at least two letters, both emphasizing the importance of conversion and salvation.[37]

That Madame de Montbazon was attractive to men cannot be doubted. Her portraits rarely do her justice, but contemporary accounts liken her to a perfectly proportioned classical statue, even if (according to the salacious account of Tallemant des Réaux) she had a tendency to put on weight, her nose was too prominent, and her mouth a little too sunken. Her breasts, he adds lubriciously, were white and firm, but half as big again as they should have been, and she had difficulty in concealing them.[38] She had very white skin and very black hair, and was tall for a woman—Tallemant went so far as to call her a colossus[39]—but carried herself with majestic dignity. Even after she had passed the age of forty she remained one of the great beauties of the court,[40] and she was still beautiful on her deathbed.[41] She herself had said that 'when a woman reaches thirty, she's good for nothing. Person-

36. See Bossebœuf, *Chateau de Véretz*, 174-176.
37. Letters 770328 and 810421.
38. Tallemant des Réaux, *Historiettes*, 2:217.
39. *Ibid.*
40. *Mémoires de madame de Motteville*, in *Collection des mémoires relatifs à l'histoire de France*, ed. Claude-Bernard and Alexandre Petitot (Paris, 1819-1829), ser. II, vol. 38, 220.
41. See the verse by Jean Loret reproduced in Tallemant des Réaux, *Historiettes*, 2:1087, n. 2.

ally, when I get there, I hope someone throws me in a river'.[42] She did, in fact, fall in a river in her early forties—we shall tell the tale in due course—but happily survived the ordeal.

She was also arrogant, selfish, immoral, indiscreet, and vindictive. On one occasion, in a long-lasting quarrel with Madame de Longueville (which we shall discuss in a moment), she threatened to have the latter's lover, the moralist La Rochefoucauld, castrated and his excised organs presented to Madame de Longueville on a silver platter.[43] Cardinal de Retz, whom she outmanoeuvred in his desire to enjoy her opulent favours, remarked that 'she loved only her own pleasure and, above and beyond her pleasure, her own interests. I have never seen anyone who preserved in vice so little respect for virtue'.[44] Her earlier attraction to the religious life seems not to have endured, for one of her numerous lovers, the naive, vain, and remarkably faithful duc de Beaufort, whom she referred to as an impotent simpleton,[45] was less disturbed by her amours than by the fact that she ate meat on Fridays.[46]

Before her liaison with Beaufort, she had been the long-time mistress of Henri II d'Orléans, duc de Longueville, and when the duke left her to marry the lovely and distinguished Anne-Geneviève de Bourbon-Condé, Madame de Montbazon was—to say the least—not pleased. The fact that it was the duke's second marriage and that his new wife (twenty-four years his junior) was indifferent to him was irrelevant. Madame de Montbazon felt herself slighted and determined to have her revenge. Nor was the situation helped by the fact that Madame de Longueville was also one of the beauties of the court and had a 'a certain indescribable languor of manner [which] made talking with her seem like the dream of a lotus-eater'.[47] She was more like an angel than a woman, said

---

42. Emmanuel de Lerne, 'Madame de Montbazon', *L'Artiste*, Sér. V, 12 (1854) 8, quoting Tallemant des Réaux, *Historiettes*, 2:217.
43. See Salmon, *Cardinal de Retz*, 139.
44. Retz, *Mémoires*, 157.
45. *Ibid.*, 315.
46. *Ibid.*

Madame de Motteville,[48] and an attack of smallpox in autumn 1642 had not affected her beauty. Both women were witty in an age when wit was more important than content, and if Madame de Longueville's conversation was more subtle and intelligent, Madame de Montbazon's was more venomous and caustic.

For Madame de Montbazon, an opportunity to oust Madame de Longueville appeared to present itself in 1643, when, at a certain *salon*, two sexually compromising letters were found. They were read out loud, much to the amusement of the company, and there was much speculation as to who had written them. Madame de Montbazon pretended to recognize the handwriting of Madame de Longueville, and, for a time, she rejoiced in the ensuing scandal. But her actions were foolish and ill-judged. The letters had actually been written by a Madame de Fouquerolles to the marquis de Maulevrier and proving this was not difficult. The handwriting was nothing like that of Madame de Longueville. The affair came to the ears of the queen who called for a retraction and public apology, and Madame de Montbazon had no choice but to rescind her accusations. But according to Madame de Motteville, her retraction was wholly insincere. The text had been diplomatically composed by Mazarin in words which would be acceptable to both parties and pinned to the back of her fan. She then further aggravated the situation by appearing at a garden party given by her step-daughter, Madame de Chevreuse, a function from which the queen had expressly forbidden her.[49] The whole business had been disastrous from the start and on 22 August 1642 Madame de Montbazon was expelled from court: a fate, save for the weather, equivalent to exile in Siberia.

Beaufort, her long-time admirer, rallied to her cause, but the more social aspects of the affair now became deeply enmeshed in politics, more precisely in the bitter feud between

47. Perkins, *France Under Mazarin* (cited in Further Reading, 196) 1:289.
48. *Ibid.*
49. *Mémoires de madame de Motteville*, 44; Cousin, *Madame de Chevreuse*, 242-243.

cardinals Mazarin and de Retz and the events leading up to the First Fronde.[50] Both Beaufort and Madame de Montbazon were violently opposed to Mazarin and all that he stood for, and both belonged to the inner circle of a group of dissidents called the *Importants* (a disparaging name bestowed on them by their opponents), one of four political parties striving for power between 1643 and 1653.[51] Now, as part of their plot to gain power, the *Importants* determined to eliminate Mazarin completely and a plan was hatched to assassinate him in his carriage.[52] That Madame de Montbazon was implicated in the plot is not in doubt, but the plan came to nothing and Beaufort was arrested and imprisoned. His place was taken by the duc de Guise, who declared his love for Madame de Montbazon and allied himself with her against Madame de Longueville. The intrigues continued through 1643 and 1644, and even when Madame de Montbazon was allowed to return to court, she foolishly continued in her opposition to Mazarin, whose power, by now, was solidly established.

She was still intriguing in 1649 when another opportunity arose to attack Madame de Longueville. The matter concerned a point of court precedence—specifically, who had the right to use a footstool or *tabouret* in the presence of the queen—and in a court whose life-blood was etiquette and precedence, this was a question of major importance. In the face of strong opposition, Madame de Longueville was seeking to enhance the position of her lover, La Rochefoucauld, by arranging for his wife to be accorded this honour, but there was strong opposition. Madame de Montbazon gleefully joined the formidable coterie of opponents (all of whom loathed Madame de Longueville), but their plans were thwarted yet again by Mazarin, who engineered an uneasy truce. Madame de

50. We discussed the matter briefly in Chapter Two. The First Fronde, the Fronde of the Parlement, lasted from 1648 to 1649 and was precipitated by a new plan for raising money proposed by Anne of Austria, mother of and regent for Louis XIV, and Cardinal Mazarin.
51. The others were the *Petits-Maîtres*, the *Frondeurs*, and the *Mazarins*.
52. For the details, see Perkins, *France Under Mazarin*, 1:291-293.

Longueville did not get her *tabouret*, but neither did she lose her position, and Madame de Montbazon's continued opposition to Mazarin and continued support for Retz was doomed.[53]

By November 1652, Retz was approaching the lowest ebb of his fortunes—by December he would be in prison—and Madame de Montbazon found it expedient to slip quietly out of Paris and retreat for a while to the country. The Second Fronde dwindled out in 1653 and the duc de Montbazon died at Couzières in October of the following year. Three years later, in 1657, the now widowed Madame de Montbazon was able to return to Paris, and still looked no more than twenty-five. Indeed, her black widow's weeds simply added to her attractiveness.[54] But her hopes of being received back into the queen's favour were doomed to disappointment, and her own life—though she did not know it—was nearing its end. A few months earlier, Larroque tells us, she had been in an accident. As she was crossing a bridge in her carriage, it had collapsed and thrown her into the river. For some time she was thought to have drowned and an anonymous *femme d'esprit* had gone so far as to compose an amusing epitaph.[55] But having escaped one brush with death, she could not escape another. In April 1657 she contracted *la rougeole*, which could have been either measles or scarlet fever (no doctor at the time could have distinguished between them), complications set in, and a few days later she was dead.

We cannot say that her life had been marked by any great accomplishments, save in the sexual field. Tallemant des Réaux reproduces an obscene street-song which satirizes both her size and her carnal appetites.[56] But she was an untrustworthy ally, a capricious lover, an indiscreet associate, and an unsuc-

---

53. See Salmon, *Cardinal de Retz*, 138-139. For details one must consult the contemporary memoirs.
54. Lerne, 'Madame de Montbazon', 8.
55. Daniel de Larroque, *Les véritables motifs de la conversion de l'abbé de la Trappe, avec quelques réflexions sur sa vie et sur ses écrits* (Cologne, 1685) 25-26.
56. Tallemant des Réaux, *Historiettes*, 2:220. The song, he says 'n'est pas trop honneste, mais il est plaisant'.

cessful intriguer. Yet we cannot blame her for using her voluptuous charms to gain the power and wealth she sought. For a woman at court, there was, effectively, no other way. As James Perkins has said, the women 'were less scrupulous even than the men as to the means by which they reached their ends',[57] and 'most of the intrigues and phases of the Fronde turned upon amours, and roundelays and pasquinades were its diplomatic correspondence'.[58] 'Women', said Madame de Motteville, 'are usually at the bottom of all State upheavals; and wars, which ruin kingdoms and empires, hardly ever occur except as a result of their beauty or their malice.'[59]

What, then, was the intelligent, ordained, and much younger Armand-Jean de Rancé doing in the company of this beautiful and worldly woman? The answer is simple. He loved her. When they first met is unknown. It could not have been earlier than 1637 when his father bought the château of Véretz (Rancé was eleven at the time), but how their relationship progressed is likewise unknown. It is not difficult to see how a pubescent boy would have sexual fantasies about a voluptuous woman in her twenties (Madame de Montbazon was at least fourteen years older than Rancé); it is more difficult to appreciate the attraction going the other way. A number of writers, therefore, have asserted that their relationship was entirely platonic and that Rancé (like Beaufort, according to Retz) loved only her soul.[60] I doubt it. At Véretz, Rancé had built for her an out-of-the-way pavilion, discreetly hidden among the oaks, and had given her the key.[61] It is improbable that they met there only for the pleasures of stimulating conversation. On the other hand, there is no evidence whatever that he was involved in her political intrigues. He would certainly have known of them and, being anti-Mazarin him-

57. Perkins, *France Under Mazarin*, 1:291.
58. *Ibid.*, 2:60.
59. Quoted in Geoffrey F. Hall, *Moths Round the Flame. Studies of Charmers and Intriguers* (New York, 1935; repr. 1969) 58.
60. Retz, *Mémoires*, 315.
61. Lerne, 'Madame de Montbazon', 8.

self, might well have approved, but his name never appears as
a political schemer. But who seduced whom, and if, and how,
and when, are all alike unknown and, indeed, irrelevant. There
is not the least doubt that Rancé was devoted to the duchess—Professor Krailsheimer speaks of his 'infatuation' with
her[62]—and there is not the least doubt that he was devas-
tated by her sudden and unexpected death. To the details of
that death we must now turn.

According to Larroque, Rancé was in the country at the
time—that is to say, at Véretz—and his servants, who had
heard of the duchess's death and knew of his affection for her,
took care to hide it from him. And so, on his return to Paris,

> he went straight up to the duchess's chamber
> which he had permission to enter at any time,
> but instead of the delights he had anticipated,
> the first thing he saw was her coffin. That it
> awaited his mistress was obvious, since he
> was confronted with the sight of her bloody
> head which, by chance, had rolled from under
> a cloth which had been carelessly thrown over
> it. It had been severed from the body at the
> neck so as to avoid the need to make a new
> and longer coffin. The one that had been made
> had been so poorly measured that it was six
> inches too short.[63]

I have shown elsewhere that, as it stands, this story is a
fabrication,[64] and so far as we know, Larroque was the first to
put it in print. It is based, however, on two facts. The first is

62. Krailsheimer, *Legacy*, 19: 'That he was infatuated with her is highly probable, that he was socially dependent on her virtually certain, but that they
had been lovers at any time remains pure conjecture.'
63. Larroque, *Véritables motifs*, 27-28.
64. David N. Bell, 'Daniel de Larroque, Armand-Jean de Rancé, and the Head
of Madame de Montbazon', cited in Further Reading, 196.

that Madame de Montbazon was indeed taller than most women (it will be remembered that Tallemant des Réaux called her *un colosse*), and secondly that her body appears to have been subjected to an autopsy. This is clearly implied by Saint-Simon,[65] and given her sudden death at a comparatively young age it is understandable. But at that time, the removal of the head was a standard accompaniment to the opening of the body, and autopsies were regularly performed in the home of the deceased.[66] It is almost certain, then, that the head of Madame de Montbazon was indeed removed after her death, and it is quite possible that, by some hideous mischance, Rancé did indeed see the eviscerated and decapitated body of the woman he loved. But Larroque's tale of the incompetent undertakers may safely be dismissed.

It seems, then, that although Larroque did not invent the story of the severed head, he certainly elaborated it. Also, as we have said, he seems to have been the first to put it into print and, once printed, the bizarre tale had an extraordinary tenacity. But bizarre though it was, the story was insufficiently bizarre for Chateaubriand who, in his *Vie de Rancé* (which we discussed in Chapter One), has Rancé come into possession of the detached skull of the duchess and take it with him to la Trappe where it was solemnly handed down to each of his successors. It is alleged to be the very skull that we see in the great portrait of Rancé painted by Hyacinthe Rigaud.[67]

But what did Rancé himself say about the story? In 1698, when he had only two more years to live, his friend and admirer, the duc de Saint-Simon, asked him about it directly. His version of the tale and Rancé's reply deserve to be quoted in full, for the english translations at present available are all incomplete.

---

65. See n. 72 below. René Rapin has a variant of the tale in which the head has been removed by the duchess's surgeon so that the body could be embalmed more easily: *Mémoires du P. René Rapin*, ed. Léon Aubineau (Paris, 1865) 2:482.
66. The evidence is presented in Bell, 'Daniel de Larroque, Armand-Jean de Rancé, and the Head of Madame de Montbazon'.
67. For details, see *ibid*. For Rigaud's portrait, reproduced as the frontispiece to this book, see Further Reading to the Introduction to this study.

It has been said (wrote Saint-Simon) that the *abbé* de Rancé (now the celebrated abbot of la Trappe) was deeply in love with Madame de Montbazon and much entertained by her. [On one occasion] he left her in Paris in the best of health to spend some time in the country [at Véretz], but when he heard she had fallen ill, he rushed back and went straight to her chamber. The first thing he saw was her head which the surgeons had removed when they opened her body [for the autopsy]. Until that moment he had not known of her death, and the shock and horror of the sight, combined with the grief it caused for a passionate and [hitherto] happy man, led to his conversion, his retreat from the world, the Order of Saint Bernard, and the reform [of la Trappe].

There is nothing true in this, save only the events [i.e. the autopsy] which gave rise to the fiction. I frankly questioned Monsieur de la Trappe on the matter—not crudely about his love for her, much less about its out-come—but about the facts, and this is what I learned.

He was indeed one of her close friends and had not left the Hôtel de Montbazon.[68] He was, in fact, friends with all the personalities involved in the Fronde: M. de Châteauneuf,[69] Mme de Chevreuse, M. de Montrésor,[70] and the whole group that then called themselves

68. The Montbazon's town-house was located on the rue de Béthisy which has now disappeared. It lay beneath the present rue de Rivoli which runs from the Place de la Concorde, past the Tuileries and the Louvre, as far as the rue Saint-Antoine which connects it with the Place de la Bastille.

69. Charles de L'Aubespine, marquis de Châteauneuf (Saint-Simon's great-uncle).

70. Claude de Bourdeilles, comte de Montrésor.

the *Importants*—especially M. de Beaufort, with whom he had often gone hunting, and Cardinal de Retz, with whom he enjoyed the closest friendship until the latter's death [in 1679]. Madame de Montbazon died just a few days after contracting *la rougeole*. M. de Rancé was at her side and never left her. He saw her receive the sacraments and was present [in the house] at her death.[71] The truth is that he was already being pushed and pulled between God and the world and had been thinking for some time of going into retreat. The impact of her sudden death on his heart and mind convinced him to carry out his intention. Shortly afterwards he went to his country house at Véretz and began his withdrawal from the world.[72]

There is no reason to disbelieve this account, and I think we may take it as an accurate report of a tragic occurrence. Rancé's only allusion to the events comes in a curious letter written in July 1682 to Mademoiselle de Goëllo (Anne d'Avaugour de Bretagne), Madame de Montbazon's younger sister. 'Your letter has given me cause for much reflexion', he wrote, 'and all the events of the past have come crowding back into my memory.'[73] Other than that, we have only the unique and not particularly helpful letter written to the comtesse de La Fayette in either October or November 1686.[74] The countess had almost certainly been reading Larroque's

71. This is how we must read '*présent à sa mort*'. Other evidence, considered in my 'Daniel de Larroque, Armand-Jean de Rancé, and the Head of Madame de Montbazon', indicates that Rancé was not actually at the duchess's bedside when she died.
72. Louis de Rouvroy, duc de Saint-Simon, *Mémoires (1691-1723). Additions au Journal de Dangeau*, ed. Yves Coirault (Paris, 1983) 1:521-522.
73. Letter 820723. Krailsheimer provides a complete english translation.
74. Letter 861022 in the english version; Letter 861122 in the french.

Véritables motifs which had been published just a year earlier
and, with more curiosity than tact, had written to Rancé
asking him what had really led him to withdraw from the
world. That Rancé even replied is surprising, but despite
portentous admonitions that what he says is to be shared
with no one, what he does say is not especially revealing.

He begins the long letter by saying that even though he
did not wholly neglect the graces which God had given him
while he was in the world, and even though he tried not to
live uselessly, he nevertheless led a very lively life. Indeed, if
he had devoted to heavenly things the time and effort he had
devoted to those of earth, he would be *'dans les airs comme les
aigles'*, 'like an eagle in the sky'. As to the precise motives
that led him to leave the world, 'I will simply say that I left
it[75] because I did not find in it what I sought'. It did not offer
him the peace he wanted, and that was just as well, for if it
had he might have looked no further. Over time the things he
had previously found so pleasant and enjoyable ceased to please
him. They appeared empty and meaningless, and he began to
view them with distaste. But since he had always preserved
his faith and trust in God, he hoped that God would come to
him and fill the great void which had been left in his heart by
his intention to separate himself from the world.

In his trouble and confusion of spirit, he retired to his
country estate at Véretz, not knowing what to do. He applied
himself to reading the type of books for which he once had no
taste; he struggled with the truths they contained; he prayed.
And eventually his eyes were opened, he let himself go in the
direction God was urging him, and 'from that moment I resolved to be as much for God as I had been for the world'.

But having made his decision, he now found himself 'in a
foreign country with neither pilot nor guide'. He passed a
number of months in confusion and disquiet, uncertain of
the path he should take. But over this period he became con-

---

75. Reading *laissai*, as on page 403 of the french edition of Letter 861122,
instead of *haïssais* in Krailsheimer, *Rancé*, 291.

vinced that his decision was right, and God gave him such powerful protection that he had no difficulty in overcoming his old habits. His first idea was to lead a simple life in his country retreat at Véretz, but God demanded more. The pleasant and peaceful life he envisaged was in no way appropriate for a man who had spent such a wild youth in the world.

Some of his friends now tried to make him change his mind, but rather than sowing doubts, his arguments with them served only to convince him that God had led him to the right decision. And so, finally,

> I saw clearly that it was God's will that I should cut myself off from all dealings with the world and, in a strict and rigorous solitude, I embraced the state in which I now am and in which I await with a keen hope the fulfilment of the promises which God has made to those who give up all things for love of him. Indeed, I may say from the peace and tranquillity I now enjoy that I have already been paid a hundredfold for all those things I could abandon.

Why he has told Madame de La Fayette all these details Rancé does not know—he has never told them to anyone else—but he trusts that she will keep them as 'an inviolable secret', which she did not.

This long letter mentions no names, neither those of his friends who sought to dissuade him from the path he had chosen, nor those whom he consulted for spiritual guidance. And it certainly makes no mention of Madame de Montbazon. It tells us, in fact, little that we do not already know: that Rancé had gradually been recognizing the vanity and emptiness of the life he had hitherto enjoyed, that he was seeking a peace which the world could not give, and that his progress from a young man about town who loved hunting and Madame de Montbazon to a cistercian monk and abbot was long, confusing, and difficult.

What, then, can we say about the death of Madame de Montbazon and its impact on Rancé? On the one hand, we may certainly dismiss most of Larroque's account. On the other, there can be no doubt that the death of the duchess had a profound effect. It was not the only tragedy which Rancé suffered at the time,[76] but it must surely have been the most shattering. Rancé's disillusionment with the world, and especially the world of scandals, intrigues, *affaires, liaisons dangereuses*, political manoeuvring, power grabbing, bedroom diplomacy, and generalized corruption assuredly began before 1657, but the tragic death of the woman he loved appears to have brought it all to a head. She herself had been no stranger to the scandals, intrigues, and so on, but save for her sexual conquests, she had not been particularly successful in any of them. She had been saved from death once, but her lucky escape had had no effect on her conduct. In her, Rancé could see the society of his times epitomized, and in her failure to gain her ends, he might also have seen the failure of that society. But true love is ultimately unaffected by the imperfections of the beloved, and the events which occurred on 28 April 1657 in an elegant house on the rue de Béthisy shook Rancé to the core. His early biographers seem to indicate that he suffered some sort of nervous breakdown, and there can be no doubt that in the months following the death of the duchess, he was wholly vulnerable. As we said earlier, he had determined to renounce the world, but had little idea what to put in its place.

It is here that we must draw attention to those whom he consulted on the question and who, when he was perhaps most susceptible to suggestion, pointed him in the direction which would ultimately lead to the solitude and silence of la Trappe. Of whom are we speaking here? Of Mother Louise Rogier of the convent of the Visitation at Tours, the Oratorians Claude Séguenot, Père Bouchard, and Pierre de Monchy, and

76. See Krailsheimer, *Rancé*, 8-10.

Arnauld d'Andilly of Port-Royal.[77] All were Jansenist either by declaration or sympathy, and the grace of conversion, in a spiritual sense, lies at the heart of Jansenism. But Mother Louise was more than that. For some years she had been the official mistress of Gaston d'Orléans, but by November 1639 he had tired of her. The situation was not helped by the fact that Louise had not restricted her favours to Gaston alone. By this time, however, she was pregnant, and in 1640 she bore a son. At about that time she, too, underwent a monumental conversion, decided to enter religion, and was professed at the convent of the Visitation in Tours in 1644. Eight years later she was superior, a position to which she was elected three times, and she spent more than sixty years in the cloister.[78] As for her son, he was unofficially adopted by Gaston's daughter. She arranged for him to be given the title of the comte de Charny, and he enjoyed a successful career as a soldier.

It was to Mother Louise, herself a convert and penitent, that Rancé went to seek guidance in the years following the death of Madame de Montbazon, and an examination of their numerous letters leaves us in no doubt of her formative influence on him. No convert is ever converted to mediocrity—the convert easily becomes the fanatic—and the advice given by a once worldly woman who had wholly abandoned the world to a once worldly *abbé* who was thinking of abandoning it can only have fallen on receptive ears. That Rancé over-exaggerated his worldly vices is probable, but that too is the way of converts. Even if he and Madame de Montbazon had enjoyed each other's bed and body as well as each other's company and conversation, it would not have mattered a great deal. *Affaires* were regarded lightly at the time, and provided one went to confession, no one worried about going to hell because of them. But converts look back on their past lives only with loathing. Molehills become mountains, and when

---

77. Krailsheimer provides details which we need not reproduce here.
78. On Mère Louise Rogier, see the excellent account in Krailsheimer, *Rancé*, 200-209.

Rancé saw himself as a man 'condemned to hell by the number and seriousness of his sins'[79], that, indeed, is what he believed. But there is, in fact, no reason whatever to assume that he was a rake, debauchee, lecher, or libertine. He may have been a somewhat immoral hedonist—most of us are to some extent—but it is infinitely unlikely that he was licentious, lustful, dissolute, and degenerate. He enjoyed the conversation and the company of the *salons*, he may well have enjoyed Madame de Montbazon, and he adored riding, but that is scarcely sufficient to make him a hardened and debauched sinner. Yet all that is irrelevant. Rancé was a convert and converts are not normal people. They have undergone something which most of us have never experienced, and their whole outlook is, of necessity, tempered by it. We may remember, too, that even after the travail of his conversion, he remained in contact with other notable and public converts: not only Cardinal de Retz, but Étienne Le Camus, Nicolas Pinette, Henri Barillon, the comte de Tréville, the comte de Brancas, the comte Du Charmel, Jean-Baptiste de Santeul, Eustache de Beaufort, Louis de Lascaris d'Urfé, Madame de La Sablière, Madame de Longueville, Madame de Saint-Loup, Mademoiselle Marie-Sylvie de La Trémouille, the marquise d'Alègre, Reverend Mother Marie-Françoise de Harlay, and Madame de La Vallière herself.[80] And there are yet others. All were converts; and if they differed in that from which they had been converted, they did not differ much in the devout piety to which they were converted. In two cases at least— the comte de Tréville and Henri Barillon—their conversions, like that of Rancé, had been associated with the sudden deaths of young, or comparatively young, women. Indeed, the case of the comte de Tréville is an almost exact parallel to that of Rancé.

Rancé's conversion, a conversion continually revitalized by his association with other converts, is fundamental to his spiri-

---

79. Letter 640630 quoted in Chapter Four, n. 13.
80. All are listed in the index to Krailsheimer's *Letters*.

tuality. What we might call 'conversion spirituality' is never lukewarm or half-hearted. It cannot be. And although it is logical, it is not (in the eyes of most people) reasonable. Indeed, it is its logic which is its problem. Rancé's logic is inexorable. You have two choices, God or the world. You cannot have both. If you choose the former you must reject the latter. If you reject the latter, you reject it completely, and from then on you are dead to the world. But dead means dead, not just moribund, and the only things you have left which you can call your own are your sins. This is an absolutist spirituality from an absolutist age, and it is not surprising that the few who read *De la sainteté et des devoirs de la vie monastique* in our politically correct twenty-first century find much with which they can happily disagree. So let us turn to the work itself. Let us examine Rancé's teaching in his *magnum opus* and see how it reflects his conversion, his character, his times, and his ideals.

FURTHER READING

The study of the psychology of religious conversion dates back to the last years of the nineteenth century with the publication in 1896 of James H. Leuba's *Studies in the Psychology of Religious Phenomena*. For this present chapter (which is not intended to be a study of conversion in general) I have restricted myself to the ideas in three books ranging in date from 1923 to 1989: (1) Robert H. Thouless, *An Introduction to the Psychology of Religion* (Cambridge, 1923, 1924 [2nd ed.], 1961 [2nd ed. with a new preface]), chs. XIII-XIV (187-224); (2) Alban J. Krailsheimer, *Conversion* (London, 1980), which includes, apart from Rancé (ch. 5 [70-81]), discussions of Augustine, Francis of Assisi, Martin Luther, Ignatius Loyola, Pascal, John Bunyan, William Booth, Charles de Foucauld, Edith Stein, and Simone Weil; and (3) Chana Ullman, *The Transformed Self. The Psychology of Religious Conversion* (New York-London, 1989), which contains a bibliography on pages 215-221. Those interested in pursuing the question further may refer to the studies by Wilfrid L. Jones (1937), Owen Brandon (1960), Joe E. Barnhart (1981), Eugene V. Gallagher (1990), Virgil B. Gillespie (1991), and Lewis R. Rambo (1993). Much could be said on this important question, but this is not the place to say it.

Religious conversion in seventeenth-century France is a separate study in its own right. As Professor Krailsheimer has said, 'the whole question of conversion in the seventeenth century is extremely complex and some of the examples quoted in the course of this book (Mme de la Vallière, Pinette, Henri Barillon, Beaufort) are sufficiently varied to make one wary of simple explanations' (Krailsheimer, *Rancé*, xv). A number of other examples are cited in the course of this chapter and the question cannot be separated from the political, social, economic, religious, and socio-psychological climate of the period. It is impossible here to present bibliographies for all the individual converts, but a useful beginning is provided by Krailsheimer in the section 'Amis et correspondants de

Rancé' in the revised french translation of his *Armand-Jean de Rancé, abbé de la Trappe 1626-1700* (Paris, 2000) 425-427.

For a stimulating discussion of Pascal's *Mémorial*, with photographs of the original and a parchment copy, see John R. Cole, *Pascal. The Man and His Two Loves* (New York-London, 1995), chs. 8-9 (104-141).

Our primary sources for the life of Madame de Montbazon are contemporary memoirs and similar material, especially the memoirs of René Rapin, Saint-Simon, Cardinal de Retz, Madame de Motteville, and Guy Joly, and the *Historiettes* of Tallemant des Réaux. The memoirs of Retz and part of the memoirs of Saint-Simon and Madame de Motteville are available in english translation. Also available in English is Tallemant des Réaux's *historiette* of Madame de Montbazon in *Miniature Portraits by Gédéon Tallemant sieur des Réaux*, tr. Hamish Miles (New York, 1926) 54-57. In secondary sources, useful (though not always entirely accurate) information is provided by Louis A. Bossebœuf, *Le Chateau de Véretz: son histoire et ses souvenirs* (Tours, 1903), ch. X (167-199) and Rancé's biographers. Emmanuel de Lerne's 'Madame de Montbazon', *L'Artiste*, Sér. V, 12 (1854) 4-9, includes some reliable data in section III (6-7), though he provides no source references, but his section IV is heavily dependent on Daniel de Larroque. The author also has Rancé dying ten months too soon. Much of the material in Henri Bremond's 'Madame de Montbazon et la conversion de Rancé', *Revue de Paris*, 36th year, vol. 2 (1929) 5-48 can be found in his *The Thundering Abbot. Armand de Rancé, Reformer of La Trappe*, tr. Francis J. Sheed (London, 1930) 27-43. His discussion is important, but must be read with a critical eye. In English, the most complete account is that which appears in the present chapter.

The cause of the duchess's death appears to have been either measles or scarlet fever (*la rougeole*). It is consistently cited as such in contemporary or almost contemporary sources, though Larroque speaks of smallpox (*Véritables motifs*, 26) which is certainly wrong. Krailsheimer, *Rancé*, 10, and those who follow him usually cite scarlet fever, but measles and scarlet fever were not differentiated until the late seventeenth century. *La rougeole* could describe either, and it is impossible to be certain which of the two was the mediate or immediate cause of death. Both diseases were more serious in the seventeenth century than they are today. For a detailed discussion of the duchess's death and the events surrounding it, see my 'Daniel de Larroque, Armand-Jean de Rancé, and the Head of Madame de Montbazon', *Cîteaux: Commentarii cistercienses* 53 (2002) 305-331, which also contains a full account of the origins, development, and persistence of the story of the severed head.

For the political events in which Madame de Montbazon was so deeply (and unsuccessfully) involved (the Retz/Mazarin conflict and the complicated intrigues of the First and Second Fronde), see (in English) the excellent study by John H. M. Salmon, *Cardinal de Retz. The Anatomy of a Conspirator* (New York, 1970), especially Salmon's index, 439-440. The old two-volume work by James B. Perkins, *France Under Mazarin with a Review of the Administration of Richelieu* (New York-London, 1886 [2nd ed.]) still contains a wealth of detail otherwise unavailable in English. Salmon's study contains a bibliography and there is a great deal of material in French. See also Further Reading to Chapter Two.

The only comprehensive history of the château of Véretz remains Louis Bossebœuf's *Le Chateau de Véretz*, cited above.

Chapter 9

RANCÉ'S MONASTICISM

THIS WILL BE A LONG chapter, and deservedly so. Rancé's *De la sainteté et des devoirs de la vie monastique* is one of the most important books written on monastic spirituality, though its length—just over a thousand pages—and stately prose do not much endear it to modern taste. John Wain's admirable comments on Samuel Johnson may equally be applied to Armand-Jean de Rancé:

> Solemn and majestic thoughts in solemn and majestic language: the emotions which a man relives in the silence of his own mind, over a greying fire at midnight, conveyed not as disjointed musings but as fully clothed, logically connected sentences: these are what Johnson offers. Our age, which prefers its writers to shriek, grunt and babble, will naturally turn away from such ordered writing. The loss is ours.[1]

One of the reasons why the sayings of the Desert Fathers find such popularity among modern aspirants to the spiritual life is precisely because they present us with such 'disjointed musings'.

To call Rancé's monasticism a penitential monasticism is to state the obvious. His spirituality was a penitential spirituality. It could be no other. It was the spirituality of his

1. John Wain, *Samuel Johnson* (New York, 1975) 166.

times and it was the spirituality of a convert. It was also a
spirituality of reaction: the reaction of the Strict Observance
against the Common; the reaction of a convert against what
he saw as the extraordinary sinfulness of his former life; and
the reaction of one who had found his God—or whom God
had found—against concupiscence of the flesh, concupiscence
of the eyes, and pride of life. Nor was there anything new in
the idea. Luther had put the matter succinctly in the very
first of his Ninety-Five Theses in 1517: 'By saying: "Do penance, etc.", our Lord and Master Jesus Christ wanted the
whole life of the faithful to be penitence . . . . Yet he does not
mean only interior [penitence]. On the contrary. Interior [peni-
tence] is nothing if it does not produce outwardly different
mortifications of the flesh.'[2] And if we may quote John Calvin:

> It is never possible for human beings to re-
> pent without the continuing help of God. For
> we are renewed from day to day and we re-
> nounce our fleshly desires little by little. We
> do not cast off the old self in one day. . . As I
> have said, we are converted to God little by
> little in specific stages (*per certos gradus*), for
> penitence has its own rate of progress.[3]

That Rancé's spirituality was penitential, therefore, is inevitable. That it was *too* penitential is a modern value judgement of no relevance and little use. For the monks who flocked
to la Trappe, and flock they did, there is not the slightest
evidence that they found it too penitential, though there were
some whose weaker constitutions were unsuited to its rigours.
As we have said earlier, one of the features continually remarked upon by a host of visitors to the abbey was the fact
that the monks were clearly happy and that they loved their

2. Martin Luther, *Luthers Werke*, ed. Otto Clemen (Berlin, 1966 [5th ed.]) 1:3.
3. John Calvin, *Praelectiones in Jeremiam*, XXXI.18; *Ioannis Calvini Opera quae supersunt omnia*, ed. Guilielmus Baum *et al.* (*Corpus Reformatorum*, LXVI; Brunswick, 1888) 38:671.

abbot as much as he loved them.[4]

What is penitence? Fundamentally, it is the imitation of Christ who was the Great Penitent.[5] On its own, however, penitence is pointless. Asceticism for the sake of asceticism is useless: less than useless, in fact, since (as Rancé says) it invariably leads to pride in one's austerities.[6] Penitence is a means, not an end, and it is primarily a means to the diminution and ultimate annihilation of *amour propre* or *voluntas propria*, self-love or self-will. Penitence, Rancé wrote to Madame de Saint-Loup (a rather tiresome woman),

> is no more than conforming our heart to that of God and it demands the total sacrifice of ourselves. It does not consist only in weeping, but in weeping for what God wants us to weep.[7]

This is important. We cannot know what God wants us to weep for unless we have some inkling of his will; and we cannot have any inkling of his will if we are full of our own will, *voluntas propria*. Thus, the more we empty ourselves of *amour propre*, the more clearly we may see what God wants us to do. But when Rancé says that penitence demands total self-sacrifice (*abnégation*), he means it. As we saw in Chapter Four, Rancé's God is a sovereign God. He is the All-Ruler and his will is omnipotent. It must inevitably follow that if his service is perfect freedom, and if perfect freedom is true happiness, our joy is to be found in saying, truly, *fiat voluntas tua*, 'your will be done'.

This complete surrender of one's own will to the will of God was, of course, most perfectly exemplified in and by Christ himself, and Rancé's spirituality is wholly Christocentric. In the Garden of Gethsemane Christ first asks

4. See Chapter Five.
5. We discussed the matter in Chapter Four.
6. See Krailsheimer, *Rancé*, 331.
7. Letter 730611a.

that the cup of his coming suffering be taken from him, but, in the end, 'not my will be done, but yours' (Lk 22:42). Only by imitating Christ can we achieve the goal he wishes us to achieve. More precisely, Rancé's spirituality is centred on Christ as Christ was envisaged by Rancé and his seventeenth-century contemporaries, and that, for the most part, is not the Christ of modern-day Christians. Few nowadays see Christ as the Great Penitent, and few nowadays would equate the imitation of Christ with humiliations, mortification, penance, and contrition. Yet many, including Rancé, would see the Incarnation as the most perfect example of humility.

What is humility? It is, as we saw in Chapter Six, no more than the recognition of our true nature. And what is our true nature? It is, on the one hand, that we are created in the image and likeness of God; on the other, it is that the likeness of the image to its prototype has been wholly obscured by sin. We now dwell in the *regio dissimilitudinis*, the 'land of unlikeness',[8] and far from giving us cause only to congratulate ourselves, the theology of creation *ad imaginem Dei* reveals to us our true grandeur and our true misery. This was a commonplace of medieval spirituality. From the Middle Ages to the nineteenth century there was a pessimistic tendency to stress the latter; nowadays we prefer, optimistically, to stress the former.

Rancé, as we have seen, had not the least doubt of his miserable and sinful condition. Nor did he have any doubt that the same was true of his monks. But what was the cause of this misery? It was, once again, that self-love and self-will which always lie at the root of sin and which, unfortunately, we fight so hard to preserve. 'We are quite happy to see everything else within us die', he wrote, 'provided self-love lives

8. The term is not uncommon in twelfth-century spiritual writing and, among the Cistercians, is especially favoured by Bernard, William of Saint-Thierry, and Aelred of Rievaulx. Étienne Gilson's lucid discussion in his *The Mystical Theology of Saint Bernard*, tr. A. H. C. Downes (London, 1940; rpt. Kalamazoo, 1990) 33-59 retains its value.

on! This is a miscalculation which has irreparable consequences!'[9]

Sometimes, however, God takes things into his own hands.
If we will not humble ourselves, he may humble us. If we will
not mortify our own concupiscence, God may mortify it for
us. Rancé, therefore, is at one with his seventeenth-century
confrères in seeing human suffering, affliction, anguish, torment, distress, and misery as a sign that God is taking notice. If your life is full of tribulations, he writes to Mother
Louise-Elisabeth Robin de La Roche, then you should be
happy, for that is how God shows his mercy.[10] It is a hidden
mercy, true, and it may not be apparent; it may even be re-
sented, but mercy it remains. Furthermore, although 'God
brings storms on the heads of those he has chosen, he can
dispel them just as quickly',[11] and he will not let his elect be
lost. Once we have accepted all these sufferings as God's will,
once we have submitted ourselves totally to his Providence,[12]
once we receive his orders 'with a resignation worthy of the
blessing we enjoy of belonging to him',[13] then we may experience that joy-in-suffering of which Saint John Climacus speaks,
that joy-in-suffering which is like honey in the comb.[14] And in
another of his letters to Mother de La Roche, he recommends
to her his own work, *De la sainteté et des devoirs de la vie
monastique*, on the grounds that it might help her in her pursuit of holiness. Let us therefore take his advice and turn our
attention to this long and important book and see how it
illustrates Rancé's understanding of the imitation of Christ
and the demands of the Christian way.

It was, after all, Christ himself who instituted monasticism. That, at least, was Rancé's view (he says so almost at
the beginning of *De la sainteté*) and it was one of those state-

9. Letter 840605a.
10. Letter 810725.
11. *Ibid.*
12. Letter 830921.
13. Letter 910730.
14. See Chapter Five, n. 63.

ments to which Larroque objected on historical grounds. Rancé
supports his idea by reference to a variety of passages from
the Gospels and concludes from this evidence that

> it cannot be doubted that Jesus Christ in-
> tended to establish a holy state within his
> Church, a state in which one could adore and
> serve him wholly dissociated from worldly
> things, with one's mind unswervingly directed
> to his divine Majesty, and with a strict and
> literal observance of all his counsels. This is
> what was perfectly achieved in the monastic
> state so long as it preserved its full vigour, so
> long as its purity was unaltered, and so long
> as the constancy and fidelity of solitaries re-
> mained unconquered by the envy, plots, and
> violent attacks of the demons. (1:7)[15]

Those who come to this state must come willingly, whole-
heartedly, and publicly. There is no place here for half mea-
sures and there is no place at all for dissimulation:

> A true religious has renounced the concerns,
> pursuits, goods, honours and pleasures of the
> world, and has done so by a public declara-
> tion authorized by the Church. As a result of
> the promise he has made to God, the use of
> these things is forever forbidden him, and
> henceforth God alone should become the ob-
> ject of his thoughts, all his affections, and all
> his desires in such a way that he cannot even
> use those things his human condition requires
> him to use without reference to God and with
> the intention of pleasing him. (1:2)

---

15. References (in parentheses) are to volume and page number/s of the first
(1683) edition of *De la sainteté*.

Rancé then proceeds to give a long account of the origin of the monastic life, both eremitic and coenobitic, illustrated and supported by an abundance of quotations from the Fathers and medieval authorities (including his favourite, Saint Bernard). His purpose, however, is not simply historical. It is to lead the reader to a discussion of the essence and perfection of the coenobitic state which, as Rancé tells us, has been designed by God to lead us most effectively to that end which God desires. God's purpose, therefore, in establishing the monastic profession

> was to establish therein those who might serve him in spirit and in truth, and who, being wholly disengaged from all things of the senses, might serve him in all purity and all holiness. One cannot but agree that the first and principal duty of a solitary is to dedicate himself to God in the tranquillity and silence of his heart, to meditate unceasingly on his law, to keep himself perfectly dissociated from everything that might distract him that from that end, and, by careful and continual application, to raise himself to that perfection to which he has been called by faithfully carrying out God's will and counsels. (1:51)

This is an eminently clear summary, and it leads Rancé to an illuminating discussion of the real meaning of poverty, chastity, and obedience in monastic life. It is true that, for us, his account is rather too cluttered with quotations—such was the style of the times[16]—but what he has to say is as impressive as it is demanding. Chastity, for example, is far more than sexual continence. It involves every single thought, word, and deed. If you have truly given yourself to Christ, then Christ should fill your whole heart, and anything you

---

16. We discussed the matter in Chapter Two.

think or say or do 'which is not Jesus Christ, or which is not done in his name, by his command, or for love of him' (1:59) should be wholly excluded.

Poverty, likewise, has little to do with money or wealth. The first thing you must get rid of is yourself, and you get rid of yourself by giving yourself wholly to God. True poverty is not poverty of pocket, but poverty of will, and that—as Saint Bernard says—means the diminution and eventual eradication of self-will or *amour propre*. And how is this to be achieved? By obedience, absolute, unquestioning obedience to one's superior, which, as Rancé makes quite clear, is of supreme importance. The life of an obedient man, he says

> is a series of victories: *An obedient man shall speak of victories* (Prov 21:28). Each and every virtue, in fact, has an opposing vice and disorder which it attacks—poverty, for example, fights avarice, meekness anger, chastity impurity, and fervour sloth—but obedience alone triumphs over all the vices at once by destroying self-love and self-will, their source and foundation. (1:101)

Larroque, as we have seen, criticized Rancé for this emphasis on absolute obedience (and Rancé will return to it later), but as we may see from the quotations he adduces, there is nothing new in what he says. It is no more and no less than the Rule of Saint Benedict, and there is not the least doubt that Saint Bernard would have agreed with him.

Then, in Chapter VI, Rancé summarizes what God requires of those who are called to the religious state. It is true, he says, that each religious Order has its own particular emphasis, but if we list those common to all, this is what we find: a fervent love of God; complete confidence in one's superior (whom religious must regard as their father); love and consideration on the part of the superior for those he regards as his children; mutual love among the brethren; assiduous prayer; a love of humiliating the spirit; the continual remembrance of death; the presence of God and his judgements; holy and salutary compunction of heart; withdrawal from the world; silence; austerity of life and mortification of the senses; manual labour; vigils; strict poverty; and the enduring of infirmities 'with a disposition worthy of the holiness of their [monastic] state' (1:108). These are, as it were, the rungs by which we climb to the top of Jacob's ladder, and they are the most certain and most effective means for achieving the perfection of the monastic profession. The rest of the book is devoted to a careful examination of each of them.

The love of God is fundamental. True, we must adore him as well as love him; the two actions are quite distinct, but both are essential. In the most general sense, the love of God should influence every action, every part, of a Christian's life; in a particular sense, it must animate every part of the monastic day. A simple observance of the law, a literal discharge of one's duties, an exact fulfilment of the exercises of piety are abortive and useless if they do not spring from the love of God, and the love of God

> is a wholly interior disposition. It may express itself in what we do [outwardly] and proclaim itself by the actions of the senses, but it resides in the heart. It is the heart which truly loves. Love is an affection of the heart, and if the heart is not moved, there cannot be true love. (1:133)

Rancé goes on to quote a lengthy passage from Saint François de Sales to illustrate his point, and then reminds us that loving obedience to God demands that one keep the *whole* of the monastic rule in all its rigour. Indeed, if a religious omits details which seem to him to be of little importance or commits faults which appear to him to be slight, then he does not truly love God. Furthermore, he is simply pandering to self-will, and we can be sure that little sins of self-will will inevitably lead to greater ones and, ultimately, to our everlasting damnation. In any case, nothing is small if it offends God. We may perhaps object that this is a counsel of perfection. Of course it is. That was the whole business of life at la Trappe.

Rancé then moves on, quite logically, to deal with the place and responsibilities of superiors. The ideas he propounds were, as we have said, anathema to Larroque, but Rancé is merely being faithful to his sources. But if a superior is indeed to have 'total and absolute government' (1:152) over his monks, as God has over the universe, he must not only know them intimately (so far as is possible he should be their only confessor) and act charitably, he must also imbue them with absolute confidence in himself. If either of these is lacking, it will simply be a case of the blind leading the blind. If both are present, we have that unity of spirit which gives to a monastic congregation 'all its truth, and all its beauty and endurance' (1:153). But does this mean that superiors, if they see fit, can relax the Rule and that their monks are still obliged to obey them? It does not.

> Even though superiors can, in some cases, give you a dispensation from some points of your Rule when real necessity or other important considerations demand it, nevertheless, if they should suggest to you that the Rule be annulled or weakened, you should give no heed to their advice nor obey their commands. In such a case you could not conform to their will without turning your back on the will of God. (1:171)

All this clearly imposes an awesome responsibility on superiors, and in Chapter IX of his work Rancé deals with precisely this question. What does it mean to be Christ's representative in the monastery? It demands, first of all, that a superior (as Saint Benedict says) must teach by both word and example. Unlike a doctor of theology or a pastor, he does not need to be learned. Doctors and pastors are lamps set up to enlighten the world and their knowledge cannot be too great. But a superior of religious? He is nothing but a lamp hidden under a bushel. His business is to direct a few chosen persons and his mission is to instill piety, not to expound doctrine. What did Saint Paul say? 'I judge myself', he said, 'to know nothing among you save Jesus Christ and him crucified' (1 Cor 2:2).

> It is there [in Christ], my brothers, that a superior will learn the nature of unbounded obedience, an unquenchable desire for reproaches and humiliations, unconquerable patience in suffering, complete resignation to the will of God, poverty without reserve, continual charity in the midst of injustice, an unswerving attachment to things eternal and the perfect renunciation of all that is transitory. (1:197-198)

Rancé is well aware that this is not everyone's view—we are dealing here with the inflammatory question of monastic studies—and he spends some time in dealing with possible objections. As Larroque pointed out, one can find inconsistencies in what he says, but his view is logical and solidly based on his patristic and medieval authorities. Whether one would or could ever find a superior with all the virtues Rancé discusses is irrelevant. What is important is that superiors should strive unceasingly to acquire them. That they will err is not to be doubted, but as they and their community become ever more united, it may be hoped that they will err less.

Rancé then moves on the discuss 'fraternal charity', the *caritas fraternitatis* of the Rule of Saint Benedict,[17] 'which is the most important commandment after that of loving God'

---

17. *Regula S. Benedicti* 72.8.

(1:445). It is true that the regular monastic life limits the number of ways in which monks can demonstrate their love for their fellows, but as their sphere is more limited, so should their zeal be greater and their love 'more all-embracing and more perfect' than that of others (1:246). And how is this to be achieved?

> The means you have for showing your love for one another can be reduced to a few main practices: prayer, for example, and showing each other all those marks of gentleness, affection, and deference that the monastic rule can permit. (1:246-247)

Of all these practices, prayer is essential. The 'necessity and utility' (1:253) of prayer demands that we pray for each other. It is through prayer that we obtain from God whatever graces we need to persevere in his service, and if it is effective for ourselves, it cannot be any less effective for our brothers. Furthermore, says Rancé,

> Do not be afraid that by asking for things for your brothers you are giving up what you need for yourselves, and that God will reduce what he gives to you in accordance with what you, through your prayers, have gained for them. Never think that the time you spend with God on their behalf is taken away from you. On the contrary. You should know that your own affairs never succeed better with God than when you commend to him those of your brothers. (1:254)

Let us not, therefore, lose any opportunity of showing our brothers how much we love them, for 'charity is the bond and foundation of monastic communities' (1:260) and prayer is 'the whole strength and power of solitaries' (1:273).

Prayer is the subject of Chapter XI of Rancé's exposition, and a magnificent chapter it is. Any religious who neglects prayer

> neglects the care of his salvation. He rejects
> the strongest and most powerful means given
> him by God for his preservation and defence.
> He is like a soldier who throws down his arms
> in the middle of battle and who can expect
> nothing but inevitable destruction. (1:273)

Rancé then deals with the meaning of Paul's injunction to 'pray without ceasing',[18] and explains that prayer is no simple intellectual creation of the mind. Prayer is the very cry of the heart and it proceeds from the inner affections and fervour of the soul. It is, in fact, the result of inspiration by the Divine Spirit of love who opens our mouths and puts the words on our lips. Prayer should be frequent, flaming, and fervent; and, as everything else in the monastic life, it demands a renunciation of ourselves, our self-love and self-will. Prayer must go hand in hand with moral progress, and during the time of prayer we must separate ourselves from the consideration of all created things. We must expel from our senses, imagination, memory, reason, and heart everything that is not God. There are two essential conditions for prayer: purity of heart and fervour; and if you wish to know whether God has heard your prayers, then look to your own conduct:

> If someone who prays becomes no better, and
> if he sees nothing in the fidelity of his life
> which can assure him of the truth of his peti-
> tions, then he must believe that his prayer is
> a mere illusion, the result of a duped imagi-
> nation. (1:291)

---

18. 1 Thess 5:17, regularly quoted by the early Fathers and ascetics.

Rancé then goes on to provide a short five-step guide to effective prayer, but adds, with eminent good sense, that if it doesn't work for you, don't use it. Use some other technique. The Spirit of God is free: 'He is not bound by human rules and practices, but communicates himself to souls and inspires them in whatever way he pleases' (1:293). There follows, finally, a consideration of distractions in prayers (and how they may be countered) before Rancé offers us a long chapter on penance and humiliations.

Penance, he says, is essential to the religious life—indeed, it *is* the religious life—but Rancé makes it perfectly clear that penance is not merely exterior penitential discipline. It is, as we have already pointed out, nothing less than the imitation of Christ himself. It is 'to monks more than any others that Christ presents the chalice of his Passion' (1:310), and it is both the duty and the joy of religious to suffer for Jesus Christ as Jesus Christ suffered for them. And if Christ was indeed the Great Penitent, of what did his penance consist? It consisted of all those things which characterize the monastic life: fasting, retreat, silence, vigils, prayer, poverty, humiliation, reproach, and so on. And a consideration of the life of Christ leads us ineluctably to the conclusion (which was also the conclusion of Luther, Jean-Jacques Olier, and almost every other *spirituel* of Rancé's generation) that there are two sorts of penance, interior and exterior:

> The soul must be afflicted as well as the body, and mortification of the spirit must be joined to mortification of the senses. That is to say, one should live at one and the same time in holy sorrow, profound humility, and rigorous austerity. You will therefore not be wrong, my brothers, if your interior penance consists of humiliation, meditation on death and the judgements of God, and compunction. And as for exterior penance, the virtues and practices which comprise its essence and founda-

tion are withdrawal from the world, silence, austerity in the matter of food, manual labour, vigils, poverty, and patience in infirmities and sickness. (1:313-314)

In other words, if we may put it mathematically, penance = the imitation of Christ = the monastic life.

Rancé now takes the four factors which comprise interior penance and deals with them in order. The rest of Chapter XII deals with humiliations, Chapter XIII with meditation on death, Chapter XIV with meditation on the judgements of God, and Chapter XV—the last chapter of Volume I—with compunction. The entirety of Volume II will be devoted to exterior penance.

His long consideration of humiliations clearly shows that we cannot take seriously his statement that the book was intended only for his monks. Had that been so, the author would not have needed to spend so much time defending his doctrine. As we have seen in earlier chapters, theological argument was not encouraged at la Trappe. Rancé, in any case, can easily support his principle by reference to appropriate authorities. If the writings of Saint John Climacus lie at the heart of his teaching on humiliations, he can also call on a number of other writers to support his case: Saint Bernard certainly ('Humiliation is the way to humility'[19]), but also Ambrose, Augustine, Basil, Benedict, Gregory the Great, and Teresa of Ávila. And if it be objected that guiding a person to perfection by love is surely better than goading them there by reproaches, then that simply indicates that one has forgotten that the way of love *is* the way of the cross. The life of Christ was an uninterrupted course of ignominy, contempt, and abasement, and the eternal Father's conduct toward his Son revealed only infinite severity and humiliation. The monastic life is, or should be, a 'continual crucifixion' (1:315).

19. *De la sainteté*, 1:317 quoting (in Latin) Bernard, *Ep.* 87.11. 'If you want the virtue of humility', Bernard continues, 'you must not avoid humiliations.'

And what is the end of crucifixion? Death—though death is only the gateway to a new and better life. The transition may be painful, but that is nothing compared with an eternity of bliss. So why do those who are in the world and of the world fear death? It is because they are so closely bound to earthly things that they can view the loss of them only with horror. But what is a religious? Someone who has renounced the world, who has no involvement with transitory things. Religious are already walking corpses. Such men and women, therefore, 'find nothing at the end of their life to cause them the slightest unease. On the contrary: they find their joy and comfort in meditating on death' (1:411). They are like the early persecuted Christians who (as Tertullian said) were always ready and willing to die. Death, after all, is no more than the end of all our sorrows and the beginning of everlasting joy. It is the ultimate goal and crowning achievement of the monastic life.

This is not a viewpoint much in favour today. We may understand it, but we do not, in general, sympathize with it. But in Rancé's France, an exhortation to meditate on death and the judgements of God (for the subjects of Chapters XIII and XIV obviously cannot be separated) would have fallen on receptive ears. As John McManners has shown so clearly,[20] Christians of all walks of life were well aware of the reality and nearness of death. All were convinced of the need to prepare for it, and all likewise were in no doubt of the importance of the disposition of one's heart in one's last hour. There was a large literature devoted to the subject—McManners notes that between 1600 and 1675 the presses turned out a hundred and five new titles, and no fewer than sixty in the following twenty-five years[21]—and such volumes as Jean

---

20. John McManners, *Death and the Enlightenment: Changing Attitudes to Death among Christians and Unbelievers in Eighteenth-Century France* (Oxford-New York, 1981, 1985). The book contains much of relevance to the seventeenth century.

21. John McManners, *Church and Society in Eighteenth-Century France, II: The Religion of the People and the Politics of Religion* (Oxford, 1998) 29.

Crasset's *La douce et la sainte mort* were the best sellers of the day. Much the same was true in England. One need only think of the immense popularity of Jeremy Taylor's *Rule and Exercises of Holy Dying* (1651), the companion volume to his *Rule and Exercises of Holy Living* (1650), and it was, in fact, simply a continuation of a late medieval tradition.[22]

Few things, says Rancé, are as beneficial as meditating on death. It expels sloth, cures inconstancy of soul, prevents the mind from wandering, makes penance pleasurable, destroys the bitterness of humiliations, kills intemperance, disengages us from all earthly things, makes our prayers more fervent, inspires pious thoughts, and preserves devotion. And that is not all, for as Saint John Climacus said, 'all the virtues are its mothers and daughters' (1:427). We must remember, too, that for sinners in seventeenth-century France, hell was not a Great Perhaps[23] but an ever-present reality. An unfortunate slip at the last moment could plunge one headfirst into its everlasting torments; and the abyss and the worm, the fire and the stench, the darkness and the chains so graphically described by Saint Bernard (and quoted by Rancé [1:434]) were not to be taken as allegories. A healthy fear of judgement, then, is a salutary thing, and if it be objected that Saint John said that 'perfect love casts out fear' (1 Jn 4:18), Rancé has a sound answer:

> In those whose love is weak, fear is a flaming fire that purifies them; and as charity increases, so fear decreases. Thus, when love is perfect, fear vanishes away, and the soul, filled with a holy ardour, is intimately united to

22. See, for example, Eamon Duffy, *The Stripping of the Altars. Traditional Religion in England 1400-1580* (New Haven-London, 1992) 301-337, and Robert N. Swanson, *Religion and Devotion in Europe, c.1215-c.1515* (Cambridge, 1995) 199-203. There is a considerable literature on the subject.
23. One may refer either to Rabelais or Browning, though Browning prefers the 'grand Perhaps'.

God by the operation of his Holy Spirit.
(1:443-444)

The brief chapter on compunction that follows this—it is less than a dozen pages—is no more than a logical extension of this theme. Meditation on death and judgement produces compunction of heart as fire produces heat and light, and much of this chapter consists of quotations from Antony of Egypt, Macarius the Great and other Fathers of the Desert, Ephraem Syrus, Basil the Great, Gregory of Nazianzus, Nilus, Jerome, the Rule of Saint Benedict, Bernard, and, of course, John Climacus. 'So take advantage, my brothers, from knowing these things':

> Weep for a few moments here to live in an eternity of joy. Wash your face unceasingly in the bitter waters of penitence. Take care only to pour out your tears, and leave it to God to wipe them away. The time will come when he will soothe your sighs, dry your eyes, and change your sorrow into infinite consolation.
> (1:458-459)

The second volume of *De la sainteté* is devoted, as we said above, to exterior penitence, the penitence of the body as distinct from that of the spirit. The questions are dealt with in detail and there is much practical instruction. For us today it may seem curious—unbalanced even—that the 460 pages of the first volume, dealing with the inner life of religious, should be exceeded by the 547 pages of the second which deals with everything from spurious reasons for leaving the cloister to details of monastic diet and what sort of work is appropriate for cloistered monks. Our own view, in this hyper-psychological age, might well be that the proportions should be reversed. Such an idea, however, misses the point: the second volume is not a treatise on bodily mortification, it is a treatise on the practicalities of the imi-

tation of Christ. It may not be the way that modern religious understand *imitatio Christi*, but it was certainly the way
the concept was understood by the great majority of the
spirituels of Rancé's time and place. It is also a volume wholly
dominated by that one essential *leitmotif* of all Rancé's writing: that a monk has severed all ties with the world and
worldly things, and is henceforth dedicated entirely and absolutely—I use the word advisedly—to the purposes of
heaven.

He begins with a lyrical description of the paradise of the
cloister and the need to separate oneself utterly from the
affairs of the world. Furthermore, once you enter the cloister
and promise stability, as Saint Benedict says,[24] then it is your
business to be stable. What does it mean to promise stability? It means that a religious is bound by his profession never
to leave his monastery. It also means that the monastery must
provide everything necessary within the monastic enclosure
so that the need to venture forth never arises.

What could be clearer? The founders of Cîteaux said the
same thing. Saint Bernard said the same thing. The
Carthusians said the same thing. And who put it more succinctly than Gratian, whom Rancé here paraphrases in French:
'A monk can no more live outside the cloister than a fish can
live out of water' (2:17). Everything else follows from that,
and the rest of this very long chapter (some one hundred
sixty pages) is devoted to discussing all the possible reasons a
monk might have for leaving the enclosure, and demonstrat-
ing that not one of them is valid. A monastery is a monk's
tomb. Do corpses leave their tombs? Not normally. Dracula
was not a monk. Nor do we leave the cloister. We do not leave
it for innocent recreation, we do not leave it to give ourselves
a break, we do not leave it for a change of scene, we do not
leave it for reasons of health, and we do not leave it to engage
in lawsuits. On this point Rancé supports his case by quoting *in extenso* seven pages of a letter of Saint François de Sales

24. *De la sainteté*, 2:13 echoing (in Latin) *Regula S. Benedicti* 58.9.

(2:54-60), and we must remember that seventeenth-century France was a virulently litigious society. Nor do we leave the cloister to look after our indigent parents. This is a matter we have discussed earlier, and (as with his chapter on humiliations) Rancé is obviously writing here not so much for his own monks—they will do what they are told—but for those outside the monastery who disagree with him. It is a long and learned discussion, solidly supported by authoritative quotations, and Rancé is well aware that his view is a minority opinion. But so what?

> In the matter of evangelical principles, the voice of the people is not the voice of God. The greatest truths are those which have the least acceptance and find the least approval among men and women. Indeed, the best justification they can have is that they are either little known or much opposed. (2:136)

We might add that the same prohibitions apply equally to superiors. They, too, are bound by their vow of stability and, as we have seen, their business is to teach as much by their example as their words. Preaching and instruction are no excuse for leaving the enclosure, and intervening in ecclesiastical affairs would simply destroy in them 'the spirit and piety of their profession' (2:153). Rancé's own life, after his return to la Trappe from Rome in May 1666, clearly demonstrates his determination to follow his own principles.

The chapter on silence that follows that on enclosure is very much shorter. The silence at la Trappe fascinated its (too) frequent visitors, but if silence is to be effective, says Rancé, it must be perpetual. If it is not, monks and nuns simply learn how to say a very great deal in a very short time. But is it not possible that these religious would find pious and edifying discourse beneficial? Yes, they might. But the disadvantages far outweigh the advantages. It is hard for us to control our tongue, and a few well-chosen words soon degenerate into useless conversation. Saint Arsenius put it in a nutshell: he could not talk to God and men at the same time. And in any case, the practice of silence sanctified the whole Cistercian Order.

What, then, of 'conferences', those strictly regulated discussion-groups held on Sundays and certain other days, when the brethren spoke of what they had found most edifying in their devotional reading? It is true that they are necessary, says Rancé, but they should be public, infrequent, simple, and holy. Above all, it is essential that they should *not* be concerned with doctrinal problems or theological controversies, for 'there is nothing more capable of producing pride, troubling the heart, and provoking disputes' (2:179).

Then, in Chapter XVIII, Rancé passes to the question of monastic diet. This, understandably, is a fairly polemical chapter which involves the essential point of contention in the War of the Observances. Rancé, in a formidable display of erudition (mocked, not unjustly, by Larroque), assembles a multitude of authorities to support his principle of a purely vegetarian diet. Again, much of it is clearly addressed to those outside the cloister—what concern could the monks of la Trappe have with the distinction, in Greek, between τάριχος and τέμαχος?—and the arguments reiterate those so long and fruitlessly bandied about between the Abstinents and the Mitigated. Not only does Rancé trace the abstinent tradition back to the apostles themselves, he also points out that a vegetarian diet is an admirable example of penitence. It does nothing to excite the passions, it moderates the ardour of the flesh and stems its irregularities, it is cheap to produce and easy to prepare, it removes occasion for murmuring and complaining, it can easily be accommodated to growing numbers, and a self-sufficient simple community can more easily help the poor. And as to guests, they should eat what the monks eat, and the abbot should not keep a separate table for their entertainment. But does this not conflict with the Rule of Saint Benedict? It does. So is it possible to dispense with a point of the Rule which has been stated so explicitly? Rancé has no doubt on the matter:

> It not only can but *should* be dispensed with!
> If the regulations laid down by the saints for
> the edification of the Church, the maintenance
> of discipline, and preservation of good mor-
> als produce the opposite effects, they no longer
> have authority and are no longer to be heeded.
> (2:252)

Indeed, if Saint Benedict himself were alive at this time and saw the extent to which his intentions have been abused, he would not change the spirit of his Rule, but he would cer-tainly change some of the details!

Rancé now turns to manual labour, one of the most widely recommended of penitential exercises. But in his day, alas,

> it has been abolished so widely that hardly
> the least trace of it is preserved even in the
> strictest observances. Indeed, there are some
> who have come to reject as something useless
> and contemptible a practice which cannot be
> commended too highly, for its basis is to be
> found in the labours of the life of Jesus Christ
> himself, and it was justified by the example
> of his apostles, the opinion of the Doctors of
> the Church, and almost all the Rules of the
> saints. (2:257)

Not only is manual labour a penitential imitation of Christ the carpenter, it is also a cure for sloth and idleness, an im-portant way of showing charity to the poor, an example of industry, and—since we are talking about ignominious manual labour—an exercise in humility. Again, Rancé introduces a wealth of sources to support the principle, and he is careful not to include among them those which would equate reading and study with the labour of one's hands. Here we find those nineteen pages—questions four to six in the chapter we are discussing—which lie at the heart of the controversy over monastic studies. Enough has been said on this topic already and there is no need here to dwell on it further. Suffice it to say that both Rancé and Mabillon were, in fact, correct; the problem was that they were arguing from different premises. For Rancé, a monk's business is penitence, not study. His task is to weep, not to teach. And if some would say that this must lead to ignorance, then Rancé replies that

> a religious cannot be considered ignorant when he knows what his profession obliges him to know. He has all the knowledge he needs when he knows how to love Jesus Christ, how to take up his cross, and how to follow and please him. This is not a science which can be acquired by study: its master and doctor is Jesus Christ, and we must learn it from him. (2:295-296)

Rancé then considers the question of whether dispensing with manual labour would not leave more time for prayer and therefore enable a monk to lead a more effective interior life. No, he says, it would not. Not only has the question been considered—and rejected—by the early Fathers, but we must also take care to balance our lives appropriately. 'Those who reject the occupations of Martha', we are told, 'do not find in exchange the pursuits of Mary' (2:315). And what sort of occupations is he speaking of here? Those (as Saint Basil says) which do not disturb one's peace and tranquillity, those which do not demand intense concentration, and those which demand an absolute minimum of conversation. And if one would prefer specific examples, Rancé is happy to provide them. You will have fulfilled your duties, he says, and imitated (so far as is possible) the ascetics of old,

> if you prepare the food the community needs,

> if you do your own laundry, clean your stables,
> carry manure, dig the ground, cultivate your
> [vegetable-] gardens yourselves, carefully and
> fervently, so that they become your main
> source of food, if you make your own clothes,
> window-panes (*sic*: *vitres*), spoons, baskets,
> shoes, and such like without having recourse
> to outside craftsmen, in short, if you neglect
> none of the services you can render to the
> monastery and joyfully embrace the meanest
> and most contemptible occupations. (2:326-
> 327)

There then follows a brief chapter on vigils. Not only is
keeping the night-watch an imitation of Christ, his apostles,
and the saints of the Church, it also reduces the hours of
sleep, and sleep (in the view of the ancient solitaries) was to
be equated with real degradation. And why? Because in sleep

> the actions of the spirit cease, and while they
> are suspended we lose our human nobility and
> excellence and become just like the other ani-
> mals over which God has given us such great
> advantages. (2:329-330)

Furthermore, vigils do away with vain thoughts and the
temptations brought by dreams. They mortify the body and
cool the heat of concupiscence. They expel nightmares, produce penitential tears, soften the heart, and clarify our mind.
At the time of the night-office, in the dark hours before dawn,
our mind is more free of distractions, our attention more
undivided, and our prayers more acceptable to God's Divine
Majesty—provided, of course, we are as awake in our soul as
we are in our body:

> Just as prayer from the mouth is nothing un-
> less it be accompanied by prayer from the

spirit, so it is not much use to keep vigil with your eyes if you do not keep vigil with your heart. There is no point in your senses being awake if your souls are languishing in drowsiness and sleep! (2:214)

The long chapter on poverty which follows this begins, once again, by asserting that in poverty lies the imitation of Christ. What is important, however, is not poverty alone, but the *love* of poverty, and that is something much more difficult. A monk must be poor in all things in all places and must utterly renounce and reject 'all the goods, superfluities, enticements, and advantages of the world' (2:338). But not only must a monk be poor, the places where he works and prays must also be poor. There is no place in the monastery, and no place in the monastic church, for rich and elaborate decoration and furnishings, and Rancé predictably invokes Saint Bernard's criticisms of Cluny. What may be perfectly reasonable—indeed, useful—for ordinary people, who are generally carnal, led by their senses and in need of exterior stimulation, is not true for monks, 'who are no longer inhabitants of Babylon, but citizens of the holy city, the heavenly Jerusalem' (2:348). Furthermore, what Saint Bernard said was not merely his own idiosyncratic opinion: it was echoed by the whole Order of Cîteaux (at least while it retained its *ancien esprit* [2:348]) and by a number of the early General Chapters. A monk is wholly separated from the world, and it is his business to have a true antipathy and sincere aversion for anything which may reflect the vanity, luxury, and superfluity of worldly people.

But not only should the monks and the Order be poor, they should also do all that they can to assist those who are likewise poor. Such was the way of the ancient solitaries, for in the poor they saw Christ himself, and in relieving the poor they relieved the poor Christ.

Under the old clothes and tattered garments

it was Christ they saw. They saw him beset
by hunger, parched with thirst, overwhelmed
with misery and fatigue; and so great was their
faith, that when they saw these things, their
own troubles, time, labours, and pains were
of no consequence, if only they could support those who stood in the place of Jesus
Christ. If they could have given their lives
for him who had poured out for them the last
drop of his blood, their joy would have been
complete. (2:352-353)

Alms-giving, therefore, in whatever form it may take, is an
indispensable monastic duty. The poor have a right to a part
of the goods and revenues of monasteries, and if you ask
what limit there should be to this charity, the answer is no
limit save impossibility alone. It is obvious, therefore, that
no religious should ever own money or private property. He
enters 'a state of perfect nakedness (*nudité*), and heaven becomes so uniquely his inheritance that he separates himself
from everything worldly' (2:367-368). And just as the individual monk must separate himself from the lure of filthy
lucre, so too must the monastery. This leads Rancé to a discussion of monastic dowries, that is to say, the practice (usual
at the time) of demanding a certain sum of money (not infre-
quently a large sum of money) as a condition for admittance
to a religious community. The final two dozen pages of the
chapter are devoted to the question and Rancé condemns it
out of hand. It is contrary to the law of God, contrary to the
example of the saints, and contrary to the teaching of the
Church. For him, it is no different from simony, and he has no
difficulty in adducing the usual plethora of examples to demonstrate his case. But when it comes down to it, the essential
reason why it is wrong could not be more simple nor have
greater authority: Christ himself said that it is not our business to turn the house of God into a den of thieves.

What, then, of sickness and infirmity? Poverty, frugality,

and good health are rarely to be found hand in hand, and Rancé was well aware of contemporary criticisms of the mortality at la Trappe.[25] But as Saint Pachomius said, 'we are never afflicted with suffering or any other pain save by the permission of God' (2:433), and if it is our business to imitate the suffering Christ, it is not our business (putting it in modern terms) to use analgesics or seek expensive or elaborate cures. Indeed, there are many examples of early monks and nuns who sought no cures at all, but left the whole matter in the hands of God. Yet this, as Rancé admits, was not universal, and he concedes that certain remedies may be used to assist or cure sick monks provided those remedies are common and cheap—he is thinking of natural or herbal cures—and provided they are commanded by the superior. If the superior does not command them, a monk has no business asking for them. To our modern sensibilities, this may appear inhuman, or at least inhumane. Given Rancé's premises, it is—once again—no more than logical.

So what if religious start dying in large numbers and we face what, to the outside world, would be an unacceptable level of monastic mortality? Rancé's answer is wholly predictable:

> Solitaries, as we have said so many times, do not come to monasteries to live, but to die, and they should be neither surprised nor frightened to see frequent deaths. What they seek is the salvation of their souls, not the preservation of their life and health. (2:459-460)

If soldiers die in battle for their king, no one is particularly astonished. That is what they are supposed to do. It is their duty. Why, then, should it be different for those in the service

25. See Chapter 5 and the balanced discussion in Krailsheimer, *Rancé*, 83-84 and 91-92.

of the King of kings? In any case, just as the early Christians actually increased in number as a result of violent persecution, so the number of monks will increase not by mitigating austerities, but by increasing them.

> The prudence of the flesh says that religious must relax [their austerities] and come down from the heights if they are to survive or increase their numbers; the wisdom of God, on the contrary, says that they must bind themselves more tightly and walk in even narrower paths. The spirit of Christ is heard in those congregations which are strict; the human spirit in those which are relaxed. (2:461)

And all, now, are relaxed. The great Order of Saint Benedict fell into laxity in the second century after its foundation, and even the Carthusians, though they maintained themselves longer than others, showed the effects of the general inconstancy shortly after their foundation. It was this and similar comments, we might add, that aroused the ire of Dom Innocent Le Masson, General of the Carthusians, and precipitated the pamphlet war between him and Rancé.[26] The purpose of the Strict Observance was to bring back the strict austerity of the past—the *premier esprit* of the Order of Cîteaux—and if these austerities bring suffering upon us and shorten our lives, so be it. The fact that many will not agree with this is not only irrelevant, but in reality a positive sign, for

> if your way of life is neither approved nor appreciated by most people, you can take comfort from the fact that it has all the features and all the marks necessary to convince you

---

26. We discussed the matter in Chapter Seven.

that it is in accordance with the Spirit of God.
(2:495-496)

As we saw earlier, as far as Rancé was concerned, 'the voice of
the people is not the voice of God' (2:136).

This examination of austerities leads logically to the last
chapter of all, which is predictable, polemical, and passionate. It is concerned with mitigations, and the essence of its
fifty pages is that mitigations are utterly indefensible. They
are nothing less than 'a violation of God's law, contempt for
his orders, a determined and wholly public resistance to his
will, a ministry of iniquity, and, consequently, a state of death'
(2:510-511). They are also stupid. If I met a man walking
west, says Rancé, and he told me he was making his way to
China or Japan, I could only conclude that he was mad, lost,
or that what he said had nothing to do with what he thought
(2:506). It is the same with monks. The way to God has been
laid out in detail by generations of saints, and to aim for
heaven by walking towards earth cannot be called rational.
The fact that most religious have decided to mitigate the primitive rules is beside the point:

> In the Old Testament, God forbade us
> through his prophet [Moses] from following
> the multitude when they abandon the truth,
> and in the New [Testament] he declares by
> the mouth of his Son that the path that leads
> to life is narrow and found by few. But that
> which leads to death is broad and spacious
> and is followed by a great number. (2:524)

This is not to say that we do not find some chosen souls,
even in the most lax and irregular congregations, who realize
that all is not well and seek, quietly and discreetly, to regu-
late their lives appropriately. They are like Noah, who retained his innocence amid the general corruption of the world.
Nor is it to say that all mitigations are unlawful. But those

which are lawful are few, and they are limited to those 'established by the authority of the sovereign Pontiffs and the constitutions of the Church' (2:527). These, and these alone, may be embraced with a clear conscience, provided one adds nothing to them and makes no further modifications.

We must remember, however, that an unthinking or unwilling asceticism is no use at all. If a monk does not love his austerities, says Rancé, there is little point in his doing them; and he cannot love them unless he has in his heart that inward spirit which is the spirit of Jesus Christ himself. A monk's business is to live as the saints have lived, but if one does not have their spirit and their devotion, it is useless to wear their habit and follow their practices. Therefore, says Rancé in a final exhortation to his beloved brothers,

> Imitate the actions of the saints and imprint them deeply in your hearts. Do not think that all those who withdraw to the cloister will open for themselves the gates of heaven. There are many who embrace this holy life, but very few who bear its yoke. According to the words of Scripture, the Kingdom of Heaven suffers violence, and it is only the violent who bear it away (Mt 11:12).
>
> Bow your heads, therefore, to receive the yoke of the Lord, bind yourselves with these blessed bonds, take this burden upon your shoulders, lighten it by the arduous exercise of the virtues, by fasting, vigils, obedience, the holy repose of solitude, the chanting of the Psalms, prayer, tears, manual labour, and by suffering every tribulation, whether it comes from the demons or from men and women.
>
> Never let the vanity of your thoughts or the pride of your heart lead you to relax any of your customary labours and austeri-

ties, for if you find yourself at the end of your course devoid of works and virtues, Jesus Christ will close the entrance of his kingdom against you.

For your comfort, say often to God what his prophet [David] used to say: 'Save us, Lord, for there are no saints left in the world; the children of men have enfeebled your truths. They speak to each other only vain things; their lips are deceitful, and they speak only to seduce those who listen to them. *Salvum me fac, Domine*' (Ps 11:2-3).

Finally, my brothers, praise God who has opened your [hearts] to his holy truths, bless him who, at the same time, has given you the desire to put them into practice, and ask him, with continual prayers, for the strength to resist the flood of contrary instructions: *Bless the God of heaven and bear witness to him in the sight of all who live, for to you he has shown his mercy* (Tob 12:6).

Let your fidelity [to your tradition] be your thanksgiving and let your gratitude be revealed in all that you do. Make your life so pure and holy, as your [monastic] state demands, that the marks of God's mercy may be found in every part of it. Let it be an edification for all, the joy of the angels, the confusion of the demons, and may it be a subject of glory and triumph to Jesus Christ for ever. (2:545-547)

Such, in essence, is the teaching of *De la sainteté et des devoirs de la vie monastique*. It is a remarkable book and in the seventeenth century (as Professor Krailsheimer has said) it 'met with enthusiasm or indignation, not indifference'.[27] As a document in the history of monasticism, he continues, it 'has an important place, as a contribution to spirituality it deserves much more serious consideration than has recently been the case'.[28] That is true, but we should note that the book is a contribution to *spirituality*, not mysticism. This, indeed, is another reason why it lacks appeal today, and we need to say a few words on the subject.

In 1814 Charles Butler published a biography of Rancé which we discussed in Chapter One, and in it he observes that prayer at la Trappe

> was both continual and fervent; but it never savoured of refinement, and, in all the agiography [*sic*] of La Trappe, a single instance of mystical excess, or even of mystical prayer, is not recorded.[29] . . . Far from endeavouring to penetrate the cloud with Moses, or to be admitted into the cellar of the Great King (such are the expressions of mystical writers), the monk of La Trappe aimed at no more, than to offer his prayer with the humble publican in the lowest part of the temple, or to fall, with the prodigal, at the feet of his offended but merciful father.[30]

This is all the more remarkable given the religious milieu of seventeenth-century France which gave birth to a variety of mysticisms (I use the plural deliberately) like so many exotic orchids. In this matter, however, I would maintain that Rancé

27. Krailsheimer, *Legacy*, 102.
28. *Ibid.*
29. This is not quite true. There are one or two very rare examples which appear in the *Relations* and Rancé both recognized and acknowledged the reality of extra-ordinary graces.
30. Charles Butler, *The Lives of Dom Armand-Jean Le Bouthillier de Rancé, Abbot Regular and Reformer of the Monastery of La Trappe; and of Thomas à Kempis, the Reputed Author of 'The Imitation of Christ'. With Some Account of the Principal Religious and Military Orders of the Roman Catholic Church* (London, 1814) 63-64.

stands firmly in the tradition of the earliest cistercian spirituality,[31] and the single recent publication which bears the
title 'Rancé mystique'[32] shows him to be a prayerful contemplative, but not a man seeking the peaks of Mount Carmel or
the inner chambers of the Interior Castle. In any case, the
monks of la Trappe had little time for individual, private
prayer. The General Chapters of 1601 and 1605 had certainly
set aside specific times for it, but an ambiguous statement in
the Rule of Saint Benedict could imply that 'private prayer'
be interpreted as 'meditation in common'. The passage in
question states that *in conventu tamen omnino brevietur oratio*,[33]
which almost certainly meant 'in community, [private] prayer
will be very brief'. But it might also be interpreted to mean
'[private] prayer will be very brief and [done] in community'. There was indeed a solid body of opinion which preferred this second interpretation, and it was an opinion shared
by Rancé. Cistercians were not Carthusians. As Mother Bernard Payne said in 1937, 'not private but liturgical prayer is
the chief occupation of the Cistercian contemplative',[34] and

> during those hours when she is engaged in
> the 'Work of God', the choral Office, the reli-
> gious is not praying as a mere individual; she
> is praying in and with the entire Mystical
> Body of Christ, both those members of it
> who are still on earth, and those already in
> eternity, and the entire Mystical Body is pray-
> ing in and through her. It is easy to see how

31. See David N. Bell, 'From Molesme to Cîteaux: The Earliest "Cistercian"
"Spirituality" ', *Cistercian Studies Quarterly* 34 (1999) 469-482.
32. [Anon.], 'Rancé mystique: la prière de saint Antoine', *Collectanea Cisterciensia*
25 (1963) 250-252. This is merely an excerpt, without introduction or notes,
from the Paris 1683 second edition of *De la sainteté*, 403-409.
33. *Regula S. Benedicti* 20.5.
34. *La Trappe in England. Chronicles of an Unknown Monastery*, by A Religious of
Holy Cross Abbey, Stapehill, Dorset [Mother Bernard Payne] (London, [1937];
rpt. Louisville KY, 1946) 186.

> such a prayer, rightly understood, emanci-
> pates the soul from the little world of its own
> individual spiritual life, introducing it into
> the incomparably vaster and fuller life of the
> Church; again, how it demands the sacrifice
> of egoism in entire self-devotion to the com-
> munity act of praising God. We are far re-
> moved here from sentimental pietism.[35]

This echoes Rancé's spirituality, and it is, at heart, the cistercian spirituality of the Middle Ages. Rancé, in fact, has much in common with Baldwin of Forde.[36] But it is far from being unique to Rancé. In his unmystical monasticism he was at one with almost all his Strict Observance confrères, and apart from the curious and important exception of Louis Quinet,[37] the 'refinements' (as Butler would say) of mystical prayer seem to have held little interest for them.[38] They are, however, of much more interest today, not least because of the easy availability of mind-altering substances, and a book on mystical rapture, the peak experience, or the highest state of consciousness will find a far wider audience than a study of monastic teaching on moral progress. And as for penance and penitence, those words, certainly, are politically incorrect.

Rancé, however, had his feet solidly on the ground. We today may not much care for the ground on which they were solidly put, but it was unquestionably familiar ground to all his seventeenth-century compatriots. Given that ground, all

35. *Ibid.*, 188.
36. See David N. Bell, 'The Ascetic Spirituality of Baldwin of Ford', *Cîteaux: Commentarii cistercienses* 31 (1980) 227-250, especially 245-248. We might also note that Baldwin is at one with Rancé in his idea that 'ascesis and mortifica- tion are simply manifestations of the love of God' (245).
37. On Louis Quinet, see the article (with bibliography) by André Derville in *DS* 12:2850-2852, and the citations in the index (259) to Louis J. Lekai's *The Rise of the Cistercian Strict Observance in Seventeenth Century France* (Washington, 1968). Quinet is an important and neglected figure and demands a proper study. His works are of the greatest interest.
38. See the useful comments by Lekai in his *Strict Observance*, 179-181.

that Rancé says follows as the night the day. Indeed, if anything can be said to characterize the two substantial volumes
of *De la sainteté*, it is their inexorable logic. Rancé was convinced that he was doing no more and no less than continu-
ing—re-forming—the tradition of the early Fathers, and especially the tradition of Saint Benedict. He was restoring the
premier esprit of the Order of Cîteaux, and if he did it in a
fashion more attuned to the seventeenth century than the
twenty-first, we can hardly blame him for that. But the essential theme of the book can be reduced to two sentences:
Christ was the Great Penitent. Imitate him.

FURTHER READING

For bibliographical details of the various editions of Rancé's *De la sainteté et des devoirs de la vie monastique*, see Part II, I.A.i [1683 *De la sainteté*]. There are two useful english summaries of the work and one complete english translation. The first summary was published in 1954 by Father Vincent Hermans in his mimeographed *Spiritualité monastique* (Rome 1954 [two volumes]) which was translated into English by 'monks of O.L. of Mepkin' in 1958 as *Monastic Spirituality. A Study of the History of Spiritual Doctrine in the Cistercian Order* (Our Lady of Mepkin, Moncks Corner SC, 1958 [mimeographed]). The summary appears on pages 376-387, but the book was never intended for general circulation and outside cistercian monasteries it is not easy to find. Far more accessible is the useful summary provided by Alban J. Krailsheimer in his *Rancé and the Trappist Legacy* (Kalamazoo, 1985), ch. 7 (87-102). It is a lucid and balanced account. My own summary presented here is intended to complement rather than supersede these earlier works.

The complete english translation of *De la sainteté* was made by 'a Religious of the Abbey of Melleray, La Trappe', who was almost certainly Dom Vincent Ryan, formerly prior of Melleray in France and subsequently first abbot of Mount Melleray in Ireland. The translation was published in two volumes in 1830 as *A Treatise on the Sanctity and on the Duties of the Monastic State. Written Originally in French by the Rev. Father Don [sic] Armand John Le Boutillier de Rancé, Abbot and Reformer of La Trappe* (Part II, I.A.i [1683]). The book admirably succeeds in conveying the spirit of Rancé's work, but as a translation it is seriously flawed. The translator had no hesitation in adding words and phrases (occasionally whole sentences), omitting words or sentences, and rephrasing and paraphrasing the actual text, and sometimes his translation is just plain wrong. All translations in this present chapter are my own, and I have a new english version of the entire work in hand. Whether I will ever finish it is quite another matter. I should add, perhaps, that in my translations here, I use 'he', 'brothers', and so on, not from an out-dated male chauvinism, but because Rancé is talking to monks, not nuns. It is quite true that he was happy to recommend his work to female religious (Reverend Mother Marie-Louise Bouthillier and Mother Louise-Elisabeth Robin de La Roche to name but two), but when he addresses '*mes frères*', that is what he means. If, however, '*hommes*' (for example) refers not specifically to male human beings but to men and women generally, then 'men and women' is how I translate it.

Translations of two brief passages from the work appeared in *Cistercian Studies* in 1973: 'Two Excerpts from de Rancé's Treatise on the Holiness and Duties of the Monastic Life', *Cistercian Studies* [*Quarterly*] 8 (1973) 53-63. The two excerpts are *De la sainteté* (1683 [1st ed.]) 1:131-140 and 196-206.

Chapter 10

UNDERSTANDING RANCÉ

IT IS TIME NOW to draw the threads together. Neither Rancé nor his monastic spirituality can be understood outside their context, and some of the criticisms often levied against him might equally be levied against almost any of his seventeenth-century french compatriots, whether friends or enemies. There is little point, for example, in drawing attention to Rancé's stark distinction between this world and the world to come, nor to his conception of monastic life as a life of penitence, nor to his insistence on the vanity of earthly concerns, nor to his pessimistic estimate of humankind, nor to his preoccupation with death and judgement. These were standard themes in *le grand siècle*, and they appear not only in the immense seventeenth-century library of hugely popular spiritual and theological writing, but in much other literature as well. To say, with surprise, that Rancé's spirituality is essentially penitential is like saying it is essentially spiritual. It is a mere tautology. And those who throw up their hands in horror when Rancé calls his monks 'gangs of criminals' only reveal their ignorance of the fact that in religious writing of the period 'crimes'—the same word in English and French—could simply be a synonym for sins.

Seventeenth-century France was not twenty-first century North America transported back three or four hundred years. We tend, today, to live in a world of varying shades of grey. Words such as 'evil' and 'wicked' are often shunned as old-fashioned, and freedom is regularly confused with license. Hell (for many of those who believe it really exists) is no longer envisaged as everlasting and excruciating torment, but merely as an unfortunate and temporary period of compensation following a life of somewhat too much indulgence, rather like a mild hangover after a good party. Satan has been reinterpreted as the personified consequences of a troubled childhood, and God, if his existence be admitted at all, is a 'Good Fellow, and 'twill all be well'.[1] On the other hand, at least in most of Europe and North America, we cannot be imprisoned without warrant or executed without cause, and—in general—we do not expect the majority of our infants to die in childhood nor ourselves to die of starvation, tuberculosis, or the plague. Such contrasts may appear obvious, but it is all too easy to look back into the past and interpret what we find there in terms of our own modern predilections. To take but two examples from the cistercian tradition, this has certainly been done with Bernard of Clairvaux and Aelred of Rievaulx, neither of whom would recognize themselves in much of the published pablum which purports to describe their ideas, ideals, and sexual orientation.

This is not, of course, to say that Rancé was no more than a clone of his colleagues. Far from it. They may all have shared certain fundamental principles, but the spiritual writers of seventeenth-century France were a decidedly diverse group of men and women, possessed of formidable intellects, utterly convinced of the rightness and righteousness of their causes, and prepared to state them at considerable length. Rancé certainly was. Once he had discovered, or once he had been shown, the straight and narrow path which led to salvation, once he had determined to bring back to his Order its *premier esprit*, nothing could deflect him from his course. In this matter he made no essential distinction between God's will and his own, and the goals he pursued were, in his view, not his but God's. In this pursuit he had a will of iron and did not care for criticism. He certainly sought approbation for

1. *The Rubáiyát of Omar Khayyám*, tr. Edward Fitzgerald (1859 [1st ed.]), stanza LXIV.

his ideas from respected colleagues, but asked-for advice is one thing; unsought criticism is quite another. There is not the least doubt that Rancé could be proud and stubborn, and his conduct in his controversies with Guillaume Le Roy, Innocent Le Masson, and others cannot be called either irenic or conciliatory. But in this, again, he was a man of his times. The absolute contrasts of the age of absolutism could be seen not only in society but in the individual. It was an age of violent and public passions and there are innumerable examples of both men and women moving from gentle persuasion to vicious attack in the blink of an eye.

Added to this was Rancé's learning and his logic. Indeed, it was his knowledge of his sources and his inexorable logic that led him into so many difficulties. We saw in Chapter Two that recourse to authority was fundamental in *le grand siècle*—novelty and innovation were anathema—and the (for us) tiresome citation of proof-texts which we find in his *De la sainteté* was standard, accepted, and necessary. The problem, of course, is that whereas the rules of logic are fixed and universal, selection of proof-texts is fluid and individual. Rancé's arguments in *De la sainteté* are effective, persuasive, and irrefutable—until one reads the effective, persuasive, and irrefutable counter-arguments of his opponents. Rancé and (for example) Dom Innocent Le Masson both knew what they were talking about—they were not mere politicians—and both knew how to argue. Both, however, combined with a great personal charm a great personal temper, and it did not take much tinder to light the fuse.

There was, however, a fundamental insecurity in Rancé. It is true that once he had convinced himself that a particular course was right, proper, and in accordance with the will of God, he pursued it unshakeably and inflexibly, but it could take him some time to come to that conviction. We may see this in the difficult years following the death of Madame de Montbazon in 1657, when he consulted a number of men and women to help him find his true path. We may see it again in his letters to Bossuet, Le Camus, Barillon, and Achille de

Harlay, seeking their views on his *De la sainteté*, and to Bossuet, Le Camus, Barillon, and Charles-Maurice Le Tellier seeking their opinions on the *Éclaircissements* of 1685. That Rancé did not always agree with their suggestions and criticisms is neither here nor there; the important thing is that he sought them. Like most of us, he needed reinforcement.

When we speak of his inflexibility, however, we must be careful not to make too sweeping a statement. It is certainly true that once he had decided that (for example) the Rule of Saint Benedict demanded the absolute stability of a monk or nun and that the needs of indigent parents did not countermand this requirement, that was that. '*J'y suis, j'y reste.*'[2] But *within* those immoveable boundaries he would do all that he could to assist and comfort his monks and alleviate the distress of the parents. It is rather like a game of chess: we cannot change either the number or disposition of the squares, but within those limits there is room for an infinity of games. There cannot be the slightest doubt that Rancé loved his monks and was loved by them. He took the deepest interest in their welfare and spiritual progress, he was clearly a superb spiritual director, and there is not the slightest reason to disbelieve Félibien des Avaux when he tells us that

> the especial care he takes for the conduct of their souls in no way offends or constrains them. Indeed, it is so much to their taste that they find it difficult to make their confession to anyone else when he gives them leave to do so. And even if he is so rigorous in correcting them that, in public, he appears [too] severe, he nevertheless addresses all their specific concerns with so great a love and tenderness that they never find greater joy than when they can talk to him.[3]

2. The remark is attributed to M. E. Patrice Maurice de MacMahon at the taking of the Malakoff on 8 September 1855.
3. André Félibien des Avaux, *Description de l'abbaye de La Trape. Nouvelle édition, avec figures* (Paris, 1689) 61.

Nor is there any reason to disbelieve the numerous visitors to the abbey who, from Rancé's lifetime onwards, testified to the radiant happiness on the faces of the monks. As Dom Dominique Georges, abbot of Val-Richer, reported to the General Chapter in 1686:

> they love their abbot in a harmony and holy understanding accompanied by sincerity and humility. They find all their joy in remaining attached to him, in revealing to him the whole of their conscience, and in obeying him in everything; and the result is that they always enjoy a profound peace, a sovereign repose, and a tranquillity that nothing can disturb.[4]

Unfortunately, love is not always combined with balanced judgement, and although Jessica might have exaggerated somewhat when she said that love is blind,[5] she did not exaggerate much. Rancé's love for his monks cannot be doubted; his judgement could be seriously flawed. We have seen examples of this earlier, not least in his choice of a successor, and Rancé's judgement of people in general tended to be unreliable. He listened too eagerly to unsubstantiated rumour; he could be too easily influenced by those he sometimes unwisely trusted (the case of Maisne is an obvious example); and he had a decided tendency to believe the worst about people rather than the best. This did not appear to have affected his renown as a spiritual director (it was, in any case, a pessimistic age), but it certainly made his life more difficult and exacerbated the controversies in which he was embroiled. Despite his charity and his undoubted concern for others, both religious and secular (witness his astonishing correspondence), he had a singular gift for making enemies.

4. Pierre de Maupeou, *La vie du Très-Révérend Père Dom Armand-Jean Le Bouthillier de Rancé, abbé et réformateur du monastère de la Trappe* (Paris, 1703 [2nd ed.]) 252.
5. William Shakespeare, *The Merchant of Venice*, vi.36.

On the other hand, Rancé was no saint. Charles Maisne might have tried to make him one, but I doubt that he himself would have been happy with the promotion. In any case, saints are saints because of some heroic virtue, not perfection—we need think only of Jerome—and to expect perfection in this world is to court disappointment. The same is true of consistency, which is ever a doubtful virtue. We need not to be too surprised, then, if Rancé, in theory wholly separated from the world, was both aware of and interested in what was going on there. He was much concerned, for example, with the consequences of the Revocation of the Edict of Nantes, and evinced an even deeper interest in the european campaigns of William III of England, William of Orange.[6] But he himself realized that his interest was inconsistent with his ideals and wrote to Henri Barillon, bishop of Luçon, saying that

> you will be surprised, Monseigneur, that I speak to you of the news of the day. I confess to you that current events make such a strong impression on me that there is nothing I think about more before God. The truth is that when God has brought peace to all Europe, and when the king's arms are triumphant, as I hope they will be, from the protection God will give them, I shall happily return to the ignorance in which I lived before these recent disturbances.[7]

Similarly, we need not believe Rancé's protestations that he did not intend his *De la sainteté* and certain other works for publication. Not to put too nice a word upon it, he is lying. Given the literary conventions of the times, it is not much of

---

6. See Letters 881013, 881017, 881100, 890126, 890414, 890903, 90/2, 920619, 920619a, and 930820.
7. Letter 920619.

a lie, but a lie it is. And there are also other occasions when what Rancé says does not quite accord with what he does. But so what? He may have been seeking perfection, but he never claimed to have achieved it, and there is no reason to throw away the two volumes of his greatest work merely because we do not wholly believe what we read in the foreword. The anomalies we see in Rancé, in fact, are minor when compared with those we see in his great friend and compatriot, Bossuet. But what Professor Krailsheimer has rightly called 'the deep gulf between [Bossuet's] private spiritual leanings and the public utterances to which his position committed him'[8] does not detract from his greatness. He, too, made serious errors of judgement and—like Rancé—his influence both during and after his lifetime was far from being invariably luminous.

Rancé was emphatically a man of his times, and his conduct, his conversion, his ideas, and his writings cannot really be appreciated outside them. Not one of his ideas is original. He did not intend them to be. As a reformer he was, in his own view, a re-former, not a revolutionary, and the superabundant proof-texts cited in *De la sainteté* bear eloquent testimony to his conception that what he said was no more than what was said by Saint Benedict and the early cistercian fathers, Saint Bernard above all. There is truth in this. As I have suggested earlier, Rancé's vision of Bernard may well have been closer to Bernard's vision of himself than we nowadays are prepared to admit. But does this mean that there is no originality at all in Rancé? It does not. It is true (I think) that all his ideas can be parallelled elsewhere, but to say, as a consequence, that his monastic spirituality is merely a second-hand spirituality is absurd. Bach and Berlioz both use the same notes and the same diatonic scale, but you can hardly mistake the music of one for that of the other. And if we rearrange the letters of DOG to form GOD, only the most

8. Alban J. Krailsheimer, *Studies in Self-Interest: From Descartes to La Bruyère* (Oxford, 1962) 173.

devoted cynophile would not see a signal difference between them. No. Rancé remains his own man, and if, inevitably, there are important areas of overlap between him and his fellow *spirituels*, the final message which emerges from the disparate ideas in his works and his letters is interconnected, impressive, and unique. There *is* a distinctly rancéan spirituality, but whether we may also call it cistercian or trappist warrants some discussion.

That it was cistercian is not, in my view, in doubt, provided we remember that there never was a single, uniform, clearly defined cistercian spirituality.[9] We cannot, for example, ransack Rancé's writings for references to the Mother of God, find hardly any,[10] and assert in consequence that he was not truly cistercian. If we were to do so, we would have to cast out William of Saint-Thierry as well. There was, rather, a series—a spectrum—of cistercian spiritualities, each reflecting the ideas and ideals of its protagonists. The spirituality of Bernard of Clairvaux was not that of Guerric of Igny, and the spirituality of Aelred of Rievaulx was certainly not that of Isaac of Stella. And when we come to the later Cistercians—people like John of Mirecourt or Pierre Ceffons of Clairvaux in the fourteenth century, Cipriano de la Huerga or Luis de Estrada in the sixteenth, or Froylán de Urosa in the seventeenth—their neglected teachings present us with a fruitful variety of spiritual themes which only add to the rich diversity of the cistercian tradition. For too long 'cistercian' has been glibly equated with 'bernardine', which does justice neither to Bernard nor to the tradition of which he was but one important representative.

What then of 'trappist'? That Rancé's spirituality was the spirituality of la Trappe in the second half of the seventeenth century is obvious, but 'trappist' has come to mean more

9. See David N. Bell, 'Is There Such a Thing as "Cistercian" "Spirituality"?', *Cistercian Studies Quarterly* 33 (1998) 455-471 and the same author's 'From Molesme to Cîteaux: the Earliest "Cistercian" "Spirituality"', *ibid.* 34 (1999) 469-482.
10. See Krailsheimer, *Rancé*, 75-76.

than that. By the end of the eighteenth century, la Trappe was a flourishing institution, but the clouds were gathering and the storm of the French Revolution was about to ravage the monastic countryside. Thus, in 1791, shortly before the suppression of the abbey, the last novice-master of la Trappe, Dom Augustin de Lestrange (1754-1827), took a group of twenty-two religious and fled from France to Switzerland. There, on 1 June 1791, he re-established the Strict Observance at la Val-Sainte, a former carthusian monastery, in the Canton of Fribourg. Three years later la Val-Sainte was recognized as an abbey by Pope Pius VI and Lestrange's resurrected observance was named the 'Congregation of Trappists'. Two years after that, in September 1796, Lestrange founded the first convent of trappist nuns—Trappistines—at Sembrancher in the Bas-Valais. From this source the Strict Observance was refounded, and, propelled by Lestrange's tireless energy, the Order slowly crept back into Europe. Its later history is not here our concern.

Lestrange was undoubtedly a remarkable organizer, and without his autocratic—dictatorial might be a better word—administration, it is quite possible that the Order would not have survived. But if Rancé was ascetic and penitential, Lestrange was superascetic and hyperpenitential. The regulations he drew up for la Val-Sainte were far more severe than those of either early Cîteaux or seventeenth-century la Trappe, and the consequences were both good and bad. On the one hand, the extraordinary asceticism attracted an extraordinary number of vocations; on the other hand, it also tended to kill them off. Dom Augustin, said a cistercian monk of the Strict Observance in 1944,

> could inspire the monks and nuns with a
> strong realizing faith and with an ardent love
> and virile courage to embrace wholeheartedly
> their life of extraordinary penance, [but] he
> could not add an iota of physical strength to
> bodies reduced by such macerations. It may

be admitted that it was a decided advantage
for many a religious of a delicate constitution
to enter into the eternal reward very shortly
after embracing that life. But it seems probable that the Church, the Mystical Body of
Christ, would have reaped greater spiritual
benefit, had they enjoyed a longer lease on
earthly existence.[11]

What Lestrange lacked, in fact, was the all-important virtue
of *discretio*: discernment. Rancé, on the other hand, in a remarkable letter to Charles de Bentzeradt, abbot of Orval,
tells him that 'discernment (*discrétion*), when free from all
laxity and fleshly indulgences, is a greater virtue than penitence',[12] and advises Bentzeradt not to get too carried away in
his desire for austerity. Lestrange would not have agreed.

The term 'Trappist', then, came to be associated, legally
and traditionally, with Dom Augustin de Lestrange, and
Lestrange's spirituality was not that of Rancé. Indeed, the
very thing of which Rancé has sometimes been accused—an
unbalanced and hyperpenitential asceticism—is far more true
of Lestrange than ever it was of the Great Reformer. Rancé,
too, could be autocratic, but he was never despotic. He was
severe, certainly, and unyielding when it came to the boundaries of the Rule, but within those boundaries, as we have
said, he demonstrated both charity and discernment. He was
also endlessly forgiving, if not to his critics, at least to those
of his brethren who showed any signs of contrition or remorse. Lestrange, on the other hand, could be as despotic as
he could be undiscerning, and although, as Augustin-Hervé
Laffay has shown,[13] it is as easy to present a caricature of
Lestrange as it is of Rancé, his understanding of the trappist

11. [Alberic Wulf], *Compendium of the History of the Cistercian Order. By a Father of the Abbey of Gethsemani, Kentucky, of the Order of Cistercians of the Strict Observance (Trappist)* ([s.l.], 1944) 267-268.
12. Letter 75/2 quoted above in Chapter Six, n. 37.
13. Laffay's detailed study of Lestrange is cited under Further Reading, 249.

life left a great deal to be desired. 'Trappist', therefore, is a term perhaps best avoided for Rancé, and it is not without cause that many—perhaps most—modern Cistercians of the Strict Observance do not care for the term.

It is sometimes said that one of the characteristics of genius is an ability to transcend one's time and place. This is not, of course, wholly correct, for we are all creatures of our time and place whether we like it or not. The works of Shakespeare may have an enduring value, but they cannot be appreciated comprehensively unless we understand something of the milieu in which they were written and from which they came. It is also true that times change and we change with them. In the world of music, for example, there are many composers whose names, nowadays, are unremembered, but who, in their time, were considered equal, and sometimes superior, to those on whom we now bestow the name of genius. Those who wish to hear a live performance of, say, Beethoven's third piano concerto will have little difficulty in finding one. It is infinitely more difficult to find a performance of the third piano concerto of Beethoven's pupil, Ferdinand Ries, which, in its day, was a popular work by a popular and celebrated composer. His concerto, in fact, was dedicated to the even more popular and celebrated Muzio Clementi, who also wrote a fine piano concerto and who ended a long and successful career by being buried in the august confines of Westminster Abbey. Mozart, it will be remembered, found only a pauper's grave.

The re-editions and reprintings of Rancé's works testify to his popularity in seventeenth-century France. Publishers did not work for love, but for money. 'In the usual course of trade', says Graham Pollard, 'a book will never be printed until someone thinks that it can be sold',[14] and that is certainly true of Rancé's favourite publisher, François Muguet, 'Imprimeur ordinaire du Roy & de Monseigneur l'Archevesque, ruë de la Harpe'.[15] But tastes have changed. Most

---

14. Graham Pollard, 'The English Market for Printed Books', *Publishing History* 4 (1978) 9.
15. As he appears on the title-page of the first edition of *De la sainteté*.

people today who seek spiritual guidance within the western christian tradition will look not to the seventeenth century but to the Middle Ages or the early Church, and publishers are well aware that a collection of maxims by the Desert Fathers or Bernard of Clairvaux (for that is what his *Sententiae* are[16]) will have far better sales than the *Maximes chrétiennes et morales* of Armand-Jean de Rancé. On the other hand, it was not so long ago that the works of pseudo-Bernard of Clairvaux were far more popular than those of the real Bernard,[17] and the wisdom of our ancestors cannot always be discarded as mere foolishness.

It would, of course, be possible to present a bowdlerized version of Rancé which would be acceptable to modern tastes. One would omit most of the material on, say, humiliations, overlook the question of monastic stability, and concentrate on what he has to say on prayer, simplicity, charity, and the love of God. But selections of this nature are dangerous things and may reveal more of the mind of the selector than of his or her source. Rancé deserves better, and we can only be ever grateful to Professor Krailsheimer for providing us with a magnificent edition of his correspondence and with offering us english translations of the most important and illuminating letters.[18]

I doubt, however, that Rancé will ever be a popular figure. There is really too great a divide between our present optimistic spirituality and the penitential pessimism of seventeenth-century France. We may esteem and admire him, but love is a different matter. He long ago took his leave of this

16. Now available in english translation in *Bernard of Clairvaux: The Parables & The Sentences*, tr. Michael Casey and Francis R. Swietek (Kalamazoo, 2000).
17. See David N. Bell, 'In Their Mother Tongue: A History of the English Translation of Works By and Attributed to Bernard of Clairvaux: 1496-1970', in *The Joy of Learning and the Love of God: Essays in Honor of Jean Leclercq*, ed. E. Rozanne Elder (Kalamazoo, 1995) 291-308.
18. Professor Krailsheimer has also provided an important overview of Rancé as a correspondent in the eighth chapter of his *Rancé and the Trappist Legacy*: 'Rancé as Seen in his Letters'.

world and we can no longer fall under the spell of his undoubted charisma. We must also remember that he was a
true convert, and it is perhaps impossible for those of us who
have not undergone such an experience to appreciate the white-
hot unquenchable fire which such an event can kindle. Rancé's
spirituality was conversion spirituality and, as we have said
earlier, conversion spirituality is never middling or mediocre.
In an age of absolute contrasts, the absolute contrast between
a sinner doomed to everlasting torment and a sinner redeemed
by the grace of God was, for the sinner in question, the greatest contrast of all. For us today sin is not viewed in quite the
same way. We have become more jesuitical, more laxist, and
Rancé would not have approved. Furthermore, the modern
christian God is seen as compassionate rather than imperi-
ous, and an overwhelming stress on his absolute sovereignty
does not fit well with our modern democratic tastes. Nor does
an overwhelming concern with death and God's judgements,
which is generally seen as morbid and unbalanced rather than
salutary and beneficial. And since Christ is never now defined
as the Great Penitent, it follows logically that the imitation
of Christ cannot be conceived in the way it was conceived by
Rancé or Bérulle or Olier or so many others in seventeenth-
century France.

It is difficult to say, then, to what extent Rancé truly tran-
scends his times. Some of the great themes, christian and
cistercian, on which he dwells are obviously of enduring value,
and if one takes the trouble to browse through his *Maximes
chrétiennes et morales*, some of them will certainly hit home.
But the broad sweep of his spiritual and monastic teaching
cannot really be understood without taking into account the
soil from which it sprang; and although this is also true of
Bernard and William and Aelred and so on, it is, I think, more
true of Rancé. His *De la sainteté* is unquestionably one of the
most important works of post-medieval cistercian monastic
writing and occupies a major place in the history of spirituality. But to what extent it may be useful to modern men and
women, whether lay or religious, is a moot point.

The Cistercians of the Strict Observance of today were raised in a world very different from that which formed those hardy souls who lived the austere life of la Trappe under the Great Reformer. Much was subsequently changed under Dom Augustin de Lestrange; much changed again in the course of the nineteenth century (a period of serious internal dissension); and much more was changed yet again in the years following the Second Vatican Council. La Trappe still exists as a thriving abbey under a discerning abbot, but Rancé would not be at home there. The buildings familiar to him were almost all destroyed during and after the French Revolution. The landscape has changed. And although the monastic day is still divided between the *opus Dei*, manual labour, *lectio divina*, prayer, eating, and sleeping in accordance with the Rule of Saint Benedict (which, following the Second Vatican Council, has been reaffirmed as the fundamental guide to monastic life), many of the actual practices of present-day cistercian life would not—could not—meet with his approval. He would find the abbey a noisy place, the liturgy hurried, the monks over-fed, and the separation between the world inside and outside the cloister far too amorphous. The abbey is not, in fact, noisy, the liturgy is not hurried, the monks are not over-fed, and the gates of the abbey are still shut against the world, but none of these are as they were in the seventeenth century. Nor should they be. Rancé himself recognized that although certain precepts of the Rule were wholly inviolate, certain others were mutable and might be changed. In his own century, some precepts, not of essential importance, had been abolished with the course of time. Some had been changed because, in their amended form, they offered greater advantage, profit, and edification than if they had been retained unchanged. Others had been abolished or modified by the authority of the Church.[19] But, as the great chinese philoso-

19. See Rancé's *La Règle de saint Benoist, nouvellement traduite et expliquée selon son véritable esprit, par l'auteur des 'Devoirs de la vie monastique'* (Paris, 1689 [2nd ed.]) 1:95-96.

pher Mencius once said, that was Then, this is Now, and the world of Now has changed in a way beyond Rancé's imagining. It is inevitable, therefore, that the Cistercian Order has also changed, sometimes dramatically; but as Father Chrysogonus Waddell has pointed out, the changes that have taken place are not of essential importance 'so long as we are sincere and reasonably successful in our attempts to be faithful, in the changed conditions of our present world, to the tradition we recognize as God's special gift to us Cistercians'.[20] We might not now agree with Rancé's teaching on humiliations, penitence, stability, and the like, and we might agree even less with the exaggerated asceticism of Lestrange; but without them and their great contributions the Strict Observance might never have survived, and the world, especially the monastic world, would be the poorer without it.

20. Chrysogonus Waddell, 'The Cistercian Dimension of the Reform of La Trappe (1662-1700): Preliminary Notes and Reflections', in *Cistercians in the Late Middle Ages*, ed. E. Rozanne Elder (Kalamazoo, 1981) 143.

FURTHER READING

For brief english summaries of the history of the Strict Observance after Rancé, see Krailsheimer, *Legacy*, 124-138, and Stephen Tobin, *The Cistercians: Monks and Monasteries of Europe* (London, 1995) 175-188. A more detailed (but biased) account may be found in Louis J. Lekai, *The Cistercians. Ideals and Reality* (Kent OH, 1977), chs. XII-XVI (153-224). The important papers in *Réformes et continuité dans l'ordre de Cîteaux: De l'Étroite Observance à la Stricte Observance. Actes du Colloque. Journées d'Histoire Monastique, Saint-Mihiel, 2-3 octobre 1992* (Brecht, 1995) are all in French, but english summaries are provided on pages 205-209. The astonishing story of the 'Monastic Odyssey' of 1798-1800 through Bavaria, Austria, Bohemia, Russia, Lithuania and the Rhineland may now be read in Marie de la Trinité Kervingant, tr. Jean Holman, *Monastic Odyssey* (Kalamazoo, 1999), though it is primarily concerned with the cistercian nuns. The book is an english translation of the same author's *Des Moniales face à La Révolution Française: aux origines des Cisterciennes-Trappistines* first published at Paris in 1989. The only comprehensive study (more than 650 pages) of Dom Augustin de Lestrange is in French: Augustin-Hervé Laffay, *Dom Augustin de Lestrange et l'avenir du monachisme (1754-1827)* (Paris, 1998). It is an excellent piece of work and there is nothing satisfactory in English. The story of the Trappistines, especially the English Trappistines, may be read in the old but still useful *La Trappe in England. Chronicles of an Unknown Monastery*, by A Religious of Holy Cross Abbey, Stapehill, Dorset [Mother Bernard Payne] (London, [1937]; repr. Louisville KY, 1946). The curious history of the trappist community at Lulworth in Dorset (England) is told in the all-too-brief paper by Dominic Aidan Bellenger, ' "A Standing Miracle": La Trappe at Lulworth, 1794-1817', in *Monks, Hermits and the Ascetic Tradition. Papers Read at the 1984 Summer Meeting and the 1985 Winter Meeting of the Ecclesiastical History Society*, ed. W. J. Sheils (Oxford, 1985) 343-350. See also the same author's 'The French Revolution and the Religious Orders. Three Communities 1789-1815', *Downside Review* 98 (1980) 25-41 (especially pages 26-34 for the Lulworth Trappists) and Jonathan Gell, 'The Return of the Cistercians to England', *Hallel* 10 (1982) 81-86. For the later history of la Trappe itself, together with an excellent account of life in the present-day monastery illustrated by superb photographs, see Dom Marie-Gérard Dubois *et al.*, *L'Abbaye Notre-Dame de La Trappe*, Collection 'Présence du Perche' (Meaucé, 2001). The same volume contains a useful succinct bibliography on pages 187-188 but, once again, there is effectively nothing in English. For reports of life at the abbey both during and after Rancé's lifetime, Tournoüer's bibliography remains indispensable: Henri Tournoüer, *Bibliographie et iconographie de la Maison-Dieu Notre-Dame de la Trappe au diocèse de Sées, de Dom A.-I. Le Bouthillier de Rancé, Abbé et Réformateur de cette abbaye, et en général de tous les religieux du même monastère* (Mortagne, 1894-1896).

PART II

An Annotated Bibliography of Works
By and Pertaining to Armand-Jean de Rancé

I: Works of Rancé.

I.A.i	Printed works (excluding letters, *dubia* and *spuria*).
I.A.ii	Unprinted and untraced works.
I.B	Letters.
I.B.i	Collected letters.
I.B.ii	Single letters.
I.C	*Dubia* and *spuria*.
I.D	Selections from the works of Rancé.

II: Biographies, biographical material, and controversial literature.

II.A	The seventeenth and eighteenth centuries.
II.B	The nineteenth and twentieth centuries.
II.C	Biographies in encyclopedias, dictionaries, and similar compendia.

✝

I) WORKS OF RANCÉ

I.A.i) PRINTED WORKS
(EXCLUDING LETTERS, *DUBIA* AND *SPURIA*)

In chronological order of publication.

Other brief compositions by Rancé will be found (i) in the pages of the early biographers—Maupeou, Marsollier, Le Nain, Gervaise, Dubois (all of whom are listed in II.A below); (ii) in the [1680?] *Recueil de plusieurs lettres du R.P. Abbé de la Trappe* and [1683] *Description de l'abbaye de la Trappe avec les Constitutions* (both listed under I.B.i); and (iii) among the documents admirably edited by Thomas Nguyên-Dình-Tuyên in his 'Histoire des controverses à Rome entre la Commune et l'Étroite Observance de 1662 à 1666', *Analecta Cisterciensia* 26 (1970) 3-247.

[1639] Ἀνακρέοντος Τηΐου τὰ μέλυ. Μετὰ σχολίων Ἀρμάνδου Ἰωάννου Βουθιλλιηρίου Ἀπχιμανδρίτου (Paris: J. Dugast, 1639, 1647; London: G. Bowyer, 1725, 1740 [editio altera]). Tournoüer, nos. 358-359.

> Listed in the 1752 catalogue of the library of la Trappe (Bell, 'Library', 150, n. 78). So far as I know, the only evidence for the 1647 edition is a comment in Maupeou's *Vie de Rancé*, 1:26, which seems to imply that it was a reprinting of the 1639 edition with a different title-page. I have never seen a copy. See further the discussion in Simon Chardon de la Rochette, 'Notice sur l'édition grecque d'Anacréon donnée par l'abbé de Rancé en 1639', in idem, *Mélanges de critique et de philologie* (Paris, 1812) 1:162-163, and Tournoüer, no. 358, who also lists early reviews. The later London editions bore the title *Anacreontis editio altera cum novis versionibus, scholiis et notis* and formed part of Michael Maittaire's edition of Anacreon. For a detailed

discussion, see Chardon de la Rochette, *Mélanges*,
1:174-182. There is some slight evidence for a french
and/or latin version of Anacreon by Rancé, but if
such a translation was ever completed, it has not survived: see *ibid.*, 1:168-170.

The only study of the Anacreon commentary (and
an excellent study it is) is the 'Notice sur l'édition
grecque d'Anacréon' by Simon Chardon de la Rochette
noted above. This first appeared in the *Magasin
encyclopédique*, V^e année, tom. 6 (June 1799) 460-496
and VIIe année, tom. 2 (February 1801) 193-203, and
was then reprinted in *idem*, *Mélanges de critique et de
philologie* (Paris, 1812) 1:144-195 (Tournoüer, no. 67).
The author presents an analysis of the book, examples
of the scholia (in greek and in french translation), a
detailed discussion of their sources, and the greek
text of the dedicatory letter to Cardinal Richelieu
together with french and latin translations. His assessment of the book is that 'it is, in general, well
done' (*Mélanges*, 150) and that it would be a useful
introduction for youngsters learning Greek. The text
of Anacreon (taken from Henri Estienne's edition)
would need revision and the commentaries would need
corrections and additions, but it could certainly be a
valuable tool. Whether the commentary is entirely
the work of the young Rancé is a moot point. Professor Krailsheimer has suggested that 'it is not necessary to believe that it is all, or mostly, R[ancé]'s own
work' (note to Letter 410110), but Rancé's authorship is defended by Dubois (1866) 1:26, Chardon de
la Rochette, *Mélanges*, 165-174, and Chrysogonus
Waddell in his 'Abbé de Rancé and Monastic Revival',
in *The Spirituality of Western Christendom, II. The Roots
of the Modern Christian Tradition*, ed. E. Rozanne Elder
(Kalamazoo, 1984) 321, n. 49. Henri Bremond, as we
might expect, denies Rancé's authorship and attributes

the work entirely to his tutor Bellérophon (see II.B
[1929] below). Rancé himself, in a letter written in
1692 (Letter 920416), says that what he produced on
Anacreon was nothing of consequence. What else, he
writes, could one expect from the pen of someone
twelve years old? 'I loved literature and took pleasure
in it: that's all.' I do not believe that the old Rancé
would say that he produced the work if he did not,
but there surely cannot be any doubt that he would
have benefited from his tutors' guidance. We might
add that the choice of Anacreon for his first essay in
publication was not especially remarkable: the poet
was popular in the France of his time.

[1665?] *Lettre du B. Fastrède, abbé de Cambron, disciple de S. Bernard et depuis 3. abbé de Clairvaux, à un abbé de l'Ordre qui sous
prétexte de faiblesse ne mangeoit que des viandes délicates et différentes
de la nourriture commune de l'Ordre, traduite en françois par M.
A.J.B.D.R., abbé de N.-Dame de la Trape, du mesme Order de Cisteaux*
([Paris?]: [s.n.], [1655?]). Tournoüer, no. 424.

> This is a quarto pamphlet of seven pages. For the
> original letter, see *PL* 182:704D-706C: 'Ep. CDXCI
> Fastredi abbatis Claræ-Vallensis tertii ad quemdam
> ordinis sui abbatem'.

[1671] *Constitutions de l'abbaye de la Trappe, avec un discours sur la
réforme*: see I.C: *Dubia* and *spuria*, [1671].

[1673] *Requeste présentée au Roy par le Révérend Père Abbé de la
Trappe* (Paris: J. Langlois fils, 1673). Tournoüer, nos. 369-370.

> = Lekai, 'Bibliography', 137, no. 152. This pamphlet
> of eight pages is often found bound with the *Requeste
> présentée au Roy par les Abbez, Prieurs, et Religieux de
> l'Estroite Observance de l'Ordre de Cisteaux. Extrait des
> registres du Conseil d'État (27 septembre 1673)* (Paris: J.

Langlois fils, 1673) (= Lekai, 'Bibliography', 137-138, no. 153). This second pamphlet then appears as pages 9-13 of the combined document. Both pamphlets are reprinted in I.B.i [1680?] *Recueil de plusieurs lettres du R.P. Abbé de la Trappe* and [1683] *Description de l'abbaye de la Trappe avec les Constitutions* listed below. For the Common Observance reactions to these *requestes*, see Lekai, 'Bibliography', 138, nos. 154-155. See also Tournoüer, no. 174. Rancé's *Requeste* is also reprinted in Louis Dubois, *Histoire civile, religieuse et littéraire de l'abbaye de la Trappe, et des autres Monastères de la même Observance qui se sont établis tant en France que dans les pays étrangers avant et depuis la révolution de 1789, et notamment de l'Abbaye de Mellerai; suivie de chartes et d'autres pièces justificatives, la plupart inédites* (Paris, 1824 [Tournoüer, no. 152]) 344-356.

For the place of these pamphlets in the War of the Observances, see (in English) Lekai, *Strict Observance*, ch. XI (143-157), especially 152. See also the brief account in Part I of this present study, Chapter Three.

[1674] *Éclaircissement sur l'état présent de l'Ordre de Cisteaux* (Paris: J.-B. Coignard, 1674).

= Lekai, 'Bibliography', 140-141, no. 168. For the Common Observance reply to this *Éclaircissement*, see Lekai, 'Bibliography', 141, no. 169, and for its place in the War of the Observances, Lekai, *Strict Observance*, 154.

[1677] *Lettre d'un abbé régulier sur le sujet des humiliations, et autres pratiques de religion*: see under this year and title in I.B.ii.

[1677] *Relations de la mort de quelques religieux de l'abbaye de la Trappe* ([Paris?]: [s.n.], 1677; E. Michallet, 1678, 1678 [2nd ed.], 1681, 1683 [3rd ed.], 1691 [new ed.], 1702; Paris: F. & P. Delaulne,

1696-1713, 1715-1718, 1717; Trévoux: Impr. de Son Altesse Sérénissime Mgr. Prince Souverain de Dombes, 1697; Paris: E. Michallet and Brussels: L. Marchant, 1702; Paris: Veuve Delaulne, 1741; Paris: G. Desprez, 1755, 1758). A reduced xeroxed facsimile (in one volume) of the four volumes of the 1741 Paris edition was published in 2000 by Father Martinus Cawley, OCSO, Guadalupe Translations, P.O. Box 97, Lafayette, Oregon 97127, U.S.A. Bourgeois/André, no. 1374; Tournoüer, nos. 373-385.

Listed (multiple copies, printed and manuscript) in the 1752 catalogue of the library of la Trappe with the (correct) note that 'plusieurs de ces Relations sont de M^r. de Rancé' (Bell, 'Library', 154, 156-157). For the 1677 edition, 'sans nom d'imp.'—the first (unauthorized) printed collection—I am dependent on Tournoüer, no. 373. The first printed edition to be authorized by Rancé was the Paris 1696 edition in two volumes. The most complete series was published in five volumes seventeen years after Rancé's death as *Relations de la vie et de la mort de quelques religieux de l'abbaye de la Trappe. Nouvelle édition, augmentée de plusieurs vies qui n'avoient pas encore paru, avec une description abrégée de cette abbaye* (Paris: G. Desprez, 1755). The 1758 edition is identical, save that it appeared in four volumes instead of five. It is the work of several authors, one of whom was certainly Rancé, and this final version includes an account of the death of Rancé himself.

At least ten celebrated *Relations* were published independently:

(i) *Instruction sur la mort de Dom Muce, religieux de l'abbaye de la Trappe* (Paris: F. Muguet, 1690), which appeared bound with the *Carte de visite faite à l'abbaye de N. Dame des Clairets, par le Révérend Père Abbé de la Trappe, le seiziesme Février 1690* listed at [1690 *Carte de visite*] below. This lurid and sensational account proved to be a popular work which, as Professor Krailsheimer has said, 'provoked a storm of criticism, several parodies, and a vigorous defence by Rancé and his friends' (Krailsheimer, *Rancé*, 93).

(ii) *Relation de la vie et de la mort de frère Palémon, religieux de l'abbaye de la Trappe, nommé dans le monde le comte de Santéna* (Paris: E. Josset, 1695, 1696 [2nd ed.]; G. Cavelier fils, 1712 [another printing of the 2nd ed.]; repr. Toulouse, 1861 [Tournoüer, nos. 408-409]). A german version of this *Relation* was published as *Wunderbarliche Lebens-Bekehrung und Todt des Bruder Palemonis* (Sraubing, [s.d.]). The only copy I know of this translation was bound with *Satzungen, wie sie beobachtet werden in denen Abbteyen zu Trappa, Buon Sollazzo, und Düssenthal nach der strengen Observanz des h. Cistercienser-Ordens* (Regensburg, 1738) and Joachim of Fiore, *Geistliches Wohlklingendes Cymbalin, das ist Merckliche Lehr-Punkten wasgestalten die sieben Tagzeiten* (Regensburg, 1738). The composite volume was offered for sale by Maggs Bros. Ltd. (London) in 2003 for US $990.95.

(iii) *Relation de la vie et de la mort du frère Albéric, religieux de la Trappe, nommé dans le monde Jean-Baptiste de Sainte-Colombe d'Oupia* (Paris: F. Delaulne, 1705).

(iv) Alexis d'Avia, *Compendio della vita di Fr. Arsenio di Gianson, monaco cisterciense della Trappa, chiamato nel secolo il conte di Rosemberg, morto nella badia di Buonsollazzo il di 21 giugno 1710* (Florence: J. Guiducci e santi Franchi, 1710 [Tournoüer, no. 24]). French translations: (by Jean-Baptiste Droüet de Maupertuy) *Abrégé de la vie de frère Arsène de Janson, religieux de l'Ordre de Cîteaux de la réforme de la Trappe, connu dans le siècle sous le nom de comte de Rosemberg, mort dans l'abbaye de Bonsolas en Toscane, le 21 juin 1710* (Avignon: Société des libraires du S.

Office, de la cité et de l'Université, 1711 [Tournoüer, no. 25]); (by Antoine Lancelot) *Relation de la vie et de la mort du frère Arsène de Janson, religieux de la Trappe, nommé dans le monde le comte de Rosemberg, mort dans l'abbaye de Buon Sollazzo en Toscane* (Paris: F. Delaulne, 1711, 1722 [Tournoüer, no. 26]).

(v) *Instructions sur la mort du frère Jean Climaque, Religieux de la Trappe, nommé dans le monde Alexandre-Claude Bosc Dubois; avec les Sentimens et les Exercices de Piété, qu'il a composés et pratiqués à la Trappe jusqu'à sa mort, arrivée le 14. de Décembre 1703* (Paris: F. Muguet, 1705 [Tournoüer, no. 77]). The *Instructions* and the *Sentimens* have separate pagination (1-107 and 1-334), but are invariably found bound together.

(vi) *Relation de la vie, de la conversion, et de la mort du frère Dorothée, nommé dans le monde François Jacob, natif de Dijon, Diocèse de Langres, & mort à la Trappe le 3. de Janvier 1716. Où l'on a ajouté des Sentimens de Piété sur les devoirs du Chrétien* (Rouen: E. Herault et Jore, 1717). The *Sentimens* appear on pages 121-154.

(vii) *Relation de la vie et de la mort du F. Colomban, Religieux Profés de l'Abbaïe de Buonsollazzo près Florence, de l'étroite observance de l'Ordre de Cîteaux, appellé dans le monde Adrien Demiannay, mort le 16 du mois de May 1714* (Paris: F. Delaulne, 1718) which also exists in an Italian translation by Dom Joseph-Dominique d'Inguimbert (see Further Reading to Part I, Chapter One), *Relazione della vita di F. Columbano* ([s.l.], 1724 [Tournoüer, no. 230]).

(viii) *Relation de la vie et de la mort du frère Alexis, religieux de la Trappe, nommé dans le monde Robert Grême* [= Robert Graham, d. 1701], *gentilhomme écossois* (Paris: F. Delaulne, 1705).

(ix) *Relation de la mort du frère Achilles, religieux de la Trappe, nommé dans le monde le chevalier d'Albergotti, natif d'Arrezzo en Toscano* (Paris: F. Delaulne, 1705).

(x) *Relation de la mort de D. Bernard Mullet.* The 1752 catalogue of the library of la Trappe (Rouen, *Bib. mun.*, MS 2240 [Coquebert de Montbret Y.4], p. 29, 167) lists six duodecimo copies of this *Relation*, but I have not traced a surviving example. The same catalogue (same reference) also lists a manuscript copy in octavo of a *Relation de la mort du f. Antoine de Perthuis, et du f. François de Charny, tous deux Religieux de La Trappe.* Antoine de Perthuis was formerly a captain in the regiment of Navarre and died in 1715; François Lotin, chevalier de Charny, died in 1716. To the best of my knowledge, neither of these *Relations* was ever published. The same is true of the duodecimo *Relation de la vie et de la mort de f. Sébastien r^x. de la Trappe* listed as a manuscript on page 71 of Paris, *Archives nationales,* F^{17} 1177 (Orne).

In 1675 Rancé wrote to the Maréchal de Bellefonds (Letter 750410) saying that he had left with him 'some rather jumbled accounts' of the circumstances of the deaths of two brothers of la Trappe and that it was of first importance that they be seen by no one but him. As usual, however, the material was leaked, first by Nicolas Pinette to whom Rancé wrote in January 1676 (Letter 760100b) regretting that he, Pinette, had divulged what was, in fact, confidential. The first edition of the *Relations* then appeared in 1677 (though it had not been authorized by Rancé), and in 1678, in a letter to his brother-in-law (Letter 781022), Rancé said that some people had been pleased with them while others found them only depressing. The next we hear of them is a decade later when Rancé sends the most recent *Relations* to Mademoiselle de Vertus

(Madame de Montbazon's sister, then ill and bed-ridden at Port-Royal) together with some other edifying works (Letter 870520). Eight years after that, in November 1695, he sent Jean Gerbais (a Doctor of Canon Law and one of the State censors) a copy of a letter from M. de Laquerre in which the latter said how edified he had been by the *Relation* of the death of the former comte de Santéna and pressed Rancé to publish more (Letter 951121). Five days later, having pondered the matter, Rancé wrote again to Gerbais proposing two volumes of ten *Relations* apiece. Next month, he wrote again to Gerbais saying that he would ask Chancellor Boucherat to send *Relations* to him for his approval (Letter 951214). This was done, and Gerbais wrote back to Rancé suggesting that the title *Relations* be changed to the more accurate *Instructions*, as had already been done in the case of Dom Muce (Letter 951218). Rancé was happy to accept the suggestion. Then, in January 1696 (Letter 960105), he wrote yet again to Gerbais saying that he had received the latter's further suggestions and would do what he could to make the necessary changes. Nevertheless, he adds, worldly people will never find much to their pleasure or their taste in reading lives which simply talk about the different ways in which certain monks have practised four or five religious virtues. Yet a considerable number have been touched by what they have read 'and I have often been asked if la Trappe has become dumb and if she will ever speak again'. Gerbais's suggestion of turning the *Relations* into *Instructions*, however, was easier said than done. Earlier in 1696 Delaulne had published two volumes containing twenty-one *Relations* and, as we may see from Letter 960614, Rancé either did not have the time or, perhaps, the inclination to turn them into *Instructions*. He is being pressed, he says, by all sorts of people and from all sides to publish accounts of the lives (and deaths) of his monks, and there can be no doubt that the *Relations* appealed strongly both to a general curiosity about life at la Trappe and a general interest in this type of literature. The fact that we today might call such an interest morbid and abnormal only reflects an ignorance of the seventeenth-century mentality. As we said in Chapters Five and Nine, 'preparation for death' was a matter of great and grave consequence to Rancé's contemporaries, and in September 1696 he wrote, again to Gerbais (Letter 960922), telling him that he had received letters from the highest in the land urging him to continue publishing the *Relations* so as to help them and others prepare for death. James II certainly seems to have profited from reading them (see Letter 970110). See further the important information in Tournoüer, nos. 373-385, and Krailsheimer, *Rancé*, 92-97.

English tr.: (i) An english translation of selected *Relations* is being prepared by Father Martinus Cawley and will be published in due course by Guadalupe Translations, P.O. Box 97, Lafayette, Oregon 97127, U.S.A.; (ii) the xeroxed facsimile of the 1741 Paris edition of the *Relations* listed above contains a long and valuable introduction (I-XL) summarizing the histories contained in the volume; (iii) in the article by Chrysogonus Waddell, 'Notes on the Mass Prayers: From the Spiritual Exercises of an 18th-Century Trappist', *Liturgy O.C.S.O.* 11 (1977) 77-87, 88-95, there is a translation of eleven pages from the *Sentimens et Exercices de Piété* of Frère Jean Climaque listed above as no. (v) of the separately published *Relations*.

German tr.: *Wunder-Werck der Göttlichen Gnad, das ist gründlich und warhaftte Beschreibung...einiger Geistlichen, dess...Closters La Trappe. Vormahls in Frantzösischer Sprach beschriben, nunmehro aber...in die Teutsche getreulich übersetzet* (Augsburg: M. Veith, 1739). Five parts in one volume. See also no. (ii) of the separately published *Relations*.

Italian tr.: *I Prodigi della Grazia espressi nella conversione di alcuni grandi Peccatori, morti da veri Penitenti, nel monastero della Trappa della stretta osservanza cisterciense. Opera trasportata della lingua franceze nell'italiana da un monaco di Buonsollazzo e dedicata a peccatori* (Firenze: J. Guiducci e S. Franchi, 1715). See further Tournoüer, no. 383. A third edition in four volumes was published by J. Mainardi at Rome in 1727.

Spanish tr.: (i) *Relación de la vida y muerte de algunos religiosos de la Abadia de la Trappa...; traducida en español por ... Juan de Sada* [Juan de Sada y Gallego] ... *de la Congregatión Cisterciense* (Pamplona: J.M. de Ezquerro, 1782). Four(?) volumes; (ii) *Vidas de los varones ilustres del Monasterio de la Trapa, escrita en francès por el ... reformador de dicha abadia Don Armando Juan Boutilier de Rancé y otros autores; traducidas en espagñol por el P.M. Don Juan de Sada y Gallego, monge cisterciense* (Pamplona: J. de Domingo, 1797-1799). Four volumes.

[1683] *De la sainteté et des devoirs de la vie monastique* (Paris: F. Muguet, 1683 [two editions], 1684 [3rd ed.], 1685, 1687?, 1701 [new ed.]; repr. Paris: B. Duprat, 1846 [one volume: see II.B (1846)]; Farnborough: Gregg, 1972 [reprint of 1st ed.]). There is also an undated second edition, Paris-Brussels: E.-H. Fricx, probably printed in 1683 or 1684. Bourgeois/André, no. 4988; Tournoüer, nos. 388-392, 394.

The 1752 catalogue of the library of la Trappe lists one copy of the work in manuscript and a number of printed copies (Bell, 'Library', 152). For a summary of *De la sainteté*, see Part I, Chapter Nine.

We first hear of the work in a letter to Bossuet written in June 1682 (Letter 820627) in which Rancé asks Bossuet not to show the manuscript to anyone. It contains, he says 'some instructions which I have given to my brethren concerning their duties and the principal obligations of their profession'. (See also Letters 870703a and 871005). But, continues Rancé, the version which Bossuet has is defective: it is not presented as systematically as it should be, there have been additions and changes which do not appear in the manuscript, some of the ideas expressed are appropriate only for la Trappe, and much of the teaching will not be approved by those outside the abbey because it no longer accords with contemporary usage and customs. Bossuet's first response to Rancé's request was prudent, but afterwards it was he, more than anyone else, who pressed Rancé to publish the work.

By December 1682 Le Camus of Grenoble had read the manuscript and had given it high praise, save for the discussion of monastic stability in which Rancé maintains that monks should not be given permission to leave their monasteries to attend to the needs of sick or indigent parents (Letter 821222a, addressed to Henri Barillon). In the same letter Rancé once more states that the manuscript is defective and that he has made many additions and corrections, but that he would value Barillon's opinion and approval. By 25 December (Letter 821225) Barillon had read the work and had replied to Rancé with suggestions that certain passages be toned down. Rancé agreed, and added that he had no doubt that many people would disagree with what he says in the book, but—like the *Relations*—there will be others who will be moved by its teachings.

By March 1683 (Letter 830311) Rancé had received further suggestions from Bossuet, Barillon, and Le Camus, and the question of the obligation of children to their parents clearly remained problematical. A detailed consideration of the matter, says Rancé, must be left for a second edition of the book which (he says) is 'impatiently awaited'.

After the book was published in March 1683 his sister, Reverend Mother Marie-Louise Bouthillier of the convent of the Annonciades in Paris, read it with approval, but Rancé wrote to her saying that other religious were trying to attack it groundlessly. As far as he was concerned, however, 'it is pure and true in all its principles and contains nothing but what has been taught by the saints' (Letter 830400a). Then, in a letter to Barillon dated 1 April 1683 (Letter 830401), he says that the book has begun to be circulated and is already finding its critics, but that does not surprise him. A letter written the next day (Letter 830402) tells us that the Procureur-Général, Achille de Harlay, comte de Beaumont, has approved it and that it contains truths once familiar but now neglected or, as Rancé says in Letter 830415, 'some very patent truths, but hardly those now in fashion'. This is a standard theme and Rancé states it again and again in a number of letters.

By August 1683 the second edition of the book had appeared, and Rancé wrote again to Barillon (Letter 830817) explaining what had been added or changed. The discussion on parental obligations had been strengthened and there were additions to the sections on prayer, charity, death, and manual labour. But it contained no new principles. As he had expected, some like the work, others do not, but the General of the Carthusians had forbidden it to be read throughout

his Order. The General at this time was Dom Innocent Le Masson who had long disagreed with Rancé
(the matter is considered in Part I, Chapter Seven),
and when one of his Carthusians asked to leave the
Order and enter la Trappe as a result of reading *De la
sainteté*, it was (as Krailsheimer says) the last straw.
That the book was not well received at Rome was, for
Rancé, hardly surprising (Letter 830626).

By December 1693 (Letter 831209) it was evident that
certain *éclaircissements* would be necessary, though in
precisely which areas was not yet clear; and by the
end of that month Rancé wrote to Barillon (Letter
831231) telling him that the book had been criticized
by Jean-Baptiste Thiers (see II.A [1694 Thiers]).
Thiers, at first, had strongly approved of it, but now,
says Rancé, with 'inconceivable eccentricity'—
bizarrerie inconcevable—he has decided to publish a
detailed critique. Rancé, however, falls back on his
usual stand—that what he says is solidly established
by appropriate authorities and that some will obviously dislike the book—but adds in a postscript that
those who are trying to discredit it are the Jansenists,
especially Pierre Nicole, who disagrees with what
Rancé says in the chapter on mitigations. This is an
odd comment and not entirely true, for the Jansenists,
on the whole, approved of the work because of its
austere and ascetic approach to the christian life. In
Letter 840124a, however, Rancé says that he prefers
to reply to the attacks on the book with silence, and
unless God makes it clear to him that he should re-
spond, he will not put pen to paper.

The third edition of the work appeared in 1684, and
in Letter 840802 Rancé wrote to Claude Nicaise saying that 'a Protestant' (the genevan doctor Daniel Le
Clerc) had appreciated it, but that that could not be

said for all Catholics. Two months later (Letter 841009a) he says that Thiers has been unable to obtain permission to have his critique printed and that if he wants it to be published, it will have to be done abroad. He may cause a scandal, says Rancé, he may do harm, he may even carry the point 'as heretics do every day in writing against the clearest and most steadfast truths of the faith', but Rancé will say no more about it for the moment.

A year later (Letter 851028) Rancé was considering a latin version of the work which he thought would be approved in Rome, but nothing came of the idea, and by that time the *Éclaircissements* (listed immediately below) had appeared in print. In the same year, 1685, there also appeared Daniel de Larroque's devastating attack on Rancé and his ideas in *Les véritables motifs de la conversion de l'abbé de la Trappe* listed below at II.A [1685 Larroque].

English tr.: (i) *A Treatise on the Sanctity and on the Duties of the Monastic State. Written Originally in French by the Rev. Father Don (sic) Armand John Le Boutillier de Rancé, Abbot and Reformer of La Trappe*, trans. by a Religious of the Abbey of Melleray, la Trappe (Dublin: R. Grace, 1830). Two volumes. The translator was almost certainly Dom Vincent Ryan, formerly prior of Melleray in France, and subsequently first abbot of Mount Melleray in Ireland; (ii) [Anon.], 'Rancé mystique: la prière de saint Antoine', *Collectanea Cisterciensia* 25 (1963) 250-252 (English translation of *De la sainteté* (1683 [2nd. ed.] 1:403-409: 'Quelle estoit la pensée de saint Antoine quand il dit, que celuy-là ne prie point véritablement, qui s'apperçoit qu'il prie?'); (iii) [Anon.], 'Two Excerpts from de Rancé's Treatise on the Holiness and Duties of the Monastic Life', *Cistercian Studies* [*Quarterly*] 8 (1973) 53-63 (English translations of *De la sainteté* [1683 (1st ed.)] 1:131-140 and 196-206).

German tr.: *Des Hochwürdigen und Gottseeligen im Leben und nach dem Todt wunderthätigen Herrn Armandi Joannis de Rancé, Abbtens und Reformators des Closters U.L. Frauen zu La Trapp, Cistercienser Ordens, welcher den 27. Octobris 1700 heilig verschiden ist, vortreffliches Werck von der Heiligkeit und denen Pflichten des klösterlichen Lebens; mit beygefügter Erläuterung und Widerlegung der dagegen gemachten Austellungen oder Einwendungen, wie auch der Lebens-Ordnung von La Trapp...* (Augsburg: M. Rieger, 1750). One volume.

Italian tr.: *La Teologia del chiostro, overo la Santità, e le Obbligazioni della Vita Monastica. Opera composta e pubblicata da un' abbate dell'Ordine Cistercense. Alla Santità di Nostro Signore Papa Clemente XII, Pontfice Ottimo Massimo* (Rome: A. de'Rossi, 1731). Three volumes, of which the third contains an Italian translation of the *Éclaircissemens de quelques difficultez que l'on a formées sur le livre De la sainteté et des devoirs de la vie monastique* listed immediately below. The translation was made by Dom Malachie d'Inguimbert. Tournoüer, no. 393.

Spanish tr.: *Santidad y deveres de la vida monastica: obra utilisima para todo religioso, y singularmente para los profesores de la regla santa, escrita en Frances por Don Armando Juan Boutiliher de Rancé, Abad reformador de el ... Monasterio de Nuestra Señora de la Trapa; traducida en español por el R.P. Mʳᵒ. Don Juan de Sada, Monge Cisterciense* (Pamplona: B. Cosculluela, 1778). Three volumes.

[1685] *Éclaircissemens de quelques difficultez que l'on a formées sur le livre De la sainteté et des devoirs de la vie monastique* (Paris: F. Muguet, 1685, 1686 [2nd ed., dated by accident 1586], 1686

[2nd ed., another printing with the correct date]; repr. Paris: Sagnier & Bray, 1847). Tournoüer, nos. 395-397.

> Listed (two copies) in the 1752 catalogue of the library of la Trappe (Bell, 'Library', 152-153). The book contains twenty-six 'difficulties' arising from *De la sainteté*, all of which are conveniently summarized in the unpaginated 'Table des Difficultez & des Eclaircissemens' which appears at the beginning of the work. On 4 January 1685 Rancé wrote to Henri Barillon (Letter 850104) saying that he knew the bishop had received copies of the third edition (1684) of *De la sainteté* and that he would now send him a copy of the *Éclaircissemens* for his opinion. They contain, he said, 'the same ideas and the same principles' as the earlier work, but 'supported and proved by different authorities and [arguments?]'. He is sure that this will correct many people's misunderstandings and convince them that his ideas are correct. His optimism, however, was unjustified and the book merely gave rise to further controversy. Meanwhile he had also sent proofs of the book to Le Tellier, archbishop of Reims, Le Camus, bishop of Grenoble, and Bossuet, bishop of Meaux, all of whom approved it. Then, on 9 April, he wrote again to Barillon (Letter 850409) asking him to make any comments in the margin of the proofs and send them on to Muguet, the publisher. He makes it clear here that *De la sainteté* had caused a considerable stir, but that—in his opinion—the difficulties and doubts that had been raised were 'unjust and unfounded'. Rancé had written nothing that was 'not in the order of God' (Letter 850802). See also Letter 850611. The second edition of the *Éclaircissemens*, he told Barillon, contained only 'some minor additions' (860131a).

> Italian tr.: *Dilucidazione di alcune difficultà formate sopra*

la teologia del chiostro, cioè sopra il libro Della santità, e delle Obbligazioni della Vita Monastica (1731), published as the third volume of Malachie d'Inguimbert's translation of the *De la sainteté et des devoirs de la vie monastique* listed immediately above.

Spanish tr.: *Suplemento primero a la obra intitulada De la Santidad y deberes de la vida monastica... traducida del frances en español ... por el R.P.M. Don Juan de Sada, Monge Cisterciense...* (Pamplona: J.M. Ezquerro, 1785).

[1686] *Les Instructions de saint Dorothée, Père de l'Église grecque, et abbé d'un monastère de la Palestine, traduites de grec en françois* (Paris: F. Muguet, 1686). Tournoüer, no. 398.

Listed in the 1752 catalogue of the library of la Trappe (Bell, 'Library', 154). In his *Vie de Dom Pierre Le Nain* (II.A [1715] below), Arnaudin incorrectly attributed this translation to Le Nain, but Le Nain himself listed it (correctly) among the works of Rancé. The work begins with a life of Dorotheus (1-62) which is followed by his *Instructions* (63-318). Some letters attributed to Dorotheus appear on pages 320-326 and these are followed (327-333) by 'De l'estat et de la disposition extérieure dans laquelle doit être un moine'. The volume concludes with an unpaginated table of chapters and instructions. According to Dubois (1866) 2:98, Rancé thought that the two existing translations of Dorotheus, one in French and one in Latin, were seriously defective, and that a new and accurate version would serve 'to revive in the souls of his monks the love of penitence and humiliations'.

[1688] *La Règle de saint Benoist, nouvellement traduite et expliquée selon son véritable esprit, par l'auteur des 'Devoirs de la vie monastique'* (Paris: F. Muguet and G. & L. Josse, 1688 [one volume; Broekaert, no. 441]; F. Muguet and G. & L. Josse, 1689 [two volumes; Broekaert, nos. 445 and 447]; F. Muguet, 1689 [two volumes in one; Broekaert, no. 446]; Veuve F. Muguet, 1703 [two volumes; Broekaert, no. 491]). For reproductions of the title-pages of the 1689 and 1703 editions, see Anselm M. Albareda, *Bibliografía de la Regla Benedictina* (Montserrat: Monestir de Montserrat, 1933) 164-165. Bourgeois/André, no. 4986; Tournoüer, nos. 400-401.

Listed (multiple copies) in the 1752 catalogue of the library of la Trappe (Bell, 'Library', 153). For the relationship of the 1688 edition to that of 1689 (which is most commonly cited), see the notes to Broekaert, no. 441, and Mensáros, 197-199. See also [1689] *La Règle de saint Benoist* below.

Rancé's new translation and commentary was (in large part) intended to defend himself against accusations that his interpretation of the Rule was unreasonable and incorrect. The most aggressive of these attacks had been made in 1687 by the learned Maurist Antoine-Joseph Mège (1625-1691) in his *Commentaire sur la Règle de saint Benoist, où les sentimens et les maximes de ce saint sont expliqués par la doctrine des Conciles, des SS. Pères...* (Paris: Veuve E. Martin, 1687 [Broekaert, no. 433; Bourgeois/André, no. 4987]). Mège (see *DLF XVII*, 837-838) had been superior of the abbey of Rethel before moving to Saint-Germain-des-Prés, and was a most erudite scholar who left (among numerous other works) a fine life of Saint Benedict. In a letter to Henri Barillon written in April 1689 (Letter 890414) Rancé says that Mège's commentary appeared 'a year ago' (by which time Rancé's own commentary had been completed in manuscript), but that it was 'full of lax ideas and principles wholly opposed to the spirit of saint [Benedict]'. It is a book that does no honour to his Congregation (Letter 890630). His own commentary, Rancé tells Barillon, contains just the same ideas and principles which he, Barillon, had already approved in *De la sainteté*. Even Dom Mège's Maurist superiors thought that he might have gone too far and, under pressure from Bossuet, they supported Rancé's intention to write his own *Explication* and, in 1689, forbade the reading of Mège's commentary. This does not mean, however, that all Benedictines approved of Rancé's work. In Letter 890502 he tells us that they were unwilling to have it read in their houses, and in Letter 891017 he says that the Benedictines and the Carthusians 'are almost the only ones who have not been pleased with it and who have tried to discredit it'. The comment is certainly true of the Carthusians, but, as Professor Krailsheimer points out, benedictine reaction was not universally hostile (note to Letter 890502).

The commentary, says Rancé in Letter 89/5, was written and published only because of pressure from his friends. He himself was reluctant to attempt it and consented only after long deliberation. Whether these comments can be taken at face value is a moot point. The commentary, he continues, took him about three months to write and Bossuet found it 'wonderful in all its parts'. In the same letter Rancé discusses, most unusually, the price of the book and the greediness of his publishers, and declares that he intends to use the proceeds 'for the poor and to set up a certain establishment with a school-master and mistress in a place where the boys and young girls have no more instruction than if they were in a country of barbarians'.

English tr.: *The Rule of Saint Benedict. Translated & Explained According to its true Spirit, by the Abbé de Rancé in 1703. In Two Volumes. Translated into English in 1835* (in manuscript). This (anonymous) translation was completed on 31 October 1835 but was never published. The two manuscript volumes of 400 pages each are at present preserved in the library of the cistercian abbey of Mount Melleray in Ireland. There is a xeroxed copy at the abbey of Gethsemani in the United States.

German tr.: *Des Hochwürdigen und Gottseeligen Herrn Armandi Joannis de Rancé, Abbtens und Reformators des Closters U.L. Frauen zu La Trapp, Cistercienser Ordens, Auslegung der Regul des heil. Benedicti nach dem wahren Geist, das ist, nach der eigentlichen Meinung dises heiligen Vatters. Aus dem Frantzösischen ins Deutsche übersetzt durch einen Priester Ord. S. Benedicti* (Augsburg: M. Rieger, 1753). Broekaert, no. 606; Tournoüer, no. 403.

Italian tr.: *La regola di S. Benedetto tradotta, e spiegata secondo il suo vero spirito. Opera da F. Malachia d'Inguimbert, Abate della stretta Osservanza dell'Ordine Cisterciense...* (Rome: G. Mainardi, 1722). Three volumes. Broekaert, no. 541. The translation was made by Dom Malachie d'Inguimbert from the French edition of 1689 (Broekaert, no. 445).

Spanish tr.: *La Regla de San Benito explicada según su verdadero espiritu por el autor de La Santidad y Deberes de la Vida Monastica. Traducido en español del francés por el Traductor de la dicha Santidad y Deberes el R.P. Maestro Don Juan de Sada, Monge Cisterciense del Real Monasterio de Santa Maria de Piedra...* (Pamplona: Viuda de Ezquerro, 1792). Two volumes. Broekaert, no. 689. The translation was made by Juan de Sada y Gallego from the french edition of 1703 (Broekaert, no. 491).

[1688] *Œuvres spirituelles de Mme. de Bellefont* (Paris: H. Josset, 1688).

For Rancé's editorial contribution to this work of

Laurence Gigault de Bellefont (or Bellefonds), reformer and superior of the benedictine abbey of Notre-Dame-des-Anges in Rouen, see Letters 870211 and 870309. As Krailsheimer observes, Letter 870309 'appears to be the sole, but conclusive, evidence that R[ancé] was the author or editor of material never hitherto attributed to him' (note to Letter 870309). For Laurence de Bellefonds, see *DLF XVII*, 130.

[1689] *La Règle de saint Benoist. Traduction nouvelle* (Paris: F. Muguet, 1689 [Broekaert, no. 443-444 (two editions in the same year)]; Brussels: E.H. Fricx, 1691 [Broekaert, no. 460]; Brussels: F. Foppens, 1704 [Broekaert, no. 493]; [Paris]: [P. Vincent], [1755] [Broekaert, no. 613]; Caen: G. Le Roy, 1786 [Broekaert, no. 677]; Paris: Lib. Rusand, 1824 [Broekaert, no. 717-718]; Cholet: F. Lainé, 1845 [Broekaert, no. 755]; Clermont-Ferrand: Lib. Catholique, 1848 [Broekaert, no. 765]; Vannes: J.-M. Galles, 1849 [Broekaert, no. 766 (selections)]; Avignon: Aubanel Frères, 1861 [Broekaert, no. 801]; Tournai: Veuve H. Casterman, 1877 [Broekaert, no. 853], 1878 [Broekaert, no. 862-863 (two editions in the same year)]). For details of these editions, Broekaert's notes *in loc.* are essential reading. Tournoüer, no. 402.

For the history of this translation of the *Regula S. Benedicti* (which Rancé made in collaboration with the Cluniac Dom Claude de Vert) and its relationship to the translations in Rancé's own commentary on the Rule ([1688] above) and Dom Augustin Calmet's *Commentaire littéral, historique et moral sur la Règle de saint Benoît* (Paris, 1734 [Broekaert, no. 558-589]), see the notes to Broekaert, no. 441, 443, 558-559, Mensáros, 196-197 (an unsatisfactory account), and the articles by Michel Pigeon, 'La traduction de la Règle par l'abbé de Rancé à l'usage des Bénédictines de La Trinité à Caen', *Cîteaux: Commentarii cistercienses* 24 (1973) 308-310 (on Broekaert, no. 677), and (especially) Chrysogonus Waddell, 'Rancé as Translator of the Rule of St Benedict', *Cistercian Studies* 17 (1982) 244-256. The two editions of 1824 (Broekaert, no. 717-718) were produced by Dom Augustin de Lestrange who reproduced Rancé's translation with Claude de Vert's *Avertissement* and notes, and added other notes of his own.

[1690] *Les Règlemens de l'abbaye de Nostre-Dame de la Trappe, en forme de Constitutions* (Paris: E. Michallet, 1690; F. & P. Delaulne, 1698, 1718 [new ed.]). Tournoüer, nos. 364-368.

'Règlemens de La Trappe, manuscrit, en un tome' and multiple copies of the printed text are listed in the 1752 catalogue of the library of la Trappe (Bell, 'Library', 153). In the same year (1690) there appeared the *Règlemens généraux pour l'abbaye de Notre-Dame de la Trappe* (Paris: F. Muguet, 1690, 1701 [Tournoüer, nos. 364, 366]), and in 1698 *Les Règlemens de l'abbaye de Nostre-Dame de la Trappe, en forme de Constitutions. Qui contiennent les exercices et la manière de vivre des Religieux* (Paris: F. & P. Delaulne, 1698, 1705 [Tournoüer, nos. 365]). The *Règlemens de l'abbaye de Notre-Dame de la Trappe, en forme de Constitutions, avec des réflexions et la Carte de visite faite à N.D. des Clairets, par le R.P. abbé de la Trappe* was published in Paris by F. Delaulne in 1718. For a listing of the contents of this last edition, see Tournoüer, no. 367, and for the revised version of the *Règlemens* used at La Val-Sainte (which is not here our concern), see *ibid.*, no. 368.

English tr.: *The Regulations of the Abbey of Our Lady of La Trappe in the Form of Constitutions. Printed at Paris, by Estienne Michallet, First Printer of the King, rue S. Jacques, at the Image of St. Paul, 1690, with the privilege of the King*, trans. John Baptist Hasbrouck (Lafayette, 1999).

Italian tr.: *La Regole della Trappa tradotte dal francese da Lorenzo Magalotti [a cura di Cesare Guasti]* (Bologna: G. Romagnoli, 1883; repr. Bologna: Forni pella Commissione per i testi di lingua, 1968 [Scelta di curiosità letterarie inedite o rare dal secolo XIII al XIX; vol. 68, dispensa 196]).

[1690] *Carte de visite faite à l'abbaye de N. Dame des Clairets, par le Révérend Père Abbé de la Trappe, le seiziesme Février 1690* (Paris: F. Muguet, 1690, 1715). The 1690 edition was printed by Muguet together with the *Instruction sur la mort de Dom Muce, religieux de l'abbaye de la Trappe* listed at [1677] above. The two works appeared bound together but with separate pagination. Tournoüer, no. 404.

Listed in the 1752 catalogue of the library of la Trappe together with 'Dernières Conférences du même en la d^{te}. Abbaye des Clairets, en un tome' (Bell, 'Library', 153). The *carte de visite* is also appended to the Paris 1718 edition of the *Règlemens de l'abbaye de la Trappe* (listed at [1690] above), the Trévoux 1697 edition of the *Relations* (listed above at [1677]), and elsewhere: see Tournoüer, no. 404. Les Clairets was a convent of nuns close to la Trappe, and in 1687 a new and aristocratic abbess was elected who was devoted to Rancé. She was Reverend Mother Françoise-Angélique d'Étampes de Valençay. At the time of her election the Visitor of les Clairets was the abbot of Val-Richer, though traditionally it had been the abbot of la Trappe; and after her election, the new abbess pleaded with Rancé to reassume the office. He himself was most reluctant to do so, but eventually succumbed to her importunity, and replaced the abbot of Val-Richer as spiritual director in September 1688. The *carte de visite* is the report of his official visitation in February 1690 (he returned for the benediction of the abbess in July) and for a full account of the visitation and a detailed summary of the contents of the *carte*, the reader must be referred to Chrysogonus Waddell, 'Armand-Jean de Rancé and Françoise-Angélique d'Étampes Valençay: Reformers of Les Clairets', in *Hidden Springs: Cistercian Monastic Women*, *Book Two*. Medieval Religious Women, Volume Three, ed. John A. Nichols and Lillian T. Shank (Kalamazoo, 1995) 599-673.

Both the *Carte* and the *Instruction* were printed without Rancé's authorization. In Letter 901026 he says that he refused to give copies of the *Carte* to those who requested it and that it was the nuns who made it public. Its publication, however, caused an uproar, primarily because of Rancé's restriction of the nuns' biblical reading to the New Testament, Psalms, and Proverbs. The rest of the Old Testament, he said, was not really suitable for nuns and there were far too many stories which had nothing to do with conventual simplicity. The resulting commotion forced Rancé to defend himself in letters to Claude Nicaise (Letter 900911) and Henri Barillon (Letter 900920), where he invokes the names of Basil the Great, Nilus, and John Cassian to support his case. It is true, he tells Nicaise, that there are possible exceptions to the prohibition and that special permission to read the Old Testament may be given to those nuns who would find it useful, but in general it is quite unsuitable for female religious. See further Waddell, 'Armand-Jean de Rancé and Françoise-Angélique d'Étampes Valençay', 639-641.

[1692] *Réponse au Traité des études monastiques* (Paris: F. Muguet, 1692). One volume in 4°; two volumes in 12°. Bourgeois/André, no. 4990; Tournoüer, no. 405.

Listed (six copies) in the 1752 catalogue of the library

of la Trappe (Bell, 'Library', 153). This is Rancé's response to Mabillon's *Traité des études monastiques* published in 1691 and listed in II.A below. The controversy over monastic studies is briefly considered in Part I, Chapter Five, of this present volume, but there is an extensive literature on the subject. The old study by Henry Didio, *La querelle de Mabillon et de l'Abbé de Rancé* (Amiens, 1892 [Tournoüer, no. 147]) retains its value though it is now (inevitably) in need of some revision. The more recent works by Blandine Barrett-Kriegel, *Jean Mabillon* (Paris, 1988) and *La querelle Mabillon-Rancé* (Paris, 1992) are both unreliable. For other secondary sources, see Bell, 'Bibliography', 281 s.v. 'Monastic studies'. For the primary sources, see below at I.A.i [1693 *Examen*]; I.A.ii [1693]; I.B.i [1846 Letters]; I.B.ii [1682 Leclercq]; II.A [1684], [1691], [1692 *Réflexions*], [1692 *Ouvrages posthumes*], [1692 *Réponse*], [1692 Sainte-Marthe], [1693 *Recueil*], [1693 A.D.P.C.E.], [1694 Vert], [1724 Gervaise], and [1761]. For a very useful compilation of relevant materials, see *Science et sainteté: l'étude dans la vie monastique par Dom Jean Mabillon*. Textes recueillis et présentés par René-Jean Hesbert (Paris [*c*.1958]). The book contains selections from the *Traité des études monastiques* and the *Reflexions sur la réponse de M. l'abbé de la Trappe*.

Latin tr.: see s.v. II.A [1692] Jean Mabillon, *Réflexions sur la réponse de M. l'abbé de la Trappe au Traité des études monastiques.*

[1693] *Examen des Réflexions du R.P. Mabillon sur la Réponse au traité des études monastiques.* 1693: see I.A.ii [1693].

[1693] *Instructions sur les principaux sujets de la piété et de la morale chrétienne* (Paris: F. Muguet, 1693, 1694 [at least two printings], 1701 [new ed.]). Tournoüer, no. 407.

As Dubois (1866) 2:747 observes, 'the basic text of this

book is indeed from Rancé's pen, but it was printed without his involvement and with a number of modifications'. The first mention of the book appears in a letter to the duchesse de Guise (Letter 931026) in which Rancé says that the volume is already being widely read and that it comprises maxims taken from his letters and other works. The collection was, however, put together without his participation, and contains 'bad expressions, bad wording, and wretched phrases' which had nothing to do with him. He had tried, unsuccessfully, to prevent its publication, and its public appearance is now a mortification he must 'swallow down'. He elaborates on the matter in a letter to Jean Gerbais (Letter 931128) describing the book as 'an assortment (*ramas*) of maxims and instructions' taken from his letters, and again saying that it was published without his involvement and against his wishes.

It seems, in fact, that the book had its origin in a manuscript by Rancé copied by Pierre de Maupeou who wished to publish it under the title *Maximes chrétiennes*, and that Rancé was indeed able to prevent its initial publication. But Maupeou then waited a few months, made certain additions and changes to the original manuscript, and resubmitted it for publication under the title *Instructions morales et chrétiennes*, pretending that, in this form, Rancé had authorized its appearance. When it was eventually published by Muguet it bore the title *Instructions sur les principaux sujets de la piété*. As to Maupeou, Rancé wrote to him in January 1694 (Letter 940108) saying that he was 'utterly scandalised' by the publication of the book, though he does not accuse Maupeou of having manipulated it.

[1697] *Conduite chrétienne, adressée à Son Altesse Royalle Madame de Guise* (Paris: D. Mariette and F. & P. Delaulne, 1697; F. Delaulne, 1703 [new ed.]). A defective edition, published without Rancé's knowledge or permission, also appeared in 1697 with the title *Conduite spirituelle, pour Son Altesse Royale M★★★. Tirée de l'Ecriture sainte* (Paris: B. Girin, 1697). Tournoüer, nos. 411-413.

Listed (one manuscript and six printed copies) as 'Conduite spirituelle' in the 1752 catalogue of the library of la Trappe (Bell, 'Library', 153). Elisabeth d'Orléans, duchesse de Guise (1646-1696), was a daughter of Gaston d'Orléans by his second marriage. She herself married Louis-Joseph de Lorraine, later duc de Guise, but her life was not happy. She had one child who died in infancy, her husband succumbed to smallpox at the age of twenty-one, her mother-in-law went mad, and her influential half-sister, la Grande Mademoiselle, hated her. Madame de Guise combined great piety with great pride and did not suffer fools gladly, and it is doubtful that anyone with less than Rancé's authority and charisma could have been her spiritual director. She often visited la Trappe and was a regular correspondent with its abbot. His 'firm and gentle guidance', says Professor Krailsheimer, 'evidently brought her comfort in a life of considerable loneliness and disappointment, and behind his invariable tone of respect one discerns a very real human affection' (Krailsheimer, *Rancé*, 303). See further *ibid.*, 298-303.

The *Conduite chrétienne* is one of many such manuals of devotion for pious lay-women to come out of the seventeenth century and it is a sensible, balanced, and humane accomplishment. In Part I of the work Rancé has much of importance to say on the nature and demands of charity and the nature and effects of prayer. The second part, which begins on page 189, contains 'des Instructions sur quelques tems & Fêtes de l'année, & sur le Jubilé. Et des sujets de Reflexions pour s'entretenir chaque jour de la semaine & du mois'. Letter 970314 makes it clear that James II of England had a manuscript copy of the work and had obviously read it carefully since he wrote to Rancé asking for clarification on certain points. One of these involved the jansenist idea that Christ died only for the elect, and Rancé corrects this, pointing out that copyists are not always reliable. He did not say that Christ came 'only for those who would walk after him in the ways he had traced'. What he said was that Christ came 'only to inspire and teach those who would come after him to walk in the ways he had traced for them'. The difference is obvious and fundamental. Madame de Guise died from cancer in 1696 and the *Conduite chrétienne* appeared the following year.

[1698] *Maximes chrétiennes et morales* (Paris: F. & P. Delaulne, 1698; Paris: D. Mariette, 1698; Delft: H. van Rhyn, 1699 [new ed.]; Paris: F. & P. Delaulne and D. Mariette, 1702 [2nd ed.]). Two volumes or two parts in one volume. Tournoüer, no. 414-415.

Listed as 'Maximes spirituelles' in the 1752 catalogue of the library of la Trappe (Bell, 'Library', 153). The work is a rather tedious compilation of more than a thousand texts culled mostly from Rancé's correspondence and earlier writings. Part I (1-256) of the 1699 edition contains 674 maxims and Part II (1-241) 669. At the end there appears a useful unpaginated 'Table des Matières'. By the time it was compiled in 1698 ill health had forced Rancé to retire to the la Trappe infirmary and he had but two more years to live. The first maxim translated in Part I, Chapter Five, n. 5, of the present volume sets the tone for the whole, but as Father Chrysogonus Waddell has pointed out, the

maxims may be very much richer than appear at first
glance: see his 'The Abbot de Rancé and Monastic
Revival' in *The Spirituality of Western Christendom, II.*
The Roots of the Modern Christian Tradition, ed. E.
Rozanne Elder (Kalamazoo, 1984) 159-162.

[1698] *Conférences ou instructions sur les épîtres et évangiles des*
dimanches et principales fêtes de l'année, et sur les vêtures et profes-
sions religieuses (Paris: F. & P. Delaulne and D. Mariette, 1698,
1702-1703 [2nd ed.], 1729). Four volumes. Tournoüer, nos.
417-418 (in no. 418, 1720 is an error for 1702).

Listed in the 1752 catalogue of the library of la Trappe
(Bell, 'Library', 152). Reprinted in Jacques-Paul Migne
(ed.), *Collection intégrale et universelle des orateurs chrétiens.*
Deuxième série (Paris: J.P. Migne, 1866) 90:13-652.

According to Dubois (1866) 2:590, Rancé's *Maximes*
chrétiennes et morales (listed immediately above) had
been widely read and much appreciated, and since
many of them had been extracted from Rancé's *in-*
structions or homilies given to his monks in Chapter,
there was a call for the publication of the homilies
themselves. Rancé was, as usual, reluctant to give his
permission, but eventually did so, and the collected
instructions appeared at the beginning of June 1698.
They are not to be confused with the formal weekly
conferences which took place at the abbey (on which
see *The Regulations of the Abbey of Our Lady of La*
Trappe in the Form of Constitutions. Printed at Paris, by
Estienne Michallet, First Printer of the King, rue S. Jacques,
at the Image of St. Paul, 1690, with the privilege of the
King, trans. John Baptist Hasbrouck [Lafayette, 1999],
35-38), and Charles Maisne, in a letter to Claude
Nicaise, says that he does not know who took the
liberty of actually calling them 'conferences'. 'It
seems', says Maisne, 'that it is the bookseller who has

done what he wanted in this matter, believing that a book bearing the title *Instructions to Monks* would not sell very well. The taste of the times is for homilies' (Dubois [1866] 2:590-591, n. 2). The taste of the times was indeed for homilies, and Maisne is probably correct. For a discussion of the content and style of the 'Instructions', see Dubois (1866) 2:590-594. See further Bernardo Bonowitz, 'Monastic Sanctification in Rancé's Conferences and Instructions on the Epistles and Gospels', *Cistercian Studies Quarterly* 35 (2000) 317-326, and David N. Bell, 'Armand-Jean de Rancé: A Conference on Spiritual Joy', *ibid.* 37 (2002) 33-46, with a translation of the conference for the third Sunday in Advent.

German tr.: *Exhortationes oder Geistliche Ermahnungs-Reden auf alle Sonn und hohe Festen des Jahrs, nebst Einkleydung und Professions-Reden, welche er...seinen Geistlichen im Capitul vorgetragen... Aus dem Französischen übersetzt* (Augsburg: M. Rieger, 1750). One volume.

Spanish tr.: *Conferencias ó instrucciones sobre las epistolas y evangelios de las dominicas y fiestas principales del año ..., escritas en francés por Don Juan Armando de Rancé ...; y traducidas a castellano por ... Hermenegildo Gutiérrez* (Madrid: R. Ruiz, 1793-1795). Four volumes.

[1698] *Règlemens pour les Filles de la Doctrine chrétienne de la ville de Mortagne, faits par le R.P. Armand Jean de Rancé, Ancien Abbé de la Trappe, et approuvez par Monseigneur Savary Evêque de Séez le 1. de May 1697* (Paris: F. & P. Delaulne, 1698). Tournoüer, no. 416.

'Monseigneur Savary' was Mathurin Savary, bishop of Séez from 1692 (though he was nominated to the see a decade earlier) to his death in 1698. For an excellent study and summary of the book, see Chrysogonus

Waddell, 'The Abbot of La Trappe and the School-
girls of Mortagne', *Cistercian Studies* [*Quarterly*] 24
(1989) 127-143. What appears to be the unique copy
of this rarest of Rancé's works is Paris, *Bibliothèque
Mazarine*, 43285. It once formed part of the episcopal
library at Séez. The school itself did not long survive
the death of Rancé, primarily because it had never
received the official approbation of Louis XIV (see
Waddell, 142).

I.A.ii) UNPRINTED AND UNTRACED WORKS

Excluding letters. For Rancéan material in manuscript, see
Tournoüer, pages 141-423, Alexandre-Charles-Philippe Vidier
and Paul Perrier, *Bibliothèque nationale. Catalogue général des
manuscrits français. Table général alphabétique* (Paris, 1939) 5:290,
and Krailsheimer, *Rancé*, 345-354 (not in the french translation).

[*c.*1670/1671] *Declarationes in Regulam Beati Benedicti ad usum
Domus Dei Beatæ Mariæ de Trappa*, in Latin with following french
translation. Manuscript: Paris, BnF, MS lat. 17,134.

Listed in the 1752 catalogue of the library of la Trappe
under the heading 'Œuvres de divers Rel[x]. de La Trappe
qui, excepté deux ou trois, ne sont point nommés' (Bell,
'Library', 155). This work was recognized by Julius
Leloczky to be a radical reworking and amplification of
the *Constitutiones Strictioris Observantiæ Ordinis Cisterciensis
in Regulam Sanctissimi Patris Nostri Benedicti*, edited by
Leloczky in his *Constitutiones et Acta Capitulorum Strictioris
Observantiae Ordinis Cisterciensis (1624-1687)* (Rome:
Editiones cistercienses, 1967). Rancé renders the
Constitutiones more austere. For a description of the work
and the manuscript, see Mensáros, 188-189.

[1690] *Tractatus de Trinitate*. Manuscript: Alençon, *Bib. mun.*, MS 147 'De Trinitate.—Quid Plato et alii nonnulli de Trinitate senserint.—1690'. 212 pages.

> Listed in the 1752 catalogue of the library of la Trappe (Bell, 'Library', 153) as two quarto volumes in manuscript. A note on the fly-leaf reads 'Ce livre est de la propre main de notre R^d. et très S^t. Père D. Armand Jean, réformateur de la Trappe, qui pour notre malheur mourut le mois passé, 31 (*sic*) Octobre 1700, comme il avoit vécu'. The date of Rancé's death given here is incorrect: he actually died between 1 and 2 pm on 27 October 1700. On this text, see the useful notes in Dubois (1869) 1:47-48, especially p. 48, n. 2.

[1693] *Examen des Réflexions que le R.P. Mabillon a faites sur la Réponse à son Traité des études monastiques*. 1693. Manuscripts: Grenoble, *Bib. comm.*, MS 5042 (dated 1718), Alençon, *Bib. mun.*, fonds Léon de la Sicotière, MS 97 (dated 1725), and Rome, *Biblioteca angelica*, fondo antico MS 1460 (s.xviii) (for this third copy, see Mensáros, 201, n. 204, who discovered it).

> This was intended as Rancé's reply to Mabillon's *Réflexions* (= II.A [1692] below), but after the reconciliation of Mabillon and Rancé at la Trappe on 27 May 1693, it was never published. A manuscript copy is listed in the 1752 catalogue of the library of la Trappe (Bell, 'Library', 153). There is, however, what looks very much like a printed and published Spanish translation of the work: *Suplemento segundo a la obra intitulada De la santidad y deberes de la vida monastica, o Examen de las reflexiones que hizo don Juan de Mabillon sobre la respuesta que dio el Abad de la Trapa a su tratado de los Estudios monasticos, escrito por el traductor de la Santidad y Deberes de la Vida Monastica* (Pamplona: Viuda de J.M. Ezquerro, 1786). The translator was the Cistercian Juan de Sada y Gallego, who also translated other

works of Rancé (see I.A.i [1677 *Relations*], [1683 *De la sainteté*], [1685 *Éclaircissemens*], [1688 *La Règle*]). *Examen de las reflexiones que hizo don Juan de Mabillon sobre la respuesta que dio el Abad de la Trapa a su tratado de los Estudios monasticos* is an exact translation of the french title, but I have not yet had an opportunity to compare the work with the french manuscript.

[?] *Tractatus de Incarnatione Verbi.*

Listed in the 1752 catalogue of the library of la Trappe (Bell, 'Library', 153) as two quarto volumes in manuscript. The manuscript seems not to have survived.

[?] *Tractatus de Gratiâ Dei.*

Listed in the 1752 catalogue of the library of la Trappe (Bell, 'Library', 153) as a single quarto volume in manuscript. The manuscript seems not to have survived.

I.B) LETTERS

Rancé's earliest extant letter, to the Jesuit Father Jacques Sirmond, the king's confessor, is dated 10 January 1641 and is written in Greek (= Letter 410110, with a french translation *in loc.* in Krailsheimer's *Correspondance*. For the greek text, see the notes to I.A.i [1639] Ἀνακρέοντος Τηΐου τὰ μέλη). It accompanied the young Rancé's edition of Anacreon. The earliest letter in which Rancé mentions la Trappe dates from 1649 and is to be found in Paris, BnF, MS français 17,391 (vol. 25 [1649] of the correspondence of Pierre Séguier), fol. 216r. It concerns the return to the abbey of a monk who, some years earlier, had shot a local peasant. It is unaccountably omitted from Krailsheimer's *Letters* and *Correspondance*, but may be found in partial transcription in Dubois (1866) 1:212, n. 3.

I.B.i) COLLECTIONS OF LETTERS

<small>IN CHRONOLOGICAL ORDER OF COLLECTION.</small>

See also II.A [1701 Maupeou]; II.B [1866 Dubois].

[1680?] *Recueil de plusieurs lettres du R.P. Abbé de la Trappe; avec la Relation de la mort de quelques autres religieux de cette maison. La Description de l'Abbaye de Sept-Fonds. Et un discours du R.P. abbé* [de Septfons] *touchant la réforme outrée qu'on dit estre dans son Monastère* ([s.l., s.d]). Tournoüer, no. 425.

> According to Tournoüer, no. 425, 'M. l'abbé Dubois en a vu un exemplaire à la Bibliothèque de Sept-Fons, portant la date de 1680' (see Dubois [1869] 1:420, n. 2), but the only copy I have seen of this very rare book (in the library of la Trappe) has neither date nor place of publication, nor the name of the printer. The Septfons copy is no longer to be found. Amongst other material the *Recueil* contains the following letters of Rancé: (1-2) [1673] *Requeste présentée au Roy par le Révérend Père Abbé de la Trappe* (pages 1-18) and *Requeste présentée au Roy par les Abbez, Prieurs, et Religieux de l'Estroite Observance de l'Ordre de Cisteaux* (19-22), both listed above at I.A.i [1673]; (3) Letter 720529 (23-30); (4) Letter 730104 (31-40); (5) Letter 730729 (41-57) to Mother Anne-Victoire de Montglat which appears only in the french edition of the *Correspondance*. In the *Recueil* it is misdated 29 July 1677; (6) Letter 801114 (58-76); (7) Letter 710723 (77-82); (8) Letter 821107 (83-86); (9) a 'Lettre à une Religieuse, sur des manquemens assez ordinaires contre le vœu de pauvreté' (83-96), with the note (page 96) that 'la lettre précédente n'est point de Monsieur de la Trappe, mais d'une personne dont la piété & la doctrine sont reconnües par les grands services qu'elle a rendue

à l'Eglise'; (10) Letter 640630 (97-100); and (11) Letter 781130 (114-130) (the famous letter to the Maréchal de Bellefonds). The other material contained in the volume is as follows: (12) 'Renouvellement des Vœux des Religieux de l'Abbaye de la Trappe' (100-102); (13) 'Désir de la Solitude' (103-108); (14) 'Extrait d'une Lettre écrite par M^r. l'Abbé de Mayne qui est en retraite à la Trappe à un Abbé de Guienne de ses amis pour le détourner de plaider' (108-114); (15) *Relations* of the deaths of brothers Bernard, Benoît, Euthime, Théodore, Rigobert, Claude, and the abbé de Châtillon (133-188); (16) 'Description de L'abbaye de Sept-Fons, avec la relation de la Mort de deux Religieux de ce monastère. Et un discours du R.P. Abbé [de Septfons] à ses Religieux touchant la réforme outrée qu'on dit estre dans sa maison' (191-242 [description] 243-275 [discours]). According to the title-page of this curious volume, it begins with the 'Lettre du R.P. Abbé de la Trappe à Monsieur Le Roy, Abbé de Haute-Fontaine. Touchant les humiliations qui se pratiquent dans les Cloîtres' (see I.B.ii [1677] *Lettre d'un abbé régulier*), but this is not the case. No such letter is to be found in the collection.

[1683] *Description de l'abbaye de la Trappe avec les Constitutions, les Reflexions sur icelles; la mort de quelques Religieux de ce Monastère, plusieurs lettres du R.P. Abbé, et une briève relation de l'Abbaye de Septfons* (Lyon: L. Aubin, 1683). Bourgeois/André, no. 321 (there attributed to Toussaint Desmares); Tournoüer, no. 142.

The contents of this important collection are as follows: Part I (unpaginated) (a) 'Discours sur la Réforme de l'Abbaye de la Trappe'; (b) Table of Contents; (c) Armand-Jean de Rancé, 'De

l'excellence de la solitude'. Part II (separate pagination) André Félibien des Avaux (but here attributed to Toussaint Desmares), 'Description de
l'abbaye de la Trappe' (1-70); (b) 'Lettre d'un
religieux bénédictin de la congrégation de S. Maur
à sa sœur religieuse sur l'excellente manière de
vivre de la Trappe, signée F.F.P.A., moine bénédictin' (71-111) (this letter, dating from 1670, is
the first, detailed, eye-witness account of la Trappe
after the reforms of Rancé. See also II.A [1670]
F.F.P.A. below); (c) 'Constitutions de l'abbaye de
la Trappe et réflexions' (112-148 [Constitutions],
149-190 [Réflexions]); (d) 'Relations de la mort
de frère Benoist, Dom Jacques, Dom Paul, Dom
Charles, Dom Urbain, Dom Augustin' (195-324);
(e) 'Relation de l'abbaye de Septfons' (325-336).
Part III (separate pagination) consists of 'plusieurs
lettres du R.P. Abbé' reprinted from the [1680?]
Recueil listed immediately above (with identical
pagination), but ending on page 96 with the spurious letter 9. Letters 10 and 11 are not included.

[1701] *Lettres de piété choisies et écrites à différentes personnes* (Paris:
F. Muguet, 1701-1702; Veuve F. Muguet, 1704). Two volumes
(vol. I omits the words 'choisies et' in the title). Bourgeois/
André, no. 1043; Tournoüer, no. 421.

The identity of the editor or editors of this
collection remains unclear, but Professor
Krailsheimer has suggested that 'the inclusion
of a large number of letters from Rancé to Mme
de Guise (d. 1696) strongly suggests that someone at least as important as Bossuet had a hand
in this first serious posthumous tribute'
(Krailsheimer, *Rancé*, 59). Whoever it was was
in a hurry, and the ordering of the more than
200 letters is a chronological disaster. Six cop-

ies are listed in the 1752 catalogue of the library of la Trappe (Bell, 'Library', 153).

[1719] Milleran, René, *Nouvelles lettres familières et autres sur
toutes sortes de sujets, avec leurs réponses, choisies de Messieurs de
Bussy Rabutin, de Furetière, de Boursault, de Fléchier, de Bouthillier
de Rancé, de l'Académie françoise, & des plus célèbres auteurs du tems*
(Brussels: J. Léonard, 1719 [new ed.]).

On René Milleran, a grammarian best known for his
suggested spelling reforms, see *DLF XVIII*, 901.

Lambert, abbé, *L'Idée d'un vray religieux dans le recüeil des lettres
de dom Paulin de l'Isle, bénédictin de la congrégation de S. Vanne et
depuis religieux, président et père maître des novices de l'abbaïe de
Notre-Dame de la Trape, avec un petit abrégé de sa vie et de celle de
François de Lisle, son frère, chanoine de Notre-Dame de Chaalons, en
Champagne* (Châlons: C. Bouchard, 1723). Tournoüer, no. 252.

According to Krailsheimer, *Rancé*, 114, n. 1, 'this
very rare book is a mine of useful information,
apparently not recorded elsewhere, on the
Vannists and also on the relations between la
Trappe and other orders towards the end of
Rancé's life'. It also contains a number of letters
(including 860926 and 861007) from Rancé to Dom
Paulin de L'Isle who began his monastic career as
a Vannist and transferred to la Trappe in 1687.
Krailsheimer (following Tournoüer, no. 252) re-
ports what may be the unique copy in the
Bibliothèque municipale of Versailles, and in 1752
there was a copy in the library of la Trappe (Bell,
'Library', 157). It is not there now.

[1741] Letters to Pierre Floriot (1673/1674), in Pierre Floriot,
*Morale chrétienne, raportée aux instructions que Jésus-Christ nous a
données dans l'oraison dominicale. Recueil de pièces concernant la mo-*

rale chrétienne sur l'oraison dominicale (Brussels: S. T'Serstevens, 1741-1745), vol. 6, pp. i-xxi, which follow page 74 of the *Recueil* with separate pagination.

> See Letter 73/7. Pierre Floriot (1604-1691) was a Jansenist, a good friend of Antoine Arnauld and Pierre Nicole, and confessor to the nuns of Port-Royal. See *DLF XVII*, 499, and the good article in *DHGE* 17:640-642.

[1846] *Lettres d'Armand-Jean Le Bouthillier de Rancé, abbé et réformateur de la Trappe*, ed. Benoît Gonod (Paris: Amyot, 1846). Tournoüer, no. 216.

> This remains a useful collection of 226 letters, all but twenty-one of which date from the period after Rancé's conversion. Gonod was librarian of Clermont-Ferrand. For an interesting, almost contemporary, review of Gonod's important edition, see Charles-Augustin Sainte-Beuve, ed. Gérald Antoine, *Portraits littéraires* (Paris, 1993 [Tournoüer, no. 446]) 991-999 (with notes on 1192-1193), 'Lettres de Rancé, abbé et réformateur de la Trappe'.

[1846] Letters to Jean Mabillon (11 September 1689 and 15 September 1699), *Ami de la Religion* 128 (1846) 522.

> = Letters 890911 and 990915.

[1865] Burnier, Eugène, *Histoire de l'abbaye de Tamié en Savoie* (Chambery: A. Pouchet, 1865). Bourgeois/André, no. 4761.

> The *Histoire* includes eight letters written by Rancé between 1666 and 1683 suggesting that the reform be introduced at Tamié and giving details as to how this might be accomplished. See the

index to Krailsheimer's Letters/ *Correspondance*, s.v. Tamié.

[1885] Ingold, Augustin-Marie-Pierre, *Archives de l'évêché de Luçon* (Paris, 1885).

> Twenty-two letters to Henri Barillon, bishop of Luçon. Copies of all twenty-two are included in the collection in Poitiers, *Bib. mun.*, MS Fontaneau 65. For a complete list of Rancé's letters to Barillon, see the index to Krailsheimer's Letters/ *Correspondance*, s.v. Barillon, Henri. Ingold's edition has now been superseded by that of Krailsheimer.

[1905] Serrant, Marie-Léon, 'Correspondance inédite de l'abbé de Rancé et de Jacques II d'Angleterre', *Revue des questions historiques* 88 (1905) 569-579.

> This was also published as an independent octavo booklet of eleven pages: Paris: Aux Bureaux de la Revue des questions historiques, 1905. See also *Letters of James the Second to the Abbot of La Trappe*, ed. John Emerich Edward Dalberg, Baron Acton (London: Philobiblon Society, 1872-1876; repr. London: Whittingham & Wilkins, 1875).

[1912] *Lettres autographes de Troussures*, ed. Paul Denis (Paris, 1912).

> Fifteen letters of Rancé. Those to Dom Robert (or Robin) Couturier, prior of Perseigne, are especially valuable (see the index to Krailsheimer's Letters/ *Correspondance*, s.v. Couturier). Denis first drew attention to these letters in 1911 in his 'Lettres inédites de Bossuet, Fénelon, Bourdaloue et de l'abbé de Rancé', *Revue d'histoire de l'Église de France* 2 (1911) 349-358.

[1923] Menjot d'Elbenne, Samuel, *Madame de La Sablière: ses pensées chrétiennes et ses lettres à l'abbé de Rancé* (Paris: Plon, 1923).

> Marguérite Hessein de Rambouillet de La Sablière (1640-1693) (*DLF XVII*, 712) was born a Protestant and after her husband's death in 1679 converted to Catholicism. In 1687 she asked Rancé to become her spiritual director, but he, as usual, refused. Many of her letters to Rancé survive, though few from Rancé to her (see Letters 88/6 [= letter 14 in Menjot d'Elbenne], 880730 [= letter 11 in Menjot d'Elbenne], 920528 [not in Menjot d'Elbenne]). She was an astonishing woman who read Greek as easily as Latin and who studied—and practised—astronomy and anatomy. Her salon was justly famed. In later life, when she had renounced the world and was dying of cancer, she took with her into hospital not only a number of books of piety and devotion, but also her astronomical telescope. She died in 1693. On her relationship with Rancé, see especially Menjot d'Elbenne, pages 176-204, and for her letters to Rancé, pages 272-335, letters 1, 2, 4-6, 9, 12-13, 15-53, 56, 59, and 61.

[1963] Tans, Joseph A.G., 'Un dialogue monologué: Lettres inédites de Rancé à Quesnel', in *Miscellanea jansenistica offerts à Lucien Ceyssens à l'occasion de son soixantième anniversaire*, ed. Hubert Willems *et al.* (Heverlee: Institut Historique Augustinien, 1963 [= *Augustiniana* 13 [1963]]) 265-306.

> More than forty letters from Rancé to Pasquier Quesnel. See the index to Krailsheimer's Letters/Correspondance, s.v. Quesnel. On Quesnel himself, see Further Reading to Part I, Chapter Six, in this present volume.

[1974] Lebrun, Jean, 'Le Camus, correspondant de l'abbé de Rancé', in *Un cardinal dans la montagne, Étienne Le Camus, évêque de Grenoble (1671-1707)*. *Actes du Colloque Le Camus, Grenoble, 1971*, ed. Jean Godel (Grenoble: Presses Universitaires de Grenoble, 1974 [Études Dauphinoises, 3]) 39-49.

> For an inventory of the correspondence of Rancé and Le Camus (thirty-four letters), see pages 48-49.

[1984] *The Letters of Armand-Jean de Rancé, Abbot and Reformer of La Trappe*, presented by Alban J. Krailsheimer (Kalamazoo: Cistercian Publications, 1984). Two volumes.

> REVIEWS:
> *Catholic Historical Review* 72 (1986) 653-654 (J.A. Bergin).
> *Church History* 54 (1985) 442 (Bede Lackner).
> *Cistercian Studies* [*Quarterly*] 21 (1986) BMS [2]-[4] (Jean Holman).
> *Cîteaux: Comm. cist.* 35 (1984) 342-343 (Edmond Mikkers).
> *Collectanea Cisterciensia* 47 (1985) BSM [570]-[572] (Yvon Petit).
> *Downside Review* 104 (1986) 253-267 (Alberic Stacpoole).
> *English Historical Review* 102 (1987) 1036-1037 (Roger Mettam).
> *Journal of Theological Studies* 37 (1986) 259-261 (Bruno Neveu).
> *Monastic Studies* 17 (1986) 245-253 (Michel Gaulin).
> *Revue Bénédictine* 95 (1985) 152 (Patrick Verbraken).
> *Studia Monastica* 27 (1985) 184-185 (Joaquim Martínez).

[1993] *Correspondance*. Édition originale par Alban John Krailsheimer (Paris: Cerf, and Cîteaux: Commentarii cistercienses, 1993). Four volumes.

The first volume includes a brief biography of Rancé by Krailsheimer (9-18), and an introduction to his spirituality by Lucien Aubry (30-42).

REVIEWS:
Collectanea Cisterciensia 55 (1993) BSM [370]-[373] (Marie-Gérard Dubois).
Joël Cornette, 'La Correspondance de l'abbé de Rancé', *Revue de synthèse* 115 (1994) 513-521. This appears as a review of Krailsheimer's edition, but it is rather a concise account, based on these letters, of Rancé's life, his reform of la Trappe, and his place in the social, religious, and political world of his time. The article concludes with 'deux exemples de lettres de Rancé', *viz.*, Letters 801114 and 821107a.
Irénée Noye, 'À propos d'une édition récente de la correspondance de l'abbé de Rancé', *Dix-septième siècle* 47 (1995) 779-782.

[1999] *Florilège de lettres, abbé de Rancé*, choix et présentation par Alban John Krailsheimer (Paris: Cerf, 1999 [Foi vivante; Les classiques, 405]).

The letters are selected from Krailsheimer's edition of Rancé's complete *Correspondance* [1993 above] and arranged according to theme: vocation, monastic life, living the christian life in the world, authority, Notre-Dame de Saint-Bernard de Comminges, prayer and sacraments, death and sickness. It is a useful and convenient florilegium. Further on Rancé's involvement in setting up the shrine of Saint-Bernard de Comminges, see Eugène Sol, *Notre-Dame de Saint-Bernard-en-Comminges. Alan-Montoulieu* (Toulouse: Impr. du Sud-Ouest, 1923).

REVIEWS:
Collectanea Cisterciensia 62 (2000) BSM [567]-[568]
(Hugues de Seréville).

I.B.ii) SINGLE LETTERS

IN CHRONOLOGICAL ORDER OF LETTERS

[1664] *Lettre de Monsieur l'abbé de la Trappe à un de ses amis, trois jours après sa profession* (cf. Letter 640630): see II.A, Pierre de Maupeou, *Éloge funèbre du très-révérend père Dom Armand-Jean Bouthillier de Rancé.*

[1672] Doinel, Jules, 'Un épisode inconnu de la vie de Malebranche, d'après une lettre inédite de l'abbé de Rancé', *Revue des questions historiques* 20 (1876) 553-559.

> = Letter 720409. This letter is our only evidence that Malebranche at one time thought of visiting la Trappe.

[1677] *Lettre d'un abbé régulier sur le sujet des humiliations, et autres pratiques de religion* (Paris: J.-B. Coignard, 1677). Tournoüer, nos. 371-372.

> The same letter also appears under two other titles: *Lettre du R.P. abbé de la Trappe à M. Le Roy, abbé de Hautefontaine, sur les humiliations et autres pratiques de religion* (Paris: J.-B. Coignard, 1677), and *Lettre du R. Père abbé de la Trappe à un ecclésiastique, &c.* (Rouen: E. Viret, 1677). It is listed in the 1752 catalogue of the library of la Trappe (Bell, 'Library', 153). The addressee of the letter was Guillaume Le Roy, commendatory abbot of Hautefontaine, and the letter is part of the controversy between Le Roy, Rancé, and others on

the question of 'fictions' which we discussed earlier in Part I, Chapter Six. The letter was actually published by André Félibien against Rancé's wishes, and Rancé wrote to Le Roy to apologize for its appearance. His apology, however, had no effect, and the result was a bitter quarrel which dragged on for years and which involved a great many people. See Letters 770414 and 770625, and Krailsheimer, *Rancé*, 40-41. For a summary of the contents of the *Lettre*, see François Vanden- broucke, 'De Rancé on Deliberate Humiliations', *Cistercian Studies* [*Quarterly*] 8 (1973) 45-52, which is a translation of the same author's 'Humiliations volontaires? La pensée de l'abbé de Rancé', *Collectanea Cisterciensia* 27 (1965) 194-201.

[1677] Barthélemy, Édouard de, *La marquise d'Huxelles et ses amis* (Paris: Firmin-Didot, 1881). Bourgeois/André, no. 1118.

> One letter from Rancé on pages 98-102. Marie Le Bailleul du Blé, marquise d'Huxelles (1626-1712) was a friend of Madame de Guise, a celebrated hostess, and a correspondent of several religious. For two of Rancé's letters to her, see Letters 771202a and 911007.

[1678] *Lettre de M. l'abbé de la Trape à M. le Maréchal de Bellefonds. Ce 30 novembre 1678* (Grenoble: F. Provensal, 1679 [with many reprintings and many manuscript copies]). Tournoüer, nos. 386-387.

> = Letter 781130. The letter is of key importance in the question of Rancé's supposed Jansenism. There is a complete english translation in Krailsheimer's Letters (English).

[1680] Debant, Roger, 'Trois lettres inédites récemment acquises par les Archives de l'Aude', *Bulletin de la Société d'études scientifiques de l'Aude* 70 (1971 [1970]) 147-151.

Contains a letter written by Rancé in 1680 to Louis-François Lefèvre de Caumartin (not in Krailsheimer's Letters/*Correspondance*).

[1682] Letter to Jean-François de Montholon, *Bulletin de Bibliophile et du Bibliothécaire* (1872) 387-388.

> = Letter 821229; Tournoüer, no. 41. Jean-François de Montholon was commendatory abbot of Saint-Sulpice-en-Bugey, the cistercian abbey near Bourg-en-Bresse (Ain) in the Rhône-Alpes.

[1682] Leclercq, Jean, 'Lettres de Mabillon et de Rancé sur saint Bernard', *Revue Mabillon* 45 (1955) 29-35.

> = Letter 820830, together with Mabillon's letter to Rancé asking him whether he thought Saint Bernard preached in Latin or in French. Reprinted in Jean Leclercq, *Recueil d'études sur saint Bernard et ses écrits* (Rome, 1966) 2:319-326.

[1686] → [1704] and [1705].

[1689] 'Lettre de M. l'abbé de la Trape à un évêque pour répondre aux plaintes et aux difficultez de dom Innocent Le Masson, général des Chartreux, au sujet des allégations faites de leurs anciens statuts dans les livres de la Sainteté et des devoirs de la Vie monastique, 20 juillet 1689', *Nouvelles de la République des Lettres* (May-June 1710) 488-519, 628-661. Tournoüer, no. 399.

> = Letter 890720. This is Rancé's reply to Dom Innocent Le Masson's attack in his *Explication de quelques endroits des anciens statuts de l'Ordre des Chartreux* listed at II.A [1683] below. The letter was written in 1689, but not published during the lifetime of either Rancé or Le Masson in obe-

dience to a royal decree prohibiting any further continuation of the dispute. For a balanced and accurate summary of the question, see Krailsheimer, *Rancé*, 162-167. The matter is also briefly discussed in Part I, Chapter Seven, of this present study.

[1689] Letter to Nicolas Malebranche, in Pierre Le Brun, *Histoire critique des pratiques superstitieuses...* (Paris: Poirion, 1701; Amsterdam: J. F. Bernard, 1733-1736 [2nd ed.]) 3:177 (in both editions). Tournoüer, no. 264.

> = Letter 890829a. This curious letter is concerned with the efficacy and legitimacy of dowsing. See also Tournoüer, no. 263.

[1690] Letter to the Maréchal de Bellefonds, in *Mercure galant* (December 1690) 192-230. Tournoüer, no. 335.

> = Letter 901129, enthusiastically describing the visit of James II of England to la Trappe on 24 November 1690. The marshal had been among his entourage. The letter was widely circulated, but not always well received (see Krailsheimer, *Rancé*, 51).

[1693] *Lettres écrites par J.-B. Bossuet, évêque de Meaux, par Armand-Jean le Bouthillier de Rancey, abbé de la Trappe et par M***, pour servir de réfutation aux bruits que les religionnaires ont répandus touchant la mort de M. Pélisson* (Toulouse: [s.n.], 1693). Bourgeois/André, no. 1836; Tournoüer, no. 406.

> See Letter 930208. On Paul Pellison-Fontanier (1624-1693), see *DTC* 12:720-721 and *DLF XVII*, 981-982. For a list of Bossuet's letters to Rancé as edited in Jacques-Bénigne Bossuet, *Œuvres complètes de Bossuet, publiées par des prêtres de l'Immaculée-*

Conception de Saint-Dizier [Haute-Marne] (Tours: Cattier, 1862-1863 [twelve volumes]) (*Correspondance de Bossuet*, ed. Charles Urbain and Eugène Lévesque [Paris: Hachette, 1909-1925 (new ed.; fifteen volumes)]), see Tournoüer, no. 56. For a comprehensive (if panegyrical) study of the relationship of Bossuet and Rancé, see Marie-Léon Serrant, *L'Abbé de Rancé et Bossuet: ou, Le grand moine et le grand évêque du grand siècle* (Paris: C. Douniol, 1903).

[1694] For Rancé's controversial letter to Claude Nicaise on the death of Antoine Arnauld (Letter 940902), see II.A [1694 Quesnel], [1697 *Recueil*], and [1792 Larrière].

[1697] *Lettre écrite à M. de Cambray par le pape. Lettre de Mgr. l'archevêque de Cambray à un de ses amis. Lettre de M^{r}. de la Trappe à M. de Meaux au sujet du livre de M^{r}. de Cambray. Réponse de M. Deslyons à un de ses amis* ([s.l.], [1697]).

In this booklet of 26 pages, M. de Cambray is Fénelon, M. de Meaux is Bossuet, the pope is Innocent XII, and the subject is Rancé's opposition to Quietism, a controversy to which he had been introduced by Bossuet in 1697: see Letters 970300, 970414, 970500, and 970703.

[1701] *Lettre de Monsieur l'Abbé de la Trappe à Madame l'Abbesse des Clairets, deux heures avant sa mort, le 26 octobre 1700*: see II.A, [1701] Pierre de Maupeou, *Éloge funèbre du très-révérend père Dom Armand-Jean Bouthillier de Rancé.*

[1704] Le Nain de Tillemont, Louis-Sébastien, *Lettre de Monsieur de Tillemont à feu Monsieur l'abbé de la Trappe, Jean-Armand Boutellier de Rancé, avec la réponse du dit abbé à Monsieur de Tillemont* ([s.l.], 1704). Tournoüer, no. 272.

Apart from Le Nain de Tillemont's letter to Rancé,

this pamphlet of 36 pages contains the (i) 'projet de lettre de feu Monsieur l'abbé de la Trappe à Monsieur de Tillemont, qui n'a pas été envoiée' (for other examples, see Tournoüer, no. 136 and 266), (ii) the actual 'réponse de Monsieur l'abbé de la Trappe à Monsieur de Tillemont' which was sent, and (iii) three other related letters enumerated in Tournoüer, no. 272. A much longer compilation (listed immediately below) with a *discours préliminaire*, notes, further letters and *pièces justificatives* was published at Nancy the following year. The letters concern Rancé's unfortunate treatment of a seventy-five-year-old Jansenist, Wallon de Beaupuis, who had been Tillemont's teacher. He came to la Trappe in 1696 to visit Rancé and Dom Pierre Le Nain, but Rancé, seeking to avoid problems with his ecclesiastical superiors, refused to see him. It must be admitted that the old man was not well treated, and Tillemont's highly indignant and critical letter was not unjustified. To this letter Rancé prepared a lengthy reply which was never sent (the *projet* noted above) and his actual reply (the *réponse*) was much briefer. For a detailed account of the incident, see Dubois (1866) 2:499-507, and for a careful and balanced account of its importance and repercussions, Bruno Neveu, *Un historien à l'école de Port-Royal: Sébastien Le Nain de Tillemont* (La Haye, 1966) 111-121.

[1705] *Idem, Lettre de M. Lenain-de-Tillemont au R.P. Armand-Jean Boutillier de Rancé, abbé de la Trappe, et les réponses de cet abbé, avec un discours préliminaire, des éclaircissemens sur les faits qui y sont rapportés, & plusieurs lettres & pièces justificatives* (Nancy: J. Nicolai, 1705). Tournoüer, no. 273.

This volume of 167 pages is discussed in the entry immediately above.

I.C) *DUBIA* AND *SPURIA*

[1656] Retz, Jean-François-Paul de Gondi, Cardinal de, *Lettre de Monseigneur l'Eminentissime Cardinal de Retz, Archevêque de Paris, à Messieurs les Archevêques et Evêques de l'Eglise de France* ([s.l.; s.n.], 1655).

> The contents of this important letter are sum-
> marized by John H. M. Salmon in his *Cardinal de
> Retz. The Anatomy of a Conspirator* (New York,
> 1970) 272-273. 'According to Joly [says Salmon],
> it was composed at Port-Royal and the draft
> brought to Retz at Ambrogiano by the abbé de
> Verjus, who was later to become the cardinal's
> secretary. There was even a rumour current later
> in the century that the abbé de Rancé was the
> author, and that Mazarin had refused Rancé pre-
> ferment because of it. But Rancé disclaimed re-
> sponsibility, and Retz, in another circular ad-
> dressed to the bishops in April 1660, claimed that
> he had composed it in Rome in December 1654.
> When the printed version of the letter appeared
> in the streets of Paris in January 1655, Mazarin
> had the *châtelet* condemn it to be burnt by the
> public executioner, and at least six published re-
> plies to it were composed by his pamphleteers'
> (*ibid.*, 272). The suggestion that Rancé was the
> author of the letter can safely be dismissed.

[1671] *Constitutions de l'abbaye de la Trappe, avec un discours sur la réforme* (Paris: M. Lepetit & E. Michallet, 1671; G. Desprez, 1688; Brussels: L. Marchant, 1674 [2nd ed.], 1694, 1701, 1702 [3rd ed.]; Avignon: A. Dupérier, 1679; Lyon: L. Aubin, 1683; Bordeaux: Henry Faye fils, [s.d.]). The *Constitutions* were also printed in the 1702 edition of the *Relations de la mort de quelques religieux de l'abbaye de la Trappe* listed in I.A.i [1677] (see Tournoüer, no. 379). Tournoüer, nos. 360-363, 319-320.

> This work appeared in numerous editions (ten copies of 'Constitutions de La Trappe, en un tome' are listed in the 1752 catalogue of the library of la Trappe [Bell, 'Library', 153]), but Rancé specifically denied any part in its production (see Letters 711212 and 810525). Nevertheless, the *Constitutions* accurately reflect the way of life at la Trappe, and, as Professor Krailsheimer has observed, what Rancé is denying is the official status of the document rather than the facts disclosed within it (Krailsheimer, *Rancé*, 87). The *Constitutions* were later revised, much expanded, and published as *Les Règlements de l'abbaye de Nostre-Dame de la Trappe, en forme de Constitutions* (listed in I.A.i [1690]). Certain of the editions listed above also contain *Réflexions sur les Constitutions de l'abbaye de la Trape* by an otherwise unknown 'abbé de Lignage' who, according to Krailsheimer, *Rancé*, 85, may have been the abbé de Villars, the nephew of the maréchal de Bellefonds. Much more work remains to be done on the *Constitutions* and *Règlements* of la Trappe, and I have not the least doubt that other editions await discovery.

[1684] *Discours de la pureté d'intention, et des moyens pour y arriver. Avec un Examen raisonné, où l'on marque dans le détail les défauts qui y sont opposez. Avec des pensées Chrétiennes sur plusieurs véritez très-importantes & très-utiles à ceux qui cherchent Dieu sincèrement. Le tout tiré des sentimens & des raisonnemens des saints Pères* (Paris: F. Muguet, 1684). Tournoüer, no. 425.

> The work was attributed to Rancé, but (according to Maupeou) he himself specifically denied authorship: 'Le livre de la pureté d'intention n'est

point de moi, mais il n'en est pas moins bon'
(Maupeou, *Vie de Rancé* [II.A (1702)] 2:104, quoted
by both Dubois [1866] 2:748, and Tournoüer, no.
425).

[1699] *Réflexions morales sur les quatre Évangiles* (Paris: F. Muguet,
1699). Three parts in four volumes. Tournoüer, no. 420.

> It is commonly held that this is not a genuine
> work of Rancé, and that may be true. It is, how-
> ever, classed among his writings in the 1752 cata-
> logue of the library of la Trappe (Bell, 'Library',
> 152) and also by Dubois (1866) 2:747. If it is not
> by Rancé, it has certainly been deeply affected by
> his ideas and is a sound witness to his spiritual-
> ity. I suspect myself that it is indeed rancéan
> material, but edited by another and unknown
> hand.

[1699] *Traité abrégé des obligations des chrétiens, par l'Auteur des
Livres de la Vie Monastique* (Paris: F. Muguet, 1699). Tournoüer,
no. 419.

> This important volume of just over 400 pages is
> almost certainly a genuine work of Rancé (his
> name appears on the title-page and in the privi-
> lege), left unfinished at his death, and then ed-
> ited and arranged by an unknown person or per-
> sons. It is attributed to Rancé in the 1752 cata-
> logue of the library of la Trappe (Bell, 'Library',
> 153) and also by Dubois (1866) 2:747. According
> to Marsollier, *La Vie de Dom Armand-Jean Le
> Bouthillier de Rancé* (II.A [1703]) 2:103, it is no
> more than an *essai*. A number of Rancé's friends,
> he tells us, 'people of eminence and influence',
> had been so impressed with what he had written
> on the duties of religious that they pressed him

to write something similar for lay Christians. He bowed to their importunities, but was prevented by illness and his other duties from completing the task. 'We must not be surprised, then, if this present work is neither as long nor as forceful as *De la sainteté et des devoirs de la vie monastique*' (*ibid.*).

Italian tr.: *Breve trattato delle obligazioni de'cristiani del P. Don Armando Giovanni Le Bouthillier di Ransé ... tradotta dall'idioma franzese in lingua toscana da Idalio Penelopeo* [Giovan-Francesco Sanminiatelli], *accademico dell'Arcadia di Roma* (Pisa: F. Bindi, 1708).

[1701] *La véritable préparation à la mort* (Paris: F. Muguet, 1701).

According to the note in *BN* 146:346, 'cet ouvrage est probablement de Rancé, le privilège placé à la fin du volume mentionnant toute la série de ses œuvres'. It also appears as an appendix to the fourth edition of the *Méditations sur la règle de s. Benoist* listed under I.D [1696] below. *Pace* the note in *BN*, I am in agreement with Dubois (1866) 2:748 that it is not from Rancé's pen, though it certainly echoes his sentiments.

[1765] Barthe, Nicolas-Thomas, *Lettre de l'abbé de Rancé à un ami, écrite de son abbaye de la Trappe* (Geneva [= Paris]: Duchesne, Panckoucke, 1765, 1766 [new ed.]). Tournoüer, no. 40.

Nicolas-Thomas Barthe (1734-1785) was a poet and playwright who never quite lived up to his early promise (see *DLF XVIII*, 128). His *Lettre de l'abbé de Rancé* is a pamphlet of sixteen pages with three illustrations by Charles Eisen. Despite its title, it is not a genuine letter of Rancé. Dubois (1869) 1:124, rightly describes it as a 'pièce

étrange, qui n'est que le récit de Larroque [see
II.A (1685 Larroque) below] mis en vers'. The
spurious letter evoked a response from another
poet and playwright, Jean-François La Harpe
(1739-1803), an eminent and widely-respected literary critic (see *DLF XVIII*, 669-671), who produced a *Réponse d'un solitaire de la Trappe à la lettre
de l'abbé de Rancé* ([s.l.; s.n.]) in 1767 (Tournoüer,
no. 249). See further Anselme Dimier, *La sombre
Trappe; les légendes et la vérité* (*Abbaye de Saint-
Wandrille*, 1946) 30-31.

Barthe's letter was rendered into english verse
by Daniel Hayes in about 1765 as *An Epistle to a
Friend: Written in a Monastery. Paraphrased from the
French by a Gentleman* (London: J. Bew and G.
Corrall, c.1765). It was then reprinted as 'An
epistle from the celebrated Abbé de Rancé' in *The
Works in Verse of Daniel Hayes, Esq.; late of the
Middle-Temple*, ed. *William Hatfield* (London: [s.n.],
1769); and reprinted again in *The Abbey of La
Trappe; or, Memoirs of The Count d'Auvergne and
Adelaide de Benavides, translated from the French of
M. Arnaud. With I. The Funeral of Arabert, Monk
of La Trappe, by Mr Jerningham* [Tournoüer, no.
239]. II. *Epistle from the Abbé de Rancé to a Friend, by
Daniel Hayes, Esq.* (Dublin: J. Rice, 1792). In this
last volume, the poem appears on pages 201-218.
Hayes' summary of the spurious letter reads as
follows: 'The conversion of the celebrated Abbé
de Rancé, is attributed to the death of the Duchess of M— [i.e. Madame de Montbazon], whom
he tenderly loved. He had been absent from her
some time, and was quite ignorant of her death;
having got into the house under cover of the night,
he went into her apartment by a back stair-case.
The first object that appeared to his view was a

coffin, which contained the body of his mistress: she had died after three days violent illness. As she was to be interred in the family vault, a leaden coffin was prepared; but it was too short, and with unheard of brutality they severed the head from the body. Struck with so shocking an event, from that instant the Abbé de Rancé renounced all commerce with the world. He retired to the monastery of la Trappe, where he became a most rigid penitent. It is from thence he writes to a friend who had long been upon his travels and is ignorant of this tragical adventure. Some works having lately appeared relating to the monastery of la Trappe, the author thought this a favourable occasion to produce his own, written long since' (201). See further David N. Bell, 'Daniel de Larroque, Armand-Jean de Rancé, and the Head of Madame de Montbazon', *Cîteaux: Commentarii Cistercienses* 53 (2002) 305-331.

[1769] *De la sainteté et des devoirs de l'épiscopat, selon les saints pères et les canons de l'Église* (Liège: Lib. Bassompière, 1769; Paris: J.-F. Bastien, 1781 [2nd ed.]). Three volumes.

The case for Rancé's authorship of this work is made by Hans Paalzov in his 'Ein unbekanntes Werk des Abtes de Rancé', in *Fünfzehn Jahre Königliche und Staatsbibliothek; dem scheidenden Generaldirector exz. Adolf von Harnack zum 31. März 1921 überreicht von den wissenschaftlichen Beamten der Preussischen Staatsbibliothek* (Berlin, 1921) 69-77. Paalzov presents a spirited argument for Rancé's authorship and demonstrates conclusively that the book must have been written between 1698 and 1707 (74); but the case remains unproven and unlikely. The copy of the work in the library of la Trappe has a hand-written note which reads

'Ouvrage de Dom Gervaise [i.e. Armand-François Gervaise (1660-1751)], abbé de la Trappe', and that seems to me much more probable. The work was certainly written by someone intimately familiar with Rancé's style and ideas.

I.D) SELECTIONS FROM THE WORKS OF RANCÉ

IN CHRONOLOGICAL ORDER OF PUBLICATION.

See also the *Florilège de lettres* (1999) listed under I.B.i above.

[1696] *Divers sentimens de piété* (Paris: A. Dezallier, 1696). Tournoüer, no. 410.

> A volume of 185 pages comprising selections and excerpts from Rancé.

[1696] *Méditations sur la règle de s. Benoist, tirées du Commentaire de Monsieur l'Abbé de la Trappe sur la mesme Règle* (Paris: F. Muguet, 1696, 1698 [2nd ed., 'augmentée de plusieurs élévations à Dieu [see Tournoüer, nos. 283-284], & d'une conduite intérieure pour se disposer à une bonne Mort']; [s.l., s.n.], 1703; Brussels: F. Foppens, 1704 [3rd ed.]; Paris: Veuve F. Muguet, 1705 [3rd ed.]; Paris: Compagnie des libraires, 1713 [4th ed.]). Two parts in one volume. Tournoüer, nos. 274-276.

> Listed in the 1752 catalogue of the library of la Trappe among the 'Œuvres de divers Rel[x]. de La Trappe' (Bell, 'Library', 155). The *Méditations* (a fine piece of work and unjustly neglected) were compiled by Pierre Le Nain. *La véritable préparation à la mort*, listed under I.C [1701] above, appears as an appendix to the fourth edition.

> German tr.: *Betrachtungen über die Regel des heiligen*

Vaters Benedicti. Aus dem Französischen übersetzt von Vital Mösl, O.S.B. (Augsburg: J. Wolff, 1766, 1782 [2nd ed.]).

Italian tr.: *Meditazioni sopra la Regola del P.S. Benedetto, estratte dal Commentario sopra la medesima Regola, steso da Monsieur Gio. Armando Boutillier, Abate della Trappa. Terza edizione. Riveduta, corretta, & accresciuta di molte Elevazioni a Dio, e di una Condotta interiore, per disporsi ad una buona Morte. ... Tradotte dal Francese, per uso delle Divote, e MM. RR. Monache dell'Ordine del medesimo P.S. Benedetto...* (Parma: P. Monti, 1709). This is a translation of the third edition of the work, published at Brussels by F. Foppens in 1704.

[1697] *Exercices de piété sur la règle de saint Benoist, avec des examens fort étendus et très utiles aux personnes qui veulent en prendre l'esprit. Retraite de dix jours* (Paris: T. Muguet, 1697, 1700). Tournoüer, no. 8.

This anonymous compilation consists primarily of selections from Rancé's commentaries on the Rule of Saint Benedict (see *Journal des savants* [July 1697] 296).

[1703] *Pensées de l'abbé de la Trappe sur divers sujets de piété, tirées de ses Lettres spirituelles* (Paris: J. de Nully, 1703).

Reprinted in a revised and enlarged edition in 1767 as *Pensées et réflexions de M. de Rancé, abbé de la Trappe* (Paris: Vente, 1767 [see s.v. [1767] below]).

[1707] *Cinq chapitres tirez du livre de la Sainteté et des devoirs de la vie monastique où il est traité: I. De l'Amour de Dieu. II. De la prière. III. De la mort. IV. Des jugemens de Dieu. V. De la componction, par M^{re}. Armand Le Bouthillier, ancien abbé de la Trappe* ([s.l.;

s.n.], [*c*.1683]; Paris: Compagnie des libraires, 1707).
Tournoüer, no. 422.

> Listed among the works of Rancé in the 1752 cata-
> logue of the library of la Trappe (Bell, 'Library',
> 152). The printing history of this compilation is
> unclear. The title-page of what appears to be the
> first edition provides only the title, omitting the
> words '*la Sainteté et des devoirs de*'. There is no in-
> dication of place, publisher, or date, but the book
> may have been published by Muguet *c*.1683 with-
> out Rancé's knowledge or permission.

[1767] *Pensées et réflexions de M. de Rancé, abbé de la Trappe* (Paris:
Vente, 1767). Tournoüer, no. 423.

> See [1703] *Pensées de l'abbé de la Trappe sur divers
> sujets de piété* listed above. The 1767 edition, a vol-
> ume of 156 pages with appendices and Rigaud's
> portrait of Rancé, ends with *Pensée* 259 (= *Pensée*
> 258 in the 1703 edition), but then goes on to in-
> clude a 'Paraphrase sur les sept Pseaumes de la
> pénitence' (119-156). According to Tournoüer, no.
> 423, 'ces pensées furent publiées par de Marsollier
> à la suite de sa vie de l'abbé de la Trappe. Paris,
> 1758. II. 499. Sous une autre forme.'

[1919] *Anthologie des écrivains catholiques prosateurs français du
XVIIe siècle*, recueillie et publiée par Henri Bremond et Charles
Grolleau (Paris: Éd. G. Crès et Cie., 1919).

> On pages 274-284 there is an excerpt from *De la
> sainteté et des devoirs de la vie monastique*, chap. XIII,
> qu. 2 ('La méditation de la mort'), and extracts
> from letters to Claude Nicaise and the duchesse
> de Guise taken from Gonod's *Lettres d'Armand-
> Jean Le Bouthillier de Rancé* (I.B.i [1846]).

[1989] *Le Soleil et les ténèbres: suivi de La solitude du désert* (Paris: Arfuyen, 1989 [Arfuyen textes mystiques, 54]).

> This little booklet of forty-seven pages contains a selection of texts taken primarily from Rancé's *Maximes chrétiennes et morales* [1698]. The section 'La solitude du désert' is an excerpt from *De la sainteté* [1683]. The booklet also includes a brief and out-of-date biography of Rancé.

[2000] Gobry, Ivan, *Rancé ou l'esprit de la pénitence* (Paris: Téqui, 2000 [L'auteur et son message, 28]).

> This fairly lengthy volume (346 pages) contains a brief and unreliable biography of Rancé followed by a selection of texts. It is somewhat better than Gobry's earlier *Rancé* (see II.B [1991] below)—a poor piece of work—but not by much.

II) BIOGRAPHIES, BIOGRAPHICAL MATERIAL, AND CONTROVERSIAL LITERATURE

II.A) THE SEVENTEENTH AND EIGHTEENTH CENTURIES

IN CHRONOLOGICAL ORDER OF PUBLICATION.

[1670] F.F.P.A., *Description de l'abbaye de Notre-Dame de la Trappe, de l'Ordre de Cisteaux, diocèse de Sées, et de l'excellente manière de vie des abbé et religieux de cette sainte maison, tirée de la lettre d'un religieux bénédictin de la congrégation de Saint-Maur à sa sœur religieuse* (Rouen: J. Hérault, 1670; [s.l.; s.n.] 1671). Bourgeois/André, no. 309; Tournoüer, no. 173.

> See also I.B.i [1683]. This letter offers the earliest, detailed, eye-witness account of life at la Trappe

after the reforms of Rancé. It also includes biographical material on Rancé himself. For an english summary, see Chrysogonus Waddell, 'The Cistercian Dimension of the Reform of La Trappe (1662-1700): Preliminary Notes and Reflections', in *Cistercians in the Late Middle Ages*, ed. E. Rozanne Elder (Kalamazoo, 1981) 123-129. Father Waddell dates the letter to about mid-September 1670; I would date it a little earlier.

[1671] [Félibien des Avaux, André], *Description de l'abbaye de la Trappe* (Paris: F. Léonard, 1671, 1672, 1677, 1678; C. Jornel, 1682 [2nd ed.]; Lyon: L. Aubin, 1683; Paris: J. Le Febvre, 1689 [new ed.]). The *Description* also appears in the *Relation contenant la Description de l'abbaye de la Trappe* (Paris: Veuve Delaulne, 1742 [Tournoüer, no. 144]) and vol. V of the Paris 1755 edition of the *Relations* (= I.A.i [1677] above). Bourgeois/André, no. 310. For details of these editions (the list is not exhaustive) and their contents, see Tournoüer, nos. 139-143.

André Félibien, sieur Des Avaux et de Javercy, was born in Chartres in 1619 and died in Paris on 11 June 1695. He was a distinguished architect and historian who enjoyed an eminent career, and was known for his scrupulous honesty and balanced judgement. His published works range from the professional (including a fine *Principes de l'Architecture, de la sculpture, de la peinture, et des autres arts qui en dépendent* [1676-1690]) to the spiritual, including a paraphrase of Lamentations (1646), a life of Luis de Granada (1668), and a translation of St Teresa's *Interior Castle* (1670). See *DLF XVII*, 473-474 (with a useful bibliography). He was a friend and admirer of Rancé who visited la Trappe a number of times, and his very popular *Description* contains interesting (if adulatory) material on its celebrated abbot. The Lyon

1683 edition—*Description de l'Abbaye de la Trappe avec les Constitutions* (= I.B.i [1683])—also contains the *Lettre d'un religieux bénédictin* listed immediately above. The Paris 1698 edition contains a *Relation historique des Constitutions de l'abbaye de Notre Dame de la Trappe* (pages 177-216). The *Description* has sometimes been attributed to the Oratorian Toussaint Desmares, but this is incorrect, and Desmares himself denied authorship (see Krailsheimer, *Rancé*, 85).

English tr.: Tournoüer, no. 139, states that the *Description* 'fut traduite en anglais', and Krailsheimer, *Rancé*, 86, observes that it was 'translated into English apparently by James Drummond (later Duke of Perth)', but adds in a footnote 'I have been unable to authenticate the story of his alleged translation'. Nor have I found any trace of it. I have in hand (and almost completed) an annotated english translation of the 1698 Paris edition.

[1674] Du Suel, François, *Entretiens de l'abbé Jean et du prêtre Eusèbe* (Paris: F. Léonard, 1674; Lyon: Chez Anisson, Posuel, & Rigaud, 1684). Tournoüer, no. 456.

On Du Suel (d. 1686) and the relevance of his *Entretiens* for the biography of Rancé, see Krailsheimer, *Rancé*, 119 and 241-242. The book 'had some success in spreading a highly favourable but scarcely lifelike impression of Rancé' (*ibid.*, 119). Du Suel was trained at the Oratory but left in 1661 to become curé of Châtres (now Arpajon) near Versailles. For his life and works, see the brief but solid article by Irénée Noye in *DS* 3:1848-1849. As curé he had visited la Trappe for three weeks in 1673 and the *Entretiens* were the result of that visit, but his account of Rancé's spiritual teaching is unreliable.

[1683] Le Masson, Innocent, *Explication de quelques endroits des anciens statuts de l'Ordre des Chartreux. Avec les éclaircissements donnez sur le sujet d'un libelle qui a été composé* [by Rancé] *contre l'Ordre et qui s'est divulgué secrètement* (La Correrie: A. Galle, [1683]). Tournoüer, no. 232.

> For Dom Innocent Le Masson, General of the Carthusians, and his bitter conflict with Rancé, see Part I, Chapter Seven, of this present study and the notes to I.B.ii [1689] 'Lettre de M. l'abbé de la Trape à un évêque pour répondre aux plaintes et aux difficultez de dom Innocent Masson', above. The quarrel between them was ended by royal command in 1689, but it still rankled seven years later (see Letter 961018). La Correrie was the residence of the lay-brothers of la Grande Chartreuse near Grenoble.

[1684] Mabillon, Jean, *Réflexions de Dom Jean Mabillon sur les "Devoirs monastiques" avec les réponses de l'auteur de ce livre*: see [1691] below.

[1685] [Larroque/La Roque], Daniel de, *Les véritables motifs de la conversion de l'abbé de la Trappe, avec quelques reflexions sur sa vie & sur ses écrits, ou Les Entretiens de Timocrate et de Philandre sur un livre qui a pour titre, Les s. devoirs de la vie monastique* (Cologne: P. Marteau, 1685). Bourgeois/André, no. 3097; Tournoüer, no. 254 (an important notice).

> See also I.B.ii [1765] above. Barthe's spurious *Lettre* is no more than a brief, versified version of the ideas of Larroque. The book contains an unpaginated preface and, on pages 201-230

(misnumbered 220), a 'Lettre à M^r. de S... sur les deux dialogues contre l'Abbé de la Trape'. This malicious but effective attack on Rancé (published anonymously) is our only source for the legend of Madame de Montbazon and the too short coffin. For a summary of the book, see Part I, Chapter Seven, of this present study, which also includes a brief biography of Larroque. For a detailed discussion of the story of the severed head, see David N. Bell, 'Daniel de Larroque, Armand-Jean de Rancé, and the Head of Madame de Montbazon', *Cîteaux: Commentarii cistercienses* 53 (2002) 305-331.

[1685] Maupeou, Pierre de, *La conduite et les sentimens de Monsieur l'abbé de la Trappe, pour servir de réponse aux calomnies de l'autheur des Entretiens de Timocrate et de Philandre sur le livre de la Sainteté et des devoirs de la vie monastique* ([Paris]: [s.n.], 1685). Tournoüer, no. 321.

This was Maupeou's rejoinder (not particularly successful) to Larroque's attack on Rancé listed immediately above. The book is extremely rare, but there is a copy at la Trappe. For Pierre de Maupeou, see Part I, Chapter One, of this present study.

[1691] Mabillon, Jean, *Traité des études monastiques divisé en trois parties; avec une liste des principales difficultez qui se rencontrent en chaque siècle dans la lecture des Originaux et un catalogue de livres choisies pour composer une Bibliothèque ecclésiastique* (Paris: C. Robustel, 1691 [one volume], 1692 [two volumes], 1693 [2nd ed.; two volumes]; repr. Farnborough: Gregg, 1967 [reprint of 1st ed.]). Bourgeois/André, no. 4989; Tournoüer, nos. 300-301.

For the controversy over monastic studies, see the notes to I.A.i [1692] above. The *Traité* had been anticipated in 1684 by a brief *Réflexions de Dom Jean Mabillon sur les 'Devoirs monastiques' avec les réponses de l'auteur de ce livre*: see François Vandenbroucke, 'L'Esprit des études dans la Congrégation de Saint-Maur', in *Los monjes y los estudios: IV semana de estudios monásticos, Poblet 1961* (Poblet, 1963) 484.

Latin tr.: (i) *Tractatus de Studis Monasticis divisus in tres partes..., gallice conscriptus a P. dom Joanne Mabillon ... nunc autem in Latinam Linguam translatus a R.P. Udalrico Standigl, celeberrimi et Exempti Monasterii Montis Sancti Audechs, congregationis SS. Angelorum Custodum Benedictino-Bavaricæ sacerdote ... juxta secundam editionem revisam et correctam* (Kempten; L. Kroniger, 1702); (ii) *Tractatus de Studiis Monasticis in tres partes distributus ... auctore P.D. Joanne Mabillon, monacho benedictino, latine versus a P.D. Josepho Porta* [= Guiseppe Porta] *Astensi, Monacho Casin. in Collegio Anselmo-Benedictino Romæ* (Venice: A. Poletti, 1705, 1729 [2nd ed.], 1745 [ed. alt.]; L. Basilium, 1770 [3rd ed.]). Tournoüer, nos. 302-306.

Spanish tr.: *Tratado de los estudios monasticos, dividido en tres partes. Con una lista de las principales dificultades que se encuentran en cada siglo en la lectura de los originales; y un Catalogo de libros selectos, para componer una biblioteca eclesiastica... Y traducido en castellano por un monge español de la Congregación de san Benito de Valladolid...* (Madrid: Viuda de M. Blanco, 1715, 1775; B. Roman, 1779).

[1692] *Idem, Réflexions sur la réponse de M. l'abbé de la Trappe au Traité des études monastiques* (Paris: C. Robustel, 1692, 1693 [2nd ed. in two volumes]). Bourgeois/André, no. 4992; Tournoüer, no. 308.

See further the useful notes in Tournoüer, nos. 307-308.

Latin tr.: (i) *Tractatus de studiis monasticis volumen tertium, complectens responsionem domni Armandi Buthilierii de Rancé, abbatis monasterii Trappæ ordinis Cisterciensis ad eundem tractatum, quæ nunc primum prodit è Gallico in Latinum sermonem conversa* (Venice: A. Poletti, 1732, 1745); and (ii) *Tractatus de studiis monasticis volumen alterum, sive appendix, complectens animadversiones D. Joannis Mabillonii in responsionem R.P. Armandi Buthilierii abbatis Trappæ ad eumdem tractatum, nunc primum latine redditas, quibus studiorum Monasticorum Praxis et Traditio validius astruuntur et ab adversariorum objectionibus omnina vindicantur. Accedit Historia Dissidii Litterarii circa hæc studia, à D. Vincentio Thuillier monacho Benedictino Gallice concinnata, et variorum Epistolis huc spectantibus ad calcem aucta et illustrata* (Venice: A. Poletti, 1730, 1745). Both translations follow the 1745 and 1770 Venice editions of Mabillon's *Tractatus de Studiis Monasticis* listed immediately above.

Idem, Ouvrages posthumes de D. Jean Mabillon et de D. Thierri Ruinart, Bénédictins de la Congrégation de Saint Maur, ed. Vincent Thuillier (Paris: F. Babuty *et al.,* 1724). Three volumes. Tournoüer, no. 467.

Dom Vincent Thuillier (1685-1736) was a most learned Maurist who taught philosophy and theology for many years at the abbey of Saint-Germain-des-Prés in Paris. Dom Denis de Sainte-Marthe, the superior-general (see [1692] immediately below), had given into his keeping all the papers of Mabillon and Ruinart, intending that Dom Thuillier should continue and complete the annals of the Order, but the latter's own literary interests took precedence and Sainte-Marthe's intentions were frustrated. Thuiller's works are listed and summarized in François, 3:136-140. Volume I of the *Ouvrages posthumes* contains a number of primary sources for the dispute over monastic studies and also Dom Thuillier's (inevitably biased) account of the history of the controversy. The 'Lettres et écrits sur les études monastiques' in 1:365-425 include Letters 920407 (400-402), 920908 (405-406), and 930607 (416-417). Thuillier's 'Histoire de la Contestation sur les Études Monastiques' is to be found in 1:365-391. For a response to this work, see below s.v. [1725] Armand-François Gervaise. Further on Dom Thuillier, see *DLF XVIII*, 1279-1280.

[1692] [Anon.], 'Réponse au *Traité des études monastiques*', *Journal des savants* (1692) 163-174.

[1692] Sainte-Marthe, Denis de, *Lettres à M^r. l'abbé de la Trappe, où l'on éxamine sa réponse au Traité des études monastiques, & quelques endroits de son Commentaire sur la Règle de saint Benoît* (Amsterdam: H. Desbordes, 1692). Bourgeois/André, no. 4991; Tournoüer, no. 447.

Dom Denis de Sainte-Marthe (1650-1725), the son of a noble family, made his profession in the Congregation of Saint-Maur in 1668 and was appointed prior of Saint-Julien in Tours in 1690. His four *Lettres* constituted a vicious attack on Rancé's *Réponse au Traité des études monastiques* listed in I.A.i above. *Inter alia*, he accuses Rancé of being filled with pride, infatuated with himself, avid for worldly relationships, and a dictatorial tyrant with regard to his monks. The letters, however, proved somewhat too much even for his Maurist superiors—François, 3:14, calls them 'trop vives, pour ne pas dire trop satiriques'—and Sainte-Marthe was removed from his post at Tours and sent back to Paris to be librarian and curé at Saint-Germain-des-Prés. It was here that he wrote his life of Cassiodorus, in which we see for the first time those qualities of great erudition and careful thought which would make him one of the foremost scholars of his generation. In 1710 he was entrusted with the publication of the *Gallia Christiana*, three volumes of which appeared before his death in 1725. In 1720 he had been elected superior-general of his Order, but the tireless energy he devoted to his duties undoubtedly hastened his death. The *Lettres* (which Rancé discusses in Letter 930306 to Claude Nicaise) do not do him justice. Jean-Baptiste Thiers came to the defence of Rancé with an equally vicious *Apologie de M. l'abbé de la Trappe contre les calomnies du P. de Sainte-Marthe* listed at [1694] below. Further on Sainte-Marthe, see the long article in François, 3:7-24 and (with bibliography) *DLF XVII*, 1135-1136.

The four letters are as follows: (i) 'Lettre à M^r. L'Abbé de la Trappe, touchant sa Réponse au Traité des Études Monastiques. Où l'on examine le style de cet ouvrage, de quelle utilité il peut estre: s'il est écrit avec assez de modération, les raisons générales & les principes qu'il y établis' (15 March 1692 [1-50], followed on pages 51-52 by 'Extraits de l'Instruction sur la mort de Dom Muce', a somewhat lurid work which had produced a great deal of criticism [see I.A.i (1677) *Relations*, no. (i)]); (ii) 'Lettre à M^r. L'Abbé de la Trappe, Où l'on examine l'Avant-propos, & les trois premiers chapitres de sa Réponse' (1 April 1692 [53-108]); (iii) 'Lettre à M^r. L'Abbé de la Trappe, Où l'on examine les principales fautes qui sont répanduës dans tout le reste de sa Réponse' (21 April 1692 [109-168]); (iv) 'Lettre à M^r. L'Abbé de la Trappe, Où, après avoir fait voir l'injustice de son procédé, l'on découvre encore quelques fautes considérables de sa Réponse, & l'on fait un examen abrégé de son Commentaire sur la Règle de saint Benoist' (26 May 1692 [169-230]).

[1693] *Idem, Recueil de quelques pièces qui concernent les quatre lettres écrites à M. l'abbé de la Trappe* (Cologne: J. Sambix l'aisné, 1693). Tournoüer, no. 447; Barbier, 4:89.

The *Recueil* contains a fifth letter of Sainte-Marthe, a letter of Rancé to Jean-Baptiste de Santeul (the hymn writer and another dramatic convert)— Letter 921105 (and see Tournoüer, no. 448)—and two other letters relating to Sainte-Marthe's attack on Rancé. For a complete list of the contents, see Tournoüer, no. 447. The *Lettres* of Sainte-Marthe and the *Recueil* are often found bound together. According to Du Jeu, *Monsieur de la Trappe* (II.B [1931]) 152, n. 3, 'ces deux libelles furent probablement édités en réalité à Tours, chez Ph. Masson'. See further Tournoüer, nos. 447-448, and the entry immediately below.

[1693] A.D.P.C.E., *Lettre au R.P. de Sainte-Marthe ... au sujet des quatres Lettres que ce religieux a écrites à M. l'Abbé de la Trappe* (Paris: [s.n.], 1693).

[1694] Thiers, Jean-Baptiste, *Apologie de M. l'abé (sic) de la Trappe contre les calomnies du P. de Sainte-Marthe* ([Grenoble]: [s.n.], 1694). Bourgeois/André, no. 1855; Tournoüer, no. 465.

See note on [1692 Sainte-Marthe] above. According to Du Jeu, *Monsieur de la Trappe* (II.B [1931])

154, n. 2, 'ce livre fut imprimé clandestinement à Lyon, sans nom d'auteur, ni d'éditeur, sans date et sans indication de provenance, en 1693. Il fut saisi et brûlé en 1694'. As a consequence, copies of the book are extremely rare. Jean-Baptiste Thiers (1636-1703) was curé of Champrond in the diocese of Chartres, and then, from 1692 to his death, curé of Vibraye (Sarthe) (see *DLF XVIII*, 1277). He wrote on an odd variety of subjects, including wigs (his *Histoire des perruques* was published in 1690), but he was a turbulent and contentious priest. He began by approving Rancé's *De la sainteté*, then attacking it (see Letter 831231), and then (changing his mind yet again) becoming Rancé's staunch but intemperate defender. He was, however, a dangerous friend and did more harm than good.

[1694] [Anon.], *Guillelmus a Sancta Amore heresiarcha redivivus in persona Armandi Joannis de Trappa* ([Dijon]: [s.n.], 1694).

William of Saint-Amour was a thirteenth-century theologian who waged a ferocious battle against the mendicants in general and the mendicant professors at the University of Paris in particular. Under Pope Alexander IV (cardinal protector of the Franciscans), William was expelled from France and his books publicly burned. In Letter 940211 Rancé writes to Claude Nicaise asking for details of this scurrilous work, and in the same letter he indicates that Jean-Baptiste Thiers' *Apologie*, listed immediately above, has been seized at Lyon (in Letter 940308, he expresses his regret at this). It seems that *Guillelmus a Sancta Amore* was considered too fierce an attack on Rancé, for the work was suppressed and I have not traced a copy.

[1694] Vert, Claude de, *Explication du chapitre XLVIII de la Règle de S' Benoist, pour servir d'éclaircissement à la question des Études Monastiques, par fr. Colomban* ([Paris]: [s.n.], [1694]). Tournoüer, no. 480.

> Claude de Vert was born in Paris in 1645 and took the cluniac habit in 1661. In 1676 he was named treasurer of Cluny, two years later he was appointed visitor of the Order, and in 1694 he became vicar-general. The following year he was given the priory of Abbeville and died there on 1 May 1708. He had a particular interest in the Rule of St Benedict, especially in its relation to the liturgy, and in his *Explication* he supports Mabillon in his view of the legitimacy of monastic studies. Dom de Vert, we might add, did not always support Mabillon (he strongly disagreed with him on the meaning of *communio* in the Rule of St Benedict), but he was a fair-minded cleric who combined great learning with great piety. See further François, 3:190-191.

[1694] Quesnel, Pasquier, *Lettre à M. l'abbé de la Trape, au sujet de la lettre que cet abbé a écrite à M. l'abbé Nicaize ... sur la mort de M. Arnaud, avec l'harangue prononcée le 9 octobre 1694, à Port-Royal des Champs, en y apportant le cœur de M. Arnaud* ([Paris]: [s.n.], [1694]).

> The 'lettre que cet abbé a écrite à M. l'abbé Nicaize' is Letter 940902 which contains what was to prove an unfortunate comment on the death of 'le grand Arnauld': see Krailsheimer's note *in loc.* On 12 January 1695 Rancé wrote again to Nicaise expressing his sadness and amazement at Quesnel's response. See also [1697] *Recueil de plusieurs pièces concernant l'origine, la vie et la mort de Monsieur Arnauld, docteur de Sorbonne*, and [1782] Noël de Larrière, *Vie de messire Antoine Arnauld*, both listed below.

[1696] Le Nain, Pierre, *Essai de l'histoire de l'ordre de Cîteaux, tirée des annales de l'ordre et de divers autres historiens* (Paris: F. Muguet, 1696-1699). Nine volumes. Tournoüer, no. 277.

> On Pierre Le Nain, see Part I, Chapter One, of this present study. The *Essai* is an uncritical work of limited scholarly value and is little more than a collection of pious biographies. See further the important notice in Tournoüer, no. 277.

[1697] [Masson, Claude], *Deux retraites de dix jours contenant chacune trente méditations, et un sermon sur les principaux devoirs de la vie religieuse, avec deux discours sur la vie des religieux de la Trape* (Paris: F. Barrois; Lyon: C. Bachelu, 1697). Tournoüer, no. 7.

> It is not entirely certain that Claude Masson composed the entire volume. The two *discours* (435-461 [I], 462-487 [II]) have sometimes been attributed to Simon-Michel Treuvé whose name appears in the 'Extrait du Privilège du Roy'.

[1697] *Recueil de plusieurs pièces concernant l'origine, la vie et la mort de Monsieur Arnauld, docteur de Sorbonne* (Liège: [s.n.], 1697). Tournoüer, no. 428.

> The *Recueil* contains an excerpt from Rancé's controversial letter to Nicaise on the death of Arnauld (see [1694] Pasquier Quesnel, *Lettre à M. l'abbé de la Trape*, listed above), a critical response to this, and Quesnel's letter on the subject.

[1700] [Addison, Joseph] *The Letters of Joseph Addison*, ed. Walter Graham (Oxford: Clarendon Press, 1941; repr. St Clair Shores, MI: Scholarly Press, Inc., 1976) 23-24 (Letter 20).

> The english essayist, poet, and statesman Joseph Addison (1672-1719) visited la Trappe in Septem-

ber 1700 when Rancé had only a month to live. He
sent an account of his visit to Dr John Hough, bishop
of Lichfield (the letter is dated Paris, Tuesday, 24
September 1700), and reported that Rancé 'has still
his senses entire, tho they are forc'd to carry him on
his Straw-bed to the Masse which he still frequents
at the most unseasonable Hours' (24).

[1701] Aquin, Louis d', *Relation de quelques circonstances des dernières
heures de la maladie et de la vie du Très Révérend Père Dom Armand-
Jean Le Bouthillier de Rancé, abbé et réformateur de l'abbaye de la
Trappe, de l'étroite observance de Cisteaux* (Paris: F. Muguet, 1701).
Tournoüer, no. 12.

Monseigneur d'Aquin (1667-1710) was bishop of Séez
and attended Rancé on his deathbed. For a brief
account of his life, see Louis Duval, *Un ami de l'abbé
de Rancé. Mgr Louis d'Aquin, évêque de Sées* (Alençon,
1902), which is a pamphlet of fourteen pages, and
for a comprehensive study, Lucien-Victor Dumaine,
Mgr Louis d'Aquin, évêque de Séez (1667-1710) (Paris,
1902). One of the bishop's companions also wrote
an account of the death of Rancé: 'Récit de la mort
de l'ancien abbé de la Trappe par une personne qui
était présente', published by Arthur Michel de
Boislisle in his edition of the *Mémoires de Saint-Simon.
Nouvelle édition* (Paris, 1879-1930), vol. VII, App. 14,
pp. 598-601 (Bourgeois/André, no. 1855). It is a useful account, though not entirely accurate.

[1701] *Idem, Imago R.P. Domni Armandi-Joannis Le Bouthillier de
Rancé, abbatis de Trappâ. Portrait de Dom Armand-Jean Le
Bouthillier de Rancé, abbé régulier et réformateur du monastère de
la Trappe, de l'étroite Observance de Cisteaux* ([s.l.; s.n.], 1701,
1741; repr. La Trappe: Ex Typis Trappæ-Majoris, 1900 'réédité
à l'occasion du deuxième centenaire de la mort du saint
Réformateur'). Latin and much amplified french paraphrase

on facing pages (at head and foot of page in the 1900 reprint). Bourgeois/André, no. 1855; Tournoüer, no. 13. The reduced xeroxed facsimile of the 1741 Paris edition of the *Relations de la mort de quelques religieux de l'abbaye de la Trappe* published in 2000 by Guadalupe Translations (see I.A.i [1677 *Relations*]) also contains an appendix giving the Latin text of the *Imago* (261-268).

> Three years later d'Aquin published his *Récit abrégé des principales circonstances de la vie et de la mort de M. de Rancé, abbé de la Trappe, en forme d'épitaphe, pour être mis en trois tables autour d'un oratoire qui est sur sa tombe* (Rouen: F. Vaultier, 1704 [Tournoüer, no. 14]); and four years after that he combined both works in his bilingual *Imago R.P. domni Armandi Joannis Le Bouthillier de Rancé, Abbatis de Trappa, ad numeros Epitaphii descripta et depingenda super parietes Ædiculæ cujusdam, qua mortales illius exuviæ terrâ sepultæ superteguntur, in gratiam Fratrum qui frequentes illic pro se primum, tum etiam pro defunctis exorant, ut a peccatis solvantur. Récit des principales circonstances de la Vie et de la Mort de Monsieur de Rancé, Abbé de la Trappe, en forme d'Épitaphe, pour être mis en trois Tables autour d'un Oratoire qui est sur sa Tombe* ([s.l.; s.n.], 1708 [Tournoüer, no. 15]).

> English tr.: [Anon.], 'Excerpt from the *Imago R.P.D. Armandi Johannis le Bouthillier de Rancé, Abbatis de Trappa*', *Cistercian Studies* [*Quarterly*] 8 (1973) 64-65.

[1701] Maupeou, Pierre de, *Éloge funèbre du Très-Révérend Père Dom Armand Jean Bouthillier de Rancé, abbé et réformateur du monastère de la Trappe* (Paris: F. Muguet, 1701). Tournoüer, no. 322.

> The eulogy is followed by two letters: (i) *Lettre de Monsieur l'abbé de la Trappe à un de ses amis, trois*

jours après sa profession (127-130) (Rancé was professed at Perseigne on Thursday 26 June 1664);
and (ii) *Lettre de Monsieur l'abbé de la Trappe à
Madame l'abbesse des Clairets, deux heures avant sa
mort* (131-132). The abbess of les Clairets in 1700
was Reverend Mother Françoise-Angélique
d'Étampes de Valençay (see I.A.i [1690 *Carte de
visite*] above), who was devoted to Rancé, and
Maupeou tells us that he began his *éloge* at her
request on 11 November 1700, finishing it about
three weeks later. Rancé actually died at about
1.30 pm on 27 October 1700, but although
Maupeou's 'deux heures' may not be quite accurate, there is no reason to doubt that the abbot
dictated the letter on his death-bed. For an english
translation, see Chrysogonus Waddell, 'Armand-
Jean de Rancé and Françoise-Angélique d'Étampes
Valençay: Reformers of Les Clairets', in *Hidden
Springs: Cistercian Monastic Women, Book Two*. Medieval Religious Women, Volume Three, ed. John
A. Nichols and Lillian T. Shank (Kalamazoo, 1995)
662-663.

[1702] *Idem*, *La vie du Très-Révérend Père Dom Armand-Jean Le
Bouthillier de Rancé, abbé et réformateur du monastère de la Trappe*
(Paris: L. D'Houry, 1702, 1703). Two volumes. Bourgeois/
André, no. 1855; Tournoüer, no. 323.

See *Journal des savants* (20 November 1702) 645-
652. This and all the following biographies are discussed in Part I, Chapter One, of this present
study.

[1703] Marsollier, Jacques, *La Vie de Dom Armand-Jean Le
Bouthillier de Rancé, abbé régulier et réformateur du monastère de
la Trappe, de l'étroite observance de Cisteaux* (Paris: J. de Nully,

1703 [first published as one volume in quarto, then, in the same year, as two volumes in duodecimo]; Paris: chez Babuty, 1758 [new ed.; two volumes]). Bourgeois/André, no. 1855; Tournoüer, nos. 315-316, 318.

> See *Journal des savants* (May 1793) 278-285. The biography proper is followed by 'Pensées de l'abbé de la Trappe sur divers sujets de piété, tirées de ses lettres universelles'. The copy of this biography in the library of the abbey of Septfons contains the note 'Le Chapitre général de 1835 a prohibé la lecture de cette vie'.

> Italian tr.: *Vita di D. Armando Giovanni Le Bouthillier di Ransé, abbate regolare, e riformatore del monastero della Trappa della stretta observanza di Cistello, raccolta da quella, che ha scritta in lingua francese il signor abbate di Marsollier, canonico della catedrale di Uzès, publicata nell'idioma italiano dall'abbate Nicolao Burlamacchi nobile Lucchese dottore si sacra teologia* (Lucca: Per i Marescandoli, 1706). According to Tournoüer, no. 317, the translator was Michele Bertacchi and the book was placed on the Index on 7 February 1718. For Niccolò Burlamacchi (d. 1732), see *DHGE* 10:1380.

[1704] Aquin, Louis d', *Récit abrégé des principales circonstances de la vie et de la mort de M. de Rancé*: see above s.v. [1701] Louis d'Aquin.

[1708] Aquin, Louis d', *Imago R.P. domni Armandi Joannis Le Bouthillier de Rancé*: see above s.v. [1701] Louis d'Aquin.

[1708] *Description du plan en relief de l'Abbaye de la Trappe présenté au Roy par le frère Pacôme, Religieux solitaire* (Paris: J. Collombat, 1708). Tournoüer, no. 348.

This is a magnificent series of engravings of life
at la Trappe, including a splendid but certainly
imaginary depiction of the death of Rancé (61-
62). For a full description, see Lucien Aubry, Eric
de Jessé, Jean Lebrun, and Philippe Siguret,
*Iconographie de l'abbaye de la Trappe et de l'abbé de
Rancé* (La Chapelle-Montligeon: Imp. de
Montligeon, 1973 [Cahiers percherons, 39]) 41,
nos. 101-109. The author also includes a copy of
'principales sentences qui sont écrites dans
l'abbaye de la Trappe et que j'ay copiées dans le
séjour que j'y ay fait, lorsque j'en ay levé le plan
pour Sa Majesté' (65-71), and certain other relevant materials listed in Tournoüer, no. 348. The
author was a parisian hermit-reformer of the her-
mitage of Sénart, where he died on 11 November
1709.

[1715] Le Nain, Pierre, *La vie du Révérend Père Dom Armand-
Jean Le Bouttillier de Rancé, abbé et réformateur de la Maison-
Dieu Notre-Dame de la Trappe, de l'étroite Observance de l'Ordre de
Cîteaux* ([Rouen]: [s.n.], 1715). Three volumes. Bourgeois/
André, no. 1855; Tournoüer, nos. 280-281.

The second edition—Paris: L. d'Hotelfort, 1719
(one volume with a slightly different title)—is
much altered, but both editions were published
posthumously and subjected to considerable editorial revision.

German tr.: *Ausführliche, lehrreiche und sehr beweg-
liche Lebens-Beschreibung des hochwürdigen und seeligen
Herrn Armandi Joannis Le Bouthillier de Rancé...
Anfangs frantzösisch beschrieben durch R.P. Petrum le
Nain, Subpriorem zu la Trappe...; nunmehro wegen seiner
Vortreflichkeit und erbaulichen Innhalts ins deutsche*

übersetzt durch einen Priester Ordinis sancti Benedicti (Augsburg: M. Rieger, 1751). Tournoüer, no. 282.

[1715] Arnaudin, [—] d', *La Vie de Dom Pierre Le Nain, religieux et ancien soûprieur de l'Abbaye de la Trappe, où il est décédé dans l'odeur de toutes les vertus, après 45. années de la plus austère pénitence. Avec deux Traitez qu'il a composez, I. Sur l'État du monde après le jugement dernier. II. Sur le Scandale qui peut arriver, même dans les Monastères les mieux règlez. Et la Liste des Religieux morts à La Trappe depuis la réforme jusqu'à présent. Par M.D.* (Paris: F. Delaulne and Saugrain l'aîné, 1715 [two editions]). Bourgeois/André, no. 1757; Tournoüer, nos. 20-21. The first treatise appears on pages 197-276 and the second on pages 277-360. The useful *Liste des Religieux* appears at the end with separate pagination (1-32).

> See Barbier, 4:990, who adds that Arnaudin (1690-1717) was 'neveu du docteur de ce nom' and that his *Vie* was based on the memoirs of the chevalier d'Espoy. Arnaudin also wrote three other books listed in Alexandre Cioranescu, *Bibliographie de la littérature française du dix-huitième siècle* (Paris, 1969), nos. 8475-8478. The life of Le Nain contains a considerable amount of information on Rancé, though it is not always reliable, and the work is included in the Paris 1755 and 1758 editions of the *Relations* (= I.A.i [1677] above).

[1718] Inguimbert, Joseph Dominique d', *Genuinus Character Reverendi admodùm in Christo Patris D. Armandi Johannis Buttilierii Rancæi, abbatis monasterii B. Mariæ Domus Dei de Trappa; ibique primigenii Spiritus Ordinis Cisterciensis Restitutoris, et pristinorum usuum Cultoris indefessi; expressus ex variis, quæ animum ipsius primùm Mundo, tùm Deo servientis optimè ostendunt* (Rome: J.M. Salvioni, 1718). Bourgeois/André, no. 1855; Tournoüer, 229.

> For a brief account of the life of Joseph

d'Inguimbert and reference to further literature, see Part I, Chapter One, of this present study and *DAC* 382-383. The last chapter of the *Genuinus Character* (168-180) simply reproduces Louis d'Aquin's *Imago R.P. domni Armandi Joannis Le Bouthillier de Rancé* listed at [1701] above. Both this work and the *Vita* listed at [1725] below were primarily intended to defend Rancé against accusations of Jansenism and to show that he was not attacking the rights and privileges of the Holy See.

[1720] Robillard d'Avrigny, Hyacinthe, *Mémoires chronologiques et dogmatiques pour servir à l'histoire ecclésiastique depuis 1600 jusqu'en 1716, avec des réflexions et des remarques critiques* ([s.l.; s.n.], 1720, 1723, 1739 [four volumes]; Nîmes: P. Beaume, 1781 [two volumes]). Tournoüer, no. 27; Barbier, 3:181-182.

For the sections relating to Rancé (the most important is to be found in 4:177-187), see Tournoüer, no. 27. The book was placed on the Index on 2 September 1727. On the Jesuit Hyacinthe Robillard d'Avrigny (1675-1719), see *DLF XVIII*, 113, and *DHGE* 5:1250.

[1722] Saint-Réal, César Vichard, abbé de, 'Apologie de l'abbé de la Trappe', in *Œuvres* (La Haye: Les frères Vaillant and N. Prévost, and Paris: Huart l'aîné, 1722) 5:173-177.

[1724] Gervaise, Armand-François, *Défense de la nouvelle 'Histoire de l'abbé Suger', avec l'Apologie pour feu M. l'abbé de la Trappe, Dom Armand-Jean Bouthillier de Rancé, contre les calomnies et les invectives de D. Vincent Thuillier, Religieux de la congrégation de Saint-Maur, répandues dans son 'Histoire des Contestations sur les Études Monastiques', insérées dans son premier tôme des 'Œuvres posthumes' de Dom Mabillon* (Paris: J.-B. Claude Bauche, 1724, 1725). Two parts in one volume. Tournoüer, no. 204.

Gervaise's *Histoire de Suger* (Tournoüer, nos. 199-201) was first published in three volumes in 1721. For Dom Vincent Thuillier and his 'Histoire des Contestations', see the notes to II.A above s.v. [1692] Jean Mabillon, *Ouvrages posthumes*. See further François, 3:137.

[1725] Inguimbert, Joseph Dominique d', *Vita di D. Armando Giovanni Le Bouthillier di Ransé, Abate Regolare, e Riformatore del Monastero della Trappa, della Stretta Osservanza Cisterciense; corretta, ampliata, e ridotta in miglior forma da F. Malachia d'Inguimbert, Monaco della Badia di Buonsollazzo della stessa Osservanza* (Rome: Stamp. del Bernabo, 1725). Tournoüer, no. 231.

Malachia was Inguimbert's name in religion. He adopted it when he took the cistercian habit at the abbey of Casamari near Rome. On Inguimbert, see the note on his *Genuinus character* listed at [1718] above.

[1738] Lancelot, Claude → II.B [1813] Schimmelpenninck, Mary A.G.

[1742] Gervaise, Armand-François, *Jugement critique, mais équitable des vies de feu M. l'abbé de Rancé, réformateur de l'abbaye de la Trappe. Écrites par les Sieurs Marsollier et Maupeou. Divisé en deux parties où l'on voit toutes les fautes qu'ils ont commises contre la vérité de l'Histoire, contre le bon sens, contre la vray-semblence* (sic), *contre l'honneur même de M. de Rancé, et de la Maison de la Trappe* (Londres [= Troyes or Reims]: aux dépens de la compagnie, 1742). Bourgeois/André, no. 1855; Tournoüer, no. 209.

According to Simon Chardon de la Rochette, 'Notice sur l'édition grecque d'Anacréon donnée par l'abbé de Rancé en 1639', *Mélanges de critique et de philologie* (Paris, 1812) 1:165, the book was printed

in Troyes. Its place in the history of rancéan biography is discussed in Part I, Chapter One, of
this present study.

[1746] Idem, *Histoire générale de la Réforme de l'Ordre de Cîteaux en
France. Tome Ier, qui contient ce qui s'y est passé de plus curieux et de plus
intéressant depuis son origine jusqu'en l'année 1726. Dédiée à Monseigneur
De la Rochefoucault Archevêque de Bourges* (Avignon: [s.n.], 1746,
1749). Bourgeois/André, no. 4983; Tournoüer, no. 212.

This is not an original work, but a revised and
up-dated version of Jean Jouaud's *Défense des
règlemens faits par les Cardinaux, Archevesques et
Evesques, pour la Réformation de l'Ordre de Cisteaux;
par Commission des Papes; à l'instance du Roy. Par les
Abbez et Religieux de l'Estroite Observance du mesme
Order* (Paris: [s.n.], 1656 = Lekai, 'Bibliography',
121, no. 65). It presents a biased and distorted
view of the Reform. See further Louis J. Lekai,
'The Unpublished Second Volume of Gervaise's
*Histoire générale de la réforme de l'Ordre de Cîteaux en
France*', *Analecta Sacri Ordinis Cisterciensis* 17 (1961)
278-283.

[1761] Irailh, Augustin-Simon, 'Dom Armand-Jean Le
Bouteillier de Rancé avec les bénédictins', in *Querelles littéraires;
ou, Mémoires pour servir à l'histoire de révolutions de la république
des lettres, depuis Homère jusqu'à nos jours* (Paris: Durand, 1761
[four volumes]) 4:224-233.

The abbé Irailh (1719-1794) was a canon of
Monistrol and then prior-curé of Saint-Vincent
in the diocese of Cahors. The *Querelles littéraires*
(his principal but not his only work) is really a
collection of anecdotes, not always historically
reliable, but written in an attractive and spritely
style. See further *DLF XVIII*, 610.

[1782] Larrière, Noël de, *Vie de messire Antoine Arnauld, docteur de la maison et société de Sorbonne* (Paris-Lausanne: S. d'Arnay et Cⁱᵉ., 1782). Two volumes. Tournoüer, no. 256.

> Larrière (*c.*1738-1802) was a jansenist layman whose jansenist writings resulted in his being exiled from France. He returned in the early days of the Revolution and collaborated in the publication of the *Nouvelles ecclésiastiques* (Tournoüer, no. 343). See *DLF XVIII*, 691. Volume 2:55-63 of his *Vie* contains an account of Rancé and his works, and on pages 375-382 we find a copy of Rancé's letter to Nicaise on the death of Arnauld (see [1694] Pasquier Quesnel, *Lettre à M. l'abbé de la Trape*, listed above).

B★★★, L. du, *Relation historique sur la célèbre abbaye de La Trappe. Plus célèbre encore par les austerités qui s'y pratiquent. Suivie d'un poëme héroïque sur le même sujet. Par Mʳ. L. du B★★★*. ([s.l.; s.n.], 1793).

> The pamphlet begins with a brief sketch of Rancé's life (5-8), including Larroque's legend of the severed head of Madame de Montbazon. This is followed by a description of la Trappe (8-14) and the story of the comte de Comminge (14-32; see II.B [1818]). The poem proper occupies pages 33-46 and begins 'Quel calme! quel désert! dans un paix profonde / Je n'entends plus mugir les tempêtes du monde! / Le monde a disparu, le temps s'est arreté / Commences-tu pour moi terrible Eternité?' It goes on to deal with Rancé's conversion, his entry into la Trappe, and his role as a loving abbot. The author may well have been Louis du Bois or Dubois.

[1886] Saint-Simon, Louis de Rouvroy, duc de, *Mémoires du duc de Saint-Simon, publiés par MM. Chéruel et Ad. Regnier fils...*

(Paris: Hachette, 1873-1886 [22 volumes]); *Mémoires de Saint-Simon. Nouvelle édition*, ed. Arthur Michel de Boislisle (Paris: Hachette, 1879-1930 [45 volumes, including indexes]); *Saint-Simon. Mémoires (1691-1723). Additions au Journal de Dangeau*, ed. Yves Coirault (Paris: Gallimard, 1983-1988 [eight volumes in the series *Bibliothèque de la Pléiade*]). Tournoüer, no. 444.

> For material relating to Rancé and la Trappe, see Tournoüer, no. 444, for the earliest edition; and vol. 8, p. 1655, s.v. Rancé in the 1983-1988 edition. What Saint-Simon says about Rancé and la Trappe remains essential, but it is not, alas, always reliable. He himself admitted that he found it impossible to be impartial, and he mingles fact with gossip in an infuriating, if entertaining, way.

> Further information on the relationship of Saint-Simon and Rancé may be found in Saint-René Taillandier, 'Saint-Simon à la Trappe', *Revue Hommes et Mondes* 4 (Mars 1949) 441-451; Hélène Himmelfarb, 'Du nouveau sur Saint-Simon: la version des Mémoires soumise à Rancé', *Revue d'histoire littéraire de la France* 69 (1969) 636-687; Georges Poisson, 'Les premières lettres connues de Saint-Simon, une correspondance inédite avec l'abbé de Rancé', *Cahiers Saint-Simon* 1 (1973) 5-13; the same author's *Saint-Simon et le Perche* (Mortagne, 1986); and Roger Judrin, 'Le portrait de Rancé', *Cahiers Saint-Simon* 1 (1973) 3-4. See also Tournoüer, no. 76.

II.B) THE NINETEENTH AND TWENTIETH CENTURIES

IN CHRONOLOGICAL ORDER OF PUBLICATION

[1813] Schimmelpenninck, Mary A.G., *Narrative of a Tour Taken in the year 1667, to La Grande Chartreuse and Alet by Dom Claude*

Lancelot, Author of the Port Royal Grammars; including Some Account of Dom Armand Jean Le Bouthillier de Rancé, Reverend Father Abbé, and Reformer of the Monastery of Notre Dame de La Trappe, with Notes; and an Appendix, containing some particulars respecting M. Du Verger de Hauranne, Abbé de St. Cyran; Cornelius Jansenius, Bishop of Ypres; and also a Brief Sketch of the Celebrated Institution of Port-Royal (London: J. & A. Arch, 1813). The second edition, considerably enlarged and with a slightly different title, appeared in 1816.

> This is a compilation and adaptation (with numerous additions) of selected excerpts from Dom Claude Lancelot's Tour to Alet, published in his *Mémoires touchant la vie de M. de Saint-Cyran* in 1738. See also Schimmelpenninck's *Select Memoirs of Port Royal, to which are appended Tour to Alet, Visit to Port Royal, Gift of an Abbess, Biographical Notices, &c., taken from Original Documents* (London: J. & A. Arch, 1829 [3rd ed.]). There were at least five editions, published both in England and the United States. I have not seen a first edition.

> On Rancé and the reform, see pages 72-94 and 252-261 (which includes an account of James II's visit to la Trappe [254-261]). Schmimmel penninck has consulted the lives of Rancé by Maupeou and Marsollier, the 1701 *Lettres de piété*, certain of the *Relations*, and some of Rancé's own works, including *De la sainteté* (see xxi-xxiv). On page 252 she mentions a life of Rancé by Joseph-François Bourgoing de Villefore (1652-1737), but this must be an error. Bourgoing de Villefore certainly wrote a life of Saint Bernard, but not, so far as I am aware, a life of Rancé (*DLF XVIII*, 222).

> On Mary Anne Schimmelpenninck, see Part I, Chapter One, of this present study.

[1814] Butler, Charles, *The Lives of Dom Armand-Jean Le Bouthillier de Rancé, Abbot Regular and Reformer of the Monastery of La Trappe; and of Thomas à Kempis, the Reputed Author of 'The Imitation of Christ'. With Some Account of the Principal Religious and Military Orders of the Roman Catholic Church* (London: L. Hansard; Longman, 1814). Tournoüer, no. 61.

> Reprinted in volume 4 of *The Philological and Biographical Works of Charles Butler, Esquire, of Lincoln's-Inn, in Five Volumes* (London: W. Clarke & Sons, 1817). The title of the book is accurate, though misleading. It is primarily a biography of Rancé; the religious and military Orders and the life of Thomas à Kempis are relegated to appendices. It is, for its time, a sound piece of work and is discussed in Part I, Chapter One, of this present study. On Charles Butler (1750-1832), see *DNB* 3:497-499. Alban Butler, of *Lives of the Saints* fame, was his brother.

[1815] Cunningham, John William, *De Rancè. A Poem* (London: T. Cadell and W. Davies, and London: J. Hatchard, 1815 [with numerous subsequent editions both in England and the United States]).

> For a discussion of this poem and its sources, together with a brief biography of its author, see David N. Bell, 'The Vicar of Harrow and the Abbot of la Trappe: John W. Cunningham and the Conversion of Armand-Jean de Rancé', *Cistercian Studies Quarterly* 35 (2000) 479-498. Cunningham's account of Rancé's conversion is dramatically wrong, but (as a learned monk of my acquaintance once said) 'if that is not how it did happen, it is certainly how it should have happened'.

[1818] [Tencin, Claudine-Alexandrine Guérin de], *History of Count de Comminge, of the Silent Order of La Trappe; Written by*

Himself: to which are added Several Interesting Particulars of the Monastery, and a Short Memoir of de Rancé, its Celebrated Reformer ([Havant]: H. Skelton, 1818). This was previously published as part of *The Memoirs of the Countess of Berci. Taken from the French by the author of the Female Quixote* [i.e. Charlotte Ramsay, afterwards Charlotte Lennox (1720-1804)] (London: A. Millar, 1756 [two volumes]).

> The *History* is a translation of the *Mémoires du comte de Comminge* (Tournoüer, nos. 459-464) by Claudine-Alexandrine Guérin de Tencin (*DLF XVIII*, 1271-1273) appended to François-Thomas-Marie de Baculard d'Arnaud's (*DLF XVIII*, 87-88) *Les amans malheureux, ou Le comte de Comminge* (Tournoüer, nos. 29-35), a popular melodrama set in the burial vault of la Trappe. For another translation by Daniel Hayes, see s.v. I.B.ii [1765] Nicolas-Thomas Barthe. Further on Tencin's *Mémoires du comte de Comminge*, see Bell, 'The Vicar of Harrow and the Abbot of la Trappe' (cited [at 1815] above) 495-496.

[1820] Göckingk, Leopold Friedrich Gunther von, *Leben des Dom Armand Johanns Le Bouthillier de Rancé, Abt's und Reformators des Klosters La Trappe. Ein Beitrag zur Erfahrungs-Seelenkunde* (Berlin: F. Maurer, 1820 [An der Spittelbrucke, 17]). Two volumes. Tournoüer, no. 215.

> This curious work, which tells us little we do not know either about Rancé or about psychology, is based primarily on Marsollier's *Vie de Dom Armand-Jean le Bouthillier de Rancé* listed above at II.A [1703].

[1842] Exauvillez, Philippe-Irénée Boistel d', *Histoire de l'abbé de Rancé, réformateur de la Trappe* (Paris: Debécourt, 1842; J. Delsol, 1868 [new ed., 'revue, corrigée et augmentée par

l'abbé R. Bonhomme, Prêtre du diocèse d'Évreux']). Tournoüer, nos. 167-168.

> The revised edition of 1868 takes into account
> Dubois's biography published in 1866 (see below).
> It also includes a useful introduction (i-xiv) giv-
> ing a brief history of rancéan biography.

> English tr.: An unpublished anonymous manu-
> script translation of the first edition of the biog-
> raphy was prepared at the abbey of Mount
> Melleray in Ireland in the second half of the nine-
> teenth century. It bears the title *The History of
> the Abbot De Rancé, Reformer of La Trappe. By
> M. D'Exauvillez. Parisian Edition in 1842. Translated
> from the French.* The only copy (so far as I am aware)
> remains at Mount Melleray.

[1844] Chateaubriand, François-René, vicomte de, *Vie de Rancé*
(Paris: H.-L. Delloye; Brussels: A. Wahlen et Cie, 1844 *&c.*).
Tournoüer, nos. 68-73.

> There are innumerable editions and translations
> of this work, but the best edition remains that
> of Fernand Letessier, *Vie de Rancé. Édition critique
> avec une introduction, des notices, des variantes et des
> notes* (Paris: M. Didier, [1955] [two volumes]).
> According to Henri Bremond, 'this biography was
> not a biography at all—but that far more valu-
> able thing—a marvellous symphony, by turns
> amusing and pathetic' (Henri Bremond, *The Thun-
> dering Abbot. Armand de Rancé, Reformer of La
> Trappe*, trans. Francis J. Sheed [London: Sheed &
> Ward, 1930] vii). An interesting contemporary
> review of the work appeared in *The Dublin Review*,
> vol. 17, no. 34 (December 1844) 297-335, and an
> even more interesting one in *La Revue nouvelle* the

following year: Jules-Gabriel Janin, 'Lettres inédites de M. de Rancé', *La Revue nouvelle* 5 (1845)
492-548, which was also published as a separate
pamphlet: Paris: [s.n.], 1858. Despite its title,
Janin's article was not an edition of Rancé's letters, but a skilled and effective rebuttal of the
portrait of Rancé as he appears in Chateaubriand.
The title of the piece results from the fact that
Janin utilized the *lettres inédites* of Rancé which
would be published the following year (1846) by
Benoît Gonod (I.B.i [1846]). Janin's conclusion
deserves to be reproduced: 'Ce [Rancé] n'était ni
un monstre ni un ange, c'était un chrétien du
temps de Louis XIV; il ressemblait à tous les
hommes du dix-septième siècle. Il s'est converti
beaucoup parce qu'il avait la foi, un peu parce qu'il
avait l'orgueil' (548).

[1846] Marie-Léandre Badiche, *Réflexions religieuses et historiques
sur l'ouvrage intitulé 'De la sainteté et des devoirs de la vie monastique'*
(Paris: A. René, [c.1846]). Tournoüer, no. 36.

This rare pamphlet was intended as a sort of introduction to the 1846 Paris reprint of Rancé's *De la
sainteté* listed above at I.A.i [1683]. Badiche discusses
the genesis of the work and its public reception, and
vigorously defends Rancé (whom he clearly esteems)
against attacks made by the Jansenists of Port-Royal.
See further Mensáros, 182.

[1864] Lapierre, Stanislas, *Circulaire de Frère Stanislas, abbé de
Septfons, au sujet de la nouvelle vie de l'abbé de Rancé de M. l'abbé
Dubois* (Clermont-Ferrand: Imp. de Mont-Louis, [1864]).
Tournoüer, no. 455.

In this unpaginated pamphlet dated 15 October
1864, Dom Stanislas Lapierre, abbot of Septfons,

deplores the inaccurate *Vie de Rancé* by Chateaubriand (which he likens to a novel by Walter Scott) and announces the forthcoming biography by the abbé Louis Dubois (listed immediately below) which appeared two years later.

[1866] Dubois, Louis, *Histoire de l'abbé de Rancé et de sa réforme, composée avec ses écrits, ses lettres, ses règlements et un grand nombre de documents contemporains inédits ou peu connus* (Paris: A. Bray, 1866; Poussielgue frères, 1869). Two volumes. Tournoüer, nos. 150-151, 627.

> On this biography, see the essential study by Louis Lekai, 'The Problem of the Authorship of De Rancé's "Standard" Biography', *Collectanea O.C.R.* 21 (1959) 157-163. Lekai demonstrates conclusively that Dubois is actually plagiarizing Dom Armand-François Gervaise. The matter is discussed in Part I, Chapter One, of this present study.

[1881] L.J.M., *La Trapa: noticias de sus más célebres monasterios y de la vida de su reformador Rancé, por L.J.M.; con un apéndice interesante precedido de un prólogo escrito por don Leandro Herrero* ([Madrid]: [Est. Rodriguez], 1881).

> I have been unable to trace the identity of 'L.J.M.' and I have not seen a copy of the book. Examples are, however, to be found in the provincial library of the *Congregación de la Misión de S. Vincente de Paúl* in Madrid and in the library of the diocesan seminary of Vitoria/Vitoria-Gasteiz in Álava/Araba.

[1892] Didio, Henry, *La querelle de Mabillon et de l'Abbé de Rancé* (Amiens, 1892).

> See notes to I.A.i, [1692] *Réponse au Traité des études*

monastiques. Despite its age, the book retains its value.

[1897] Büttgenbach, Franz, *Armand-Jean de Rancé, Reformator der Cistercienser von la Trappe und erster Abt der Trappisten* (Aachen: I. Schweitzer, 1897).

> Büttgenbach provides neither source-references nor a bibliography, but he has obviously based his account on Dubois's *Histoire de l'abbé de Rancé*. The work contains nothing new.

[1897] Schmid, Bernhard, *Armand Jean Le Bouthillier de Rancé, Abt und Reformator von la Trappe, in seinem Leben und Wirken dargestellt* (Regensburg: National Verlagsanstalt, 1897; repr. Frankfurt am Main: P. Kreuer, 1900 [Frankfurter zeitgemässe Broschüren. Neue Folge. Bd. 19, Hft. 12 (Zur zweiten Centenarfeier des Todes desselben)].

> This is a substantial volume of 437 pages based primarily on the *Histoire de l'abbé de Rancé* of Dubois and the *Vie de Dom Armand-Jean Le Bouthillier de Rancé* of Marsollier. The author has also used the unreliable *Vie de Rancé* by Chateaubriand, the sound *Histoire civile, religieuse et littéraire de l'abbaye de la Trappe* by Louis Dubois (Paris, 1824 [Tournoüer, no. 152]), and Henri Didio's excellent *La querelle de Mabillon et de l'Abbé de Rancé* (Amiens, 1892 [Tournoüer, no. 147]).

> REVIEW:
> *Cistercienser-Chronik* 9 (1897) 192 (B. Hene).

[1903] Serrant, Marie-Léon, *L'Abbé de Rancé et Bossuet: ou, Le grand moine et le grand évêque du grand siècle* (Paris: C. Douniol, 1903).

> This is an over-adulatory study, but it contains

useful material unavailable elsewhere. See also s.v.
I.B.ii, [1693] *Lettres*.

[1929] Bremond, Henri, *'L'Abbé Tempête': Armand de Rancé*,
Réformateur de la Trappe (Paris: Hachette, [1929] ['Figures du
Passé']).

> The impact of this book, which caused a storm
> of protest, is discussed in Part I, Chapter One, of
> this present study. Francis Sheed, the english
> translator, notes its 'peculiar quality' and writes
> that 'it is precisely as a Reformer—who was nearly
> always wrong—and as a Founder—who was be-
> low the level of his foundation—that Rancé draws
> the abbé Bremond's slightly murderous fire' (v).
> 'As founder of the Trappist reform', he contin-
> ues, '[Rancé] appears not as a great monk but as
> an instrument powerfully used by God for ends
> that he never really comprehended' (vi). I cannot
> myself subscribe to this view, but there are plenty
> of people who will.

> English tr.: *The Thundering Abbot. Armand de Rancé*,
> *Reformer of La Trappe*, trans. Francis J. Sheed (Lon-
> don: Sheed & Ward, 1930).

[1930] Simon, Georges-Abel, *Réponse à 'L'Abbé Tempête'*, *ou*
l'Abbé de Rancé et son nouvel Historien (*A propos du Livre de M. H.*
Brémond) (La Chapelle-Montligeon: Impr. de Montligeon, 1930,
1938 [revd. ed.]).

> This is a useful pamphlet of a dozen pages di-
> rected against Bremond's portrait of Rancé. In
> the revised edition of 1938, 'nous n'avons guère
> ajouté que les citations tirées des Lettres et
> Conférences, et la majeure partie du dernier
> paragraphe' (12, n.).

[1930] Cherel, Albert, *Rancé* (Paris: Flammarion, [1930] ['Les Grands Cœurs']).

> Cherel's biography is dedicated to his brother-in-law 'Pierre du Roure, en religion Rév. Père Robert, moine profès de l'abbaye de Notre-Dame de Cîteaux'. In the preface, Cherel points out that despite the date of his book (1930) the manuscript had been in the hands of the printer for some months before Bremond's *L'Abbé tempête* was published. Unlike Luddy's biography (listed immediately below), it is not therefore intended as a refutation of Bremond.

[1931] Luddy, Ailbe J., *The Real de Rancé: Illustrious Penitent and Reformer of Notre-Dame de la Trappe* (London & New York: Longmans, Green & Co., and Dublin & Cork: The Talbot Press, 1931).

> This was intended as a rebuttal of the biased portrait presented by Bremond, but it lacks Bremond's force and pungency. 'As a biography of Rancé', says Luddy, Bremond's work 'can only be characterised as a travesty of truth. How anyone could seriously offer this ugly amalgam of half-truths, suspicions, insinuations, and "likely guesses" as a study of De Rancé passes comprehension' (vi). Bremond, he continues, 'represents the illustrious Reformer as a liar, a coward, a tyrant, a hypocrite, a shallow-minded pedant intoxicated with self-conceit, who could nevertheless so impose upon the world as to be regarded as a saint and a genius. Facts are accepted, rejected, or modified, according as they help or hinder this view. The method is simplicity itself, and infallibly efficacious' (xiii). Luddy's indignation may lead him into some exaggeration, but he

does not exaggerate much. A brief overview of earlier biographies appears on pages 312-313.

French tr.: *L'abbé de Rancé. Son vrai visage* (Brehan-Loudéac: Abbaye de Timadeuc, 1931). This anonymous translation was not intended for publication and circulated in mimeographed form only within the cistercian Order. There is a copy in the library of the abbey of Cîteaux.

[1931] Du Jeu, E., vicomte, *Monsieur de la Trappe* (*Essai sur la vie de l'abbé de Rancé*) (Paris: Librairie Académique Perrin, 1931 [two editions]).

Du Jeu's biography is a balanced account (save when he is speaking of trappist observances, for which he has no time at all), but it is also clearly pro-Rancé. The author makes good use of Rancé's letters and provides a brief but judicious assessment of the abbot at the end of the volume (207-210).

[1939] Toppino, Antonio, *L'Abate di Rancé, grande asceta moderno.* Tesi di laurea patrocinata dal Chiar.mo Prof. U.A. Padovani e sostenuta dal Sac. Antonio Toppino il giorno 8 novembre 1939 all'Università Cattolica del Sacro Cuore di Milano. Typescript.

After a first chapter on the nature of the *via ascetica*, Chapter II is entitled 'L'ambiente storico dell'Abate Rancé', Chapter III 'La vita di Rancé e la sua conversione eroica', and Chapter IV 'La riforma della Trappa'. The thesis contains sound and interesting material, but was never published. I have used the copy in the library of the abbey of Septfons.

[1959] Simon, Georges-Abel, *L'Abbé de Rancé* (Notre-Dame de

Bonne Espérance, 1959 [mimeographed]). Two volumes with continuous pagination (1:1-210; 2:211-429).

> This very sound study (of which there is a copy in the library of la Trappe) is marked 'Pour usage privé' (underlined in the original) and was never intended for general circulation.

[1974] Krailsheimer, Alban J., *Armand-Jean de Rancé, Abbot of la Trappe. His Influence in the Cloister and the World* (Oxford: Clarendon Press, 1974).

> This masterly work remains the finest and most balanced account of Rancé, his importance, and his influence.

> French tr.: *Armand-Jean de Rancé, abbé de la Trappe 1626-1700* (Paris: Cerf, 2000). This is a revised and corrected edition of the 1974 publication and is therefore to be preferred to the original. The translation, which appears as anonymous, was actually prepared by Frère Elie Levie, a monk of la Trappe (who died in 1990), revised by Frère Hugues de Seréville, then prior of la Trappe and now abbot of Abbaye Notre-Dame des Neiges, and checked by Professor Krailsheimer before his death in 2001.

> REVIEWS:
> *American Historical Review* 81 (1976) 155-156 (Norman Ravitch).
> *Choice* 12 (1975) 411 (Anon.).
> *Cistercienser-Chronik* 83 (1976) 107-120 (Bernardin Schellenberger).
> *Cîteaux: Comm. cist.* 26 (1975) 216-221 (Yves Chaussy).
> *Collectanea Cisterciensia* 37 (1975) BSM [691]-[692]

(Chrysogonus Waddell).
Dix-septième siècle 120 (1978) 211-213 (Bruno Neveu).
Downside Review 94 (1976) 159-162 (Daniel Rees).
English Historical Review 91 (1976) 645 (Bernard Plongeron).
Historical Journal 19 (1976) 787-792 (Dermot Fenlon).
Historisches Zeitschrift 223 (1976) 165-166 (R. Reichardt).
Journal of European Studies 4 (1975) 395-396 (T. Dawson).
Journal of the Australasian Universities Language and Literature Association 45 (1976) 125-127 (A.R. Clark).
Listener 92 (1974) 345 (Louis Allen).
New Statesman 88 (1974) 830 (John Raymond).
Review for Religious 34 (1975) 498-499 (M. Basil Pennington).
Revue d'histoire de la spiritualité 53 (1977) 178-180 (Jean Lebrun).
Theologische Zeitschrift 33 (1977) 54-55 (W.A. Schulze).
Times Literary Supplement (13 December 1974) 1424 (A.H.T. Levi).

[1978] [Apostles of the Infinite Love], *The Holy War or The Story of Abbot de Rancé* (St-Jovite, Québec: Éd. Magnificat, 1978 [2nd ed.], 1991); *La Guerre sainte ou L'histoire de l'abbé de Rancé* (St-Jovite, Québec: Éd. Magnificat, 1982).

> This is the same work in both French and English. The Apostles of Infinite Love are the members of The Order of the Magnificat of the Mother of God which (I quote their website) 'was requested by the Blessed Virgin at La Salette (France) in 1846, and was founded in Canada in 1962'. (http://www.magnificat.ca/english/).

The Holy War is based on Dubois's biography supplemented by the works of Maupeou, Marsollier, Le Nain, and Gervaise, with limited reference to Chateaubriand, Serrant, Bremond, Cherel, and Du Jeu. The book also uses the 'Manuscrit de Septfons' which 'includes the notes of Dom de la Tour, and the writings of Dom Anselm and other religious contemporaries of Abbot de Rancé. ... Kept at La Trappe until 1791, at which time there was a forced emigration; these folios were then transported from one country to another, finally coming into the possession of the Abbey of Septfons in 1845. The collection is comprised of 12 folios' (172).

The *Holy War* is the War of the Observances. After a brief introduction, the book is essentially divided into three sections. The first section (22-85) begins with Rancé's arrival at la Trappe in 1662 and continues with an account of the political manoeuvring of the Abstinents and the Mitigated in Rome, together with Rancé's role in the events. The second section (86-133) begins with a sketch of the 'spectacular protest by the Reformed' in 1667, the spread of the Reform, and the concerted opposition to its success, especially from the abbey and abbots of Cîteaux. The third and final section (135-162) opens with the appeal to the king in 1673 and continues with the reform at Leyme (under Madame de Vieuville), the first real sign that the wind was turning with the positive report of the official visitor, Dom Hervé Du Tertre, the astonishing conversion of abbot 'de Saumon' (i.e. Jean-Antoine de la Forêt de Somont, abbot of Tamié), the final years of Rancé, Innocent XI's formal approbation of the Reform, and the pope's intention to grant a cardinal's hat to

Rancé (135-162). 'History must inscribe his name in a place of honor among the restorers of monastic life, while awaiting the wished-for day when the Church, forgetting hurt feelings, will grant him the honor of the altars' (i.e. his canonization) (13).

There is nothing new in any of this, and the book is written from the standpoint of piety. But it contains good english translations of a considerable amount of material unavailable elsewhere.

[1985] Krailsheimer, Alban J., *Rancé and the Trappist Legacy* (Kalamazoo: Cistercian Publications, 1985).

'When I first began to study Rancé', wrote Professor Krailsheimer, 'my concern was primarily historical, and the nature of my research into archive material so specialised that my first book on the results of that research (*A.J. de Rancé*, Oxford, 1974 [see above]) was mainly addressed to scholars. By the time I had finished my second book devoted to Rancé, an edition of his letters, I had come to realise that the subject was much more relevant to the interests of non-specialists than I had originally believed.' *Rancé and the Trappist Legacy* was the result. It is an excellent study.

REVIEWS:
Catholic Historical Review 73 (1987) 629-630 (F. Ellen Weaver).
Church History 57 (1998) 238-239 (Philip F. Gallagher).
Cîteaux 38 (1987) 382-383 (Colette Friedlander).
Collectanea Cisterciensia 48 (1986) BSM [135]-[137] (Yvon Petit).
Église et théologie 18 (1987) 140-141 (Kenneth C. Russell).

Monastic Studies 17 (1986) 245-253 (Michel Gaulin).
Review for Religious 46 (1987) 631-632 (Charles
Cummings).

[1985] Caneva, Anna Maria, *A.-J. Le Bouthillier de Rancé, la sua
vita, le sue opere* (Roma: Pontificia Universitas Lateranensis,
1985 [Theses ad Doctoratum in Sacra Theologia]).

> Anna-Maria (Maria-Laura) Caneva's 'A.-J. Le
> Bouthillier de Rancé: Aspetti del suo
> insegnamento spirituale; la guida spirituale',
> *Cîteaux: Comm. cist.* 40 (1989) 333-354, is excerpted
> from this dissertation.

[1991] Gobry, Ivan, *Rancé* (Lausanne: L'Âge d'homme, 1991).

> For an important and highly critical review (by
> Lucien Aubry) of this out-of-date and disappoint-
> ing work, see *Collectanea Cisterciensia* 54 (1992) BSM
> [263]-[264]. It is difficult to see why the book was
> ever published. It is certainly not worth reading.
> Gobry's *Rancé ou l'esprit de la pénitence* (see I.D
> [2000]) is not much better.

[1996] Caneva, Anna Maria, *Il riformatore della Trappa. Vita di
Armand-Jean de Rancé* (Roma: Città Nuova, 1996).

> French tr.: *Le Réformateur de la Trappe. Biographie
> de L'Abbé de Rancé*, trad. Jean-Marie Wallet
> (Nouvelle Cité, 1997). The french translation is a
> revised, corrected, and expanded version of the
> italian original.

> REVIEWS:
> *Gregorianum* 78 (1997) 288 (Maria Cecilia Zaffi).
> *Collectanea Cisterciensia* 59 (1997) BSM [270]-[271]
> (Marie-Gérard Dubois).

II.C) Brief Biographies in Encyclopedias, Dictionaries, and Similar Compendia

I have not included here those entries in encyclopedias and dictionaries which are entirely derivative and add nothing useful, either in content or approach, to the subject. Entries in early *compendia* from 1734 to 1882 are listed in Tournoüer, nos. 44, 59, 138, 146, 162-164, 179, 225, 237, 246-247, 250, 255, 297, 336, 339, 344, 427, and 441.

[1688] Baillet, Adrien, in *Des enfans devenus célèbres par leurs études ou par leurs écrits. Traité historique* (Paris: A. Dezallier, 1688) 358-362. Tournoüer, no. 37.

> For Adrien Baillet (1649-1706), see *DLF XVII*, 94-95.

[1708] Dupin, Louis-Ellies, in *Bibliothèque des auteurs ecclésiastiques du 17ᵉ siècle* (Paris: A. Pralard, 1708 [seven volumes]) 4:158-197.

> For Louis-Ellies Dupin (1657-1719), see *DLF XVII*, 416-419.

[1714] Hélyot, Pierre, in *Histoire des ordres monastiques, religieux et militaires et des congrégations séculières de l'un et de l'autre sexe qui ont esté établies jusqu'à présent...* (Paris: J.-B. Coignard, 1714-1719 &c. [eight volumes]) 6:1-15. Tournoüer, no. 228.

> For Pierre Hélyot (1660-1716), known in religion as *père Hippolyte*, see *DLF XVIII*, 592. His account (by his own admission) is entirely dependent on Marsollier's *Vie de Rancé* listed above at II.A [1703], but his presentation is of interest.

[1726] Beaunier, Charles, *Recueil historique, chronologique et topographique des archevêchez, évêchez, abbayes et prieurez de France, tant d'hommes, que de filles...* (Paris: A.-X.-R. Mesnier, 1726 [two volumes]) 2:762-770. Tournoüer, no. 45.

> The same volume and page numbers in the second (1734) and third (1743) editions, though the third edition has a slightly different title: *État des archevêchez*, etc. For Dom Charles Beaunier (1676-1737), see *DLF XVIII*, 154.

[1811] Weiss [——], in [Joseph-François Michaud & Louis-Gabriel Michaud], *Biographie universelle, ancienne et moderne* (Paris, 1811-1862) 35:166-169. Tournoüer, no. 336.

[1822] Richard, Charles-Louis & Giraud, Jean-Joseph, *Bibliothèque sacrée, ou Dictionnaire universel historique, dogmatique, canonique, géographique et chronologique des sciences ecclésiastiques* (Paris: Méquignon fils aîné, 1822-1827) 5:237-240.

[1846] Raulin (abbé), in *Le Plutarque français; vies des hommes et des femmes illustres de la France, depuis le cinquième siècle jusqu'à nos jours, avec leurs portraits en pied gravés sur acier; ouvrage fondé par M. Éd<ouard> Mennechet. Deuxième édition, publiée sous la direction de M. T. Hadot* (Paris: Langlois & Leclercq, 1844-1847) 4:207-220. The first edition of this work (which I have not used) appeared between 1835 and 1841.

[1860] Frère, Edouard-Benjamin, in *idem, Manuel du Bibliographie Normand ou Dictionnaire bibliographique et historique* (Rouen: A. Le Brument, 1858-1860; repr. Geneva, Slatkine, 1971) 2 (1860):432.

[1911] Obrecht, Edmond M., in *The Catholic Encyclopedia* (New York, 1911) 12:639.

[1936] Carreyre, J., in *Dictionnaire de théologie catholique* (Paris, 1903-1972) 13:1652-1656.

[1949] Ausenda, Renata O., in *Enciclopedia Cattolica* (Città del Vaticano, 1949) 2:1992-1993 s.v. 'Bouthiller [*sic*] de Rancé'.

[1949] Lenssen, Seraphin, in *Hagiologium Cisterciense* (Tilburg: [s.n.], 1949) 2:25-45.

[1963] Elsen, Christophorus, in *Lexikon für Theologie und Kirche* (Freiburg, 1963) 8:988-989.

See also s.v. Karl S. Franck below.

[1967] Lekai, Louis J., in *The New Catholic Encyclopedia* (New York-Toronto-London, 1967) 12:78-79.

[1973] Vandenbroucke, François, in *Dizionario degli Istituti di Perfezione* (Rome, 1973) 7:1205-1208.

[1975] Brouette, Émile, in *Dictionnaire des auteurs cisterciens*, ed. Émile Brouette, Anselme Dimier, et Eugène Manning (Rochefort: Abbaye Notre-Dame de St-Remy, 1975-1979 [La Documentation cistercienne, 16]) 594-598.

[1980] Heimbücher, Max, in *Die Orden und Kongregationen der katholischen Kirche* (Paderborn-München-Wien: F. Schöningh, 1980 [4th ed.]) 1:363-365.

[1988] Krailsheimer, Alban J., in *Dictionnaire de spiritualité* (Paris, 1937-1995) 13:81-90; repr. without revision in *Spiritualité cistercienne: Histoire et doctrine* (Paris: Beauchesne, 1998) 415-429.

[1990] Michaux, Gérard, in *Dictionnaire du Grand Siècle*, ed. François Bluche (Paris: Fayard, 1990) 1300-1301.

[1990] Dimier, Anselme, in *Catholicisme: hier, aujourd'hui, demain* (Paris, 1990) 12:478-479.

This is a disappointing entry with more than one error.

[1996] Robert, Léon, revd. Dominique Descotes, in *Dictionnaire des lettres françaises: le XVIIe siècle*, ed. Albert Pauphilet *et al.*, revd. under the direction of Patrick Dandrey by Emmanuel Bury *et al.* (Paris: Fayard, 1996 [orig. ed. 1951]) 1070-1072.

> Descotes has added to the original entry a volume by Henri-Georges Gaignard, *Visages de Rancé* (Paris: F. Lanore, [*c*.1983]). This is incorrect. The title of the volume is actually *Visages de Rance*—i.e. the Rance valley in Britanny—and has nothing to do with the abbot of la Trappe.

[1997] [Anon.], in *The Oxford Dictionary of the Christian Church*, ed. Frank L. Cross & Elizabeth A. Livingstone (Oxford: Oxford University Press, 1997 [3rd ed.]) 1364.

[1999] Franck, Karl S., in *Lexikon für Theologie und Kirche* (Freiburg, 1999) 8:825-826.

[2001] Bell, David N., in *Encyclopedia of Monasticism*, ed. William M. Johnston (Chicago: Fitzroy Dearborn, 2000) 1056-1057.

INDEX

This index does not include the names of all authors mentioned *en passant* in the Further Readings to each chapter, nor does it include the names of all authors cited in Part II (the Bibliography). It does, however, include those names of which something significant is said.

ABBREVIATIONS

abb.	abbot	pr.	prior
abp.	archbishop	RM	Réverénde mére
bp.	bishop	RP	Réverénd pére
comm.	commendatory	sup.	superior

Abandonment (*abandon*) 91-93
Abbots, their position and responsibilities 102-104, 131, 156, 161, 206-207
Abelard, Peter: see Peter Abelard
Abstinents 61-70, 131, 217, 347
Acey (abbey) 45
Addison, Joseph xxiii, 323-324
Aelred of Rievaulx 235, 241, 246
Agathange, frère: see Gervaise, Armand-Jean
Albani, Cardinal Annibal d' 9
Albergotti, chevalier d' (frère Achilles), monk of La Trappe 260
Albon, RM Louise-Henriette d', sup. of the Visitation (Riom) 41-42, 113

Alègre, Jeanne-Françoise de Garande, marquise d' 192
Aleman, Mateo 149
Alexander IV, Pope 321
Alexander VII, Pope 66, 81
Alms-giving and monastic hospitality 222
Ambrose of Milan 41, 211
Anacletus II (antipope) 134
Anacreon 253-255
        see also s.v. Rancé, Commentary on Anacreon
Angoulême 27
Annat, François 149
Annonciades, Les (Parisian convent) 31, 45
Antony the Great 159, 214
Apatheia 128

Aquin, Louis d', bp. of Séez xxiii, 5, 9, 16, 22, 25, 324-325, 327, 330

Aquinas, Thomas, OP 112

"Archweeper": see Jean de Hauteville

Aristophanes 159

Arnaudin, d' 7, 25, 270, 329

Arnauld, Antoine (*le grand Arnauld*) 37-38, 42, 137, 149, 150, 291, 300, 322, 323, 333

Arnauld, Catherine 42

Arnauld, RM Jacqueline-Marie-Angélique, abbess of Port-Royal 42

Arnauld d'Andilly, Robert 38, 82, 122, 123, 127-128, 139, 191

Arnolfini, Octave, comm. abb. of La Charmoye 60-61

Arsenius 217

Articles of Paris (*Articuli Parisienses*) 57

Athanasius of Alexandria 41, 149, 158

Aubry, Lucien, OCSO 33, 109

Aucour, Jean Barbier d' 149

Augustine of Hippo 35, 36, 41, 74-75, 82, 85, 109, 110, 113, 117, 211

Austerities 223-227
see also s.v. Penitence and penance

Autopsies in 17th-century France 185-186

Autun, Jacques d' 45

Auxonne, Ursulines of 45-46, 98

Babylon 221

Baculard d'Arnaud, François-Thomas-Marie de 337

Badiche, Marie-Léandre 339

Baillet, Adrien 350

Baldwin of Forde 101-102, 230

Balzac, Guez de 30

Barillon, Henri, bp. of Luçon xviii, 92, 113, 156, 162, 164, 165, 166, 168, 175, 192, 194, 236, 237, 239, 264, 265, 266, 269, 271-272, 277, 292

Barrett-Kriegel, Blandine 167, 278

Barthe, Nicolas-Thomas 305-306, 314

Basil the Great 112, 113, 211, 214, 219, 277

Bavent, Madeleine (Ursuline) 45

Bayle, Pierre 148

Beaufort, Eustache de, abb. of Sept-Fons 192, 194

Beaufort, François de Vendôme, duc de 175, 179-181, 183, 187

Beaunier, Charles, OSB 351

Beaupuis, Wallon de 301

Beethoven, Ludwig van 244

Bellefonds, Bernardin Gigault, maréchal de 260, 288, 297, 299, 303

Bellefonds, Laurence Gigault de, sup. of Notre-Dame des Anges (Rouen) 273-274

Bellérophon, Jean de 255

Benedict of Nursia 110, 211, 224, 231, 240
Order of Saint Benedict 224
see also s.v. Rule of Saint Benedict

Benedict XII, Pope 132

Benedictines 55, 113, 272

Benserade, Isaac de 44

Bentzeradt, Charles de, abb. of Orval 243

Berman, Constance H. 71

Bernard of Clairvaux 19, 41, 47, 52, 88, 110, 113, 128, 131, 133-136, 138, 143, 174, 186, 203, 204, 211, 213, 214, 215, 221, 235, 240, 241, 245, 246, 298

Bernard of Clairvaux, *Pseudo-* 76-77, 87, 245

Bertacchi, Michele 327

Bérulle, Pierre de, Cardinal, Cong. Or. 41, 77-78, 79, 90-91, 137, 139, 246

Bible in 17th-century France 41, 80

Black Mass 46

Blois, Ordonnance of (1579) 54

Blunt, Hugh F. 172

Bocquillot, Lazare André, *curé* of Châteleux 139

Bodin, Jean 45

Boguet, Henri 45

Boileau-Despréaux, Nicolas 30

Bonaventure, OFM 112

Bonowitz, Bernardo, OCSO 103

Bosseboeuf, Louis 177, 195, 196

Bossuet, Jacques-Bénigne, bp. of Meaux 7, 8, 10, 30, 43, 47, 50-51, 91, 103, 107, 136, 139, 148, 156, 162-164, 236, 237, 240, 264, 265, 269, 272, 289, 299-300

Bouchard, RP, Cong. Or. 190

Boucherat, Louis 261

Boucherat II, Nicolas, abb. of Cîteaux 62, 68

Bouhours, Dominique, SJ 149

Boullé, RP Thomas 46

Bourbon-Condé, Anne-Geneviève de 179

Bourdaloue, Louis, SJ 30-31

Bourgoing de Villefore, Joseph-François 335

Bouthillier, Denis xvi, 27, 183

Bouthillier, Denis-François xvi-xvii, 173

Bouthillier, RM Marie-Louise-Isabelle, nun of Les Annonciades (Paris) 165, 233, 265

Bouthillier, Victor, abp. of Tours xviii, 29, 35, 152

Brancas, Charles, comte de 192

Bremond, Henri 18-20, 21, 23, 26, 95, 195, 254-255, 338, 342, 343, 347

Brothels for the clergy 40

Buonsolazzo (abbey) 9

Burlamacchi, Niccolò 327

Burnet, Gilbert 29

Bursfeld: see s.v. Congregations

Butler, Charles 14-15, 22, 228, 230, 336

Büttgenbach, Franz 18

Buvée, Barbara, sup. of the Ursulines of Auxonne 45-46

Calmet, Augustin, OSB (Vannist) 274

Calvin, John 36, 198

Caneva, Anna Maria, OCSO 22, 349

Canivez, Joseph-Maria, OCSO 52

Capuchins 41

Caritas fraternitatis: see Charity, fraternal

Carmelites 176

Carpentras 9

Carta Caritatis: see Charter of Charity

Carthusians 146-147, 215, 224, 229, 272, 314
see also s.v. Le Masson, Innocent

Casamari (abbey) 331

Cassian: see John Cassian

Cassinese: see s.v. Congregations

Cassiodorus 319

Casuistry 80-81, 96

Caumartin, Louis-François Lefèvre de 298

Caussade, Jean-Pierre de, SJ 91-92

Cawley, Martinus, OCSO 93

Ceffons, Pierre, monk of Clairvaux 241

Chambre Ardente, affair of the 46

Champvallon, François de Harlay de, abp. of Paris 31, 67

Chantal, Jeanne-Françoise de, founder of the Visitation 42, 92, 106
Chapelain, Jean 149
Chardon de La Rochette, Simon 253-254, 331-332
Charity, fraternal 101-102, 207-208
Charles VIII, king of France 57
Charny, François Lotin, chevalier de, monk of La Trappe 260
Charny, comte de 191
Charter of Charity 58, 130, 131, 132
Chastity, nature of 203-204
Chateaubriand, François-René, vicomte de 15, 18, 19, 21, 23, 26, 185, 338-339, 340, 341, 347
Châteauneuf, Charles de L'Aubespine, marquis de 186
Chaussy, Yves 23
Cherel, Albert 19, 21, 343, 347
Chevreuse, Claude de Lorraine, duc de 177
Chevreuse, Marie de Rohan, duchesse de 177, 180, 186
Choiseul, Duplessis-Praslin, Gilbert de, bp. of Comminges xx
Christ, imitation of 89-90, 99, 127, 199-200, 210-211, 214-215, 220, 221, 223, 231, 246
    as the Great Penitent 89-90, 99, 199-200, 210, 218, 231, 246
Chrysogonus, Saint 171
Chrysostom, John: see John Chrysostom
Cirey, Jean de, abb. of Cîteaux 56-57
Cîteaux (abbey and Order) ch. 3 *passim* (esp. 52, 54, 55, 56, 58, 59, 60, 62, 63, 66, 68, 69), 128, 130, 132-133, 215, 221, 224, 231, 242, 347

Clairets, Les: see Les Clairets
Clairvaux (abbey) 54, 56, 60, 61, 62, 100
Classicism (*classicisme*) 34, 49
Clement I, Pope 171
Clement IX, Pope 66
Clement X, Pope 67
Clement XI, Pope 9
Clement XII, Pope 9
Clement of Alexandria 141
Clementi, Muzio 244
Climacus, John: see John Climacus
Cluny (abbey) 221
Collège d'Harcourt (Paris) xvii
Collège Saint-Bernard (Paris) 57
Cologne 148, 165
Colombe, La: see La Colombe
Columba, Saint 158-159
Commendatory system 53-55, 57-58, 69, 72-73
Comminge, comte de 333, 336-337
Comminges, shrine of Saint-Bernard de 295
Communion: see Eucharist
Compunction 214
Concupiscence 109-110, 198, 201, 220
Condren, Charles du Bois de, General of the Oratory 90, 139
Conferences at La Trappe 217, 282
Confessional, importance of 104-105, 206, 237
Congregations 72, 132
    Benedictine 55, 70
    Bursfeld 55
    Cassinese 55
    Castile 58
    Cistercian 58-59
    Congregation of Trappists 242
    Feuillants 59, 61, 70, 72
    Valladolid 55

Conversion ch. 8 *passim*
    psychology of 169-174,
    192-193, 194, 198
    moral, intellectual, and
    mystical 170-171
    'Conversion spirituality'
    169-176, 246
Copenhagen 148
Corneille, Pierre 30, 43
Corsini, Cardinal 9
Cotheret, Nicolas, librarian of
    Cîteaux 57
Councils
    Aix-en-Provence (1585)
    159
    Carthage IV (411?) 159
    Lateran IV (1215) 56
    Lateran V (1514) 54
    Trent (1545-1563) 41, 54,
    59-60, 69, 87
Couturier, François, abb. of Port-du-
    Salut 16-17
Couturier, Robert/Robin, pr. of
    Perseigne 292
Couzières 177, 182
Cragg, Gerald 30, 49
Crasset, Jean, SJ 149, 212-213
Cunningham, John William, vicar of
    Harrow 336
Cyprian of Carthage 149
Cyril of Alexandria 141
Cyril of Jerusalem 141

De Grox, Marie-Pierre 119
Death, meditation on 212-214, 246,
    262
Deification 128
Del Rio, Martin Antón, SJ 45
Demiannay, Adrien (frère Colomban),
    monk of Buonsollazzo 259
Demonic possession in 17th-century
    France 44-47, 51

Demonologists, 17th-century French
    45-46
Descartes, René 30, 150
Desert Fathers 110, 111, 113, 122,
    128, 129, 133, 136, 158,
    197, 214, 245
Desmares, Toussaint, Cong. Or. 313
Desprez, Guillaume 43
Detachment 98-101, 108-109, 114,
    124, 162, 207, 221
    see also s.v. Renunciation
Didio, Henri 18, 167, 278, 340-341
Diet at La Trappe 109-110
Dijon 46
Discernment (*discrétion*) 133, 243
Dorotheus of Gaza 123, 127, 270
Dowries, monastic 222-223
Dowsing 299
Drummond, James, duke of Perth 313
Du Charmel, Louis de Ligny, comte
    de 192
Du Jeu, vicomte 19, 21, 320-321, 344,
    347
Du premier esprit de l'Ordre de Cisteaux:
    see Paris, Julien
Du Roure, Pierre, monk of Cîteaux
    19, 343
Du Suel, François, *curé* of Châtres
    149, 313-314
Du Tertre, Hervé, abb. of Prières 347
Du Verger, Léonore de Rohan, dame
    177
Dubois, Alexandre-Claude Bosc
    (frère Jean Climaque),
    monk of La Trappe 259
Dubois, Louis 16-18, 20, 21, 22, 26,
    31, 340, 341, 347
Dupin, Louis-Ellies 350

Eden, Garden of 74-75
Edict of Nantes 148, 168, 239
Eisen, Charles 305

Ephrem Syrus 113, 128, 214
Equiprobabilism 96
Escobar y Mendoza, Antonio de 149
Essenes 162
Estienne, Henri 254
Estrada, Luis de 241
Estrées, L': see L'Estrées
Eucharist 37-38, 91, 148
Eudes, John, founder of the Congregation of Jesus and Mary 78, 90
Eugene IV, Pope 58
Eusebius of Caesarea 41, 141
Exauvillez, Philippe-Irénée Boistel d' 15, 17
Executions 32-33, 45

Fastred, abb. of Clairvaux 255
Faure, dom Muce, monk of La Trappe 257-258, 261, 319
Favier, Jean xvii, xx, 31, 82
Félibien des Avaux, André 31, 104-105, 115, 126, 139, 237, 289, 312-313
Fénelon, François de Salignac de La Mothe, abp. of Cambrai 300
Feuillants, Congregation of 59, 61, 70, 72
"Fictions", controversy over: see s.v. Humility and humiliations
Filles de la Doctrine chrétienne (Mortagne) 283-284
Fléchier, Esprit, bp. of Nîmes 30-31
Floriot, Pierre 108, 139, 290-291
Foisil, Zozime, abb. of La Trappe xxiii, 10
Foreknowledge, divine: see s.v. Predestination
Fouquerolles, Mme de 180
Free will 83-85
French Revolution 14, 242, 247, 333
'French School' of spirituality 90-91, 95

Fronde, First and Second 28, 29, 35, 44, 49, 181-183, 186, 196

Gallia christiana 319
Gallicanism 42-43, 137
Gaston d'Orléans: see Orléans, Gaston, duc d'
General Assembly of the Clergy (1655) xviii, 35
General Chapter 10, 52-59, 61, 66, 68, 131, 132, 221
  Benedictine 55
Georges, Dominique, abb. of Val-Richer xxi, 64-65, 238
Gerbais, Jean 261-262, 279
Germany, Cistercian abbots in 64, 67
Gervaise, Armand-Jean, abb. of La Trappe xxiii, 10-14, 16, 22, 25, 308, 330-332, 340, 347
Gibbon, Edward 7
Gilbert de la Porrée 134
Gobry, Ivan 22, 349
Göckinck, Leopold Friedrich Gunther von 15
Goëllo, Anne d'Avaugour de Bretagne, Mlle de 187
Gondi, Paul de: see Retz, Cardinal de
Gonod, Benoît 20, 291
Grace, doctrine of 75, 83-86, 92, 137
Graham, Robert (frère Alexis), monk of La Trappe 259
Grand siècle, le ch. 2 passim (esp. 32-35), 103, 109, 126, 175, 193, 234, 236
Grandier, Urbain, curé of Saint-Pierre-du-Marché (Loudun) 45, 51
Gratian 215
Gregory I, Pope (Gregory the Great) 41, 113, 211
Gregory XV, Pope 61
Gregory of Nazianzus 141, 214
Gregory of Nyssa 141
Grégy 10

Guémenée, Anne de Rohan, princesse de 175

Guerric of Igny 241

Guibourg, *abbé* 46

Guise, Élisabeth d'Orléans, duchesse de 279-280, 289, 297, 310

Guise, Louis-Joseph de Lorraine, duc de 181, 280

Hagiography 42

Harding, Stephen, abb. of Cîteaux 130

Harlay, Achille de, comte de Beaumont 236-237, 265

Harlay, RM Marie-Françoise de (Visitandine) 192

Hayes, Daniel 306, 337

Head of Mme de Montbazon: see s.v. Montbazon, Marie d'Avaugour de Bretagne, duchesse de

Hell 213, 234-235

Hélyot, Pierre, OFM (Third Order) 350

Henry IV, king of France 27, 59-60

Hermans, Vincent, OCSO 118-119, 232

Hermant, Godefroi, canon of Beauvais 139

Herodotus 141

Hincmar, abp. of Reims 83-84, 96

Homer 141

Honnête homme, conception of 39

Hospitality, monastic: see Almsgiving

Hôtel-Dieu (Paris) 139

Hough, John, bp. of Lichfield xxiii, 324

Humility and humiliations xxii, 106, 116, 117, 125-128, 135-136, 145-146, 200-201, 207, 210-211, 218, 245, 248, 296-297

Hundred Years' War 52, 55

Huxelles, Marie Le Bailleul du Blé, marquise d' 297

Image and likeness of God 200

Importants 181, 187

In suprema (apostolic constitution) 65-66

Inguimbert, Joseph-Dominique d', bp. of Carpentras 9, 25, 329-330, 331

Innocent II, Pope 134

Innocent III, Pope 77, 87

Innocent VIII, Pope 56

Innocent XI, Pope 67, 81, 347

Innocent XII, Pope 300

Irailh, Augustin-Simon, pr. of Saint-Vincent (Cahors) 332

Isaac of Stella 241

Isidore of Pelusium 141

Isocrates 141

Ivan the Terrible 39

Jacob, François (frère Dorothée), monk of La Trappe 259

James II, king of England 262, 281, 292, 299, 335

Janelle, Pierre 87, 96

Jansen, Cornelius, bp. of Ypres 35-36, 42, 43

Janin, Jules-Gabriel 339

Jansenism and Jansenists xxii, 7, 8, 9, 35-39, 42-43, 50, 67, 80, 82-83, 85-86, 96, 121, 136-138, 144, 146, 149, 151, 157, 191, 266, 281, 301, 333

Jardin du Luxembourg (Paris) 32

Jean de Hauteville (the 'Archweeper') 87

Jerome 41, 149, 214, 239

Jerusalem, heavenly 221

Jesuits xxii, 8, 36, 38-39, 41-43, 80-83, 85-86, 92, 96, 149, 150-151, 158, 246

John, Saint 213

John Cassian 41, 112-113, 128, 277

John Chrysostom 41, 141, 149

John Climacus 41, 79, 93, 112-114, 121-128, 130-131, 137-138, 143, 162, 201, 211, 213, 214

John of the Ladder: see John Climacus

John of Mirecourt, monk of Cîteaux 241

Johnson, Samuel 197

Joly, Charlotte xvi, 27, 173

Joly, Guy 195

Jouaud, Jean, abb. of Prières 62, 63, 65, 66, 332

Joy, spiritual and monastic ch. 5 *passim*, 127, 199, 201, 214

Judgements of God, meditation on 212-214

Kempis, Thomas à: see Thomas à Kempis

Knox, Ronald 176

Krailsheimer, Alban J. xv, xxi, xxv, xxvii, 7, 18, 20-23, 33, 38, 39, 65, 112, 121-122, 137, 146, 165, 167, 172-174, 184, 194-195, 227-228, 232, 240, 245, 254, 258, 266, 274, 280, 289, 290, 294-296, 303, 313, 345-346, 348-349

La Barrière, Jean de, comm. abb. of Feuillant 59, 72

La Bruyère, Jean de 30

La Charmoye (abbey) 60

La Colombe (abbey) 10

La Correrie 314

La Cour, Jacques de, abb. of La Trappe xxiii, 12

La Fayette, Marie-Madeleine de La Vergne, comtesse de 30, 44, 187, 189

La Ferté (abbey) 54, 56, 62

La Fontaine, Jean de 30

La Harpe, Jean-François de 306

La Huerga, Cipriano de 241

La Reynie, Nicolas de 46

La Roche, RM Louise-Élisabeth Robin de (Visitandine) 201, 233

La Rochefoucauld, François, duc de 30, 43, 179, 181

La Rochefoucauld, François de, Cardinal 61, 62

La Sablière, Marguerite Hessein de Rambouillet, Mme de 44, 175, 192, 293

La Salette 21, 346

La Tour, Jean-Baptiste de, pr. of La Trappe 6-11, 347

La Trappe (abbey) *passim*
    Bibliography xxvi
    La Trappe before Rancé xx
    Rancé as regular abbot xxi
    Earliest mention of La Trappe by Rancé 286
    Earliest description of La Trappe after Rancé's reform 289, 311-312
    As fortress, prison, and tomb 107-108, 110, 130, 215
    Novitiate 104
    Mortality at La Trappe xxii, 109-110, 223-224
    Library 123, 139-141, 144
    Library catalogue (1752) 140
    Perpetual silence 161, 216-217
    Poltergeist activity 47, 51, 98
    Visitors to La Trappe 115, 198-199, 238
    Expulsion of monks from La Trappe 13-14

La Trémouille, Marie-Sylvie de 192
    La Vallière, Louise-
    Françoise Le Blanc de La
    Baume, duchesse de 175,
    176, 192, 194
La Val-Sainte (abbey) 59, 242
La Vieuville, Anne d'Orvilliers de,
    abbess of Leyme 347
Ladder of Divine Ascent: see John
    Climacus
Laffay, Augustin-Hervé 243, 249
Laigues, Geoffroy, marquis de 175
Lancelot, Claude, osb 150, 335
Lancre, Pierre de 45
Lapierre, Stanislas, abb. of Sept-Fons
    16, 339-340
Laquerre, M. de 261
Largentier, Abraham 60
Largentier, Denis, abb. of Clairvaux
    60-62
Larrière, Noël de 333
Larroque, Daniel de 3, 15, 147-166,
    167-168, 176, 184, 187,
    190, 195, 204, 206, 207,
    217, 267, 305-306, 314-
    315, 333
Larroque, Mathieu de 148
Launoy, Jean de 149
Laxism 80-81, 82, 86, 96, 246
Le Camus, Étienne, bp. of Grenoble
    xviii, 113, 156, 162, 164,
    168, 175, 192, 236, 237,
    264, 265, 269, 294
Le Clerc, Daniel de 266
Le Loyer, Pierre 46
Le Maître, Claude, abb. of Châtillon
    66
Le Masson, Innocent, General of the
    Carthusians xxii, 146-147,
    164, 165, 167, 224, 236,
    265-266, 298-299, 314

Le Nain, Pierre, sub-pr. of La Trappe
    xxiv, 7-8, 9, 13, 14, 16, 21,
    22, 25, 82-83, 270, 301,
    308, 323, 328-329, 347
Le Nain de Tillemont, Sébastien 7,
    300-301
Le Reclus (abbey) 12-13
Le Roy, Guillaume, comm. abb. of
    Hautfontaine xxii, 38, 69,
    106, 126, 146, 164, 167,
    236, 288, 296-297
Le Tellier, Charles-Maurice, abp. of
    Reims 156, 237, 269
Leclercq, Jean 101, 102, 111
Lectio divina 112, 131
Lekai, Louis, O.Cist. 16-17, 23, 25,
    26, 61, 62, 65, 68, 70, 128,
    340
Leloczky, Julius, ocso 284
Lenoncourt, Madeleine de 177-178
Leo I, Pope (Leo the Great) 137
Lerne, Emmanuel de 195
Les Clairets (abbey) 3, 11, 276-277
Lestrange, Augustin de, abb. of La
    Val-Sainte 59, 242-243,
    247, 248, 275
L'Estrées (abbey) 10-11
Levie, Élie, ocso 345
Lignage, *abbé* de 303
Liancourt, duchesse de 31, 115
Library at La Trappe: see s.v. La
    Trappe (abbey)
L'Isle, Paulin de, osb (Vannist),
    then monk of La Trappe
    290
Literature, religious, in 17th-century
    France 40-43
London 148
Longueville, Anne-Geneviève de
    Bourbon, duchesse de 44,
    175, 179-181, 192

Longueville, Henri II d'Orléans, duc
    de 179
Loudun, Ursulines of 45, 51, 98
Louis XI, king of France 54
Louis XIII, king of France 27
Louis XIV, king of France 10, 11, 12,
    29-30, 35, 46, 48, 62-64, 66-
    68, 147, 151, 284
Louviers, nuns of 45, 98
Love, nature of 105-106, 213-214, 280
    see also s.v. Self-will and
    self-love
Love of God, defined 205
    as fundamental 205
    and one's neighbour 101-
    102, 107
Luddy, Ailbe J., ocso 19-20, 343-344
Luis de Granada, op 41
Lully, Jean-Baptiste 157
Lulworth, Dorset (abbey) 249-250
Luther, Martin 198, 210
Luynes, Louis-Charles d'Albert, duc
    de 177, 178

Mabillon, Jean, osb (Maurist) xxii,
    112-113, 133, 145, 219,
    278, 285, 291, 298, 314,
    315-316, 322
Macarius the Great 214
Magnificat of the Mother of God,
    Order of the 21
Maisne, Charles, monk of La Trappe
    3-8, 11, 12, 25, 238, 239,
    282-283
Malachie, Dom: see Inguimbert,
    Joseph-Dominique
Malebranche, Nicolas 296, 299
Malherbe, François de 30, 43
Manicheanism 109
Manual labour 218-220, 226
Marie de Médicis, queen of France 27

Marsollier, Jacques, archdeacon of
    Uzès 6-7, 9, 13, 14, 15, 16,
    18, 21, 22, 25, 31, 304, 310,
    326-327, 335, 337, 341,
    347, 350
Marteau, Pierre 147-148
Martin V, Pope 53
Martin, Henri-Jean 40
Mary, the Virgin 241
Mary Magdalen 88
Mary, Pierre, abb. of Cadouin 68
Masson, Claude, Cong. Or. 323
Maugier, Étienne 60, 62, 69
Maulevrier, marquis de 180
Maupeou, Grégoire, monk of La
    Trappe 3
Maupeou, Pierre de, monk of La
    Trappe, then *curé* of
    Nonancourt 3-5, 7, 13, 14,
    16, 21, 22, 25, 165-166,
    279, 303-304, 315, 325-
    326, 335, 347
Mazarin, Jules, Cardinal xviii, 28-29,
    48, 152, 162, 180-182, 183,
    196, 302
McManners, John 212
Meat eating 60-61, 65, 131, 158-159,
    217-218
    see also s.v. Abstinents
Medina, Bartolomé de, op 81
Mège, Antoine-Joseph, osb
    (Maurist) 147, 167, 271-
    272
Mencius (Mêng-Tze) 248
Mensáros, Aurel, O. Cist. 19
Merton, Thomas, ocso 172
Milleran, René 290
Mitigations (of the Rule of Saint
    Benedict) 133, 206, 217-
    218, 224, 225-226, 247,
    266

Molière, Jean-Baptiste Poquelin, known as 30

Molina, Luis de, sj 83, 85

Molinism 83, 85-86, 96, 113

"Monastic Odyssey": see s.v. Trappistines

Monastic studies, controversy over xxii, 13, 111-114, 117, 121, 127, 147, 162, 167, 207, 219, 278, 315-320, 322

Monasticism, ch. 9 *passim*
instituted by Christ 155, 162, 201-203
demands of 204-205
purpose of 203
as a continual crucifixion 211

Monchy, RP Pierre de, Cong. Or. 190

Monk, definition of 98, 108-109, 124

Montbazon, Anne de 178

Montbazon, Hercule de Rohan, duc de 177, 182

Montbazon, Louis de Rohan VI, prince de Guémené, comte de 177

Montbazon, Marie d'Avaugour de Bretagne, duchesse de xviii, 15, 38, 39, 45, 46, 121, 153, 165, 166, ch. 8 *passim*, 236, 306-307, 315, 333

Montbazon, Marie-Éléonore de 178

Montbazon, Hôtel de (Paris) 186, 190

Montespan, Françoise-Athénaïs de Rochechouart, marquise de 46, 175

Montglat, RM Anne-Victoire, abbess of Gif 287

Montholon, Jean-François de, comm. abb. of Saint-Sulpice-en-Bugey 298

Montmorency-Laval, François de, bp. of Québec 10-11

Montrésor, Claude de Bourdeilles, comte de 186

Moorhouse, Geoffrey 161

Morimond (abbey) 54, 56, 62

Mortification: see Penitence and penance

Moses 225, 228

Motteville, Françoise Bertaut, Mme de 180, 183, 195

Mozart, Wolfgang Amadeus 244

Muce: see Faure

Muguet, François 244, 269, 279, 310

Mullet, Bernard, monk of La Trappe 260

Mysticism, distinguished from spirituality 228-229

Narbonne 39-40

Neo-Platonism 79, 91

Newman, John Henry, Cardinal 87-88

Nicaise, *abbé* Claude 141, 266, 277, 282, 300, 310, 319, 321, 322, 323, 333

Nicole, Pierre, solitary of Port-Royal 82, 149, 150, 266, 291

Nilus of Ancyra 214, 277

Nivelle, Pierre, abb. of Cîteaux 62-63

Noah 225

Nonancourt 3

Novices, Cistercian 132

Nuns' reading, Rancé's views on 277

Obedience 102-103, 105-107, 116, 124-125, 204, 205, 207, 226

Oblates 133

Old Testament, nun's reading of 277

Olier, Jean-Jacques, *curé* of Saint-Sulpice 78, 79, 89-90, 210, 246

Original guilt 76

Original sin, doctrine of 74-76, 78, 83

Orléans, Gaston, duc d' 140, 191, 280

Orval (abbey) 70

Paalzov, Hans 307

Pachomius 223

Pacôme, frère 327-328

Padway, Lazarus of 56

Paris, Julien, abb. of Foucarmont xxi, 121, 122, 128-133, 136, 137, 138, 143

Pascal, Blaise 30, 36, 38, 81, 137, 171, 195

Paul, Saint 84, 99, 111, 207

Paul the First Hermit 155

Pausanias 141

Pavillon, Nicolas, bp. of Alet 38, 39, 153

Payne, RM Bernard, abbess of Holy Cross (Stapehill) 229-230, 249

Pelagius 74

Pellison-Fontanier, Paul 299

Penitence and penance *passim*, but esp. 88-90, 93, 99, 114-115, 118, 129, 131, 133-135, 137, 176, 197-200, 210-211, 214, 214-215, 218, 234, 245, 248

Penitence, exterior and interior 210-211

Perkins, James 183, 196

Perseigne (abbey) xx, 48, 122, 129, 139

Perthuis, Antoine de, monk of La Trappe 260

Pétau, Denis, sj 149

Peter, Saint 88

Peter Abelard 134

Petit, Jean, abb. of Cîteaux 66

Petitcolin, Marie-Gabriel, ocso 119

Pezzoli, Denise 119

Philo of Alexandria 141, 160, 162

Pinette, Nicolas 140, 163, 175, 192, 194, 260

Pirot, Georges, sj 81

Pius VI, Pope 242

Poitiers 32

Pollard, Graham 244

Polybius 141

Pontigny (abbey) 54, 56, 62

Populations, monastic 54-55

Port-Royal (abbey) 14, 38, 42, 43, 141, 149, 150, 157, 177, 191, 291, 302, 335, 339

Post-mortems: see Autopsies

Poverty, nature of 204, 207, 221
    love of 221
    and obligations to the poor 221-222

Prayer 112, 116-117, 127, 131, 208-210, 219, 220-221, 226, 245, 280
    defined 209
    conditions for 209
    communal and private 229-230
    unceasing 209

Preaching in 17th-century France 30-31, 50, 283

Predestination, Single and Double 35-36, 50, 75, 83-86, 138

Prières (abbey) 128

Printing of religious works in 17th-century France 40-43, 50

Probabilism 80-81, 86, 96

Probabiliorism 96

Prophecy, Old Testament 160

Providence 91, 92, 122, 201

Pyrenees, Treaty of the 29

Querelle des Anciens et des Modernes, le 34

Quesnel, Pasquier, Cong. Or. 90, 137-138, 144, 145, 293, 322

Quietism 91-92, 300

Quinet, Louis, abb. of Barbery 230

Racine, Jean 30

Rader, Matthew 123

Rambouillet, Catherine de Vivonne, marquise de 43
Rambouillet, Hôtel de (Paris) 43
Rancé, Armand-Jean de, abb. and reformer of La Trappe
    Portait by Hyacinthe Rigaud xxvi, 310, and frontispiece
    Birth xv, xvi
    Family xvi-xvii, 27-28
    Education xvi-xviii
    Interest in astrology, alchemy, and occultism 46, 51
    Delegate at the General Assembly of the Clergy xviii, 35
    As horseman 31-32
    As preacher 31-32, 43, 45
    And the Parisian *salons* 43-44
    His conversion xix-xx, 152, ch. 8 *passim*, 336
    And Mme de Montbazon ch. 8 *passim*
    Novitiate at Perseigne xx-xxi
    Becomes regular abbot of La Trappe xx-xxi
    Reading of his will at La Trappe 139
    In Rome xxi, 64-65, 216
    At the General Chapter of 1667 66
    Sickness and death xxiii, 281, 285, 324, 328
    His intended canonization 3, 5, 160, 347-348
    His character xxiii-xxiv, 235-240
    His views on indigent parents 108-109, 124, 157-158, 216, 237, 264-265
    His view of monks as gangs of criminals 79, 107, 127, 234
    His biographers ch. 1 *passim*
    As spiritual director 238
    As a *spirituel*, not a mystic 171
    His literary ambitions 163-164, 239-240
    His originality 117, 240-241
    And Jansenism 37-39, 82, 118, 136-138, 297, 301, 330, 339
    And Gallicanism 43
    And Molinism 83
    And Quietism 91-92
    And the 'French School' of spirituality 91
    And the revocation of the Edict of Nantes 148, 168, 239
    His enemies ch. 7 *passim*
    His reading and learning ch. 6 *passim*
    His writings (the following references are to Part I of this study only):
        Commentary on Anacreon (1639) xvii, 27-28, 34
        Requeste présentée au Roy (1673) 66, 154, 164
        Éclaircissement sur l'état présent de l'Ordre de Cisteaux (1674) 67
        Relations de la mort de quelques religieux de l'abbaye de la Trappe (1677) 110-111, 163

Lettre d'un abbé régulier sur le sujet des humiliations (1677) 126, 146
De la sainteté et des devoirs de la vie monastique (1683) xxiv, 101, 109, 116, 133, 138-139, 146, 148, 150, 152, 154-155, 157, 159, 160, 162-165, 193, ch. 9 *passim*, 236, 237, 239, 240, 246
Éclaircissemens de quelques difficultez que l'on a formées sur le livre De la sainteté et des devoirs de la vie monastique (1685) 164, 237
La Règle de saint Benoist, nouvellement traduite et expliquée selon son véritable esprit (1688) 132-133
Conduite chrétienne adressée à Son Altesse Royalle Madame de Guise (1697) 116
Maximes chrétiennes et morales (1698) 99, 245, 246
Sermon on Saint Bernard 134-136
Correspondance/Letters 20, 245
Rapin, René, sj 185, 195
Reclus, Le: see Le Reclus
Reform of the Cistercian Order ch. 3 *passim*, 128-134
Regio dissimilitudinis 200
Régnier-Desmarais, François-Séraphin, comm. pr. of Grandmont 42
Regula Sancti Benedicti: see Rule of Saint Benedict
Remy, Nicolas 45

Renunciation (*désoccupation*) 123-124, 129
    see also s.v. Detachment
Rethel (abbey) 271
Retz, Paul de Gondi, Cardinal de xviii, 28-29, 152, 162, 175-176, 177, 179, 181, 183, 187, 192, 195, 196, 302
Richelieu, Armand-Jean Du Plessis, Cardinal xvi, xvii, 27-28, 62-63, 254
Richer, Edmond 149
Ries, Ferdinand 244
Rigaud, Hyacinthe xxvi, 185
Rigorism 80-82, 96, 133
Robert of Molesme 130
Robillard d'Avrigny, Hyacinthe, sj 330
Rodriguez, Alonso, sj 42, 82-83, 113
Rogier, RM Louise-Françoise, sup. of the Visitation (Tours) 122, 174, 175, 190-191
Romanticism (*romanticisme*) 34
Rosemberg, comte de (frère Arsène de Janson), monk of La Trappe 258-259
Rosweyde, Heribert, sj 149
Rouen 45
Rufinus 149
Ruinart, Thierry, osb (Maurist) 317
Rule of Saint Benedict 34, 52, 60, 102, 103, 116, 130-133, 135, 145, 147, 158, 161, 163, 164, 204, 206, 214, 215, 217-218, 237, 247, 270-272, 309, 322
Ryan, Patrick, ocso 113
Ryan, Vincent, abb. of Mount Melleray 232, 267

Sablé, Madeleine de Souvré, marquise de 44

Sacy, Isaac-Louis Le Maistre de, solitary of Port-Royal 42-43, 139, 149

Sada y Gallego, Juan de, ocso 285-286

Saint-Cyran, Jean Du Vergier de Hauranne, *abbé* de 36, 38, 137, 139, 149, 150

Saint-Évremond, Charles de Saint-Denis, sieur de 43

Saint-Joseph, Madeleine de 90

Saint-Loup, Diane Chasteignier de La Roche-Posay, marquise de 192, 199

Saint-Simon, Louis de Rouvroy, duc de 12, 30, 185-187, 195, 333-334

Saint-Sulpice, Society of 78, 90

Saint-Victor (abbey) 7

Sainte-Chapelle (Dijon) 141

Sainte-Colombe d'Oupia, Jean-Baptiste de (frère Albéric), monk of La Trappe 258

Sainte-Marthe, Denis de, osb (Maurist) 147, 167, 317-320

Sales, François de, co-founder of the Visitation 41, 42, 103, 105-106, 113, 205, 215-216

Salmon, John H.M. 196, 302

Salons, Parisian 36, 38, 43-44

Santéna, comte de (frère Palémon), monk of La Trappe 258, 261

Santeul, Jean-Baptiste (Victorine) 139, 192, 320

Satan and Satanism in 17th-century France 44-47, 98, 111, 235

Saumur, Château de 148

Savary, Mathurin, bp. of Séez 283

Schimmelpenninck, Mary Anne 14, 26, 334-335

Schmid, Bernhard 18

Schola caritatis 107

Scholasticism, spirituality of 112

Scott, Sir Walter 16, 340

Séguenot, RP Claude, Cong. Or. 38-39, 190

Séguin, *abbé* Jean-Marie 15

Self-will (*volonté propre*) and self-love (*amour propre*) 100, 103, 106-107, 124-125, 199-201, 204-206, 209
    see also s.v. Love

Sembrancher 242

Sept-Fons (abbey) 14, 16, 21, 70, 287, 288, 289, 347

Sermons: see Preaching

Seréville, Hugues de, ocso 345

Serrant, Marie-Léon 21, 300, 341-342, 347

Sévigné, Marie de Rabutin-Chantal, marquise de 30

Sévigné, Renaud de 175

Shakespeare, William 244

Sheed, Francis 342

Sickness and remedies 223-224

Simon, Georges-Abel 18-19, 342, 344-345

Sin ch. 4 *passim*
    as homicide and deicide 78
    mortal and venial 80
    as *crime* 79

Sinai, Monastery of Mount 122, 124

Sirens 141-142

Sirmond, Jacques, sj 286

Sixtus V, Pope 59

Sleep, its ill effects 220

Socrates 149

Somont, Jean-Antoine de la Forêt de, abb. of Tamié 347

Soubise, François de Rohan-Montbazon, prince de 178

Spinoza, Baruch 160

Spirituality, 17th-century French ch. 4 *passim* (esp. 87-93, 95), 98, 111
    'Cistercian' and 'Trappist' 241

Stability (*stabilitas*), monastic 108, 117, 124, 215-216, 245, 248, 264
Strict Observance, rise of ch. 3 *passim*, 256, 347-348
see also s.v. Abstinents
Sydow, Max von 39, 44

Tabouret, affair of the 181-182
Tallemant des Réaux, Gédéon 178, 182, 185, 195
Tamié (abbey) 70, 291-292
Tansillo, Luigi 88
Tauler, Johannes, OP 41
Taylor, Jeremy 213
Tears, spirituality of 87-89, 114, 122, 127, 214, 219, 226
Tencin, Claudine-Alexandrine Guérin de 336-337
Terence 141
Teresa of Ávila (Discalced Carmelite) 41, 67, 211
Tertullian 212
Theodoret of Cyrrhus 149
Theology, Rancé's views on 111-113, 127, 211, 217
see also s.v. Monastic studies
Thiers, Jean-Baptiste, *curé* of Champrond, then Vibraye 266, 267, 319, 320-321
Thirty Years' War 28
Thomas à Kempis, OSA 14, 41, 149, 336
Thouless, Robert 169-171, 194
Thucydides 141
Thuillier, Vincent, OSB (Maurist) 13, 317-318, 331
Toppino, Antonio 344
Torcy, Jean-Baptiste Colbert, marquis de 148
Tournoüer, Henri xxvi, 250
Tours xviii, 29, 35, 57, 152

Trappistines 242, 249
'Monastic Odyssey' of (1798-1800) 249
Tréville, Henri-Joseph de Peyre, comte de 192
Tutiorism 81-82, 96

Ullman, Chana 171-172, 194
Unigenitus Bull (8 Sept 1713) 138, 144
Urfé, Louis de Lascaris d' 192
Urosa, Froylán de, O.Cist. 241
Ursulines 45-46, 51, 98

Valençay, Françoise-Angélique d'Étampes de, abbess of Les Clairets 3, 11, 26, 276-277, 300, 326
Valladolid: see s.v. Congregations
Val-Richer (abbey) 276
Valvason, Erasmo di 88
Vargas, Martin 58
Vatican Council, Second 247
Vaussin, Claude, abb. of Cîteaux 63, 66
Véretz xvii, xviii-xix, xx, 46, 51, 146, 177, 183, 184, 186-189
Véritables motifs de la conversion de l'abbé de la Trappe, Les: see Larroque, Daniel de
Versailles 32
Vert, Claude de, OSB (Cluniac) 274, 322
Vertus, Catherine-Françoise d'Avaugour de Bretagne, Mlle de 177, 260-261
Vigils 220-221, 226
Vincent-Buffault, Anne 88
Virey, Pierre de, abb. of Clairvaux 56
Visitation, abbatial 58
Visitation, convent of the (Riom) 41-42 (Tours) 122, 191
Visitation, Order of the 105

47, 51

Xenophon 141

Vitré (Brittany) 148
Voiture, Vincent 44

Waddell, Chrysogonus, OCSO xxiv,
100-101, 119, 248, 254,
281-282, 312
Wain, John 197
Wars of Religion 53, 55, 57, 59

Westminster Abbey 244
William III, king of England 239
William of Saint-Amour 321
William of Saint-Thierry 241, 246
Witchcraft in 17th-century France 44-
47, 51

Xenophon 141